INCEST IN CONTEMPORARY LITERATURE

Manchester University Press

Incest in contemporary literature

Edited by
Miles Leeson

Manchester University Press

Copyright © Manchester University Press 2018

While copyright in the volume as a whole is vested in Manchester University Press, copyright in individual chapters belongs to their respective authors, and no chapter may be reproduced wholly or in part without the express permission in writing of both author and publisher.

Published by Manchester University Press
Altrincham Street, Manchester M1 7JA, UK
www.manchesteruniversitypress.co.uk

British Library Cataloguing-in-Publication Data is available
A catalogue record for this book is available from the British Library

ISBN 978 1 5261 2216 2 hardback
ISBN 978 1 5261 4810 0 paperback

First published 2018

Published in paperback 2020

The publisher has no responsibility for the persistence or accuracy of URLs for any external or third-party internet websites referred to in this book, and does not guarantee that any content on such websites is, or will remain, accurate or appropriate.

Typeset by Out of House Publishing

Contents

Notes on contributors   *page* vii

Acknowledgements   x

Introduction   1
Miles Leeson with Emma V. Miller

Part I Behind closed doors

1 Text, image, audience: Adaptation and reception of Andrea Newman's *A Bouquet of Barbed Wire* (1969)   21
Frances Pheasant-Kelly

2 Assuming a 'manly position': The crisis of masculinity in Ian McEwan's early fiction   47
Justine Gieni

3 'Waking in the dark': Remembering incest in *A Thousand Acres* (1991), *Exposure* (1993) and *Beautiful Kate* (2009)   69
Rebecca White

Part II Incest and the child protagonist

4 'The word is incest': Narrative, affect and judgement in and across the *Lolita*s   97
Matthew Pateman

5 Appropriate or anathema? The representation of incest in children's literature   117
Alice Mills

6 '[B]orn to make a real life, however it cracks your heart': Creative women and daydreaming in Margo Lanagan's *Tender Morsels* (2008)   133
Emma V. Miller

Part III Incest as a political conceit

7 The desire for power and the power of desire: The case of Pier Paolo Pasolini   161
Michael Mack

8 'Our close but prohibited union': Sibling incest, class and national identity in Iain Banks's *The Steep Approach to Garbadale* (2007)   180
Robert Duggan

9 Is posthuman incest possible? Science fiction and the futures of the body   198
Alistair Brown

Part IV The rhetoric of narrating incest

10 'Is't not a kind of incest?' Metaphor and relation in the poetry of Ted Hughes and Sylvia Plath   225
Charles Mundye

11 '[T]he thing that makes us different from other people': Narrating incest through '*différance*' in the work of Angela Carter, A.S. Byatt and Doris Lessing   246
Emma V. Miller and Miles Leeson

12 Avuncular ambiguity: Ethical virtue in Iris Murdoch's *The Black Prince* (1973) and Simone de Beauvoir's *The Mandarins* (1954)   269
Miles Leeson

Index   289

Notes on contributors

Alistair Brown is Associate Lecturer in the Faculty of Arts and Social Sciences at the Open University, and Teaching Fellow in the Department of English Studies at Durham University. His research falls broadly within contemporary literature and the digital humanities, with recent publications including studies of communication technologies and narrative, postmodernism and video games, research impact and social media, and the value of English in the creative and digital industries. He is currently writing a monograph on video games and literature. He can be found on twitter @alibrown18

Robert Duggan is Senior Lecturer in Modern and Contemporary Literature at the University of Central Lancashire. He received his PhD from the University of Kent and has previously held academic posts at the University of Chichester and Keele University. His research focuses on literary form and experiments in genre in current writing and he has published on a range of contemporary authors including Angela Carter, Martin Amis, Iain Banks, Toby Litt, Rupert Thomson and China Miéville. His monograph *The Grotesque in Contemporary British Fiction* (Manchester University Press) was published in 2013, and he is currently working on a new project on the politics of space in contemporary literature.

Justine Gieni is a University Instructor in English Studies at the University of Regina and St. Thomas More College. She earned her PhD in English from the University of Saskatchewan. Her research areas include narratives of sexual trauma, abjection, hysteria and gender studies. Her writing has been published in *MP: Online Feminist Journal* (2012), *Forum: Postgraduate Journal* (2011), *Journal of Monsters and the Monstrous* (2012), as well as a forthcoming essay in the collection, *Reading in the Dark: Horror in Children's Literature and Culture* (University Press of Mississippi, 2017).

Miles Leeson is Director of the Iris Murdoch Research Centre at the University of Chichester as well as Visiting Research Fellow at the University of Kingston. He is the lead editor of the *Iris Murdoch Review* and has published widely on her work. His monograph *Iris Murdoch: Philosophical Novelist* (Continuum) was published in 2010 and he has also written on Woolf, Nabokov and Queneau. His latest work is the collection *Iris Murdoch: A centenary Celebration* (Sabrestorm, 2019).

Michael Mack is Reader (Associate Professor and tenured Research Fellow) in English Studies and Medical Humanities at Durham University. He is the author of *Anthropology as Memory: Elias Canetti and Franz Baermann Steiner's Responses to the Shoah* (Niemeyer, 2001); *German Idealism and the Jew. The Inner Anti-Semitism of Philosophy and German Jewish Responses* (University of Chicago Press, 2003), *Spinoza and the Specters of Modernity: The Hidden Enlightenment of Diversity from Spinoza to Freud* (Continuum, 2010), *How Literature Changes the Way we Think* (Continuum, 2012) and *Philosophy and Literature in Times of Crisis: Challenging our Infatuation with Numbers* (Bloomsbury, 2014).

Emma V. Miller is a writer and academic based at Durham University. She specialises in the study of gender and trauma literature dating from the nineteenth century to the present day. She has published in numerous journals and edited collections, most recently contributing to the Cambridge University Press Critical Concepts series on Trauma and Literature. Her monograph on incest in the novels of Iris Murdoch is forthcoming with McFarland & Company, Inc.

Alice Mills is Adjunct Professor of Literature and Children's Literature at Federation University, Ballarat, Australia. She has published widely as a scholar of fantasy and children's literature, with a particular interest in psychoanalytic and Jungian approaches to literature. She has published a book on Mervyn Peake and edited two further scholarly books (one in conjunction with Jeremy Smith) and a number of anthologies of literature for children.

Charles Mundye is Head of Academic Development in the Department of Humanities at Sheffield Hallam University. He is editor of *Keidrych Rhys, The Van Pool: Collected Poems* for Seren (2012), and co-editor of Robert Graves and Laura Riding's *A Survey of Modernist Poetry and A Pamphlet Against Anthologies* for Carcanet (2002). He is currently President of the Robert Graves Society and a Fellow of the English Association.

Matthew Pateman is head of department at Edge Hill University. He has written and published on a wide range of topics including contemporary fiction, Quality Television, aesthetics and transgressive texts. His monograph *Joss Whedon* was recently published in the MUP Television Series.

Fran Pheasant-Kelly is MA Film Studies Course Leader and Reader in Screen Studies at the University of Wolverhampton, UK. Her research spans terrorism, space, science and abjection in film and television. She is the author of numerous publications including two monographs, *Abject Spaces in American Cinema: Institutions, Identity* *and Psychoanalysis in Film* (I.B. Tauris, 2013) and *Fantasy Film Post 9/11* (Palgrave, 2013), and the co-editor of *Spaces of the Cinematic Home: Behind the Screen Door* (Routledge, 2015).

Rebecca White is a tutor in the Department of English at Durham University. Her AHRC-funded doctorate explored classic-novel screen adaptation from 1995 to 2009, and she has published widely on Austen, Dickens, the Brontës, and Gaskell. She is a reviewer for *The Year's Work in English Studies*, and her most recent publications include a critical introduction for *Charles Dickens: Complete Novels* (Anthem Press, 2016) and a chapter in *Fan Phenomena: Jane Austen* (Intellect, 2015). She is currently researching Austen on YouTube for a Special Issue of *Women's Writing*, and investigating the reception of nineteenth-century fiction in the First and Second World Wars.

Acknowledgements

The editor and contributors wish to thank and acknowledge the support and assistance they have received from Andrea Newman, Ashley Pearce, Stephen Parton, Mammoth Screen Ltd, ITV Ltd and Mammoth Screen Productions, Abbie Weinberg, Rachel Ward, Jane Smiley and Lynn Pleshette, Screen Australia, Screen New South Wales, the South Australian Film Corporation, Leah Churchill-Brown, Faber & Faber, Farrar, Strauss and Giroux (Macmillan) and all at HarperCollins, Pathé Production, Luisa Fisher, Simon J. James, Pamela Osborn, Mark Sandy, Colin Theakston, Patricia Waugh, Sarah Wootton and Frances White.

We are grateful to David Miller, Editor of the *Journal of Literary and Trauma Studies*, and to Nebraska Press, for allowing us to draw upon content for the introduction covered previously in Emma V. Miller's article ' "We must not forget that there was a crime": Incest, domestic violence and textual memory in the novels of Iris Murdoch', *Journal of Literature and Trauma Studies* 1:2 (University of Nebraska Press, Fall 2012), pp. 65–94, doi.org/10.1353/jlt.2012.0014.

None of this would be possible without the support of our colleagues and families.

This work owes much to the vision and endeavour of Emma V. Miller, without whom the collection would not have come to fruition: it is dedicated to her.

Introduction

Miles Leeson with Emma V. Miller

Literature has always had a fractious and convoluted relationship with the depiction of incest. From the sexual relations between Lot and his daughters in Genesis to the stories of Byblis, Myrrha and Philomela – perhaps best known today through Ovid's *Metamorphoses* – tales of incest have been disseminated for thousands of years. In the myths and legends we associate with Western culture, incest has continually played a significant role. A number of versions of the fall of King Arthur, including those described in *The Post-Vulgate Cycle* and Thomas Malory's *Le Morte d'Arthur* indicate that the eventual demise of Camelot can be traced to Arthur's incestuous liaison with his sister.[1] Incest, in this instance, can be interpreted as a political metaphor whereby the behaviour or the condition of the monarch, reflects upon the state of the nation.[2] In the Renaissance, incest in literature was, as Elizabeth Archibald puts it in relation to Shakespeare's *Pericles*, 'intertwined with the theme of good and bad kingship … In Renaissance drama the incestuous protagonists tend to drag everyone else down with them as for instance in Ford's *'Tis Pity She's A Whore* and Middleton's *Women Beware Women*. There can be no recovery from consummated incest in these plays; villains and victims alike must die.'[3] For the Romantics, in the words of Percy Shelley, incest 'may be the excess of love or hate',[4] and incest appears repeatedly as a motif in both Romantic and Gothic writing, as a depiction of forbidden desire and of horror, from Matthew Gregory Lewis' infamous tale of sexual transgression, *The Monk* (1796), to the yearning of a sister for her brother in Chauteaubriand's novella, *René* (1802), to Shelley's depiction of father-daughter abuse in his tragedy, *The Cenci* (1819). Indeed, although often not explicitly depicted, incest has been read in the literature of gothic-romance throughout the Victorian age, in fictions such as Emily Brontë's *Wuthering Heights* (1847) and Bram Stoker's *Dracula* (1897).[5] As Paul A. Cantor asserts 'incest epitomizes the transgressive force of the Gothic, its implacable urge to go beyond all boundaries, especially the bounds of conventional law and morality.'[6] Literature has provided readers with a means to consider this ultimate taboo, to enforce the prohibition, to find a means to narrate suffering, sometimes to provide comfort, but also to cause a sensation, and even as a trope to explore something else entirely.

Building upon the integral role that incest has had in literary history, this collection of essays focuses on the variety of approaches that fictional practitioners have undertaken in the last sixty years or so to highlight the varying notions of incest that are inextricably linked to the contemporary debate. The diverse range of literary treatments of incest in this collection include: as a Freudian theory of adolescent developmental fantasy; as sexual abuse; as a conceit for political adaptation; as a tool for discussing and investigating cultural identity – but this is not an exhaustive list. Indeed, this collection is interested in the multifarious nature of the depiction of this most sensitive and controversial of taboos within contemporary literature, and how current psychological and sociological debates have informed current artistic practice and fictional poetics. The research in this volume addresses a variety of media and cultural figures, all of whom – implicitly or explicitly – have highlighted something important about the incest taboo. Our collection emerges from historical representations of, and discourses about, incest, but it also aims to engage dynamically with contemporary debate, and to examine critically how recent cultural and artistic considerations of incest have evolved from those of the past.

Beth Bailey has stated that, 'While notions of childhood innocence were first clearly articulated in the 1760s and did not reach their sentimental apogee until the early nineteenth century, by the mid-eighteenth century, historians can already find a 'new feeling for childhood,' most particularly in relation to sexual crimes.'[7] She writes of the increase in accusations of rape committed on 'prepubescent girls' between the 1600s and the end of the 1700s in Paris and states that even so, 'charges of incest were almost non-existent.'[8] Bailey dates the 'first child protection organization' as originating in New York in 1874[9] and just over two decades later, Freud made his proposal that hysteria resulted from sexual abuse in infancy. Debates about raising the age of consent in the UK and the USA also intensified during this period. The age of consent in the UK was increased 'from ten to twelve in 1861', 'then again to thirteen in 1875'.[10] However, parliament resisted raising it to sixteen until a journalist named W.T. Stead brought the plight of child sex workers such as Elizabeth Armstrong to public attention in the 1880s. Armstrong was just thirteen when she was bought with the intention of using her as a sex worker and then subdued using chloroform.[11] As historian, Lloyd deMause, observed in 1976, '[t]he history of childhood is a nightmare from which we have only recently begun to emerge. The further back in history one goes, the lower the

Introduction

level of child care, and the more likely children are to be killed, abandoned, beaten, terrorised, and sexually abused.'[12]

Concern about child abuse in the UK can perhaps be traced even further back, to what is thought to be the first 'reference to an age of consent' in 1275.[13] Kathryn Cullen-Dupont explains how in the United States the age of consent 'was originally set at ten by common law' until 1864 when pressure from women's rights activists provoked change. Cullen-Dupont expands on this with an overview of the history of consent in the States, saying that Oregon was first to increase the age of consent to fourteen, but in some areas the reaction to women's campaigns was not to raise the age but to lower it, with Delaware amending it in 1872 to just seven years of age. Delaware did eventually increase the age of consent to fifteen 'but on the condition that rape be treated as a misdemeanour.' Similarly, 'Wisconsin raised the age of consent to fourteen in 1887 in response to women's demands', yet just twenty-four months later the state reacted to 'male complaint' and subsequently 'reduced both the age of consent (to twelve) and the punishment' with a proviso that there should be 'a lighter sentence "if the child shall be a common prostitute."'[14] Yet, while the campaigns to protect children from sexual offences were gaining in momentum, specific legislation on the subject of incest did not appear until the twentieth century. The Punishment of Incest Act was passed in England in 1908, but Scotland did not criminalise incest until 1986,[15] yet it was not until the 2003 Sexual Offences Act that the specific offences of 'sexual activity with a child family member and inciting a child family member to engage in sexual activity' were created.[16] As Judith V. Becker and Emily M. Coleman explain, 'the social problem of incest has been clouded by many myths. Initially, it was believed that incest was limited to certain geographical areas (e.g. Appalachia) and to only lower socioeconomic families. Incest was thought to occur only once or twice and not to be an ongoing pattern.'[17] Yet, even when the Kinsey Reports were published in two volumes in 1948 and 1953 respectively, and their findings on the sexual behaviour of American citizens, 'shocked experts and the public alike'[18], as Judith Herman asserts, '[t]he public, in the judgement of these men, was not ready to hear about incest'.[19] The Kinsey Reports were the work of a group of researchers led by Indiana University zoologist, Alfred Kinsey, and their findings suggested that 'the majority of the nation's citizens had violated acceptable moral standards as well as state and federal laws in pursuit of sexual pleasure.'[20] Yet, Judith Herman writes that, '[w]hile Kinsey and his associates dared to describe a vast range of sexual behaviours in exhaustive detail … On the subject of incest, apparently, they felt the less said the better.'[21] It is difficult to believe now that while some aspects of the report were received with shock, the statistic that '24 per cent of white, middle-class married women reported sexual abuse … was downplayed',[22] and even when another work detailing the prevalence of incest was published in 1955, S. Kirson Weinberg's *Incest Behaviour*, 'no sensation, in fact no public response of any kind, attended its publication.'[23]

During this period, even when it was accepted that intrafamilial sexual abuse had occurred, blame was in a number of cases directed to other members of the family, including underage victims, as Joseph E. Davis writes:

> In fact without denying the pathology of the 'incest prone' father ... for some systems theorists it was the mother who despite her formal innocence in the sexual events, actually served as the 'cornerstone in the pathological family system' ... By effecting the role reversal with the daughter, by refusing sex with the father, and by denying the incest, the mother 'set up' the incest and made its perpetuation possible.

He goes on to describe how '[i]n the family systems model, the daughter was seen to play a complying role in the incest behaviour. She returned hostility, theorists argued, to her overly demanding mother and helped to reverse their roles'.[24] The emphasis on a perceived family rivalry has clear echoes in Freud's Oedipus complex theory. In *A Secure Base: Clinical Applications of Attachment Theory*, the psychologist and psychoanalyst, John Bowlby suggests that Freud's change of direction, led to 'the concentration in analytic circles on fantasy and the reluctance to examine the impact of real-life events', something he states, 'has much to answer for.'[25] Developing his argument he writes:

> It is not an analyst's job, so the conventional wisdom has gone to consider how a patient's parents may really have treated him, let alone to entertain the possibility, even probability, that a particular patient may have been the target for the violent words and violent deeds of one or both of his parents. To focus attention on such possibilities, I have often been told, is to be seduced by our patients' prejudiced tales.[26]

However, it is Jeffrey Moussaieff Masson's *The Assault on the Truth: Freud's Suppression of the Seduction Theory* (1984) that has perhaps become the best-known polemic on Freud's rejection of the Seduction Theory. Masson highlights the 'icy reception' Freud describes when he presented the findings that led to 'The Aetiology of Hysteria', and how Freud states that fellow psychiatrist, Richard von Krafft-Ebing likened his theory to, 'a scientific fairytale'.[27] Masson quotes Freud detailing how shortly after he had presented his ideas, he felt 'isolated', and that he had 'written down in full' his ideas '[i]n defiance of my colleagues'.[28] However Freud might have come to his decision to so dramatically alter his professional stance, as Florence Rush asserts in her critique of Freud, 'The Freudian Cover-Up', his choice went on to profoundly influence the way that reports of sexual violence in the home were received by professionals and the general public alike.[29]

Introduction

Proving the occurrence of incest, like many sexual crimes, relies heavily upon the testimony of the victim, and therefore upon convincing the listener or reader of this testimony to believe their account. Yet, even if the actuality of incest is not disputed in general, individual narrators still must contend with a multitude of further challenges, as Chris O'Sullivan and Deborah Fry explain: 'Children often do not disclose sexual abuse because they believe the situation is normal, blame themselves, are afraid of the consequences, and/or fear they will not be believed. These barriers to reporting are often reinforced by the perpetrator.'[30] Furthermore, as Vikki Bell details, 'the incest prohibition' has been viewed 'as a gateway which once passed, takes one into a world of deviancy and illusions. ... [I]ncest is seen as a problem that will lead to the female survivor becoming a "problem" for society (she will become "anti-social").'[31] This suggests a cyclical problem, whereby even if a victim's account is believed they may then be subject to being judged themselves.

However, a cultural shift is identifiable in the latter decades of the twentieth century. Building concern regarding women's rights at this time, in their intimate relationships as well as in the wider sphere, helped to direct the conversation towards the rights of children, as '[f]eminists linked spousal abuse with child abuse'[32]. Nancy Whittier has described how, although

> [f]eminists continued to cast child sexual abuse as a crime against women and an example of the pervasiveness and violence of men's control of women' rather than 'as a unique issue. As activists in various locations began to expand their analysis of and work against child sexual abuse, and as the growing national women's movement brought them into increasing contact with each, the events and institutions in the late 1970s laid the groundwork for a broader movement against abuse in the 1980s.'[33]

In 1971 John Rawls' *A Theory of Justice* was instrumental in the debate of 'what is owed to children as a matter of justice'[34] and in 1973 C. Hardman published an article calling for children to be viewed 'as people to be studied in their own right, and not just the receptacles of adult teaching'.[35] Later in the same decade, during the International Year of the Child (1979), Michael Freeman gave a public lecture where he concentrated 'for the first time directly on children's rights' and 'identified "rightlessness" as a root cause of child abuse.'[36] However, it was not until the late 1980s and early 1990s that the 'paradigm shift' in attitudes on children's rights happened,[37] a change that was signified by the United Nations Convention of the Rights of the Child (1989).

As discussions surrounding the occurrence of incest as a social reality grew amongst feminist writers, so did the number of other kinds of publications, including Maya Angelou's autobiography of her own experience of abuse in the home, *I Know Why the Caged Bird Sings* (1969) and in 1972 Virginia

Woolf's memoirs, 'A Sketch of the Past' and '22 Hyde Park Gate' were released in full. Literary works concerned with incest also proliferated, with examples such as: Vladimir Nabokov's *Lolita* (1955 Paris & 1958 New York), Doris Lessing's *The Golden Notebook* (1962), Angela Carter's *The Magic Toyshop* (1967), Nabokov's *Ada or Ardor* (1969), Ian McEwan's *The Cement Garden* (1978) and Jane Smiley's *A Thousand Acres* (1991), to name just a few.[38]

However, despite developments in medical and cultural understanding of the reality of sexual abuse in the West, recent news coverage has revealed it has still continued to be prevalent. News coverage of events alleged to have occurred at the BBC (specifically the Savile cases but other investigations are on-going)[39] in the UK during the 1950s and 1960s illustrates how attitudes to accusers, victims and/or survivors of sexual abuse has altered very recently in many ways. In Austria in 2008, the Fritzl case, concerning the systematic imprisonment and incestuous rape of Elisabeth Fritzl by her father Joseph, resulting in seven offspring and one miscarriage, highlighted both the shocking nature of repeated, forced incest and also the changing media dynamic. A great deal of attention was – rightly – paid to the case due to the chain of events over twenty-four years which, to the media, was the direst apogee that incest could attain, with *Der Standard* reporting: 'The whole country [Austria] must ask itself just what is really, fundamentally going wrong.'[40]

That Freud chose to name his theory of sexual development and incestuous fantasy after a mythical literary character has further complicated the relationship between the real life occurrence of intra-familial abuse and the literary depiction of incest. The Oedipus complex is a term used – and indeed misused by the media and others – in everyday discourse today, yet it undermines the actuality of sexual violence in the home, both in its definition and also by its reference to Oedipus. It suggests that incest is a fiction and also undercuts the power of fiction to educate and assist: the damage is twofold. However, literature has been instrumental in helping to break through the taboo of talking of incest and thereby paving the way for survivors of abuse to speak out. It has also undoubtedly assisted in helping survivors find a space within the existing narratives to tell a different account of the experience of incest. Indeed the rise of autobiographical work by incest survivors is a growing area of publishing – Elisabeth Fritzl is, according to a report in the *Austrian Times*, writing hers for publication[41] – and this too is an area ripe for academic discussion. Until very recently literature on incest generally did one of the following: disguised incest as something else so that it was suggested rather than made explicit in the text; depicted it as a historical rather than a current possibility; indicated that it could only be seen as an allegory for a political problem; or presented it in erotic rather than abusive terms. In order to seek assistance, those suffering from abuse required a means to explain

Introduction

their experiences, a way of speaking of what was for many years unspeakable, and literature helped to shape a means to do this, both in terms of finding a new way of telling but also by providing re-readings and rewritings of existing motifs of incest. Where literature, though, arguably encounters problems, is, ironically, in its inherently fictional nature. A work of fiction may be able to explore and project the actual experience of an individual more effectively than many other means, it may be able to reach a wide audience and thereby influence a great number of people but how can a mode of art – that is in its very name fictive – assist those whose voices are most doubted? Literature may have increased awareness of incest in society, but whether it will ultimately assist or hinder the furtherance of understanding of the circumstances of incest becomes less clear with every development in the field.

This is a crucial concern, and raises questions about the very purpose of literature and its moral and social responsibility. Such concerns specifically connected to incest and trauma became more problematic in the 1990s with the allegations of False Memory Syndrome (FMS). Supporters of the FMS movement suggested that individuals had been coerced by their therapists to believe and report incidents of abuse, where none had occurred. The term False Memory Syndrome was coined in 1992 by Peter and Pamela Freyd, as a result of an allegation made against Peter, by their adult daughter after re-accessing what she understood to be a repressed memory.[42] Michael Salter includes the False Memory Syndrome Foundation in his discussion of the 'backlash' against the change in attitudes towards reports of sex offences, which had 'created alternative testimonial opportunities for victimised children and women away from the medico-legal traditions that had trivialised their accounts.'[43] He describes this new state of affairs as 'a challenge not only to established expertise but to the project of governmentality itself and the gender order it legitimises'.[44] Raiit and Zeedyk include a list of those who have 'depicted the FMS movement as a backlash to the shame and guilt aroused through the uncovering of endemic child abuse in the Western world.'[45] Although strongly defended as a concept by the False Memory Syndrome Foundation, it is also virulently contested by proponents of recovered memory theory and treatment. The work of Elizabeth F. Loftus and J.E. Pickrell does indeed indicate that memory can be tampered with. Of particular note is the 'familial informant false narrative procedure' research exercise, whereby subjects were encouraged to believe they were once 'lost in a mall', and which demonstrates that persuasive 'interviewing' can in some cases lead to reports of memories of occurrences that did not happen in reality.[46] Yet the relevance of this investigation to the issue of sex abuse has been questioned by, amongst others, Pope and Brown (1997), and research suggests that women with a documented background of abuse are not always able (or perhaps willing) to recall the event in years to come. Indeed it has been concluded that the inability to engage with such events until a period of years has passed, if at all, may be to do with the nature of the event itself and the continued power of the abuser (Kelly, 1998).[47] An incorrect allegation of abuse would undoubtedly be a distressing scenario and one that ought to be guarded against for the benefit of all concerned, yet the widespread discussion of False Memory Syndrome led not just to protecting the innocent but also to deterring actual sufferers of abuse from seeking assistance. FMS continues to be a subject of intense debate, and one that can be seen to have informed literary examinations and responses to the topic of incest.

Incest in contemporary literature: The collection

This volume explores some of the literature that has depicted incest since the 1950s to the present day, asking crucially: Why incest? Why this particular presentation? And why at this point in time? This collection can only provide a sampling of the literary responses to this sensitive, convoluted and expansive topic, but we hope it will contribute to the debate commenced by others, such as Janice Doane and Devon Hodges in their book, *Telling Incest: Narratives of Dangerous Remembering* (2001) and by Elizabeth L. Barnes in her edited collection, *Incest and the Literary Imagination* (2002). We have deliberately sought to juxtapose authors who are well-known for writing on incest such as Ian McEwan, with those that have not been exposed to extensive critical consideration regarding this theme, such as Margo Lanagan, and we have extended our understanding of the literary 'text' to include the literary adaptation, as the televisual or filmic interpretation of a work of fiction can provide a culturally influential 'reading' of the literary object. There are literary examples included which may seem as if they do not meet the popular definition of 'incest', as they do not include sexual relations between blood relatives, but rather those that act in the stead of relations, such as step-father and step-daughter, such as Humbert Humbert and Dolores Haze in Vladimir Nabokov's *Lolita*. Yet under the Sexual Offences Act of 2003 in the UK, the definition of family includes those who act as a parent or who have been brought up in close proximity as if family.[48] We therefore feel that this is an important inclusion. We have also incorporated depictions of what is known as 'emotional incest' or 'covert incest', which is defined as follows:

> According to Maloney ... it 'occurs when a child becomes the object of a parent's affection, love, passion and preoccupation. The boundary between caring and incestuous love is crossed when the relationship with the child exists to meet the needs of the parent rather than the need of the child.' It includes excitatory and sexualised relationships, even when there is no clear-cut, explicit sexual activity between the individuals.[49]

Introduction

This collection, however, is not intended to cover every type of literary depiction of the taboo, indeed, within the constraints of such a volume, it would be quite impossible. We are also literary critics, not psychologists or sociologists who may interpret the texts quite differently, but we have made every effort to be responsible with the subject matter, as even if literature does not pretend to constitute a factual history it is hugely influential and often reflects life. Literature can also convey the emotional experience of people in a way that the reportage of historical or scientific facts alone cannot.

We are aware that there continues to be debate regarding the most accurate or indeed, preferable terminology to describe the sexual relationships this book considers. We have decided to use 'incest' for the title as it is the term most easily understood by the majority of people to refer to sexual activity between family members and it includes all types of such activities, whether these can be argued to be potentially consensual or forced. The contributors have chosen the terms they think most suitable to the specific depictions of incest they refer to in their particular chapters, and this includes whether to refer to those subject to abuse, as 'victims', 'survivors', 'complainants' or one of the other less frequently used terms. As this is a text designed to encourage debate on literature and language we have not prioritised any lexical items, and for the sake of expediency we have not provided a list of alternative terms at every point the need for such a noun has arisen. Describing incest from the perspective of the victim/survivor/complainant of domestic sexual violence is a positive but relatively new phenomenon and a continually evolving process and so in this respect we have issued no restriction beyond observing an appropriate academic style of expression.[50]

The collection is divided into four parts, which we consider cover four of the dominant literary presentations of incest in the latter half of the twentieth century. The essays within each of these parts seek to showcase the variety of literary presentations of incest which pertain to the group's overarching theme, while being distinct enough individually to act as a catalyst for critical discussion. In so doing the collection aims to provide not only an overview of incest narratives in the post-war period – as outlined above – but to enhance the reader's perception of both theoretical and historical constructs from within, and indeed beyond literature.

Part I, 'Behind closed doors', explores how incest has been narrated in terms of the everyday domestic environment, both as an exceptional occurrence but also, in some cases, as an event that is part of the 'ordinary' and understood framework of existence. Frances Pheasant-Kelly discusses Andrea Newman's novel *A Bouquet of Barbed Wire* (1969) and the two subsequent television adaptations of this text, and in doing so she engages with adaptation theory and contemplates the contemporaneous reaction of audiences to all three presentations of the narrative. She considers the characters' repression of incestuous desires, and their associated concerns regarding loss, absence and grief. Introducing new interview material with Andrea Newman, unique to this collection, Pheasant-Kelly presents a timely reassessment of the fall-out of this controversial work. Justine Gieni follows this chapter by looking at Ian McEwan's early short stories and his novel, *The Cement Garden* (1978). She explores these fictions by interrogating the relationship between gender performance and domestic abuse. Through a discussion of the conflicts of masculine subjectivity in its dependence on and desire for the woman-mother, Gieni brings gender theory and feminist critique into conversation with established readings of McEwan's early work. The third essay in this part is by Rebecca White, who considers the debates surrounding memory and sexual trauma, and the specific conflict between the Recovered Memory Movement and the False Memory Syndrome Foundation in relation to Jane Smiley's *A Thousand Acres* (1991), Kathryn Harrison's *Exposure* (1993) and Rachel Ward's 2009 film adaptation of Newton Thornburg's novel, *Beautiful Kate* (1982).

Part II, 'Incest and the child protagonist', begins with Vladimir Nabokov's infamous depiction of child abuse between step-father, Humbert Humbert and the orphaned Dolores Haze, *Lolita* (1955). Matthew Pateman examines the complex relationship between the text's sensitive content and its use of incest as a rhetorical device. He develops his argument to include the narratological presentations of this text in its various filmic incarnations, exploring the ethical implications of each of these independent and yet, arguably, interconnected interpretations of one of the most controversial novels of the twentieth century. In the next essay in Part II, Alice Mills explores whether literature intended for children does, or indeed, should, examine the issue of child abuse in the home, and whether literature has a responsibility to educate the child reader on how to deal with such a situation if it should occur. She examines a variety of the existing literature for children and young people in this respect, before providing a detailed extrapolation of Gary Crew and Annmarie Scott's *In My Father's Room* (2000). To conclude this part, Emma V. Miller examines Margo Lanagan's *Tender Morsels* (2008). As a text marketed toward the young adult group of readers, the violent sexual content of *Tender Morsels* has been subject to intense debate in the media and by parents and young readers alike. Miller considers whether the text can be defined as a work of trauma fiction, its relationship to its fairy-tale heritage and, in its presentation of reality and fantasy, how far it can be considered a work of feminist literature.

Part III, 'Incest as political conceit' is a consideration of one of the most established means of addressing incest in literary history, as a conceit for political unrest. Michael Mack begins this group of discussions, by reading the works of Pablo Pasolini as political allegory, whereby the scandal and the violence of his *oeuvre* arguably aim to expand the awareness of the reader or viewer, and illuminate the controversial and disturbing aspects of the world. Mack focuses his

Introduction

discussion on the depictions of incest in Pasolini's literary and filmic output, and argues that through approaches such as allegory, a means for political improvement might be found. Robert Duggan follows this chapter by examining Iain Banks's 2007 novel *The Steep Approach to Garbadale*, by focussing on how Banks relates the novel's sibling incest to the text's complex concern with national identity. He explains that Banks has also been part of a wider preoccupation in contemporary Scottish writing regarding the habitation of border zones, where the border ceases to be an idealised geometric line and instead becomes a site that one can reside in and/or the ground against which the figure emerges. Incest too, is a topic concerned with borders, familial, sexual and cultural. Alistair Brown concludes this group by examining science fiction, which challenges our understanding of humanness and by extension the human family, by presenting the possibility of a posthuman environ, and questions whether in such a setting incest is even possible. He also explores scientific medical developments in the known world, and how they might impact upon our concept of family. His texts are Kaitlyn O'Connor's *Abiogenesis* (2012), Wyndham Lewis' *Plan for Chaos* (c.1951) and William Gibson's *Neuromancer* (1984). These essays all investigate the connections and the disjunctures between the personal and the political.

In the final group of essays, 'The rhetoric of narrating incest', Charles Mundye continues with the discussion of incest as metaphor, by exploring the concept of incest in the poetry of Ted Hughes and Sylvia Plath. He also seeks to situate their work in a long literary history of the manipulation of incest as a literary trope in Ovidian mythology, Bibical narratives and the writing of William Shakespeare. Mundye argues that Hughes's late work on Ovid's tales of incest, and on the various significances of metamorphosis, creatively engages in a complex dramatic exchange with Plath's poetry. The nature of this exchange is considered in terms of the conceptualisation of sibling relationships, and father–daughter relations in and between their poems. The second chapter in this group by Emma V. Miller and Miles Leeson, examines the efforts by characters in literature to romanticise incest, using its rarity, its alleged exclusivity, as a means to support their argument. Leeson and Miller examine this problematic depiction of incest under the lens of the Derridean concept of *différance*, considering how every word, even incest, no matter how it is presented is arguably unable to escape its context: linguistically, culturally, criminally and artistically. The authors concentrate their discussion on Doris Lessing's *The Golden Notebook* (1962), Angela Carter's *The Magic Toyshop* (1967) and A.S. Byatt's *Morpho Eugenia* (1996). Miles Leeson then concludes the collection by examining the presentation of incest in the novels of Iris Murdoch and Simone de Beauvoir, with a particular focus on Murdoch's *The Black Prince* (1973) and Beauvoir's *The Mandarins* (1957). He examines the philosophical interaction between virtue, desire and sexual choice in the texts, and the role of such frictions within the fictional form.

The central issue here is one of intent; do both Beauvoir, and Murdoch – who exhibited a much greater artistic interest in incest than her French counterpart – depict incest as merely a narrative device or, rather, as a tool by which to promote a certain type of moral seriousness? It appears clear that both authors engage in each presentation of the incest taboo, but it is the ethics of writing incest which is at the centre of the discussion here.

We have sought to address what we consider to be the dominant literary depictions of incest in the latter half of the twentieth century, and those presentations that are of central concern to literary critics. We hope that this volume will inform and further the existing academic interest in this field and that it will prompt further investigation in what continues to be a dynamic and continually developing area of interdisciplinary studies.

Notes

1 For a discussion on incest in Arthurian literature see: Elizabeth Archibald, *Incest and the Medieval Imagination* (Oxford University Press, 2001), pp. 7, 216.
2 Carolyne Larrington writes that 'the Post-Vulgate, mediated through Malory to Boorman, saw the incest as the cause of the Round Table's collapse.' See: Carolyne Larrington, *King Arthur's Enchantresses* (I.B. Tauris, 2006), p. 188.
3 Archibald, *Incest and the Medieval Imagination*, p. 236.
4 Percy Bysshe Shelley, 'Letter to Mrs Gisbourne' (16 November 1819), in Mrs Shelley (ed.), *Essays, Letters from Abroad, Translations and Fragments* (Edward Moxon, 1845), p. 137.
5 For more on reading incest in *Wuthering Heights* see: Eric Solomon, 'The incest theme in Wuthering Heights', *Nineteenth Century Fiction* 14:1 (June, 1959), pp. 80–3. For a discussion of incest criticism regarding *Dracula* see: William Hughes, *Bram Stoker's Dracula: A Reader's Guide* (Bloomsbury) pp. 44–8, 96. Also see: Emma V. Miller, '"We must not forget that there was a crime": Incest, domestic violence and textual memory in the novels of Iris Murdoch', *Journal of Literature and Trauma Studies* 1:2 (Fall, 2012), pp. 65–94, doi.org/10.1353/jlt.2012.0014 (accessed 30 March 2017).
6 Paul A. Cantor, 'The fall of the House of Ulmer: Europe vs. America in the gothic vision of The Black Cat', in Thomas Fahy (ed.) *The Philosophy of Horror* (The University Press of Kentucky, 2010), p. 143.
7 Beth Bailey, 'The vexed history of children and sex', in Paula S. Fass (ed.), *The Routledge History of Childhood in the Western World* (Routledge, 2013), p. 196.
8 *Ibid.*, p. 196.
9 *Ibid.*, p. 197.
10 *Ibid.*, p. 198.
11 *Ibid.*, p. 198. For more detail on this and the debates regarding the age of consent in the UK and the USA see: Bailey, 'The vexed history of children and sex', pp. 196–9.

Introduction

12 Lloyd deMause, 'The evolution of childhood', in Lloyd deMause (ed.), *The History of Childhood* (Rowman & Littlefield, 1974), p. 1.
13 Alisdair Gillespie and Suzanne Ost, 'The 'higher' age of consent and the concept of sexual exploitation', in Alan Reed et al. (eds), *Consent: Domestic and Comparative Perspectives* (Routledge, 2017), p. 163.
14 For all references to this author in this discussion, see: Kathryn Cullen-DuPont, *Encyclopedia of Women's History in America*, 2nd edn (Facts on File, 2000), p. 7.
15 Vikki Bell, *Interrogating Incest* (Routledge, 1993), p. 126.
16 Kim Stevenson and Anne Davies, *Blackstone's Guide to the Sexual Offences Act 2003* (Oxford University Press, 2004), p. 103.
17 Judith V. Becker and Emily M. Coleman, 'Incest', in Alan S. Bellack et al. (eds), *Handbook of Family Violence* (Springer, 1988), p. 188.
18 Miriam G. Reumann, *American Sexual Character* (California University Press, 2005), p. 1.
19 Judith Herman, *Father-Daughter Incest* (Harvard University Press, 1981), p. 18.
20 Reumann, *American Sexual Character*, p. 1.
21 Herman, *Father-Daughter Incest*, p. 17.
22 Maria C. Sauzier, 'Memories of trauma in the treatment of children', in Paul S. Appelbaum, Lisa A. Uyehara and Mark R. Elin (eds), *Trauma and Memory* (Oxford University Press, 1997), p. 378.
23 Herman, *Father-Daughter Incest*, p. 18. Also see: Emma V. Miller, 'Literary Incest: Intertextuality and Writing the Last Taboo in the Novels of Iris Murdoch' (PhD dissertation, Durham University, 2011), http://etheses.dur.ac.uk/1400/ (accessed 15 February 2017) pp. 8–12. Miller, '"We must not forget that there was a crime"', pp. 68, 65–94.
24 Joseph E. Davis, *Accounts of Innocence* (University Press of Chicago, 2005), p. 50–1.
25 John Bowlby, *A Secure Base* (Routledge, 1988), p. 87.
26 *Ibid.*, p. 87.
27 Sigmund Freud, quotation from 'Letter to Wilhelm Fliess' (26 April 1896), in Jeffrey Moussaieff Masson, *The Assault on Truth* (Fontana, 1992), p. 9.
28 Freud, quoted from letters to Wilhelm Fliess (4 May 1896; 30 May 1896) in Masson, *The Assault on Truth*, p. 11.
29 Florence Rush, 'The great Freudian coverup', *Feminism and Psychology* 6:2 (May 1996), pp. 260–76. Miller, '"We must not forget that there was a crime"', pp. 68–9.
30 Chris O'Sullivan and Deborah Fry, 'Sexual assault victimization across the life span: Rates, consequences and interventions for different populations', in Robert C. Davis, Arthur J. Lurigio and Susan Herman, *Victims of Crime* (Sage, 2007), p. 37.
31 Bell, *Interrogating Incest*, p. 137.
32 John Douard and Pamela D. Schultz, *Monstrous Crimes and the Failure of Forensic Psychiatry* (Springer, 2013), p. 100.
33 Nancy Whittier, *The Politics of Child Sexual Abuse* (Oxford University Press, 2009), p. 28.

34 David Archard and Colin M. Macleod, 'Introduction', in David Archard and Colin M. Macleod (eds), *The Moral and Political Status of Children* (Oxford University Press, 2002), p. 1.
35 Michael Freeman, *The Moral Status of Children* (Martinus Nijhoff, 1997), p. 3.
36 *Ibid.*, p. ix.
37 *Ibid.*, 'Preface'.
38 Miller, '"We must not forget that there was a crime"', pp. 8–12.
39 BBC News, *Jimmy Savile scandal: Report reveals decades of abuse*, BBC, 11 January 2013, www.bbc.co.uk/news/uk-20981611.stm (accessed 7 February 2013).
40 Quoted by Matthew Weaver and Kate Connolly, 'Austrian cellar case man admits abduction and incest', *Guardian*, 28 August 2008, www.guardian.co.uk /world/ 2008/apr/28/austria.internationalcrime2 (accessed 31 January 2013).
41 Thomas Hochwarter, 'Elisabeth Fritzl has plans to write a book', *Austrian Times*, 18 March 2009. http://austriantimes.at/index.php?id=11889 (accessed 17 March 2013).
42 Alison Winter, *Memory* (University Press of Chicago, 2012), p. 226.
43 Michael Salter, *Organised Sexual Abuse* (Routledge, 2013), p. 61.
44 *Ibid.*, p. 61.
45 Raiit, Fiona E. and M. Suzanne Zeedyk, *The Implicit Relation of Psychology and the Law* (Routledge, 2000), p. 135.
46 Brendan E. Depue, 'False Memory Syndrome', in Irving B. Weiner and W. Edward Craighead, *Corsini Encyclopedia* vol. 2, 4th edn (John Wiley and Sons, 2010), pp. 645–6.
47 For this extended discussion see: Weiner and Craighead (eds), *Corsini Encyclopedia*, vol. 2, 4th edn, pp. 645–6.
48 Sexual Offences Act 2003, London, UK © Crown Copyright 2003, The Stationery Office Limited under the authority and superintendence of Carol Tullo, Controller of Her Majesty's Stationery Office and Queen's Printer of Acts of Parliament, p. 17. www.legislation.gov.uk/ukpga/2003/42/section/25 (accessed 25 May 2017).
49 Richard B. Gartner, *Betrayed as Boys* (Guilford Press, 1999), p. 26.
50 See: Karen Corteen, 'Victims, survivors or complainants', in Karen Corteen, Sharon Morley, Paul Taylor and Jo Turner (eds), *A Companion to Crime, Harm and Victimisation* (Policy Press, 2016), pp. 264–9.

Bibliography

Fiction

Angelou, Maya, *I Know Why The Caged Bird Sings* (Virago, 2004)
Brontë, Emily, John S. Whitley (introd. and notes), *Wuthering Heights* (Wordsworth Editions Ltd., 2000)
Chateaubriand, François-René, de, Irving Putter (trans.), *Atala and René* (University of California Press, 1952)

Introduction

Ford, John, Sonia Massai (ed.), *'Tis Pity She's a Whore* (Bloomsbury, 2011)
Kelly, Liz, Sheila Burton and Linda Regan, *Supporting Women and Challenging Men: Lessons From the Domestic Violence Intervention Project* (Policy Press, 1998)
Lacy, Norris J. (ed.), *Lancelot–Grail: The Old French Arthurian Vulgate and Post-Vulgate in Translation*, vols. 1–5 (D.S. Brewer, 2010)
Lacy, Norris J. (ed.), E. Jane Burns (introd.), Carol J. Chase (trans.), *The History of the Holy Grail, Lancelot-Grail: The Old French Arthurian Vulgate and Post-Vulgate in Translation*, vol. 1. (D.S. Brewer, 2010)
——., Rupert T. Pickens (trans.), *The Story of Merlin, The History of the Holy Grail, Lancelot-Grail: The Old French Arthurian Vulgate and Post-Vulgate in Translation*, vol. 2. (D.S. Brewer, 2010)
——., Samuel N. Rosenberg (trans. I), Carleton W. Carroll (trans. II), *Lancelot I & II, The History of the Holy Grail, Lancelot-Grail: The Old French Arthurian Vulgate and Post-Vulgate in Translation*, vol. 3. (D.S. Brewer, 2010)
——., Samuel N. Rosenberg (trans. III), Roberta L. Krueger (trans. IV), *Lancelot III & IV, The History of the Holy Grail, Lancelot-Grail: The Old French Arthurian Vulgate and Post-Vulgate in Translation*, vol. 4. (D.S. Brewer, 2010)
——., William W. Kibler (trans.), *Lancelot V, The History of the Holy Grail, Lancelot-Grail: The Old French Arthurian Vulgate and Post-Vulgate in Translation*, vol. 5. (D.S. Brewer, 2010)
——., E. Jane Burns (trans.), *The Quest for the Holy Grail, The History of the Holy Grail, Lancelot-Grail: The Old French Arthurian Vulgate and Post-Vulgate in Translation*, vol. 6. (D.S. Brewer, 2010)
——., Norris Lacy (trans.), *The Death of Arthur, The History of the Holy Grail, Lancelot-Grail: The Old French Arthurian Vulgate and Post-Vulgate in Translation*, vol. 7. (D.S. Brewer, 2010)
——., Martha Asher (introd. and trans.), *The Post-Vulgate Merlin Continuation, The History of the Holy Grail, Lancelot-Grail: The Old French Arthurian Vulgate and Post-Vulgate in Translation*, vol. 8. (D.S. Brewer, 2010)
——., Martha Asher (trans.), *The Post-Vulgate Quest for the Holy Grail & The Post-Vulgate Death of Arthur, The History of the Holy Grail, Lancelot-Grail: The Old French Arthurian Vulgate and Post-Vulgate in Translation*, vol. 9. (D.S. Brewer, 2010)
Lewis, Matthew Gregory, Matthew MacLachlan (ed.), *The Monk* (Penguin, 1998)
Malory, Thomas, Helen Cooper (ed., notes and introd.), *Le Morte Darthur* (Winchester Manuscript, Oxford World Classics, Oxford University Press, 1998)
Middleton, Thomas, Richard Dutton (ed.), *Women Beware Women, and Other Plays* (Oxford University Press, 2009)
Morrison, Toni, *The Bluest Eye* (Vintage, 2016)
Nabokov, Vladimir, *Ada or Ardor* (Penguin, 2011)
Ovid, A.D. Melville (ed.), E.J. Kenney (introd. and notes), *The Metamorphoses* (Oxford University Press, 1998)
Shelley, Percy, Zachary Leader and Michael O'Neill (eds, introd and notes), 'The Cenci', in *The Major Works* (Oxford University Press, 2009), pp. 314–99

Stoker, Bram, Maurice Hindle (introd. and notes), Christopher Frayling (preface), *Dracula* (Penguin, 2010)

Troyes, Chrétien, de, Burton Raffel (ed.), Joseph L. Duggan (afterword), *Perceval: The Story of the Grail* (Yale University Press, 1999)

Non-fiction

Archard, David and Colin M. Macleod (eds), *The Moral and Political Status of Children* (Oxford University Press, 2002), pp. 1–18

Bagley, Christopher and Kathleen King, *Child Sexual Abuse: The Search for Healing* (Tavistock/Routledge, 1990)

Bailey, Beth, 'The vexed history of children and sex', in Paula S. Fass (ed.), *The Routledge History of Childhood in the Western World* (Routledge, 2013), pp. 191–210

Barnes, Elizabeth (ed.), *Incest and the Literary Imagination* (University Press of Florida, 2002)

Becker, Judith V. and Emily M. Coleman, 'Incest', in Alan S. Bellack, Michael Hersn, R.L. Morrison, Vincent B. Van Hassalt (eds), *Handbook of Family Violence* (Springer, 1988), pp. 187–206

Bell, Vikki, *Interrogating Incest: Feminism, Foucault and the Law* (Routledge, 1993)

Bowlby, John, *A Secure Base: Clinical Applications of the Attachment Theory* (Routledge, 1988)

Brownmiller, Susan, *Against Our Will: Men, Women and Rape* (Bantam, 1976)

Cantor, Paul A., 'The fall of the House of Ulmer: Europe vs. American in the gothic vision of The Black Cat', in Thomas Fahy (ed.), *The Philosophy of Horror* (University Press of Kentucky, 2010), pp. 137–60

Campbell, Robert J., *Campbell's Psychiatric Dictionary* (Oxford University Press, 2009)

Cullen-Dupont, Kathryn (ed.), *Encyclopaedia of Women and History in America* (Da Capo Press, 1998)

Davis, Joseph E., *Accounts of Innocence: Sexual Abuse, Trauma and the Self* (The University of Chicago Press, 2005)

Depue, Brendan E., 'False Memory Syndrome', in Irving B. Weiner and W. Edward Craighead (eds.), *Corsini Encyclopedia* (John Wiley and Sons, 2010), pp. 645–6.

deMause, Lloyd, 'The evolution of childhood', in Lloyd deMause (ed.), *The History of Childhood* (Psychohistory Press, 1974), pp. 1–74

Doane, Janice L. and Devon Hodges, *Narratives of Dangerous Remembering From Stein to Sappho* (University of Michigan Press, 2001)

Douard, John and Pamela D. Schultz, *Monstrous Crimes and the Failure of Forensic Psychiatry* (Springer, 2013)

Duggan, Joseph J., *The Romances of Chrétien de Troyes* (Yale University Press, 2001)

Freeman, Michael, *The Moral Status of Children: Essays on the Rights of the Child* (Martinus Nijhoff, 1997)

Freud, Sigmund, James Strachey (trans.), *The Interpretation of Dreams* (Avon, 1965)

———, James Strachey and Anna Freud with Alix Strachey and Alan Tyson (trans.), 'The aetiology of hysteria', in *Early Psychological Publications, Complete Psychological Works of Sigmund Freud*, vol. III (Vintage, 2001), pp. 189–221

———., James Strachey and Anna Freud with Alix Strachey and Alan Tyson (trans.), 'The development of the libido and the sexual organisations', *Introductory Lectures on Psycho-Analysis (Part III), The Standard Edition of the Complete Psychological Works of Sigmund Freud*, vol. 16 (Vintage, 2001), pp. 320–38

Friedan, Betty *The Feminine Mystique* (Norton, 2001)

Gartner, Richard B., *Betrayed as Boys: Psychodynamic Treatment of Sexually Abused Men* (Guilford Press, 1999)

Gillespie, Alisdair and Suzanne Ost, 'The "higher" age of consent and the concept of sexual exploitation', in Alan Reed, Michael Bolander, Nicola Wake and Emma Smith (eds), *Consent: Domestic and Comparative Perspectives* (Routledge, 2017), pp. 161–76

Herman, Judith with Lisa Hischman, *Father-Daughter Incest* (Harvard University Press, 1981)

Larrington, Carolyne, *King Arthur's Enchantresses: Morgan and Her Sisters in Arthurian Tradition* (I.B. Tauris, 2006)

Laschinger, Bernice, 'Attachment Theory and the John Bowlby Memorial Lecture 2006 a short history', in Sarah Benamer and Kate White (eds), *Trauma and Attachment: The John Bowlby Memorial Conference Monograph 2006* (Karnac Books, 2008)

Masson, Jeffrey Moussaieff, *The Assault on Truth: Freud's Suppression of the Seduction Theory* (Fontana, 1992)

Miller, Emma V., 'Literary Incest: Intertextuality and Writing the Last Taboo in the Novels of Iris Murdoch' (PhD dissertation, Durham University, 2011), http://etheses.dur.ac.uk/1400/ (accessed 15 February 2017)

———., ' "We must not forget that there was a crime": Incest, domestic violence and textual memory in the novels of Iris Murdoch', *Journal of Literature and Trauma Studies* 1:2 (University of Nebraska Press, Fall 2012), pp. 65–94, doi.org/10.1353/jlt.2012.0014 (accessed 30 March 2017)

O'Sullivan, Chris and Deborah Fry, 'Sexual assault victimization across the life span: Rates, consequences and interventions for different populations', in Robert C. Davis, Arthur J. Lurigio and Susan Herman (eds), *Victims of Crime* (Sage, 2007), pp. 35–54

Raiit, Fiona E. and M. Suzanne Zeedyk, *The Implicit Relation of Psychology and the Law* (Routledge, 2000)

Reumann, Miriam G., *American Sexual Character: Sex, Gender, and National Identity in the Kinsey Reports* (California University Press, 2005)

Rush, Florence, 'The great Freudian coverup', *Feminism and Psychology* 6:2 (May 1996), pp. 260–76

Sacco, Lynn, *Unspeakable: Father-Daughter Incest in American History* (Johns Hopkins University Press, 2009)

Salter, Michael, *Organised Sexual Abuse* (Routledge, 2013)
Sauzier, Maria C., 'Memories of trauma in the treatment of children', in Paul S. Appelbaum, Lisa A. Uyehara and Mark R. Elin (eds), *Trauma and Memory: Clinical and Legal Controversies* (Oxford University Press, 1997), pp. 378–93
Shelley, Percy Bysshe, 'Letter to Mrs Gisbourne' (16 November 1819), in Mrs Shelley (ed.), *Essays, Letters from Abroad, Translations and Fragments* (Edward Moxon, 1845)
Stevenson, Kim and Anne Davies, *Blackstone's Guide to the Sexual Offences Act 2003* (Oxford University Press, 2004)
Whittier, Nancy, *The Politics of Child Sexual Abuse: Emotion, Social Movements and the State* (Oxford University Press, 2009)
Winter, Alison, *Memory: Fragments of a Modern History* (University Press of Chicago, 2012)
Woolf, Virginia, 'A sketch of the past' and '22 Hyde Park Gate' in *Moments of Being*, Jeanne Schulkind (ed. and introd.) (Chatto & Windus, 1976), pp. 69–138; 140–56

Websites

BBC News, *Jimmy Savile scandal: Report reveals decades of abuse*, BBC, 11 January 2013, www.bbc.co.uk/news/uk-20981611.stm (accessed 7 February 2013)
Hochwarter, Thomas, 'Elisabeth Fritzl has plans to write a book', *Austrian Times*, 18 March 2009, http://austriantimes.at/index.php?id=11889 (accessed 17 March 2013)
Sexual Offences Act 2003, London, UK © Crown Copyright 2003, The Stationery Office Limited under the authority and superintendence of Carol Tullo, Controller of Her Majesty's Stationery Office and Queen's Printer of Acts of Parliament, p. 17. www.legislation.gov.uk/ukpga/2003/42/section/25 (accessed 25 May 2017)
Weaver, Matthew and Kate Connolly, 'Austrian cellar case man admits abduction and incest', *Guardian*, 28 April 2008, www.guardian.co.uk/world/2008/apr/28/austria.internationalcrime2 (accessed 31 January 2013)
Weinraub, Judith, 'Germaine Greer, "opinions that may shock the faithful", Review of *The Female Eunuch*, 22 March 1971, *New York Times* www.nytimes.com/books/99/05/09/specials/greer-shock.html (accessed 23 March 2017)

Part I

Behind closed doors

1

Text, image, audience: Adaptation and reception of Andrea Newman's *A Bouquet of Barbed Wire* (1969)

Frances Pheasant-Kelly

Although Andrea Newman's novel, *A Bouquet of Barbed Wire* (1969),[1] received largely positive reviews on its initial publication, it garnered immediate notoriety on its dramatisation as a television series in 1976. This first adaptation was, nevertheless, highly successful, attracting 26 million viewers, while a more recent television version in 2010 achieved 13 million viewers over its three episodes.[2] The furore surrounding London Weekend Television's (LWT) 1976 production centred on Peter Manson's (played by Frank Finlay) apparently incestuous desire for his nineteen-year-old daughter, Prue (played by Susan Penhaligon), with whom he seems obsessed. Aside from Manson's displays of jealousy towards Prue's husband, the drama's portrayal of sadomasochism and infidelity both attracted and scandalised audiences and reviewers alike – for instance, Penny Perrick of the *Sun* commented 'Let's hope that plastic people with horrible habits like the Mansons are banished from the screen forever',[3] whereas *Times* reviewer, Michael Church, assigned the series 'a curious magic'.[4] Also telling of the drama's 1970s' contexts was *Times* reviewer, Michael Ratcliffe's comment that, 'bright spots included … two sharp blows across the face for Prue, from the sorely provoked Gavin'.[5] Whereas the first adaptation followed the novel closely, the second differed both narratively and visually, with its less oppressive aesthetics seeming to reflect changed attitudes towards incest since the 1970s. In respect of the latter, Joan Lynch observes how, '[t]he shroud of secrecy, silence, and lies woven by patriarchy was ripped in the late 1970s by feminists, many of whom were psychologists, who revealed their and others' pain as survivors of incest'.[6] In a related vein, Euan Ferguson of the *Observer* suggests that the unmentionable nature of incest was one of the reasons that made the 1976 version so popular, leading him to ask, 'why remake this? I know incest, even the thought of it, is still taboo, but in the mid-70s it was seriously taboo and thus entrancing viewing'.[7]

The novel's narrative, however, does not entail actual incest, but rather problematises a father–daughter relationship without directly depicting the taboo, since Prue actively invites the attention of her father, and takes delight in provoking him emotionally. In many ways, the novel and its adaptations explore the boundary between paternal affection and incestuous desire. Indeed, in interview, both the novel's author, Andrea Newman,[8] and director of the second adaptation, Ashley Pearce,[9] contend that Peter Manson would have been shocked by any suggestion of incest. Nonetheless, the implication of mutual attraction between father and daughter is an undeniable central feature. More contentiously, the mode of its signification in both novel and first adaptation (through fantasised scenarios and imaginary dialogues), together with Prue's provocative behaviour, recalls Freud's notion of childhood phantasy and its inference of child desire.

The latter superseded his earlier Seduction Theory, in which he attributed symptoms of hysteria in adult women to previous abuse, and instead suggested that children had imagined or fantasised such mistreatment. As Judith Herman reports, a number of surveys from the 1950s to the present day, including the 1953 Kinsey report, which was based on 4,000 interviews,[10] discredit this suggestion and indicate that incest is, and has long been, a real and widespread phenomenon. Yet, the information from these reports was not prioritised at the time because, according to Herman, 'The public, in the judgement of these men, was not ready to hear about incest.'[11] In the 1970s, however, feminist social science scholars and psychologists again uncovered evidence of extensive child abuse, their work illustrating the contentious historical tensions of the incest debate. For, at one end of its spectrum lie the patriarchal sensibilities promoted by Freud and, at the other, these feminist responses, which disclosed the on-going suppression of child abuse reports. The recent media attention given to paedophilia concerning a number of such cases that occurred during the 1970s – notably regarding Jimmy Savile – typifies the suppression of child abuse, with a significant lapse in time occurring between suspicions of crime, and subsequent police investigation.[12]

The way in which the father–daughter relationship in *Bouquet of Barbed Wire* is represented, principally through claustrophobic settings, close framing, and editing, also lends itself to analysis using Raymond Williams's concept of a 'structure of feeling'[13]. Williams suggests that the dominant ideas at any given time manifest pervasively across visual culture though may only be recognised retrospectively. He explains this phenomenon as 'the continuity of experience from a particular work, through its particular form, to its recognition as a general form, and then the relation of this general form to a period'.[14] Even though it is not possible to directly correlate a single drama's aesthetics with either generalised attitudes towards incest, or broader cultural emotions at any given time, there is nonetheless a line of travel between the oppressive scenarios of the novel and 1976 versions of *Bouquet of Barbed Wire* and the censorship of similar concurrent contentious (but more explicit) material (*Brimstone and Treacle*[15] and *Scum*[16] for instance) in a reflection of society's 'felt sense of the quality of life at a particular place and time'.[17] The unstable political landscape during the 1970s is telling in this respect – as Lez Cooke observes, 'The cultural shift from the 1960s to the 1970s, from liberalism to conservatism and from consent to coercion, was reflected in the television drama produced during the decade'.[18] While Cooke goes on to explain how television programmes such as the period drama enabled viewers a means to 'escape'[19] such political tensions, one might also correlate such conservatism with the visual strategies evident at the time. Indeed, Williams himself specifies a correspondence between the enclosed aesthetics of the post-war televised play with both the technological limitations of the period and the contemporaneous 'structure of feeling'[20] and suggests Bergman's *The Lie*[21] as a late example of this.

Accordingly, this essay argues that the varying representations of father–daughter desire in the novel and its dramatisations correspond with their respective zeitgeists, these reflecting differences in attitudes towards incest. In sum, the 1976 version conveys the child figure as seductive and manipulative in line with Freudian concepts of phantasy, as if cohering with concurrent patriarchal perceptions of incest. Here, incest remains implicit, its suppression being signalled through technical aspects such as framing, cinematography and *mise-en-scène*, and conveying a 'feeling' of repression in relation to father–daughter desire. In contrast, the open aesthetics of the second drama correlate with the changed socio-cultural climate, which is reflected across visual culture and broader regimes more generally and ranges from tendencies towards exposing physical and psychological interiority in art to the dismantling of entrenched institutional practices. This is in line with claims by Anna Meigs and Kathleen Barlow who note the emergence

> in the 1970s and [which] continues to this day an important American literature on the surprising frequency and traumatic consequences of "incestuous abuse" … Overall, this new literature signals a paradigm shift in American public consciousness: It is less acceptable to view incest as an infrequent and obscure act more or less effectively controlled by its taboo.[22]

In examining the differences between the three versions of *Bouquet of Barbed Wire*, this chapter further considers audience responses and critical reception, connecting the socio-cultural and legislative climate regarding child abuse at the time of their production with the overall 'structure of feeling'.

Freud, Seduction Theory and the Oedipus complex

Though incest is taboo for most cultures, a long purported facet of child–parent relationships is Freud's theory of the Oedipus complex, which describes a child's desire for the parent of the opposite sex.[23] Prior to proposing the Oedipus complex, however, Freud[24] postulated a 'theory of seduction' based on his studies of hysteria whereby he contended that trauma arose because of repressed memories of sexual abuse by an older individual, usually a father figure. As Pamela Thurschwell points out, however, even at this point, the term Seduction Theory implies the child is motivating the abuse. By 1897, 'Freud found himself obliged to abandon his Seduction Theory [when] his almost simultaneous discovery of the Oedipus Complex … led inevitably to the realization that sexual impulses operated normally in the youngest children without any need for outside stimulation'.[25] Significantly, according to this theory the initiator of these desires was clearly the child rather than the parent, such an attraction arising when the child realises that it is not the sole object of its parental affections, but that his/her parents are also important to each other. Accordingly, '[t]he desolate child encounters a new crisis of sexual desire and jealousy … [and] will develop an erotic love for the parent of the opposite sex and a rivalrous hatred for the parent of the same sex who seems to monopolise the other, desired, parent'.[26] If Freud's articulation of this desire shifted from the daughter (as implicated in Seduction Theory) to denote a male child's desire for his mother, he later provided a revised version that accommodated a young girl's desire for her father.

At first sight, *A Bouquet of Barbed Wire* does not appear to fit either Seduction Theory or the Oedipal scenario, because firstly, Prue does not express resentment of her mother, and secondly, Manson returns her feelings, suggesting their relationship to be something different. Given that there is no evident sexual contact between them, their relationship might arguably constitute emotional incest rather than its physical counterpart. In such circumstances, Patricia Love explains, 'a child is chosen by a parent to be a primary source of emotional support', with the result that the parent–child relationship becomes too close, or 'enmeshed'.[27] However, both the novel and 1976 drama accentuate Prue's knowingness and seductiveness, and her representation coheres with historical patriarchal assumptions concerning incest, which were promoted by Freud. As Herman explains, the concept of 'the seductive daughter' is one that has informed both literary and religious traditions as well as underpinning clinical literature and observes that: 'In general, these investigators tended to focus on qualities in the child victims which might have fostered the development of an incestuous relationship. They, too, conjured up the image of the magical child, the nymphet, who has the power to entrap men'.[28] Moreover, a significant element of the parent–child axis in all three versions involves Prue's masochistic tendencies. For example, she implores Gavin to hurt her, whilst visualising her father's face. Freud elaborates on masochism in his essay 'A Child is Being Beaten', which specifically addresses the notion of sexual pleasure associated with suffering pain. He explains this as one of a series of interrelated fantasies in which 'the wording runs: "*I am being beaten by my father*" [original emphasis] [and] involves a 'high degree of pleasure ... of an unmistakeable masochistic character',[29] with self-punishment arising because of guilt about desire for the father figure. This seems relevant to *A Bouquet of Barbed Wire*, with Prue's behaviour clearly conforming to concepts of the 'seductive daughter' and her guilt resulting in masochistic tendencies that mirror the feelings of real victims of incest. For, as Herman reports of incest victims, 'in many cases, they seemed to feel that they deserved to be beaten'.[30] In sum, therefore, the visual style of the novel and 1976 adaptation constitutes part of a broader structure of feeling that, according to Williams, focused on the entrapment of interior life, and feelings of enclosure and also reflected attitudes towards incest, a topic which was suppressed by the public and clinicians alike.

Andrea Newman's A Bouquet of Barbed Wire (1969)

Andrea Newman's *A Bouquet of Barbed Wire* was first published in 1969, with later editions in 1976 and 2010 (contemporary to the respective television adaptations), the back cover of the latter version highlighting the controversy that the 1970s' adaptation had prompted. Its storyline of incestuous desire was not unique, being one of a number of other post-war incest fictions of the time. In a list of narratives compiled by Janet Walker, which included television fictional films, documentaries, and talk show sessions that featured incest in an 'atmosphere of recognition and change',[31] arguably, *Bouquet*'s best-known post-war contemporary was Vladimir Nabokov's novel *Lolita* (1955) (which is discussed by Matthew Pateman in Chapter 4 of this collection). Similarly to *A Bouquet of Barbed Wire*, *Lolita* was adapted as a film in 1962 (dir. Stanley Kubrick) and later directed by Adrian Lyne in 1997, although it featured a much younger child, and unfolded mostly from the perspective of her stepfather. In contrast, the child protagonist of *A Bouquet of Barbed Wire* is nineteen years old, and, whereas *Lolita* involved actual abuse, the incest in Newman's novel was merely intimated by the interior reflections of its characters.

Despite its contentious subject matter, Newman's novel received good reviews, its endorsements describing it as 'enormously readable',[32] having a 'fizzling style'[33] and a 'passionate excess'[34], while *The Financial Times* stated that it, 'forces on us with new vigour Andrea Newman's belief in the primitive animal savagery that lies so very near the civilised surface'.[35] Michael Church of *The Times* too praised the novel, stating that, '[Newman] has, at the most fundamental level, a crystal ball penetration as to what we are really like'.[36] The book's later editions also attracted positive commentaries, the *Sun* considering it: 'Tense, well written and utterly absorbing,[37] while Nancy Banks-Smith of the *Guardian* declared that, 'Andrea Newman has an entertaining ability to shock'.[38] Personal correspondence to Newman was similarly complimentary, with readers from as young as fourteen years old stating that they had enjoyed reading it.[39]

The plot mostly unfolds through various third-person internal 'monologues', chiefly those of Manson and Prue but also of Cassandra (Cassie), Manson's wife. It follows Manson's obsession with his daughter, and his jealousy and disapproval of her marriage to Gavin, indicated, for example, when Cassie informs Manson of Prue's deliberate decision to become pregnant, and we learn that 'Manson felt sick'.[40] Prue's internal reflections imply that she reciprocates Manson's desires, and reveal that she deliberately incites violence between the two men: 'I wanted to see a fight, a fight over me, a fight between them, my two men. But I wanted Daddy to win'.[41] Another of her internal meditations offers further insight: 'Was there something wrong with her perhaps? She became mildly excited at the very idea. It might be interesting to have something wrong with her. Did this explain why she tormented her father – did she want him to strike back?'[42] She also enjoys Gavin hitting her, suggested by the text, 'It was neither a heavy blow nor a light one but it took all the breath from her body with shock. It was not the pain, such as it was, that she minded: there was even a faint sense of pleasure in the stinging sensation and the knowledge that Gavin had caused it'.[43]

While Andrea Newman states that she did not consciously internalise the various characters' musings, nonetheless, their concealed form in contrast to direct speech is relevant to the theme of incest. In this way, the suppressed nature of much of the text echoes its taboo subject matter at the time of the novel's writing and signals a generalised reluctance to address the subject of incest openly. As well as disclosing Prue's inappropriate affections for the father, these internal revelations also inform the reader of her desire for masochistic violence, Prue constantly inviting her partner, Gavin, to hit her as she fantasises about her father. Such desire is made explicit in a third-person narration that reveals, 'Prue found now that when Gavin made love to her she could not shut her eyes for a second without seeing her father's face'.[44]

In a different vein, Manson's obsession with Prue instead associates paternal desire with loss, and there are persistent references to absence and grief emerging throughout. Predominantly, this centres on a fear of aging, with Manson's incestuous thoughts linked to a yearning for lost youth. The link to ageing gains the empathies of the viewer, and circumvents the sexualisation of Prue. Textually, the language used enforces a sense of loss whilst linking youth to his obsession with Prue. For example, in Chapter 1, Manson's internal monologue notes, 'And now the fine Spring rain, for her first day back',[45] connecting Prue to the words 'Spring' and 'first'. Moreover, while Manson's fascination with youth primarily emerges in his attraction to Prue, it later arises in relation to her 'substitute', his secretary, Sarah Francis. "'I just feel – oh Cass, I just feel so *old* "[46] Manson tells his wife. In later discussions with Cassie about his resentment of Gavin, he muses, 'The world belongs to the young and you're a fool if you resent it. They're the new elite'.[47] Later, he contemplates how,

> Everything went back to age. It was as if he was on some hideous roundabout, perpetually passing the same point, unable to jump off. He lay in the dark and let the words revolve in his mind: too old, times have changed, they're young, accept the inevitable, things are different now, on and on, digging an endless division. Not a family anymore but two generations at war.[48]

Cassie too reflects on the passing years: 'It isn't the actual child you want, in the end, just the knowledge that you're capable of having one' she tells Manson.[49] Although Andrea Newman was thirty when she wrote *A Bouquet of Barbed Wire*, she explains that this attention to age was 'how I imagined a midlife crisis would be'.[50]

Manson's obsession with Prue is especially apparent in the internal monologue of Chapter 1. The first indication of his longing occurs in the text, 'when he finally heard her voice',[51] the word 'finally' conveying an impatience to speak to her and further emphasised by the text, 'there must still be time'.[52] Thereafter, the reader learns that he manages to speak to her by telephone: 'In the middle of it, the phone. Prue',[53] his thoughts typifying the truncated rhythms that articulate his suppressed feelings. "'Hullo, darling"'[54] Manson addresses her, whilst the intensity of his emotion emerges when he tells her, '"Are you all right now?" How hard it was not to betray insane anxiety',[55] and 'He shook his head, forgetting she could not see him, drunk with the pleasure in her voice',[56] the words 'insane' and 'drunk' corresponding with romantic passion rather than paternal affection. Moreover, the text that describes her voice as, 'full of childish excitement and adult mystery. It was a very feminine sound to him',[57] further conflates fatherly love with sexual desire. The second chapter persists with allusions to romance, and we learn that 'They kissed'.[58] 'How direct she was. Much too direct and logical. Coming right out with it. Like that other time' the truncated enunciation of his conscious internal thoughts giving way to lengthier exposition in direct prose. For example, Manson informs Prue, "'I'm ashamed to admit it, but it hurts me when you mention the flat as home. There now. My secret is out, and I know it's quite indefensible, that's why I didn't tell you"'.[59] Further intimations of incestuous desire emerge at the end of Chapter 2 when Manson tells Prue, '"And I love you". How seldom this was said after childhood: what curtain of restraints descended?' "And I love you too"',[60] responds Prue, their declarations once more akin to romantic lovers rather than father and daughter.

Prue's reciprocation of Manson's feelings becomes evident in Chapter 4 where the narrative now unfolds from her perspective. The text, 'Prue, putting the phone down, thought: I exploit him, I know I do. Or victimise him even. Now Mummy's different ... But Daddy I take advantage of, even more than I used to. I simply can't avoid it: an irresistible urge to play the little girl, to see how far I can go',[61] discloses that she consciously provokes the affections and attention of her father. In fact, her later thoughts reveal that she enjoys, and even promotes the conflict between her father and Gavin.[62] A major source of disquiet and anger for Manson is Prue's revelation of her pregnancy, confounded by Cassie's disclosure that Gavin "'wasn't the first.'"[63] As a result, 'Manson was suddenly aware of the empty glass in his hand and the desire to break it',[64] the words 'desire' and 'break' not only conveying jealousy but also implying a connection between violence and desire, another controversial theme that emerges when Gavin later beats Prue and Cassie admits to masochistic tendencies.[65]

Indeed, Gavin unambiguously identifies Manson's incestuous desires, stating "'Sure your dad wants to screw you, baby. Sticks out a mile ... I don't mean he's aware of it. He's got it all buried *way* down.'"[66] Prue's internal reflection is equally revealing, as the text states, 'The trouble was that she got vivid mental pictures of everything Gavin said'.[67] Her masochistic desire for violence relates to sex, emerging in a passage that states, '[t]he night was very still and then the only sounds she could hear were his blows to her face and his tortured breathing, curiously similar to making love. She was panting in exactly the same way'.[68] Thus, although the novel does not entail actual incest between Manson and Prue, there are distinct articulations of their mutual desire through simile, metaphor, and syntax, these occasions often entailing sadomasochism.

Bouquet of Barbed Wire (dir. Tony Wharmby, 1976)

In 1976, LWT screened the first television adaptation of Newman's novel as a seven-part serial. Despite some negative critical reviews, audiences responded enthusiastically to the series and defended such criticisms. As noted earlier, *Sun* reviewer Penny Perrick slated the series, stating, 'Andrea Newman, who wrote the series, thinks that watching these goings-on will help us identify our own problems and maybe solve them. But I'd say that *Bouquet of Barbed Wire* did more harm than good'. Perrick goes on to declare that 'they behaved in a way that nobody else does. So they were as convincing as cardboard cut-outs'.[69] Perrick's review provoked angry retaliation from a number of viewers, one comment stating 'Penny Perrick's outburst against *Bouquet of*

Barbed Wire made me and others furious. I have a very wide circle of friends who thought this serial was one of the BEST' [capitals in original].[70] Others agreed, with one viewer commenting, 'if it included a bit of incest – well, if it exists, let's bring it out into the open'[71] whilst another responded with, 'we six cannot understand why the serial was so condemned. It was one of the best we have watched for a long time'.[72] In personal correspondences to Newman, viewers consistently praised the drama, with one viewer stating, 'Peter and Cassie for me were real. They repeated what I experienced in my life, in my marriage'.[73] Another article by *Daily Mail* reviewer, Lynda Lee Potter similarly provoked retaliatory responses from fans of the series, with one viewer writing to Newman, 'I think you have been very successful in conveying, in both an entertaining and thought-provoking way, the deep often tangled relationships people can become involved in with each other, and the intensity of feeling people can experience when those relationships are disturbed by external forces'.[74] *Observer* critic, Clive James, also responded positively, stating that 'if you can accept the fact that *Bouquet of Barbed Wire* (LWT) is the house of Atreus transferred to Peyton Place on a long low loader, there are worse serials to get hooked on … there is plenty of solid middle-class adultery and incest. Sheila Allen is having a whale of a time as the Older Woman who has welcomed her daughter's husband into her bed, which is roughly what her husband (Frank Finlay) would like to do with the daughter'.[75]

Retrospectively, the 1976 version is still held in high regard, with Damien Timmer (joint managing director of Mammoth Screen Productions which oversaw the remake), commenting, '[t]he original TV version of *Bouquet of Barbed Wire* was one of the most controversial dramas of its era, busting taboos which still have the power to shock decades later'.[76] John Lloyd of the *Financial Times* described it as 'steamy' and 'a breakthrough'[77] while Hermione Norris, who plays Cassie in the 2010 remake, commented that, 'I was nervous of it, to be honest … because every time you mention *Bouquet of Barbed Wire*, people kind of gasp, and mention the 1970s' production which wiped the floor with people'.[78]

Tony Wharmby directed and produced the drama, while Newman wrote the script and, according to Newman, '[t]he late great Cyril Bennett was head of LWT then and once we had his blessing we were away. There was no interference'.[79] Consequently, the 1976 version followed the novel closely, mobilising the same sense of suppressed emotion that characterised Newman's novel. This intensity proved attractive to audiences and as Newman suggests, 'it wasn't the subject matter that was scandalous – if you study it there wasn't actually that much sex in it, certainly not in the book – but it was the atmosphere that was shocking. There was a very erotic feel to it'.[80]

Mostly drawing on the original text, and partly replicating the protagonists' mental reflections by means of highly stylised flashbacks and echoing voiceover, the series achieves the claustrophobic atmosphere wrought by the relationship between Prue and her father through its camerawork and framing. In particular, their mutual desire translates into close framing. For example, episode one presents their first lunchtime meeting in a series of extreme close ups, with both characters tightly framed. Camera angles are also important – one shot from immediately behind Prue with Manson's face partially obscured by her hat gives the appearance that he is almost kissing her, although this close framing partly stems from certain technological constraints.

As Karen Lury explains about television of the 1970s, 'the composition of the television image … is defined in part through its relationship to the frame',[81] the 1.33:1 standard aspect ratio typically deployed in television producing a 'squarer' image than the more recent widescreen format, meaning that there is inherently less space around the characters. In contrast, the director of the later 2010 version, Ashley Pearce used a ratio of 1.77:1, which, as Lury notes, is 'more close to the dimensions of the film image'.[82] Lury explains that the 'wider aspect ratio may save money, as single setups and shots incorporating several actors at a time effectively substitute for the current practice of labour and time-intensive 'single shots''.[83] She concludes that a consequence of greater frame space is a 'more populated image'.[84] However, *Bouquet of Barbed Wire* varies from this convention with the 2010 version affording more space around its characters while the framing of Prue and Manson in the 1976 version is undeniably claustrophobic, its extreme close-ups of them together replacing the usual convention of shot-reverse-shot.

Partly, the use of the close-up, as Lury[85] further explains, was vital to early broadcasting because of the smallness of the television screen. However, with recently expanded screen sizes, the deployment of the close-up has arguably become more cinematic than televisual, perhaps explaining the 2010 adaptation's proclivity for 'open' framing. Lury also suggests that the long shot is less common in television than cinema since close-ups enable a focus on talking and characters' faces.[86] Yet, a number of long shots occur in the 1976 version, its use serving several functions. Partly, counterpointing the extreme close-ups deployed in filming Prue and her father, physical distance between other characters conveys their respective emotionally detached relationships. For example, in episode one, 'Homecoming', cinematography and framing imply an emotional gulf between Manson and both Cassie (Sheila Allen), and his son-in-law, Gavin Sorenson (James Aubrey). The framing of Gavin and Prue is also less constricted, while camera shots tend to intercut between Cassie and Manson rather than feature them in the same frame. When Cassie and Manson are framed together, they invariably appear in long shot to emphasise the physical (and by extension, emotional) distance between them. Their conversation often supports this visual signification of detachment, typified in episode two when Cassie says to Manson, 'I feel as if everything is slipping

Text, image, audience

away from us'. She also states that, 'you can hardly bear [Prue] out of your sight'.[87] Indeed, a constant motif during filming of Cassie is a photograph of Prue in the background, signifying her persistent presence in their relationship while an early close-up of a photograph of Prue in Manson's office hints at his obsession. Moreover, conversations between Manson and Cassie (as well as other characters) centre almost exclusively on Prue.

A second function of the long shot is to render Prue as childlike since when she appears in long shot to the rear of the frame, she seems physically much smaller in relation to Manson and Cassie, who mostly dominate the foreground of the frame. A typical example arises in episode one, when, in the restaurant scene, Prue is positioned to the rear of the frame, while Manson dominates the foreground, portraying her as a small child. In a subsequent scene in episode one, a similar arrangement discloses a bikini-clad Prue standing in the kitchen with Cassie occupying the immediate foreground and Prue to the rear of the frame so that she again appears small and vulnerable. In a further example, a series of long and medium shots display Prue sunbathing as Gavin massages oil into her abdomen and neck. These intercut with a zoom in to close-up of Manson's sunglasses, suggesting that they are concealing the fact that he is watching Prue and Gavin. The sequence proceeds to intercut between increasing close-ups of Prue's body and Manson's sunglasses, conveying the latter's intense jealousy. A low angle close-up of Prue reveals her eyes opening slightly to glance first at Gavin and then Manson, indicating her awareness of how she is consciously manipulating her father's feelings.

As well as cinematographic techniques that position her as a child, Prue's figure behaviour and speech are also childlike – she refers to her parents as 'Daddy and 'Mummy', and her verbal articulation is demanding, repetitive, and often overly candid. For example, in the restaurant scene in episode one, as she describes a fainting episode to Manson, she continually eats as she talks, much as a child would. These visual and narrative strategies for suggesting Prue as a child persistently enable incest to be suggested whilst mitigating the outcry that may have resulted had she been actually younger. Indeed, as noted earlier, Cooke acknowledges a particular sensitivity to the content of television dramas of the time, with pressure groups reacting to the permissiveness of the 1960s.[88] Consequently, the BBC production of Dennis Potter's *Brimstone and Treacle*, also intended for broadcast in 1976, was withdrawn because of concerns over its controversial rape of a mentally afflicted young woman.[89]

In line with Lury's observations, Raymond Williams too correlates television's technological limitations with its aesthetics and meaning, and aligns it with the dominant structure of feeling. He suggests that in its early form, especially where the television play re-enacted the staged play, 'the technical possibilities that were commonly used corresponded to this structure of feeling: the enclosed internal atmosphere; the local interpersonal conflict; the close-up on private feeling. Indeed these emphases could be seen as internal properties of the medium itself when in fact they were a selection of some of its properties according to the dominant structure of feeling'.[90] These properties were not confined to television but permeated other cultural forms – for instance, artwork of the post-war period, which had been dictated by both frame and gallery (such as the crowded collage of Richard Hamilton's *Just What Is It That Makes Today's Home So Different, So Appealing* [1956], Andy Warhol's *Soup Cans* [1962], and Lucian Freud's intimate portraits) began to move away from the enclosure of gallery space into public libraries, streets and the landscape itself. Works such as Robert Smithson's *Spiral Jetty* (1970) and Andy Goldsworthy's *Sheepfolds* (1996–2003) typify the rejection of gallery space and further demonstrate the gravitation towards a shift in the dominant structure of feeling, a juncture at which *Bouquet of Barbed Wire* was produced. As Walker notes, the 1970s was an interim period which saw the mood change from one of optimism to pessimism and whose art was characterised by a 'repoliticization and feminization'.[91]

John Ellis expands further upon the technological effect on a drama's aesthetics, noting that the change from video to film had an additional implication. Ostensibly, the change liberated the television drama from the studio because, 'the adoption of 16 mm film extended the physical reach of television drama production into real locations. Video at that time was not the portable format that it became in the 1980s, so effectively producers had the choice between two production routes: studio/video or location/film'.[92] Certainly, much of the 1976 version of *Bouquet of Barbed Wire* takes place indoors whilst the 2010 adaptation entails more kinetic cinematography and diversity of camerawork compared to the protracted, static takes of the 1976 version when video tape recording (VTR) was used.[93]

Williams also discusses the serialisation of dramas noting that, 'serials and series have advantages for programme planners: a time slot … can be filled for a run of weeks, and in their elements of continuity the serial and the series encourage attachment to a given station or channel'.[94] Cooke elaborates more specifically on the tendency towards serialisation during the 1970s as being one of economic necessity.[95] A significant aesthetic effect of the seven-part serialisation of *A Bouquet of Barbed Wire* was the way that it enabled the development of character complexity, as well as conveying an intensification of suppressed emotion and, as Brian Viner points out, 'allowed room for the misery to develop properly'.[96] Correspondingly, the shortened three-part structure of the 2010 version has an inherently faster-paced narrative, while its 'mystery element changes motivation and to some extent character'.[97]

In relation to such serialisation, John Ellis explains that '[b]roadcast TV narration has a more dispersed narrational form than cinema: it is extensive rather than sequential'.[98] Because of this, television series maintain continuity

Text, image, audience

by linking various segments together. According to Ellis, this can occur in several ways – he explains that there does not necessarily have to be temporal unity between segments. One alternative is that 'it is also possible to produce effects of alternation and contrast between segments: the contrasting pastimes of two connected characters, or an anticipatory alternation between the tranquil life of one character and the arrival of another who will cause an upset'.[99] Ellis goes on to exemplify this continuity with the opening scenes of *Bouquet of Barbed Wire*. He discusses the crosscutting sequence which switches between scenes of Manson walking home, and Prue and Gavin's return from honeymoon stating, '[p]eaceful scenes of Frank Finlay walking through the sunlit park back to his office are intercut with scenes of arrival at Victoria Station, crowds, train noises, doors slamming, station announcements. Discontinuity on the soundtrack indicates that this alternation is meaningful, that the arrival constitutes a disturbance'.[100] Indeed, the two parallel events are contrasted in various ways: for example, distinctions arise between urban/rural, taxi/walking, and youth/age. Nonetheless, they each comprise 'overpopulated' frames, with Peter Manson's journey visually dissected by 'entrapping devices' including tennis court nets, and mesh fencing, thereby contributing to the overall sense of enclosure that pervades the series.

The theme of incest is also relevant to Sarah Francis's (Deborah Grant) relationship with Manson, because she essentially becomes a substitute for Prue. 'You really love her', Sarah comments to Manson. 'Yes, of course, but not in the way that I love you, that's quite different' he responds, seemingly unaware of his incestuous traits.[101] In fact, his infidelity with Sarah occurs in Prue's bed, with Sarah commenting, 'it seemed unnatural, us in her bed'.[102] As Herman notes, this substitution is typical of incestuous relationships.[103] Father–daughter incest is further intimated by Sarah's relationship with her father. In episode two, 'Introductions', her father warns her about the dangers of boyfriends and, like Manson, displays a jealous disposition, replicating the motif of obsessive father–daughter relationships. Furthermore, similar to the framing of Manson and Prue, that of Sarah and her father is also claustrophobic. However, in the brief scene of their limited encounter, she has her back turned to him, reinforcing her dislike of him as he refers to Sarah and her sister as 'my two little girls', a comment which further alludes to the conflation of paternal feelings with incestuous desire (since both 'little girls' are in fact adults).[104]

Bouquet of Barbed Wire (Ashley Pearce, 2010)

The second television adaptation of the novel, made in 2010 by Mammoth Screen Productions, and directed by Ashley Pearce, deviates significantly from both the original text and the first series. Narratively, its plotline varies, whilst its *mise-en-scène* features contemporary London settings and cityscapes.

Overall, there are differences in the way that the novel and first series mostly take place in claustrophobic indoor locations, while more of the later series occurs outdoors. Characterisation is different while its alternative visual strategies also include rapid editing, slow motion flashbacks, and scenes of graphic injury and explicit sexual activity. Lighting too is more distinctive in the second series, with noir-style illumination exacerbating the sense of threat that permeates its secondary plot. Director Ashley Pearce explains these visual effects as part of a 'deliberately bigger canvas' in which 'the back-story was more complex, part thriller and part family in crisis',[105] Pearce further describes how its camerawork, while portraying the vastness of the city, often involved extreme low angle shots and high angle viewpoints that relate to Peter Manson's (Trevor Eve) occupation as an architect. Pearce explains that he intended such viewpoints to convey the city as a 'hollow place'. In short, while the *mise-en-scène* often features vast cityscapes as a 'deliberate stylistic motif', he intended to depict Manson's solitude by representing him as a solitary figure against the vastness of the city. The expansiveness of city space contrasts with the scenes of home life, and differs markedly to the oppressive domestic settings of the 1976 version.

Pearce also forges a change in Manson's characterisation, and while the character was 'quite predatory in 1976, this is a new study of a man who didn't understand his desire and was a victim, driven by events'.[106] In the 2010 version, Pearce states that, 'Manson has laudable paternal qualities, the drama exploring what happens if he doesn't know where the line is and when his protectiveness becomes an inappropriate obsession'.[107] Manson's open displays of anguish are consistent with the less oppressive aesthetics of the second version, Fisun Gunner attributing this to 'Trevor Eve's ability to play complex, nuanced characters far better than the stiff, granite-faced Frank Finlay'.[108]

Other characterisations also deviate from the original television drama. Whilst in the novel and 1976 television series, Prue is controlling and manipulative, Imogen Poots' characterisation is less knowing. Pearce explains that the casting of Imogen Poots as Prue was influenced by her professional profile and constituted a 'significant coup for the production'.[109] Visually, the choice of Poots conveys a more innocent version of Prue since she is more fragile-looking than Susan Penhaligon. Her long blond hair and innocent young looks heighten this fragility, with Pearce suggesting that 'her pre-Raphaelite hair and fantastic smile helped us to see her from Manson's perspective'.[110] Camerawork and editing contribute to this effect, exemplified in the scene at the series' opening where the camera observes Manson looking at Prue, before it cuts to close-up and enables his point of view. The scene unfolds in slow motion, with backlighting enhancing her innocence and beauty, and the way in which Manson reacts to that moment thus becomes understandable for viewers. Indeed, the use of slow motion to present Manson's memories of Prue, as well as fast motion and time-lapse effects, are distinctive visual strategies of the 2010 series.[111] A constant image is one of Prue playing with blue balloons, seen in slow motion. Manson's viewpoint of Prue persists throughout the series, and in episode one, they go bowling together. As she bends over, the viewer observes her from Manson's perspective, eroticised because her short dress exposes the tops of her legs. Manson then sweeps her off her feet and twirls her round as a parent might a small child, the use of slow motion once more temporally extending the scene and thereby focusing attention on the moment. When Prue returns home, her mother asks, 'please tell me you didn't wear that awful coat all through the evening Prue'. 'It smells of Daddy' responds Prue, thereby replicating the mutual inferences of desire that permeated the novel and 1976 version.[112] In a later restaurant scene, we again see Prue sexualised from Manson's perspective when her dress slips off her shoulder. At the same time, she drinks through a straw and crunches her food noisily as she eats (akin to Susan Penhaligon's characterisation in the earlier version), and is thereby presented as simultaneously childlike. Therefore, rather than an objective perspective that frames the two closely (as in the 1976 version), the viewer repeatedly experiences Manson's subjective viewpoint, which consistently sexualises her, but is encouraged to understand his feelings towards her. In other words, her youthfulness (she appears younger than Susan Penhaligon's character) and a distinctly sexualised perception of her as articulated through the father's eyes, suggest her as innocent victim rather than the consciously 'seductive daughter' of the earlier version. The relationship between Manson and Prue remains one of sexual ambiguity, and in the scene where they kiss, they appear to do so as lovers rather than father and daughter. The scene is extended, and Manson holds Prue's face whilst he kisses first one cheek, then the other, and then hovers centrally as if to kiss her on the lips, the slowly unfolding sequence heightening its significance.

Gavin Sorenson's character too is different, and he is now cast with a Yorkshire accent (rather than American). He is Prue's schoolteacher and, despite having similar financial concerns to the character of 1976, a class difference seems more distinct in the 2010 version. Gavin is portrayed as a sadomasochist and traumatised character, exemplified in the scene when he deliberately burns his arm and violently beats Prue, while in the series' finale, we learn that he was subject to abuse by his stepfather. (The secondary plot centres on his stepfather's abuse of his sister, Paula, who is, in actual fact, Manson's daughter from another relationship). Akin to the first drama, Sarah Francis remains a substitute for Prue, indicated as Manson takes her to the same restaurant so that the substitution motif is replicated from the original series, the analogy perpetuated when he almost rapes her.

Cinematography varies from the first adaptation, the series opening with a rapidly edited sequence of a car crash. We witness Manson walking towards the accident site, his approach filmed in slow motion. The series then unfolds in flashback, revisiting the events of the previous four months that preceded the crash. The *mise-en-scène* persistently moves beyond the home with cityscapes and rural panoramic shots afforded by a more mobile camera. Certainly, kinetic camerawork tends to follow the characters rather than merely framing them in the static takes typical of the 1976 version. There is also conspicuous deployment of diverse camera angles with multiple perspectives, especially canted, low and high angle shots, as well as framing of groups of characters outside of the family. Corresponding with the earlier drama, some scenes occur in Manson's workplace, though locations external to the home now include Cassie's workplace, disclosing her professional life as a marriage guidance counsellor (in contrast with the 1976 series and the novel where Cassie was educated but stayed at home) and reflecting the real-world circumstances of women going to work. Less attention is afforded framing as a technique to convey the closeness between characters that typified the original version. Instead, the oppressive intensity of concealed feelings transforms into animated expressions of anger and grief, especially in the less self-controlled depiction of Manson.

Yet, there is some visual and narrative parity with the first series – for example, Prue misses school to meet her father for lunch (paralleling Prue's missing of lectures in the 1976 version). In this early lunchtime encounter, the restaurant scene again sees a number of shots that similarly situate Prue and her father in close proximity within the same frame. However, the aspect ratio here determines a less constricted presentation. Additionally, the use of backlighting once more gives a 'halo' effect to Prue, portraying her as ethereal and angelic (and innocent victim). Since the viewer observes her from Manson's perspective, when he comments on her beauty, the viewer is also encouraged into this viewpoint. Thematically, the recent series lacks the focus on the loss of youth that pervades the novel and the first series.

If the representation of incestuous desire in the 2010 version derives from the director's formal and aesthetic choices that were facilitated by newer technologies, it simultaneously reflects the less repressive socio-cultural contexts of its production and its more liberated audiences. Its externalisation of the theme of incest, and lack of internal feelings and voiceovers in comparison to the novel and first series, compares to the high media profile of recent incest cases as well as emerging widespread revelations of paedophilia in the public domain and a certain familiarity with such scenarios. In fact, as Brian Viner notes, 'these days the reaction would be, and indeed, is a lot more ho-hum … Times have changed, and we've changed with them. It's early days in *Bouquet of Barbed Wire* mark 2, and I imagine there's plenty of sex, sado-masochism and incestuous yearnings to come, but it won't have the nation earnestly discussing it in banks and at bus-stops, in school corridors and

Text, image, audience

supermarket aisles, like it did in 1976'.[113] Nonetheless, the remake received good critical reviews, *Observer* critic, Mike Bradley, describing it as 'a tense, engaging tale',[114] while Gunner declares that, 'age has not withered *Bouquet of Barbed Wire*'.[115] Brian Viner further comments on the first episode that, 'Guy Andrews has written excellent, and admirably sparse dialogue; Ashley Pearce's direction is clever without being overly tricksy; even the background music, which besmirches so much television drama these days by forgetting its place and crashing the foreground, is just about right. And most conspicuously of all, the casting is spot-on and the acting utterly splendid'.[116]

Conclusion

Newman's 1969 novel depicts mutual desire between a father and daughter, the truncated rhythms of its text together with significant internal monologue, whether deliberate or not, reflecting the taboo nature of incest. The 1976 television adaptation, also scripted by Newman, follows the novel closely, with camerawork, framing, and *mise-en-scène* conveying the repressive aspects of the novel, though its visual style also resulted from technological limitations and restricted camera mobility. The sense of suppression evoked by this imagery also corresponds with the unspoken-about nature of incest at that time, while the characterisation of Prue conforms to perceptions of the 'seductive daughter' promoted first by Freud, and subscribed to more generally by subsequent literary depictions and clinical practitioners. These aspects conspire to reflect the atmosphere of inhibition and moral campaigning associated with the 1970s' conservative zeitgeist. In contrast, Ashley Pearce's remake in 2010 conjures a much more open aesthetic in the way that it lacks the claustrophobic framing of the first drama and moves out of domestic settings. Consequently, it is more visually diverse, its tendency for open spaces, kinetic camerawork, and less cramped framing being enabled by new technologies, while the narrative itself is compressed into three episodes. Consequently, it is faster paced and limits the build-up of emotional intensity that characterised the earlier adaptation. At the same time, the production corresponds with a heightened media focus on cases of incest and paedophilia in an increasingly child-sensitive society. Certainly, in recent decades, there has been an intensification of public consciousness surrounding issues of paedophilia and incest, both culminating in, and stemming from a comprehensive updating of child legislation. If Newman's novel and its first adaptation came out at a time when incest and paedophilia were less conspicuous in the media, the 2010 drama followed a decade of media revelations concerning child abuse. Accordingly, as Samantha Lay notes in her study of British social realism, the increased social awareness of children and their problems has led to an emphasis on their representation in film and television.[117] Lay ascribes this awareness to media initiatives (such as BBC's *Children in Need*[118]), and improved campaigning as well as revisions in legislation concerning child welfare.[119] As Karen Lury observes, 'it has only recently become a crime to physically assault your child' (2010: 55). Certainly, The Children Act of 1989 was far-reaching in its changes and set a precedent for revisions, updates, and new legislation, evident in the legal changes following the murders of Victoria Climbie in 2000, and Jessica Chapman and Holly Wells in 2002.[120] Lay further locates the heightened focus on children within a context of 'sporadic moral panics',[121] citing the murder of Jamie Bulger, Stephen Lawrence, Damilola Taylor, and Victoria Climbie as major sources of this concern.[122] She also comments on the high media profile of cases concerning systematic abuse at Cleveland and Clwyd.[123] In recent years, additional cases of child abduction and significant, long-standing abuse have emerged,[124] whilst the case of Jimmy Savile has dominated headlines of late, the alleged stifling of previous abuse reports and the apparent refusal to acknowledge the nature of his acts at the time reflecting earlier attitudes towards child abuse.

While such cases often involve younger children, *Bouquet of Barbed Wire* centres on a nineteen year old. Yet, Prue is conveyed as childlike in both novel and the two dramas, either visually, through cinematography or framing, figure behaviour, or by appearance. Such representation enables the narratives to deal with sensitive issues of incest in a way that would have been unacceptable had young children been involved. Even so, the second version presents Prue as more innocent and vulnerable and less knowing than the 1976 drama, in line with changed attitudes and legislation towards children and a move away from the 'seductive daughter' trope that Freud instigated. Even as discussion is currently more open about incest and child abuse, such crimes are less tolerated. This openness does not occur in isolation but follows other general patterns of transparency and accountability (for example, in the uncovering of institutionalised racism and the dismantling of male-dominated medical hierarchies that led to medical cover-ups).[125] Even as such uncovering stems from radical political shifts and equal rights during the 'decade of the determined minority',[126] it reflects a swing in the dominant structure of feeling, namely, from a repressive, patriarchal society to one that is generally more liberated, transparent, equitable and increasingly child-sensitive.

Notes

1 The title of the television versions is *Bouquet of Barbed Wire*, which differs from that of the novel.
2 John Plunkett, 'More than 5.5m put Spooks under surveillance', *Guardian*, 20 September 2010, www.guardian.co.uk/media/2010/sep/21/spooks-tv-ratings (accessed 20 October 2012).

3 Penny Perrick, 'Home sweet home? It was never like this', *Sun* (1976). Personal Cuttings Collection of Andrea Newman.
4 Michael Church, 'Another Bouquet', *The Times*, 15 January 1977, p. 11.
5 Michael Ratcliffe, 'Bouquet of Barbed Wire', *The Times*, 17 January 1976, p, 9.
6 Joan Driscoll Lynch (2002) 'Incest discourse and cinematic representation', *Journal of Film and Video*, 54:2/3 (2002), p. 43.
7 Euan Ferguson, '*Observer* Review: *Bouquet of Barbed Wire* ITV1', *Observer*, 12 September 2010, p. 23.
8 Andrea Newman, 'Interview between Andrea Newman and Frances Pheasant-Kelly', 2 November 2012.
9 Ashley Pearce, 'Interview between Ashley Pearce and Frances Pheasant-Kelly', 20 November 2012.
10 Judith Lewis Herman, *Father-Daughter Incest* (Harvard University Press, 2000), p. 12.
11 Herman, *Father-Daughter Incest*, p. 18.
12 BBC, 'Jimmy Savile scandal: Report reveals decades of abuse', 11 January 2013, www.bbc.co.uk/news/uk-20981611.stm (accessed 7 February 2013).
13 Raymond Williams, *Drama from Ibsen to Brecht* (Penguin, 1968), p. 9.
14 *Ibid.*, p. 9.
15 *Brimstone and Treacle* (writ. Dennis Potter, 1976).
16 *Scum* (writ. Roy Minton, 1977).
17 Raymond Williams, *The Long Revolution* (Greenwood, 1975), p. 47.
18 Lez Cooke, *British Television Drama* (Palgrave Macmillan, 2015), p. 123.
19 *Ibid.*, p. 123.
20 Raymond Williams, *Television* (Routledge, 2003), p. 53.
21 *The Lie* (writ. Ingmar Bergman, trans. Paul Britten Austin, dir. Paul Britten Austin, 'Play for Today', BBC, 29 October 1970).
22 Anna Meigs and Kathleen Barlow, 'Beyond the taboo: Imagining incest', *American Anthropologist* 104:1 (2002), p. 38.
23 Sigmund Freud, James Strachey et al. (trans.), *Totem and Taboo* (Vintage, 2001).
24 Sigmund Freud, James Strachey et al. (trans.), *Early Psychoanalytical Publications* (Vintage, 2001).
25 Editor's note in Sigmund Freud, James Strachey (trans. and general editor), Anna Freud with Alix Strachey and Alan Tyson (trans.), *A Case of Hysteria* (Vintage, 2001b), p. 128.
26 Pamela Thurschwell, *Sigmund Freud* (Routledge Critical Thinkers) (Routledge, 2000), p. 46.
27 Patricia Love with Jo Robinson, *The Emotional Incest Syndrome* (Bantam Books, 1990), p. 8.
28 Herman, *Father-Daughter Incest*, p. 39.
29 Sigmund Freud, James Strachey et al. (trans.), *An Infantile Neurosis* (Vintage, 2001), p. 185.
30 Herman, *Father-Daughter Incest*, p. 101.
31 Janet Walker, *Trauma Cinema* (University of California Press, 2005), pp. 52–3.

32 [Fragment], *Sunday Telegraph*, 1969, Personal Cuttings Collection of Andrea Newman.
33 Michael Scott, 'Recent fiction', *Daily Telegraph*, 19 October, 1969, Personal Cuttings Collection of Andrea Newman.
34 [Fragment], *Glasgow Herald*, 1969, Personal Cuttings Collection of Andrea Newman.
35 [Fragment], *Financial Times*, 1969, Personal Cuttings Collection of Andrea Newman.
36 Michael Church, 'Another Bouquet', p. 11.
37 [Fragment], *Sun*, 1976, Personal Cuttings Collection of Andrea Newman.
38 Andrea Newman, *The Telegraph*, 2010, https://www.telegraph.co.uk/culture/tvandradio/7980317/I-never-set-out-to-shock-Andrea-Newman.html.
39 Andrea Newman, Personal Documents, Letters from viewers (1976) [details omitted to protect authors' identities] (accessed 12 November 12).
40 Andrea Newman, *A Bouquet of Barbed Wire* (Serpent's Tail Press 2010), p. 31.
41 *Ibid.*, p. 22.
42 *Ibid.*, p. 94.
43 *Ibid.*, p. 91.
44 *Ibid.*, p. 82.
45 *Ibid.*, p. 1.
46 *Ibid.*, p. 32.
47 *Ibid.*, p. 55.
48 *Ibid.*, p. 57.
49 *Ibid.*, p. 58.
50 Newman, Interview with Frances Pheasant-Kelly.
51 Newman, *A Bouquet of Barbed Wire*, p. 1.
52 *Ibid.*, p. 3.
53 *Ibid.*, p. 3.
54 *Ibid.*, p. 3.
55 *Ibid.*, p. 4.
56 *Ibid.*, p. 5.
57 *Ibid.*, p. 4.
58 *Ibid.*, p. 6.
59 *Ibid.*, p. 11.
60 *Ibid.*, p. 12.
61 *Ibid.*, p. 21.
62 *Ibid.*, p. 22.
63 *Ibid.*, p. 31.
64 *Ibid.*, p. 31.
65 *Ibid.*, p. 235.
66 *Ibid.*, p. 67.
67 *Ibid.*, p. 67.
68 *Ibid.*, p. 216.
69 Perrick, 'Home sweet home'.

70 Susan Jennings, 'Hands off our Barbed Wire', Audience responses to Penny Perrick's review, *Sun*, Personal Cuttings Collection of Andrea Newman, 1976.
71 C.F. Allen, 'Hands off our Barbed Wire', Audience responses to Penny Perrick's review, *Sun*, Personal Cuttings Collection of Andrea Newman, 1976.
72 Mrs. Denman, 'Hands off our Barbed Wire', Audience responses to Penny Perrick's review, *Sun*, Personal Cuttings Collection of Andrea Newman, 1976.
73 Anon., Letter, Personal Cuttings Collection of Andrea Newman.
74 Lynda Lee-Potter, [Fragment], *Daily Mail*, 1976, in Newman, Personal Cuttings Collection.
75 Clive James, *Visions Before Midnight* (Picador, 1977), p. 153.
76 Damien Timmer, quoted in Leigh Holmwood, 'ITV1 to screen new version of A Bouquet of Barbed Wire', *Guardian*, 21 September, 2009, https://www.theguardian.com/media/2009/sep/21/itv-bouquet-barbed-wire-trevor-eve (accessed 8 February 2018).
77 John Lloyd, 'Serious intentions and steamy intrigues', *Financial Times*, 11 September 2010, p. 21.
78 Hermione Norris quoted in Anon, 'Bouquet of Barbed Wire: Best Drama', *Western Mail*, 4 September 2010.
79 Andrea Newman, 'I never set out to shock', *Daily Telegraph*, 4 September 2010, www.telegraph.co.uk/culture/tvandradio/7980317/I-never-set-out-to-shock-Andrea-Newman.html (accessed 20 October 2012).
80 Newman in Jenny Johnston, '*Bouquet of Barbed Wire* scandalised seventies viewers – but will a remake have the same impact?' *Mail Online*, 10 November 2010, www.dailymail.co.uk/femail/article-1308475/Bouquet-Of-Barbed-Wire-scandalised-Seventies-viewers--remake-impact.html (accessed 10 November 2012).
81 Karen Lury, *Interpreting Television* (Hodder Arnold, 2005), p. 21.
82 *Ibid.*, p. 23.
83 *Ibid.*, p. 24.
84 *Ibid.*, p. 24.
85 *Ibid.*, p. 30.
86 *Ibid.*, p. 27.
87 *Bouquet of Barbed Wire* (writ. Andrea Newman, dir. Tony Wharmby, LWT, © ITV Studios Ltd., 1976).
88 Cooke, *British Television Drama*, pp. 106–7.
89 *Ibid.*, p. 106.
90 Williams, *Television*, p. 53.
91 John Walker, *Left Shift* (I.B. Tauris, 2002), p. 2.
92 John Ellis, 'Importance, significance, cost and value', in Catherine Johnson and Rob Turnock (eds), *ITV Cultures* (Open University Press, 2005), p. 49.
93 Andrea Newman, 'Bouquet Then and Now', Interview, *Daily Telegraph*, 2010, Personal Document of Andrea Newman, Complete transcript of interview.
94 Williams, *Television*, p. 57.

95 Cooke, *British Television Drama*, p. 104.
96 Brian Viner, 'Last night's TV – Spooks, BBC1; Bouquet of Barbed Wire, ITV1; Coronation Street, ITV1', *Independent*, 20 September 2010, www.independent.co.uk/arts-entertainment/tv/reviews/last-nights-tv--spooks-bbc1-bouquet-of-barbed-wire-itv1-coronation-street-itv1-2084682.html (accessed 20 October 2012).
97 Andrea Newman, 'I never set out to shock', *Daily Telegraph*, 4 September 2010, p. 29 www.telegraph.co.uk/culture/tvandradio/7980317/I-never-set-out-to-shock-Andrea-Newman.html (accessed 20 October 2012).
98 John Ellis, *Visible Fictions* (Routledge, 1992), p. 147.
99 *Ibid.*, p. 150.
100 *Ibid.*, p. 150.
101 *Bouquet of Barbed Wire* (writ. Andrea Newman, dir. Tony Wharmby, LWT, © ITV Studios Ltd., 1976).
102 *Bouquet of Barbed Wire* (© ITV Studios Ltd., 1976).
103 Herman, *Father-Daughter Incest*, p. 94.
104 *Bouquet of Barbed Wire* (writ. Andrea Newman, dir. Tony Wharmby, LWT, © ITV Studios Ltd., 1976).
105 Pearce, Interview.
106 *Ibid.*
107 *Ibid.*
108 Fisun Gunner, 'A Bouquet of Barbed Wire ITV 1', the*arts*desk.com, 7 September 2010, www.theartsdesk.com/tv/bouquet-barbed-wire-itv1 (accessed 11 November 2012).
109 Pearce, Interview.
110 *Ibid.*
111 At these points, slow motion and time-lapse effects were filmed on 16 mm.
112 *Bouquet of Barbed Wire* (writ. Guy Andrews and Andrea Newman, © Mammoth Screen Ltd., 2010).
113 Brian Viner, 'Last night's TV–Bouquet of Barbed Wire, ITV 1; Grandma's House, BBC2', *Independent*, 7 September 2010, www.independent.co.uk/arts-entertainment/tv/reviews/last-nights-tv--bouquet-of-barbed-wire-itv1-grandmas-house-bbc2-2072100.html (accessed 10 November 2012).
114 Mike Bradley, 'Review: Bouquet of Barbed Wire ITV1, 9pm', *Observer*, 5 September, 2010.
115 Gunner, 'A Bouquet of Barbed Wire ITV1'.
116 Viner, 'Last night's TV–Bouquet of Barbed Wire, ITV 1; Grandma's House, BBC2'.
117 Samantha Lay, *British Social Realism* (Wallflower Press, 2002), p. 108.
118 A major charity in Britain. See http://www.bbc.co.uk/corporate2/childreninneed (accessed 8 February 2018).
119 Lay, *British Social Realism*, p. 109.
120 NSPCC Factsheet: 'An introduction to child protection legislation in the UK', May 2012, www.nspcc.org.uk/inform/research/questions/child_protection_legislation_in_the_uk_pdf_wdf48953.pdf (accessed 20 October 2012).

121 Lay, *British Social Realism*, p. 109.
122 *Ibid.*, p. 109.
123 *Ibid.*, p. 109.
124 These include Josef Fritzl in 2008 and reports of child abuse by the Catholic Church.
125 Cortney Franklin, 'Male peer support and the police culture', *Journal of Women & Criminal Justice* 16:3 (2008), pp. 1–2. Rosemary Pringle, *Sex and Medicine: Gender, Power and Authority in the Medical Profession* (Cambridge University Press, 1998).
126 Norman Shrapnel quoted in Walker, *Left Shift*, p. 19. Norman Shrapnel, *The Seventies* (Constable, 1980), p. 173.

Bibliography

Fiction

Nabokov, Vladimir, Craig Raine (afterword), *Lolita* (Penguin, 2000)
Newman, Andrea, *A Bouquet of Barbed Wire* (Serpent's Tail Press, 2010)

Non-fiction

Allen, C.F, 'Hands off our Barbed Wire', *Sun* (1976), Audience responses to Penny Perrick's review, *Sun*, Personal Cuttings Collection of Andrea Newman
Anon, 'Coming soon … Bouquet of Barbed Wire', *Daily Mail*, 3 September 2010
Anon, 'Bouquet of Barbed Wire: Best Drama', *Western Mail*, 4 September 2010
Bradley, Mike. 'Review: Bouquet of Barbed Wire ITV1, 9pm', *Observer*, 5 September 2010
Butler, Jeremy, *Television Style* (Routledge, 2010)
Church, Michael, 'Another Bouquet', *The Times*, 15 January 1977
Cooke, Lez, *British Television Drama: A History* (Palgrave Macmillan, 2015)
Denman, Mrs, 'Hands off our Barbed Wire', *Sun* (1976), Audience responses to Penny Perrick's review, *Sun*, Personal Cuttings Collection of Andrea Newman
Ellis, John, *Visible Fictions* (Routledge, 1992)
——., 'Importance, significance, cost and value', in Catherine Johnson and Rob Turnock (eds), *ITV Cultures: Independent Television Over Fifty Years* (Open University Press, 2005), pp. 36–56
Ferguson, Euan, '*Observer* Review: *Bouquet of Barbed Wire* ITV1', *Observer*, 12 September 2010
Franklin, Cortney, 'Male peer support and the police culture', *Journal of Women & Criminal Justice* 16:3 (2008), pp. 1–25
Freud, Sigmund, Jeffrey Moussaief Masson (ed. and trans.), *The Complete Letters of Sigmund Freud to Wilhelm Fleiss: 1887–1904* (Harvard University Press, 1985)
——., James Strachey (ed.) and Anna Freud with Alix Strachey and Alan Tyson (trans.), *Early Psychoanalytical Publications, The Standard Edition of the Complete Psychological Works of Sigmund Freud*, vol. 3 (Vintage, 2001)

———., James Strachey (ed.) and Anna Freud with Alix Strachey and Alan Tyson (trans.), *A Case of Hysteria, Three Essays on Sexuality and Other Works, The Standard Edition of the Complete Psychological Works of Sigmund Freud*, vol. 7 (Vintage, 2001)

———., James Strachey (ed.) and Anna Freud with Alix Strachey and Alan Tyson (trans.), *Totem and Taboo and Other Works, The Standard Edition of the Complete Psychological Works of Sigmund Freud*, vol. 13 (Vintage, 2001)

———., James Strachey (ed.) and Anna Freud with Alix Strachey and Alan Tyson (trans.), *An Infantile Neurosis and Other Works, The Standard Edition of the Complete Psychological Works of Sigmund Freud*, vol. 17 (Vintage, 2001)

Herman, Judith Lewis, *Father-Daughter Incest* (Harvard University Press, 2000)

James, Clive, *Visions Before Midnight* (Picador, 1977)

Jennings, Susan, 'Hands off our Barbed Wire', *Sun* (1976), Audience responses to Penny Perrick's review, *Sun*, Personal Cuttings Collection of Andrea Newman

Johnson, Catherine and Rob Turnock (eds), *ITV Cultures: Independent Television Over Fifty Years* (Open University Press, 2005)

Lay, Samantha, *British Social Realism: From Documentary to Brit Grit* (Wallflower Press, 2002)

Lloyd, John, 'Serious intentions and steamy intrigues', *Financial Times*, 11 September 2010

Love, Patricia with Jo Robinson, *The Emotional Incest Syndrome: What To Do When A Parent's Love Rules Your Life* (Bantam Books, 1990)

Lury, Karen, *Interpreting Television* (Hodder Arnold, 2005)

———., *The Child in Film: Tears, Fears and Fairytales* (I.B. Tauris, 2010)

Lynch, Joan Driscoll, 'Incest discourse and cinematic representation', *Journal of Film and Video* 54 (2002), pp. 43–55

Meigs, Anna and Kathleen Barlow, 'Beyond the taboo: Imagining incest', *American Anthropologist* 104 (2002), pp. 38–49

Nannicelli, Ted, 'Ontology, intentionality and television aesthetics', *Screen* 53 (2012), pp. 164–79

Newman, Andrea, Personal Documents – Letters from viewers [details omitted to protect viewers' identities] (1976) (accessed by chapter author 12 November 2012)

———., 'Bouquet Then and Now', Interview, *Daily Telegraph*, 2010, Personal Document, Complete transcript of interview

———., 'Interview between Andrea Newman and Frances Pheasant-Kelly', 2 November 2012

———., 'Interview between Ashley Pearce and Frances Pheasant-Kelly', 20 November 2012

Perrick, Penny, 'Home sweet home? It was never like this', *Sun* (1976), Personal Cuttings Collection of Andrea Newman

Potter, Lynda Lee, *Daily Mail* (1976), Personal Cuttings Collection of Andrea Newman

Pringle, Rosemary, *Sex and Medicine: Gender, Power and Authority in the Medical Profession* (Cambridge University Press, 1998)

Ratcliffe, Michael, 'Bouquet of Barbed Wire', *The Times*, 17 January 1976

Scott, Michael, 'Recent fiction', *Daily Telegraph*, 19 October 1969, Personal Cuttings Collection of Andrea Newman
Shrapnel, Norman, *The Seventies: Britain's Inward March* (Constable, 1980)
Thurschwell, Pamela. *Sigmund Freud*, Routledge Critical Thinkers (Routledge, 2000)
Walker, Janet, *Trauma Cinema: Documenting Incest and the Holocaust* (University of California Press, 2005)
Walker, John, *Left Shift: Radical Art in 1970s' Britain* (I.B. Tauris, 2002)
Williams, Raymond, *Drama from Ibsen to Brecht* (Penguin, 1968)
——., *The Long Revolution* (Greenwood, 1975)
——., *Television* (Routledge, 2003)

Film and television

Bouquet of Barbed Wire (writ. Andrea Newman, dir. Tony Wharmby, LWT, © ITV Studios Ltd., 1976)
Bouquet of Barbed Wire (writ. Guy Andrews and Andrea Newman, © Mammoth Screen Ltd., 2010)
Brimstone and Treacle (writ. Dennis Potter, dir. Barry David, BBC, 1987)
Lie, The (writ. Ingmar Bergman, trans. Paul Britten Austin, dir. Paul Britten Austin, Play for Today, BBC, 29 October 1970)
Lolita (writ. Vladimir Nabokov, dir. Stanley Kubrick, Metro-Goldwyn-Mayer, Seven Arts Pictures, A.A. Productions Ltd., Anya, Harris-Kubrick Productions, Transworld Pictures, 1962)
Lolita (writ. Vladimir Nabokov (novel), Stephen Schiff (screenplay), dir. Adrian Lyne, Guild, Lolita Productions and Pathé, 1997)
Scum (writ. Roy Minton, dir. Alan Clarke, BBC, 1977)

Websites

BBC News, 'Child's body found at care home', 23 February 2008, Available at http://news.bbc.co.uk/1/hi/world/europe/jersey/7260625.stm (accessed 20 October 2012)
BBC News, 'Profile: Josef Fritzl', BBC, 19 March 2009, http://news.bbc.co.uk/1/hi/world/europe/7371959.stm (accessed 20 October 2012)
BBC News, 'Jimmy Savile scandal: Report reveals decades of abuse', BBC, 11 January 2013, www.bbc.co.uk/news/uk-20981611.stm (accessed 7 February 2013)
Burrell, Ian, 'Revealed: *Newsnight* emails that accuse BBC of Jimmy Savile cover up'. *Independent*, 20 October 2012, www.independent.co.uk/news/uk/crime/revealed-newsnight-emails-that-accuse-bbc-of-jimmy-savile-coverup-8218971.html (accessed 25 November 2012)
Fisun, Gunner, 'A Bouquet of Barbed Wire ITV 1', The *Arts* Desk.com, 7 September 2010, www.theartsdesk.com/tv/bouquet-barbed-wire-itv1 (accessed 11 November 12)

Holmwood, Leigh, 'ITV1 to screen new version of A Bouquet of Barbed Wire', *Guardian*, 21 September 2009, www.independent.co.uk/arts-entertainment/tv/reviews/last-nights-tv-spooks-bbc1-bouquet-of-barbed-wire-itv1-coronation-street-itv1-2084682.html (accessed 19 October 2012)

Johnston, Jenny, '*Bouquet of Barbed Wire* scandalised seventies viewers – but will a remake have the same impact?', *Mail Online*, 10 November 2010, www.dailymail.co.uk/femail/article-1308475/Bouquet-Of-Barbed-Wire-scandalised-Seventies-viewers-remake-impact.html (accessed 10 November 2012)

Newman, Andrea, 'I never set out to shock', *Daily Telegraph*, 4 September 2010, www.telegraph.co.uk/culture/tvandradio/7980317/I-never-set-out-to-shock-Andrea-Newman.html (accessed 20 October 2012)

'NSPCC Factsheet: An Introduction to child protection legislation in the UK, May 2012, www.nspcc.org.uk/inform/research/questions/child_protection_legislation_in_the_uk_pdf_wdf48953.pdf (accessed 20 October 2012)

Plunkett, John, 'More than 5.5m put Spooks under surveillance', *Guardian*, 20 September 2010, www.guardian.co.uk/media/2010/sep/21/spooks-tv-ratings (accessed 20 October 2012)

'Sexual Offences Act 2003', www.legislation.gov.uk/ukpga/2003/42/part/1/cross-heading/sex-with-an-adult-relative (20 October 2012)

Viner, Brian, 'Last Night's TV- Bouquet of Barbed Wire, ITV 1; Grandma's House, BBC2', *Independent*, 7 September 2010, www.independent.co.uk/arts-entertainment/tv/reviews/last-nights-tv-bouquet-of-barbed-wire-itv1-grandmas-house-bbc2-2072100.html (accessed 10 November 2012)

——., 'Last Night's TV – Spooks, BBC1; Bouquet of Barbed Wire, ITV1; Coronation Street, ITV1'. *Independent*, 20 September 2010, www.independent.co.uk/arts-entertainment/tv/reviews/last-nights-tv-spooks-bbc1-bouquet-of-barbed-wire-itv1-coronation-street-itv1-2084682.html (accessed 20 October 2012)

2

Assuming a 'manly position':[1] The crisis of masculinity in Ian McEwan's early fiction

Justine Gieni

Ian McEwan's early fiction, including his short story collections *First Love, Last Rites* (1975) and *In Between the Sheets* (1978), as well as his novel *The Cement Garden* (1978), are frequently characterised as 'shock lit': a phrase that denotes lurid subject matter, including stories of rape, incest, molestation, sadomasochism, and murder.[2] Dominic Head and Jack Slay Jr. situate McEwan's early fiction, in its portrayals of violence, in contemporary society, alongside other 'shock lit' authors like Martin Amis, Kathy Acker, Angela Carter and Bret Easton Ellis.[3] McEwan's depictions of post-war Britain frequently expose the depravity that lies beneath civilised society. Although the British Press has described his work as sensational,[4] his focus on the monstrously ordinary is perhaps the most disturbing feature of his work.[5] His fiction delves into the disturbing drives and desires of ordinary men and women. By probing the psyches of his characters, McEwan reveals how it can often be ordinary anxieties, immaturity and isolation that compel seemingly 'normal' people to commit horrifying violence. While not exclusively male (the perpetrators are notably female in 'Pornography' and 'Disguises'), within the contexts of McEwan's early work, it is frequently male protagonists who commit sexual violence to gain power. As evidenced in 'Homemade', *The Cement Garden*, and 'In Between the Sheets', it is male characters that feel ineffectual, vulnerable or weak and are thus driven by an apparent cultural imperative with the goal of gaining patriarchal dominance. In this way, these characters expose the fragility of the social order, as apparently ordinary Oedipal-incestuous anxieties transform into monstrous transgressions.

McEwan's 'shock lit' interrogates the conflicts of post-war Britain. During a period of economic hardship and labour unrest in Britain (1973–1979), McEwan's early fiction examines the widespread discontent, and, through his descriptions of urban wastelands, abandoned buildings and decrepit houses, his work reflects the hardship that characterised this period of British history. This socio-political decline in British culture can be associated with the moral 'sickness' of patriarchal gender roles. Specifically, this post-war period is indicative of a 'crisis of masculinity', wherein the traditional roles and expectations of patriarchy were no longer secure. According to Kaja Silverman, the Second World War and the recovery period initiated a historical crisis that resulted in 'a radical loss of belief in the conventional premises of masculinity.'[6] At this time, masculine subjectivity was vulnerable and threatened by sources that disturbed the 'dominant fiction' of patriarchal mastery: the 'dominant fiction' being what Silverman identifies as the 'commensurability of penis and phallus' or denial of male castration.[7] Economic turmoil, political strife, and perhaps most importantly, the women's liberation movement during the post-war years destabilised traditional gender roles, initiating a crisis that can be interpreted in Oedipal terms to be a crisis of castration. McEwan's early fiction reflects this crisis by depicting male characters struggling not only with the breakdown of patriarchal order, but also with the taboo of incestuous desire.

The women's liberation movement, which gained prominence in Britain throughout the 1970s, directly challenged traditional structures of patriarchy, including the social organisation of the family unit. According to Stephen Brooke, 'the family was the primary site' of controversy during this period of social change.[8] The women's liberation movement began to question and challenge traditional family structures and their relationship to the production and persistence of patriarchal power. Ideologies of male dominance were viewed as rooted in the traditional sexual division of labour, structuring men's roles as breadwinners and women's roles as domestic caregivers. Women's entry into the paid labour force, alongside access to contraception and abortion, enabled women to gain greater freedom and autonomy.[9] Social changes brought about by feminist activists such as women's paid labour and higher education had the effect of undermining and destabilising male dominance, leading to an antagonistic backlash against feminism and 'masculinity crisis.'[10] Set against this context of social change and cultural anxiety, McEwan's early fiction illustrates the reactionary violence of certain men (and boys) when confronted by changing gender roles and expectations.

McEwan strongly suggests in all three works discussed that Oedipal anxieties underlie men's sexual violence against women. To maintain the 'dominant fiction' of patriarchal power requires symbolic acts of violence against women to define and defend the boundaries of traditional gender roles; this violence is symptomatic of Oedipal castration anxieties. As Silverman describes, it is only through the 'incest taboo … that the paternal legacy will be transmitted in an orderly way from father to son'.[11] Patriarchal power thus requires the repression of incestuous desires for the mother to consolidate the powers of the actual and symbolic father in cultural and familial structures.[12] Denial of male castration and displacement of lack onto the female body also determine the male subject's successful emergence out of the Oedipal complex.[13] Kiernan Ryan addresses how, in McEwan's work, 'the survival of patriarchal culture depends on the disavowal of the feminised flesh, [as] maleness must be forced into being over and over again through acts and attitudes fuelled by hatred and fear, through a pathological obsession with keeping vulnerability at bay'.[14] McEwan's male characters are plagued by anxieties and taboo desires, as if unable to fully emerge from the Oedipal dilemma. In an interview with John Haffenden, McEwan asserts that fear, rather than hatred, underlies misogyny: 'There is among men a fear of women and of their power ... I see this defensiveness as a burden for men, and not just as the thing men do to women.'[15] Through repudiation and performance, McEwan's male characters deny their fears of castration and violently defend the boundaries of manhood.

McEwan's early fiction portrays Oedipal-incestuous drives to expose the fragile boundaries separating ordinary manhood from monstrosity. The incest depicted in all three McEwan texts instantiates the unresolved conflicts of gender identity: in particular, the fear of and desire for the Woman-Mother. Ordinary Oedipal-incestuous anxieties become monstrous when distorted by patriarchal pressures to control and dominate the female Other. As evidenced in Gothic literature and film, including Hitchcock's *Psycho* (1960), Shelley's *Frankenstein* (1818), and Poe's 'The Fall of the House of Usher' (1839), the Oedipal anxieties of male protagonists have a history of monstrous consequences when explored in the arts. McEwan draws upon this Gothic history in 'Homemade' and *The Cement Garden* to re-envision adolescent 'rites of passage' in the bildungsroman genre as an initiation into patriarchal violence. The narrator in 'Homemade' and Jack in *The Cement Garden* act out their anxieties through violence against women. For example, in 'Homemade', an adolescent male's initiation into sexual maturity culminates with the rape of his ten-year-old sister. Without remorse, the protagonist commits incestuous rape to assert a 'manly position';[16] similarly, in *The Cement Garden*, a fifteen-year-old boy tries to enact a paternal role by physically violating his older sister. Sexual anxiety is also present in 'In Between the Sheets,' when a father reacts to the 'coming of age' of his adolescent daughter. In each of these stories, McEwan 'shocks' his audience by revealing how patriarchy corrupts relationships in the family unit, between brothers and sisters, and father and daughter.

'Homemade'

'Homemade' begins where it ends: a girl weeping as she sits on the side of the bathtub, having been sexually violated by her older brother. As horrific as this scenario is, perhaps more disturbing still is the boy's sense of achievement in losing his virginity, which eclipses any remorse he feels for his sister's suffering. In his mature reflection on the event, the narrator recognises that it was his relationship with Raymond, his boyhood friend, mentor and rival, rather than his sister, who was the catalyst of this act. Together, Raymond and the narrator exemplify a homosocial bond that is reinforced through the sexual exploitation of his ten-year-old sister Connie. Male homosociality becomes the determining factor in the narrator's sexual violence. Michael S. Kimmel argues that male homosociality uses women as 'a kind of currency' for men 'to improve their ranking on the masculine social scale'.[17] The narrator recalls his homosocial bond with Raymond, a boy, 'a year older ... who conducted my education ... who initiated me into the secrets of adult life'.[18] Ironically, Raymond is not suited for his position as an authority on adult life, as it is the narrator who experiences 'a variety of pleasures ... rightly associated with the adult world'.[19] These adult pastimes become trials or tests of their masculinity. The younger, more ignorant narrator enjoys adult vices such as drinking and smoking, and revels in succeeding when Raymond fails. The narrator measures his own successes or failures as a man against Raymond. In these trials of masculinity, the narrator surpasses his mentor in the race for sexual dominance.

Implicit in the boys' relationship is an element of homosocial sexuality. The boys' friendship is fuelled by their emergence as sexual beings. The narrator describes this period of adolescence as 'the dawn of my sexual day'.[20] A sexual awakening occurs while in 'a cellar on a bomb site', a locale that reflects Britain's patriarchal militarism, when Raymond 'began to rub his prick with a coruscating vigour, inviting me to do the same'.[21] The two boys masturbate, leading to the narrator's ejaculation onto Raymond's jacket pocket. The latent homoeroticism of this episode supports the idea that Raymond is the real love interest in the story, as it is his approval that the narrator seeks in all of his trials of adult initiation, especially with regard to his sexual expertise. In fact, the narrator only wants to lose his virginity to gain Raymond's approval: 'it was the right thing to do because Raymond beamed'.[22] It is Raymond's 'exhilaration'[23] for sexual conquest that spurs the narrator's own emerging sexuality. In this way, Raymond is the one who inspires the narrator to new realms of fantasy and longing.

The narrator's socialisation is also guided by the workmen who frequent the local café. From these men, Raymond and the narrator listen to stories of 'cunts, bits, skirt, of strokings, beatings, fuckings, suckings, of arses and tits', but also of the 'attendant diseases, of pus and swellings, cankers and regrets'.[24] This catalogue of sexual triumphs and tribulations illustrates how objectification forms the basis of the boys' knowledge of adult sexual relationships. Illustrative of male homosociality, the bravado and the objectification of sex contribute to the narrator's decision to rape his sister. From these conversations, the narrator learns to view sex as removed from morality and emotional intimacy. As representative of the patriarchal imagination, these conversations draw sex together with abject bodily processes of disease, filth, and leaking bodily fluids. As Julia Kristeva describes in *Powers of Horror*, how to maintain patriarchal order 'the abjection of those flows' – 'urine, blood, sperm, excrement' – it is necessary to separate the 'proper-clean' male subject from the 'improper-dirty' female body.[25] However, as these conversations reveal to the narrator, sex is a confrontation with not only abject bodily processes, but also with the desired, yet threatening female body.

The angst associated with adolescence is also a crucial determinant of the narrator's decision. Peer pressure and anxiety contribute to the narrator's homosocial rivalry and bond with Raymond. As McEwan illustrates, adolescence can be a time when sexual knowledge is both desired and feared. The narrator relates his adolescent burden, saying how he 'resented' his 'virginity' and describing it as 'my malodorous albatross'.[26] While his virginity is a burden and an obstacle to achieving manhood, sexual knowledge remains 'terrifyingly obscure' to him.[27] The fears surrounding sexuality, and particularly the female body, fuel his desire to attain manhood at whatever cost. In this sense, the narrator's boyhood quest for sexual knowledge is also a form of conquest over the terrifying, yet desired, female body. As premised in 'The Laugh of the Medusa,' Hélène Cixous describes men's sexual possession of the female body as a means 'to penetrate' and 'pacify' the 'dark continent' of the female body.[28] According to Cixous's argument then, as unknown and mysterious, female sexuality remains something potentially dangerous and a threat to the construction of masculine subjectivity and patriarchal power. To pacify fears of inadequacy, men enact the sexual conquest of the female body and fortify their own power by identifying with the phallus. To conquer his fear, the narrator must gain first-hand knowledge of what is termed in the text, the 'Fleshly Grail,' that is, knowledge of female genitalia.[29] As Linda Broughton argues, this reference to the 'Holy Grail' situates the narrator's search for knowledge amid a Romantic quest tradition;[30] in a way, Lulu's genitalia is divine and powerful in that her sexuality is shrouded by an aura of mystery and allure. However, McEwan ironises the sacred quest of the 'Holy Grail' in Christian mythology, as the narrator's search for knowledge is motivated by a profane desire for sexual power. For the cost of a shilling, he would be able to 'glimpse ... Dinky Lulu's pussy'.[31] Lulu Smith, the girl whose sexual reputation is shrouded in fantasy, represents the mysteries of the female body in the male imagination; Lulu is referred to by names that connote fear and desire. She is also referred to as a variety of other names including, 'Zulu Lulu.'[32] In this latter epithet, the narrator exoticises Lulu by suggesting her likeness to a Zulu warrior. She becomes an exotic/erotic Other whose sexual mystery must be conquered.[33] Lulu's rumoured sexual ability is a focus for the boys along with her physical form. The narrator refers to '[h]er wobbling girth and laughing piggy's eyes', calling her a 'heaving, steaming leg-load of schoolgirl flesh'.[34] In their fleshly presence, Lulu and also the narrator's mother and sister are associated with an animalistic, abject vision of femininity. The narrator's mother is described as 'vast and grotesque, the skin hanging from her like flayed toad-hides' and his sister Connie as an 'ugly bat'.[35] Here, McEwan draws from elements of Gothic body horror to depict the female body as grotesque and degraded in its association with animals (pig, toad and bat). Indeed, within Gothic literature, the monstrous female body is often likened to an animal, such as when Lucy transforms into a child-killing predator in Stoker's *Dracula* (1897)[36] or the monstrous powers of Queen Ayesha are likened to a snake in H. Rider Haggard's *She* (1887).[37] Lulu, Connie, and the narrator's mother are symbolically unified in his imagination as abject. Yet, the narrator desperately desires to experience female flesh for himself. In this way, the degraded Lulu is transformed into the 'divine Lulu Smith':[38] her mysterious power derived solely from her possession of 'cunt'.[39]

For the narrator, female genitalia is a representation of unconquered territory. Reminiscent of the violence and oppression of Britain's colonial conquest of parts of Africa, the narrator wants to conquer the 'dark continent'[40] of Lulu's sexuality. His desire to possess this knowledge becomes an obsession, saying that he 'saw' 'cunt' 'in the smile of the conductress, I heard it in the roar of the traffic, I smelt it in the fumes from the shoe-polish factory, conjectured it beneath the skirts of passing housewives'.[41] The narrator is fixated on this obsession, yet it remains just outside his reach. Without a female accomplice, the narrator is unable to complete his initiation into manhood. Ironically and tragically, the narrator uses his sister, rather than Lulu, as the source of his enlightenment into the female body allowing him to 'face the awesome Lulu with zeal and abandon'.[42] With knowledge, the narrator will be 'armed' in battle against the terrifying 'Zulu Lulu' as he struggles to overcome his anxieties.[43] By manipulating his sister into a sexualised version of her favourite game of 'Mummies and Daddies',[44] the narrator enacts a disturbing perversion of Oedipal development. Through this seemingly innocuous game, in its mimicry of adult relationships, Connie is violated. Implicit in this game is the acting out of an Oedipal drama, where brother and sister take up the social-sexual roles of their parents. As his sister enacts the role of mummy, she is redefined by the narrator as a sexually viable partner for him in his mimicry of the daddy role. During the game, Connie is transformed for her brother

Assuming a 'manly position'

into 'something more than a sister'.[45] The game allows each of the children to engage in fantasy scenarios: for Connie, it is at first the fantasy of being the happy housewife; for the narrator, it is a more sinister, sexual fantasy of rape and conquest.

At first, the game makes Connie 'happy' and empowers her: 'She was the inter-galactic-earth-goddess-housewife, she owned and controlled all around her'.[46] In this domestic fantasy, Connie takes on a role of Woman-Mother. As Linda Broughton argues, Connie assumes 'the mythic, symbolic status of woman'.[47] In her role, Connie embodies wholeness for her brother who states, 'I have never seen another human so complete'.[48] His sister appears to possess everything that he does not; where he lacks confidence, Connie is complete, even divine. The narrator's emasculation is directly tied to his sister's symbolic association with womanhood. As long as female sexuality remains unknown, the narrator's sense of manhood will be incomplete. Only by conquering her sexually will the narrator achieve the phallic mastery that he understands to be the basis of patriarchal dominance. Connie's transformation, in her brother's mind, from degraded, 'ugly bat'[49] to desirable, powerful Woman, illustrates the contradictions of the feminine in the patriarchal imaginary spectrum, with the juxtaposition of the female as divine alongside the female as degraded Other. McEwan's narrator seeks to investigate and demystify his sister's femininity by conquering her sexually. In this sense, rape reveals a psychological conflict deeply rooted in masculine subjectivity: by raping his sister, he conquers the female Other. According to Susan Brownmiller, this conquest over the female body is a foundation of manhood: '[Man's] forcible entry into her body, despite her physical protestations and struggle, became the vehicle of his victorious conquest over her being, the ultimate test of his superior strength, the triumph of his manhood.'[50] In this feminist understanding of sexual violence, rape is a signifying act used to incite fear in women and prove male dominance. It is an assertion of power over another, and not an act of desire, love, or sexual longing.

The game takes a sinister turn when the narrator tries to convince Connie that the most important thing that grown-ups do is to "'fuck'" and that her game of 'Mummies and Daddies' should mimic this activity as well.[51] Despite his manipulation, the phallic persona of the narrator is emasculated. The boy is bumbling, pathetic, and a failure in his sexual attempts. From his crude explanation of sex to his lack of finesse in the act of penetration, the narrator's incompetence is readily apparent. After explaining to Connie how they will get a "'nice feeling'" from sex, he fails to follow through. Connie's reaction of 'boredom' and her repetition that "'I'm not getting any feeling'" satirises the 'manly position' that the narrator attempts to gain.[52] At one point, Connie bursts out in laughter at the sight of her brother's penis, mocking the phallus and describing it more than once as "'silly'".[53] The narrator's masculinity is reduced to abjection: a 'lonely detumescent blankness, numbed by this final humiliation'.[54] As Connie subjects her brother's sexuality to her critical gaze there is a breakdown of masculine self-definition. Connie's laughter indicates her brother's inadequacy and reflects a subversive feminine power. When Connie laughs at her brother, it humiliates him in an expression of her own agency. Her ascent to sexual authority culminates when she tells her brother, "'I know where it goes'".[55] Her knowledge of the female body enables her brother to fulfil his mission: 'With her hand she guided me'.[56] If we are to trust the narrator's description of the event, Connie acts as a guide through the act. With this final irony, Connie is conveyed as unwittingly initiating her own rape. McEwan's narrator does not specify how or from whom Connie has learned this adult knowledge, but it is a disturbing detail that further deepens the profound betrayal of trust between brother and sister. The narrator implies that his sister was asking for it, a claim so often made against victims of rape. Brownmiller addresses female complicity as a 'deadly male myth of rape', illustrating how a rapist 'shifts the burden of blame from himself to his victim' by arguing that the female victim 'was asking for it'.[57] This 'blame the victim' mentality often constructs the female victim in particular as unconsciously wishing for sexual advances or not taking proper care in preventing the sexually aggressive actions of male perpetrators. However, as feminist theorist Laura S. Brown has argued, 'the dominant culture, its forms and institutions' needs to be understood as perpetuating not only the biases against female victims (or minority groups), but also the social conditions that lead to trauma.[58] This diversion of blame onto Connie is certainly a means for the narrator to avoid feeling guilt and shame, yet it also implicates a wider context of patriarchy as a culture that perpetuates violence through domination.

Having literally and figuratively penetrated the mysteries of the female body, the boy feels accomplished, although he admits that it was 'one of the most desolate couplings'.[59] His masculinity is restored from abjection to a 'manly position'.[60] Desiring affirmation from his peers, the narrator wishes there were others to witness the act, particularly Raymond but also 'all my friends, all the people I knew'.[61] By raping his sister, the narrator thinks he has proven his masculinity. As he states, 'I felt proud, proud to be fucking ... to be lying there in that manly position'.[62] However, his triumph is undermined when he reaches orgasm in a 'miserable, played-out, barely pleasurable way'.[63] While disparaging of his younger self, the adult narrator does not seem to acknowledge the severity of his actions; rather, the episode is recalled as a befuddled sexual conquest and not a traumatic act of rape. There remains a lack of moral integrity in the narrator, who conveys his emotional detachment from the violation. According to the DSM-IV, the narrator's lack of

Assuming a 'manly position'

empathy and disregard of his sister's rights indicate a pathological social disorder.[64] Indeed, as Brownmiller argues, such disregard of women's rights is endemic in patriarchal society, where rape has 'played a critical function … of intimidation by which all *men* keep all *women* in a state of fear'.[65] In this way, the narrator's act of sexual violence is monstrously ordinary as an act of conformity with patriarchal norms.

Although the boy feels pride. McEwan makes it clear that this episode was traumatic for both children. Connie's trauma is more obviously displayed as she cries in the bathroom; however, the narrator implies that the experience was also traumatic for him, albeit to a lesser degree. Overwhelmed by the experience, the narrator declares that he wants nothing to do with the adult sexual world for an indefinite period of time and determines to cancel the meeting with Lulu unless Raymond wishes to see her independently, which he is certain he will not. Indeed, a latent masochism in masculine homosociality is implied throughout the story, even if it is only at the end of this sexual episode that the narrator experiences for himself the self-destructive drive that underlies male bonding. As McEwan illustrates throughout 'Homemade', there is a sadomasochistic undercurrent in patriarchal masculinity that victimises girls and women, but also causes men to 'self-abuse'[66] through their conformity, competition and attempts at mastery. Situated within a Gothic context, this story of the transformation of a boy becoming a man through rape is twisted into a shocking nightmare wherein the boy comes to embody a monstrous version of masculinity collapsing into abjection.

The Cement Garden

Sadomasochism and incest are also exemplified amongst the siblings in *The Cement Garden*. Similar to 'Homemade', the male protagonist of *The Cement Garden* reflects on his adolescence, recalling his transition from boyhood to maturity. Once again, McEwan disturbs the coming-of-age narrative by positing depravity and misogyny at the borderline of 'normal' masculinity. McEwan dramatises the Oedipal scenario through sibling relationships, when Jack and his siblings must adopt new roles after the deaths of their parents. Jack attempts to fill the patriarchal role as the male head of the household and his older sister, Julie, becomes the family's mother-surrogate. In conformity with patriarchal roles, Jack's performance of masculinity is rigid and abusive. Like the narrator of 'Homemade', Jack does not make a distinction between his sisters and other women, regarding them all as erotic objects and 'invention[s]' of his imagination.[67] Yet beyond Jack's outward persona of toughness, there is an emotionally fragile boy who struggles with feelings of inadequacy and clings to his older sister. Jack masks feelings of inadequacy through violence, acting out in ways that degrade female authority.

However, unlike 'Homemade' where the male narrator attempts to affirm his power through incestuous rape, in *The Cement Garden*, it is Julie, who expresses her authority over the family by initiating incestuous sex with Jack. Specifically, Julie's embodiment of womanhood, as simultaneously mother, sister, wife and lover to Jack provides a subversive challenge to the patriarchal convention of the nuclear family. Just as McEwan pathologises the coming-of-age of the narrator in 'Homemade' by representing his sexual rite of passage as wretched and sadistic, he once again critiques male dominance in his depiction of incest in *The Cement Garden*. Here, incest is used as a counter-discourse to patriarchal rule, illustrating the undercurrent of desire that exists at the threshold of hegemonic masculinity: namely, men's desire and dependency on the woman-mother.

After the death of their mother, the children's home 'seemed to have fallen asleep'[68] as they repress the knowledge of her death and their actions of burying her in the trunk. Here, the sleepy atmosphere of the household recalls the common trope of Gothic tales such as 'Briar Rose' and 'Rip Van Winkle', where slumber is suggestive of suspended time and otherworldliness. Peter Childs identifies this burial as repression of their mother's death and 'of Jack's desires'.[69] Specifically, by burying his mother, Jack is also symbolically burying his Oedipal-incestuous desires. In the months that follow, the children attempt to return to normalcy, yet the insidious scent of decay pervades the family's home. There is suspense when Derek, Julie's new boyfriend, traces this foreboding scent to its source, the trunk that holds the body of their deceased mother. Yet the discovery of this buried body is not the only 'return of the repressed'[70] in McEwan's novel, rather, the death of their mother gives rise to something even more disturbing: the incestuous relationship between Jack and Julie.

The incidence of their mother's death, increases the children's rebellion against social norms, and their transgressive behaviour escalates to the point of committing incest. Although they do not immediately act on their desire, sexual tension between the siblings exists even before their parents' deaths as evidenced in a childhood game. Like the game of 'Mummies and Daddies', through the siblings' erotic game McEwan suggests that there exist latent Oedipal-incestuous drives, which underlie the traditional family structure. As McEwan describes in interview with Ian Hamilton, 'in the nuclear family ... if you remove the controls, you have a ripe anarchy in which the oedipal and the incestuous are the definitive emotions'.[71] It is the 'controls' of patriarchy that enforce the incest taboo on the family unit. Indeed, all of the men within *The Cement Garden*, including Jack, Jack's father, and Julie's boyfriend, Derek, vie against each other for control over the family, attempting to assert their dominance they also degrade female authority and repudiate any traces of emasculation. In this masculine performance, there is disavowal of dependence and desire for the maternal body, an infantile desire that is repressed in the individuation process of becoming a man. Beginning with Jack's father, a rigid and authoritarian man who dominates his wife and ridicules his children, there is a pattern of patriarchal rule that begins to crumble throughout the novel. As the family patriarch, Jack's father imposes his will not only on his wife and children, but also on his garden. By structuring his garden through 'neatness and symmetry',[72] Jack's father attempts to master and control nature. Following a heart attack, which leaves him a 'semi-invalid',[73] his authority begins to diminish along with the deterioration of his 'special world'.[74] Without the father's imposing presence, the children, like his garden, become unruly. At this time, Jack's father becomes the object of ridicule for Jack and Julie. He must also 'compete' in an Oedipal rivalry with his youngest son, Tom, 'for Mother's attention'.[75] The father's regression from patriarchal authority to a 'semi-invalid', dependent on his wife's nurturing attention, illustrates his emasculation.[76] Like his father, Jack will attempt to assert his dominance, only to be undermined by his dependence on Julie's love and attention.

However, replacing his father as the male head of the household is not a smooth transition for Jack, as both Julie and her new boyfriend Derek become potential rivals. Julie seems to easily claim the responsibilities and authority of the maternal role during their mother's illness and subsequent death. Julie takes up the maternal role when she allows Tom, the youngest sibling at age six, to pretend to be a baby. In this infantile subject-position, Tom garners Julie's love and attention by becoming needy and dependent. As a maternal figure, Julie occupies that role of love object for the infantile child. Indeed, Tom's regression foreshadows the transformation that occurs in Jack, as he too grows to accept his dependence and, this time, erotic attachment to Julie as a mother-substitute. The parallels between Tom and Jack are another way that McEwan disturbs the patriarchal model of dominance in the novel. Under Julie's authority, traditional gender roles are undermined, as evidenced by her consenting to Tom's request to dress like a girl:[77] 'We should let him be a girl if he wants to.'[78] While Tom enjoys being treated passively like a baby and dressing like a girl, Jack initially struggles to accept Julie as an authority figure. As Julie's power over her family grows, Jack enacts his contempt for her in a violent game: 'I dragged her by the arm on to her bed. She lay with her knees drawn up, her hands raised to protect her throat ... Now there was an edge of panic in her thrashing about. She could not breathe in.'[79] The game ends when Julie, panic-stricken, urinates on the bed, her laughter having 'tailed away into tired weeping'.[80] Jack's game escalates into sadistic violation. As Angela Roger argues, the power struggle between Jack and Julie contains a sexual element, which is 'suggestive of rape'.[81] Jack is frequently violent, terrorising his siblings with threats of abuse and, "'always about to hit someone'",[82] Jack also lashes out in anger when Julie tells him what to do. Although Jack wants to be the family's father-figure, it is Julie who is "'in charge'"; this imbalance of power leaves Jack feeling 'cheated'[83] and emasculated. He is forced to come to terms with the fact that Julie has taken control of what has become *her* family.

Derek, Julie's boyfriend, is also a rival to Jack for control over the household. With his facial hair, strong build, and flashy red sports car, Derek embodies a form of masculinity that Jack both desires to emulate and rebels against. Notably, Derek's clean and proper body is a stark contrast to Jack's pimpled complexion and poor hygiene. Like Commander Hunt, a character in Jack's favourite novel, Derek becomes an ideal, primarily because he garners Julie's love and attention. Derek's 'manliness' is proven when he takes Jack to the snooker hall: 'a dark, male, adolescent world where [Derek] can rule the roost'.[84] At the snooker hall, Derek shows off his proficiency of the game and humiliates Jack under the gaze of male peers: 'I stared at Derek fiercely and without blinking. But … though I snatched at the tear as soon as it rolled out, I knew they had seen it.'[85] Although Jack presents a tough exterior, he cannot hide his childlike vulnerability. The reader is reminded that despite his performance, Jack is still very much a child who is struggling with loss.

From Derek's perspective, the incest between Jack and Julie is perceived as "'sick'" and unnatural.[86] Derek's intervention, his discovery of the mother's body and the incestuous relationship between Jack and Julie, disturbs the union of the siblings. By notifying the authorities, Derek performs the 'Law of the Father',[87] the patriarchal order that enforces the boundaries of the incest taboo and regulates gender roles. Julie's subversive authority is contained as the arrival of the police at the home suggests the status quo of patriarchal order will be restored. In this portrayal of the children's circumstances, the reader may sympathise with their dilemma, to such an extent that Derek's intervention may seem like a violation of their familial bond in the aftermath of such personal disturbance and unhappiness. As Carmen Callil and Colm Toibin argue, what is most disturbing about *The Cement Garden* is how McEwan enables the reader to identify with the closed off world that the children create: 'Their world has been so perfectly created that you feel miserable at the prospect of it being broken up.'[88] One can go so far as to argue that McEwan's novel dramatises for the reader the conflicts of infantile attachment to the mother and the traumatic separation that occurs in the anxieties of the Oedipal complex. As a counter-discourse to patriarchy, the strength of the children's bond affirms the central and founding position of the mother as the locus of familial unity – a bond that is disavowed in preservation of male dominance. Indeed, the novel strongly suggests that for patriarchy to exist at all, Oedipal-incestuous desires must be repudiated as a threat to the constitution of masculine dominance; specifically, patriarchy must overthrow and usurp the power of maternal influence. As McEwan's novel exemplifies, this shift in power marks a brutal and traumatic loss that is never completely healed.

'In Between the Sheets'

Like 'Homemade' and *The Cement Garden*, McEwan's short story, 'In Between the Sheets', indicates that incestuous desire is a component of familial attachment. In 'Homemade' and *The Cement Garden*, Oedipal-incestuous drives between siblings expose latent, libidinal desires and anxieties of masculinity. 'In Between the Sheets' continues McEwan's critique of male dominance, while presenting incestuous feelings in a filial relationship between father and daughter. By exposing the father's desire for his daughter, McEwan once again undermines the 'Law of the Father', which makes patriarchy possible.[89] In the story, Stephen Cooke, a middle-aged writer who has suffered the emasculation of a failed marriage due to sexual incompatibility, confronts his feelings of desire and anxiety around his daughter's burgeoning sexuality. Stephen struggles to uphold the propriety of his patriarchal role, as he is seduced by his daughter's sexuality. Yet unlike the teenage boys in 'Homemade' and *The Cement Garden*, the adult male protagonist of 'In Between the Sheets' is able to successfully negotiate the psychosexual terrain of incestuous desire in affirmation of the patriarchal order. Rather than succumb to his desires, Stephen preserves the boundaries of his daughter's sexual autonomy, and sublimates his inappropriate desires into the creative process of his writing. Whereas the narrator of 'Homemade' and Jack experience the angst of adolescence, the male protagonist of 'In Between the Sheets' is middle-aged. However, despite his age and experience, Stephen is not exempt from the crisis of masculinity. Stephen acknowledges his inadequacies and his unrealistic ideals – both of which relate to his problematic relationship to female sexuality. Stephen takes much of the blame for his failed marriage: 'I never satisfied my wife in marriage ... Her orgasms terrified me'.[90] Stephen is emasculated by his ex-wife who 'hated him for his fearfulness, his passivity and for all the wasted hours between the sheets'.[91] Stephen's sexual inadequacies are amplified now that his ex-wife has taken 'a vigorous lover'[92] and his daughter, who is turning fourteen, is on the brink of womanhood.

In their interactions, Stephen's ex-wife exudes confidence and aggression, in contrast to Stephen's ineffectuality: his wife complains of his choice of restaurant, asks him not to cry, and reveals that Miranda, their daughter, does not want to spend time with him. She is also sexually liberated and empowered by their divorce. In contrast, Stephen appears emasculated and weak. McEwan reinforces Stephen's inadequacy in description of his physical body: 'His cock was small in his hands … wrinkled by the cold, or perhaps the fear. He felt sorry for it'.[93] The patriarchal equation of penis and phallus is undermined in the inadequacy and abject state of Stephen's body. Arguably, there is both pathos and an element of critique in Stephen's failings, as McEwan counters the fiction of men's innate power and privilege. Rather than affirm patriarchal masculinity and its fiction of phallic mastery, McEwan portrays Stephen's manhood in relation to inadequacy and fear. Just as the narrator in 'Homemade' fears the sexuality of Lulu Smith, and Jack feels threatened by Julie's authority, Stephen also expresses similar gender anxiety. Like the narrator of 'Homemade,' Stephen repudiates his fears of female sexuality by engaging in transgressive fantasies. Following a meeting with his ex-wife, when they were served by a child waitress, Stephen has a wet dream about the girl. In the dream, the girl 'took a cup and held it to the machine. But now *he* was the machine, now *he* filled the cup'.[94] Stephen's erotic desire, and the fantasies it initiates are clearly paedophilic. As these erotic fantasies emerge, Stephen sublimates his inappropriate desires into the creative process of his writing. Having written down the dream in his journal, Stephen assuages his anxiety: the dream 'worried him less now'.[95] He aims to transform the dream into a story. As van der Kolk and van der Hart identify in their discussion of repression, the creation of narrative is a necessary mental schema to integrate 'unassimilated scraps of overwhelming experiences'.[96] In other words, once transformed into narrative language or an integrated story, traumatic experiences or feelings can be contained; the traumatic content no longer disrupts or intrudes as nightmares, flashbacks or hallucinations.[97] In this way, Stephen subdues his erotic fantasies of paedophilia; however, the emergence of repressed incestuous desires for his teenage daughter are more difficult to quell.

Stephen's fantasising involves both paedophilia and incestuous desire directed at his fourteen-year-old daughter Miranda and projected onto her friend Charmian, who 'stood no more than 3 foot 6'.[98] Charmian seems to embody many of Stephen's conflicted feelings about the female body: like a child, Charmian is diminutive and described as 'doll-like'[99] when she wears a 'child's dress'.[100] Yet, like his ex-wife, Charmian is also confident and voices her opinions, which in turn, causes Stephen to become nervous: 'The tiny girl gazed patiently into [Stephen's] eyes and he felt for a moment poised on the edge of total confession'.[101] As a joke, Charmian blocks the door to Stephen's home, an act that reflects an earlier episode where his ex-wife stood in the doorway of his previous home, and she 'glared down at him'.[102] Instead of waiting for Charmian to move, he tries to 'lift her high in the air like a child', but rather than acquiesce to this treatment she 'thumped his hand with her fist and shouted' at him.[103] In this instance, Stephen attempts to treat

Charmian as a child, yet she asserts her autonomy. Charmian's presence seems to defy Stephen's infantilisation of her, as noted when she gazes at Stephen and Miranda like 'a wise old woman'.[104] Much like Julie, Charmian heightens Stephen's gender anxieties in her symbolic association to iconic womanhood, wherein she embodies femininity at every age: childhood, adolescence, maturity and old age.

Stephen's fears of the female body are projected onto Charmian. Repulsed by Charmian's physical presence, Stephen considers her an example of abject femininity when compared to his daughter: '[O]ur lovely daughter with a friend who belongs by rights in a circus or silk-hung brothel serving tea ... is it not perverse?'[105] Derived from prejudices and stereotypes related to dwarfism, Stephen's views of Charmian illustrate his anxiety. Stephen's perceptions of women remain confined by patriarchal imagination, where women are either idealised or degraded. Ironically, it is not Charmian's friendship with Miranda that is shown to be perverse, but rather Stephen's own feelings for his daughter that transgress the boundaries of normative familial attachment. Stephen's incestuous desires are apparent as he awkwardly avoids Miranda's breasts when they embrace and contemplates buying her lingerie. Stephen does not understand the girls' relationship and is threatened by it. His fears are realised when he awakes in the middle of the night after hearing sounds of his daughter's sexual pleasure and likens it to 'the sound of his wife in, or approaching, orgasm'.[106] Stephen identifies 'the frame of all [his] anxieties' to be his wife's cries of arousal.[107] It is this sound of the female body in sexual pleasure that he hears coming from his daughter's bedroom. Stephen's fears of female sexuality can be associated with a fear of women's empowerment and agency. In regards to his daughter, Stephen's fears are evident: he fears losing his daughter's love, just as he lost the love of his wife; he also fears his daughter's emergence as a sexual being – as Miranda's 'coming of age' will further the dissolution of his patriarchal control. In Stephen's anxiety, the boundaries of sexuality and identity are blurred, as his daughter and his wife merge into one person, as indicated by the identical sound of their sexual pleasure. Miranda appears to occupy an ambiguous position in Stephen's mind as she straddles the boundaries of child and woman, daughter and wife: 'She could be a child or a woman, she could be any age'.[108] As John Haffenden identifies, '[McEwan] places the reader very close to [Stephen's] consciousness, especially when at night he overhears what he takes to be [his daughter's] romantic restlessness, to the point where one is convinced that incest will take place'.[109] The reader is led to believe that Stephen will act upon the incestuous desires for his daughter.

However, rather than act on his 'violent and confused ideas towards his daughter',[110] Stephen stops, snapping himself out of this dream-like state: 'Her father stood in front of her, very still, very massive, one foot in front of the other as though frozen mid-step, arms limp by his side'.[111] Like a sleepwalker or 'dreamer',[112] Stephen has approached the boundary of his unconscious desires, yet he does not cross this line. The final image of the story is Stephen studying his daughter's face as she sleeps. He stares at 'the pallor of her upturned throat' and recalls a childhood memory, wherein he stood in front of 'a field of dazzling white snow which he, a small boy of eight, had not dared scar with footprints'.[113] This image of 'white snow'[114] reiterates his daughter's sexual innocence, and presents Stephen's moral decision not to violate his daughter. Unlike the adolescent male characters in 'Homemade' and *The Cement Garden*, Stephen does not cross the threshold of incestuous desire in violation of the female Other.

Throughout McEwan's early fiction, he employs shocking and disturbing depictions of men and boys using violence to assuage anxiety. When situated in its historical context of post-war Britain, these early works of fiction illuminate the widespread 'crisis of masculinity', wherein men's claims to power and privilege were undermined on multiple levels, including the cultural 'coming of age' of women's liberation during the second wave of feminism.[115] Violence, in the form of incestuous rape, whether real or imagined, is exhibited by the male characters in McEwan's stories as a means to expose latent fears and desires in men's dependency on the Woman-Mother. Specifically, male characters in McEwan's fiction use violence to elevate their social status in their homosocial peer group, to deny gender anxiety including 'unmanly' feelings such as vulnerability or ineffectuality, and to challenge the power and autonomy of women. In each story, 'Homemade', *The Cement Garden* and 'In Between the Sheets', McEwan challenges the status quo of patriarchy by representing Oedipal-incestuous desires that lurk just below the surface of social order – in particular, in the founding structure of the nuclear family. In this way, McEwan shocks his readers by blurring the line between hegemonic masculinity and pathological violence, by confronting the ordinary monstrosity of patriarchal relations.

Notes

1 Ian McEwan, 'Homemade', *First Love, Last Rites* (Vintage, 2006), p. 43.
2 Dominic Head, *Ian McEwan* (Manchester University Press, 2007), p. 25.
3 See: Jack Slay Jr., *Ian McEwan* (Twayne, 1996), pp. 3, 11, 22, 24, 10, 87, 116; and Head, *Ian McEwan* (2007), p. 34.
4 Bruce Finney, 'Briony's stand against oblivion', *Journal of Modern Literature* 27:3 (2004): p. 68.
5 The term 'monstrously ordinary' is used here to refer to the inherent capabilities of human nature to destroy and cause pain.
6 Kaja Silverman, *Male Subjectivity at the Margins* (Routledge, 1992), p. 53.
7 Silverman, *Male Subjectivity*, p. 15.

8 Stephen Brooke, *Sexual Politics* (Oxford University Press, 2011), p. 191.
9 *Ibid.*, p. 191.
10 Judith Kegan Gardiner, 'Introduction', in Judith Kegan Gardiner (ed.), *Masculinity Studies and Feminist Theory* (Columbia University Press, 2002), p. 6.
11 Silverman, *Male Subjectivity*, p. 37.
12 *Ibid.*, p. 37.
13 *Ibid.*, p. 40.
14 Kiernan Ryan, *Ian McEwan* (Northcote House, 1994), p. 12.
15 Ian McEwan, 'Interview with John Haffenden', in John Haffenden (ed.), *Novelists in Interview* (Methuen, 1985), p. 177.
16 McEwan, 'Homemade', p. 43.
17 Michael S. Kimmel, *The Gender of Desire* (SUNY Press, 2005), p. 186.
18 McEwan, 'Homemade', p. 24.
19 *Ibid.*, p. 27.
20 *Ibid.*, p. 26.
21 *Ibid.*, p. 26.
22 *Ibid.*, p. 23.
23 *Ibid.*, p. 24.
24 *Ibid.*, p. 29.
25 Julia Kristeva, L.S. Roudiez (trans,), *Powers of Horror* (Columbia University Press, 1982) pp. 53, 72.
26 McEwan, 'Homemade', p. 29.
27 *Ibid.*, p. 30.
28 Hélène Cixous, 'The laugh of the Medusa,' *Signs* 1:4 (1976): p. 877.
29 McEwan, 'Homemade', p. 32.
30 Linda Broughton, 'Portrait of the subject as a young man: The construction of masculinity ironized in 'male' fiction', in Philip Shaw and Peter Stockwell (eds), *Subjectivity and Literature from the Romantics to the Present Day* (Pinter 1991), p. 140.
31 McEwan, 'Homemade', p. 32.
32 McEwan, 'Homemade', pp. 28, 30.
33 R.G. Thompson, *Freakery: Cultural Spectacles of the Extraordinary Body* (New York University Press, 1996), p. 15.
34 McEwan, 'Homemade', p. 28.
35 *Ibid.*, pp. 30–1.
36 Bram Stoker, David Rogers (introd. and notes), *Dracula* (Wordsworth, 2000), p. 175.
37 H. Rider Haggard, Daniel Karlin (ed., introd., biblio., and notes), Dennis Butts (biblio. and chronology), *She* (Oxford University Press, 2008), p. 144.
38 *Ibid.*, p. 35.
39 *Ibid.*, p. 35.
40 Cixous, 'The laugh of the Medusa', p. 877.
41 McEwan, 'Homemade', p. 35.

42 *Ibid.*, p. 35.
43 *Ibid.*, pp. 35, 30.
44 *Ibid.*, p. 38.
45 *Ibid.*, p. 35.
46 *Ibid.*, p. 39.
47 Broughton, 'Portrait of the subject', p. 4.
48 McEwan, 'Homemade', p. 39.
49 *Ibid.*, p. 31.
50 Susan Brownmiller, *Against Our Will* (Bantam, 1976), p. 5.
51 McEwan, 'Homemade', pp. 39, 38.
52 *Ibid.*, pp. 40–1, 43.
53 *Ibid.*, p. 42.
54 *Ibid.*, p. 42.
55 *Ibid.*, p. 42.
56 *Ibid.*, p. 42.
57 Brownmiller, *Against Our Will*, p. 312.
58 Laura Brown, 'Not outside the range: One feminist perspective on psychic trauma', *American Imago* 48 (1991): p. 122.
59 McEwan, 'Homemade', p. 43.
60 *Ibid.*, p. 43.
61 *Ibid.*, pp. 42–3.
62 *Ibid.*, p. 43.
63 *Ibid.*, p. 43.
64 *DSM-IV-TR* (Diagnostic and Statistical Manual of Mental Disorders, Hefner Media Group, 2004), http://dsm.psychiatryonline.org/doi/abs/10.1176/appi.books.9780890420249.dsm-iv-tr (accessed 26 April 2013).
65 Brownmiller, *Against Our Will*, p. 5.
66 McEwan, 'Homemade', p. 23.
67 McEwan, *The Cement Garden* (Vintage, 2006), p. 26.
68 *Ibid.*, p. 71.
69 Peter Childs, *The Fiction of Ian McEwan* (Palgrave, 2006), p. 40.
70 See Sigmund Freud, James Strachey (ed.) and Anna Freud with Alix Strachey and Alan Tyson (trans.), *An Infantile Neurosis and Other Works, The Standard Edition of the Complete Psychological Works of Sigmund Freud*, vol. 17 (Vintage, 2001), note 72.
71 McEwan, Ian, 'Points of departure [Interview with Ian Hamilton]', *The New Review*, 5:2 (1977), p. 19.
72 McEwan, *The Cement Garden*, p. 15.
73 *Ibid.*, p. 13.
74 *Ibid.*, p. 15.
75 *Ibid.*, p. 13.
76 *Ibid.*, p, 13.
77 In the short story, 'Disguises', (1975) McEwan also draws on the ideas of cross-dressing and incestuous relations.

78 McEwan, *The Cement Garden*, p. 47.
79 *Ibid.*, pp. 30–1.
80 *Ibid.*, p. 31.
81 Angela Roger, 'Ian McEwan's portrayal of women', *Forum for Modern Language Studies* 32:1 (1996), p. 14.
82 McEwan, *The Cement Garden*, p. 98.
83 *Ibid.*, p. 53.
84 Childs, *The Fiction of Ian McEwan*, p. 42.
85 McEwan, *The Cement Garden*, p. 106.
86 McEwan, 'Homemade', p. 136.
87 Jacques Lacan, Brucee Fink (ed.), *Écrits: A Selection* (Norton, 2002), p. 582.
88 Carmen Callil and Colm Toibin, *The Modern Library* (Picador, 1999) p. 113.
89 J. Gallop, 'The father's seduction', in Robyn R. Warhol and Diane Price Herndl (eds), *Feminisms Redux: An Anthology of Literary Theory and Criticisms*, (Rutgers University Press, 1995), pp. 159–60.
90 Ian McEwan, 'In Between the Sheets', in Ian McEwan, *In Between the Sheets* (Jonathan Cape, 1978), p. 98.
91 *Ibid.*, p. 100.
92 *Ibid.*, p. 100.
93 *Ibid.*, p. 104.
94 *Ibid.*, p. 99.
95 *Ibid.*, p. 99.
96 Van der Kolk, Bessel A. and Onno van der Hart, 'The intrusive past: The flexibility of memory and the engraving of trauma', in Cathy Caruth (ed.), *Trauma: Explorations in Memory* (Johns Hopkins University Press, 1995), p. 176.
97 *Ibid.*, p. 163.
98 McEwan, 'In Between the Sheets', p. 97.
99 *Ibid.*, p. 97.
100 *Ibid.*, p. 98.
101 *Ibid.*, p. 98.
102 *Ibid.*, p. 95.
103 *Ibid.*, p. 101.
104 *Ibid.*, p. 103.
105 *Ibid.*, p. 100.
106 *Ibid.*, p. 104.
107 *Ibid.*, p. 104.
108 *Ibid.*, p. 105.
109 McEwan, 'Interview', in Haffenden, *Novelists in Interview*, p. 171.
110 *Ibid.*, p. 171.
111 McEwan, 'In Between the Sheets', p. 105.
112 *Ibid.*, p. 105.
113 *Ibid.*, p. 106.
114 *Ibid.*, p. 106.

115 Michael S. Kimmel, *Manhood in America: A Cultural History*, 3rd edn (Oxford University Press, 2012), pp. 189–210.

Bibliography

Fiction

Grimm, Jacob and Wilhelm Grimm, Maria Tatar (trans., pref. and notes), A.S. Byatt (introd.), 'Briar Rose' (Norton, 2012), pp. 238–45

Irving, Washington, Jennifer Donnelly (introd.), *Rip Van Winkle and Other Stories* (Puffin, 2010), Digital Edition

McEwan, Ian, 'Disguises', in *First Love, Last Rites* (Vintage, 2006), pp. 123–57

——., 'Homemade', in *First Love, Last Rites* (Vintage, 2006), pp. 23–44

——., 'In Between the Sheets', in *In Between the Sheets* (Jonathan Cape, 1978), pp. 89–106.

——., 'Pornography', in *In Between the Sheets* (Jonathan Cape, 1978), pp. 11–28.

——., *The Cement Garden* (Vintage, 2006)

Haggard, H. Rider, Daniel Karlin (ed., introd., biblio. and notes), Dennis Butts (biblio. and chronology), *She* (Oxford University Press, 2008)

Stoker, Bram, David Rogers (introd. and notes), *Dracula* (Wordsorth, 2000)

Non-fiction

Brooke, Stephen, *Sexual Politics: Sexuality, Family Planning, and the British Left from the 1880s to the Present Day* (Oxford University Press, 2011)

Broughton, Linda, 'Portrait of the subject as a young man: The construction of masculinity ironized in "male" fiction', in Philip Shaw and Peter Stockwell (eds), *Subjectivity and Literature from the Romantics to the Present Day* (Pinter, 1991), pp. 135–45

Brown, Laura S., 'Not outside the range: One feminist perspective on psychic trauma', *American Imago* 48:1 (1991), pp. 119–33

Brownmiller, Susan, *Against Our Will: Men, Women and Rape* (Bantam, 1976)

Callil, Carmen and Colm Toibin, *The Modern Library* (Picador, 1999)

Childs, Peter, *The Fiction of Ian McEwan* (Palgrave, 2006)

Cixous, Hélène, 'The laugh of the Medusa', *Signs* 1:4 (1976), pp. 875–93

Finney, Bruce, 'Briony's stand against oblivion: The making of fiction in Ian McEwan's *Atonement*', *Journal of Modern Literature* 27:3 (2004), pp. 68–82

Freud, Sigmund, James Strachey (ed.) and Anna Freud with Alix Strachey and Alan Tyson (trans.), 'Repression', and 'Mourning and melancholia', *On the History of the Psychoanalytic Movement, Papers on Metapsychology and Other Works, The Standard Edition of the Complete Psychological Works of Sigmund Freud*, vol. 14 (Vintage, 2001), pp. 141–58; pp. 237–58

——., James Strachey (ed.) and Anna Freud with Alix Strachey and Alan Tyson (trans.), 'The development of the libido and the sexual organisations', *Introductory*

Lectures on Psycho-Analysis (Part III), *The Standard Edition of the Complete Psychological Works of Sigmund Freud*, vol. 16 (Vintage, 2001), pp. 320–38

Gallop, Jane, 'The father's seduction', in Robyn R. Warhol and Diane Price Herndl (eds), *Feminisms Redux: An Anthology of Literary Theory and Criticisms* (Rutgers University Press, 2009), pp. 146–62

Head, Dominic, *Ian McEwan* (Manchester University Press, 2007)

Horrocks, Roger, *Masculinity in Crisis: Myths, Fantasies, and Realities* (St. Martin's Press, 1994)

Kegan Gardiner, Judith, 'Introduction', in Judith Kegan Gardiner (ed.), *Masculinity Studies and Feminist Theory* (Columbia University Press, 2002), pp. 1–30

Kimmel, Michael S., 'Masculinity as homophobia: Fear, shame, and silence in the construction of gender identity', in Harry Brod and Michael Kaufman (eds), *Theorizing Masculinities* (Sage Publications, 1994), pp. 119–40

——., *The Gender of Desire: Essays on Male Sexuality* (SUNY Press, 2005)

——., *Manhood in America: A Cultural History* (Oxford University Press, 2012)

Kristeva, Julia, L.S. Roudiez (trans.), *Powers of Horror: An Essay on Abjection* (Columbia University Press, 1982)

Lacan, Jacques, Bruce Fink (ed.), *Écrits: A Selection* (Norton, 2002)

Logan, Carol, *Counterbalance: Gendered Perspectives for Writing and Language* (Broadview, 1997)

McEwan, Ian, 'Points of departure [Interview with Ian Hamilton]', *The New Review*, 5:2 (1977), pp. 9–21

——., 'Interview with John Haffenden', in John Haffenden (ed.), *Novelists in Interview* (Methuen, 1985), pp. 168–90

Nadal, Marita, ' "The Fall of the House of Usher": A master text for (Poe's) American Gothic', *Journal of English Studies* 7 (2009), pp. 55–70

Roger, Angela, 'Ian McEwan's portrayal of women', *Forum for Modern Language Studies* 32:1 (1996), pp. 11–27

Ryan, Kiernan, *Ian McEwan* (Northcote House, 1994)

Silverman, Kaja, *Male Subjectivity at the Margins* (Routledge, 1992)

Slay Jr., Jack, *Ian McEwan* (Twayne, 1996)

Thompson, Rosemarie G., *Freakery: Cultural Spectacles of the Extraordinary Body* (New York University Press, 1996)

Van der Kolk, Bessel A. and Onno van der Hart, 'The intrusive past: The flexibility of memory and the engraving of trauma', in Cathy Caruth (ed.), *Trauma: Explorations in Memory* (Johns Hopkins University Press, 1995), pp. 158–82

Websites

'Dinky', in Walter Rader (maintainer of site), '*The Online Slang Dictionary*, 10 March 2011, http://onlineslangdictionary.com/meaning-definition-of/dinky (accessed 26 April 2013)

DSM-IV-TR: Diagnostic and Statistical Manual of Mental Disorders, 4th edn, *American Psychiatric Association* (Hefner Media Group, 2004), http://dsm.psychiatryonline.org/doi/abs/10.1176/appi.books.9780890420249.dsm-iv-tr (accessed 26 April 2013)

McEwan, Ian, 'Interview by Helen Whitney', 'Faith and Doubt at Ground Zero', *Frontline, PBS.org*, April 2002, www.pbs.org/wgbh/pages/frontline/shows/faith/interviews/mcewan.html (accessed 26 April 2013)

3

'Waking in the dark':[1] Remembering incest in *A Thousand Acres* (1991), *Exposure* (1993) and *Beautiful Kate* (2009)

Rebecca White

'By day and night he wrongs me',[2] laments Goneril in *King Lear*, her anguish defining Shakespeare's portrait of 'Father against child'.[3] As 'property of blood',[4] her voice is framed by the patriarchal power epitomised by her sire; she is simultaneously suppressed as daughter and subject, and consequently, ultimately deprived of mind and body by a male discourse that constricts the female presence as 'ever soft, / Gentle, and low'.[5] '[B]ound to th' father',[6] the patriarchy becomes a prison within which Goneril and her sister Regan are castigated by the cultural weight of Lear's 'majesty',[7] derided as 'unnatural hags'[8] and marginalised by centuries of Shakespeare scholarship.[9] It is such critical and cultural 'lacunas in memory', however, that Jane Smiley interrogates in her feminist re-visioning of *King Lear*, as *A Thousand Acres* (1991) seeks to unveil an interrelationship between suffering and silence, finally illuminating the 'wrongs' of the father.[10]

Acting as 'lawyer for Goneril and Regan' ('Ginny' and 'Rose' in *A Thousand Acres*), Smiley proposes 'a different narrative of their motives and actions that casts doubt on the case Mr Shakespeare was making for his client, King Lear'.[11] In allowing the female voice to break 'the unbroken surface of the unsaid',[12] and thereby expose Lear's 'undivulgèd crimes',[13] the 'disease that's in [his] flesh'[14] is revealed as 'incestuous'[15] desire; setting 'all at odds',[16] Smiley reworks Lear's imaging of women as 'centaurs', and instead casts the King into the 'darkness', 'the sulphurous pit' of his 'burning, scalding' male covetousness.[17]

Significantly, Smiley's adaptation of Shakespeare's text, together with Kathryn Harrison's novel *Exposure* (1993) and Rachel Ward's film version of Newton Thornburg's *Beautiful Kate* (2009), embodies many of the complexities and controversies that surround the 'evil' that she perceives in *King Lear*, as the often tense interplay between the 'real' and the reconstructed characterises debates about incest and memory. *A Thousand Acres* and *Exposure* were published within a context of conflict, during the 'Memory Wars' that divided psychological and legal discourse throughout the 1990s. The women's liberation movement, shaped during the 1970s, enabled female victims to voice their stories, their empowerment challenging the culturally sanctioned concealment of incest and the patriarchally endorsed silencing of women – the propriety need to "'pretend nothing happened'".[18] Consequently, following the African American authors who disclosed the 'gross crime'[19] of incest from the 1970s onwards (including Toni Morrison in *The Bluest Eye* – 1970 – and Alice Walker in *The Color Purple* – 1982), the late-twentieth century witnessed an outpouring of incest narratives.[20] During this time, the writing of novelists and memoirists was encouraged, and their claims reinforced, by the work of Recovered Memory Movement psychologists such as Judith Herman, whose book *Father-Daughter Incest* (1982) became a landmark in promoting discussion of a taboo that had, arguably, been evaded by Freud decades earlier.

Incest, however, is 'a volatile subject'.[21] This is discernible not simply in its link with hierarchical gender relations (as Vikki Bell's 1993 research suggests, the 'daughter', for example, can be seen as defined and therefore 'owned' by the father), but also in its association with conflicting concepts about memory.[22] Whereas psychologists such as Herman and Lisa Hirschman (1982), and authors such as Laura Davis and Ellen Bass (1988), stress the plausibility of remembered incidents of incest abuse,[23] opposing theories of memory have been propounded which highlight the elusiveness of recollection, and the possibility of implanting ideas in the brain. Elizabeth Loftus (1995), in particular, has challenged the Recovered Memory Movement. Her psychological experiments have demonstrated that individuals 'can be led to believe that entire events happened to them after suggestions to that effect', consequently 'leading to the creation of false memories'.[24] As Fiona E. Raitt and M. Suzanne Zeedyk have written: 'Those most sceptical of the notion of repressed memories (e.g. Underwager and Wakefield, 1994) consider women who claim to recover memories of childhood abuse to be suffering from delusions. These "delusions" or "mistaken memories" are categorized as "false memories", and those who have them are said to be suffering from a pathological condition: False Memory Syndrome.' The term is 'in large part the currency of the organization called the False Memory Syndrome Foundation', which was founded in the early 1990s.[25]

Indeed, the roots of False Memory Syndrome can arguably be discerned in the work of Freud.[26] As Judith Herman notes, although he maintained that he 'was able to recognise in this phantasy of being seduced by the father that expression of the typical Oedipus conflict', 'Freud was never comfortable with his discovery, because of what it implied about the behaviour of respectable family men … Recognising the implicit challenge to patriarchal values, Freud refused to identify fathers publicly as sexual aggressors'.[27] Set within a tradition of scepticism against 'hysterical' women, this protective privileging of masculinity is seen by feminists, such as Rosaria Champagne, as underpinning the motivations behind the False Memory Syndrome Foundation; concerned largely with defending fathers from abuse allegations, it has been read as maintaining an ideology that upholds the primacy of the male.[28] Certainly, although Katha Pollitt notes that '[t]he danger of the repressed memory attacks politically is that they are used to discredit what we now know about childhood incest', it is 'unfortunate' that 'certain feminist individuals … think that if a woman says it … testimony is its own proof'.[29] At the same time, however, the very existence of the 'Memory Wars', sparked as a condemnatory response to feminist debate, can be seen, in part, as embodying patriarchal dictates in itself. Indeed, as Doane and Hodges assert, women's incest narratives 'continue to elicit sharply corrective analyses', subjected to the 'social power of normative views about women's hysteria, tendency to lie, and vulnerability to manipulation'.[30]

This simultaneous intertwining of women's speech and suppression has been further complicated by legal discourses concerning incest and memory. Echoing John Henry Wigmore's *A Treatise on the Anglo-American System of Evidence in Trials at Common Law*, which postulated the female predisposition to make false allegations against men, Herman notes the 'Crisis of Disclosure' that continued to confront women in late-twentieth-century male-dominated (American) law courts.[31] Indeed, Smiley's appropriation of legal language in adapting Shakespeare – she acts as 'lawyer for Goneril and Regan'[32] – provides an implicit reference to the wider, potentially oppressive framework in which her novel is set; just as 'truth' is presented as a punishment in *King Lear* – a demeaning 'dower' for Cordelia – honesty does not necessarily elicit reward in *A Thousand Acres*.[33] Tellingly, by making 'Goneril [her] star witness', the 'desired verdict was not "innocent", but rather "not guilty", or *at least* "*not proven*"' [my italics], the ambiguity of her 'court' paralleling, in Smiley's novel, the law's evasion of incest as emblematised by Caroline.[34]

Embodying the complex double-binds of speech and silence, autonomy and ownership that colour the incest debate, Shakespeare and *King Lear* remain 'a kind of past, a locus of cultural authority structuring the novel [*A Thousand Acres*], that can be powerfully reinterpreted but not easily shed'.[35] Just as Ginny and Rose 'could not unknow what [they] knew', Shakespeare's canonical presence continues to possess Smiley's novel.[36] The literary indeed becomes a further complex – and often contested – backdrop in remembering abuse. Just as Ginny's canning and pickling in *A Thousand Acres* implies both preservation and distortion, *telling* incest couples the ambiguities of memory with the constructedness of narrative – as Ned exclaims in *Beautiful Kate*, his written 'evidence' of his relationship with his sister is 'fiction'.

Moreover, Cathy Caruth, developing Freud, stresses both the latency of trauma (and, by implication, incest) and its essential incomprehensibility and inexpressibility; 'the traumatic event is not experienced as it occurs, it is fully evident only in connection with another place, and in another time'.[37] As Rose exclaims in *A Thousand Acres*, ' "I know what I was saying, but I don't know what it means, exactly. Or how to tell you what it means" '.[38] Following Caruth, Marinella Rodi-Risberg argues that if 'traumatic experience eschews linguistic reference, then linguistically speaking, trauma is thought of in non-representational terms', raising 'issues of representation, memory and witnessing with specific implications for literary studies ... [I]f trauma ... manifests itself as an epistemological crisis that destroys the perceptions of time and space and instead repeatedly returns as intrusive images and compulsive behaviour ... then how can it be testified to, represented, read, and ... textually worked over?'[39] This struggle to articulate trauma and memory is likewise signified in the shifting popular and critical responses to the incest narrative as a genre. Although, as Rodi-Risberg asserts, 'Literature becomes the forgotten unforgettable place of trauma that it so urgently needs', the proliferation of stories led to an indictment of incest as 'the plat-du-jour in the 90s' marketplace'.[40] At the same time, 'a ghastly trauma of childhood has been turned into an all-purpose literary ingredient';[41] recalling the objectification of women – 'we were just his, to do with as he pleased'[42] – the incest story has been commodified (exemplified by the very title of a *New York Times* article: 'Incest as a selling point' – 1997).[43] Incest has, as such, become 'a touch too predictable', 'too fashionable, too overworked in fiction, especially when it comes through recovered memory', numbing its power; editors argue that 'It's not a riveting plot device. There's something opportunistic about it' – "I'm not shocked by it, I'm bored'.[44] Caught between remembering and recoiling, the vociferousness of incest narratives has ironically re-cast a veil over the subject.

A Thousand Acres (both Smiley's novel and Jocelyn Moorhouse's film adaptation), *Exposure* and *Beautiful Kate* explore many of the traits of incest abuse as outlined by Herman. Above all, Herman asserts that women who expose incest are frequently vilified by a male discourse that constricts their voices and, recalling Shakespeare's 'hags', defines them as 'bitches'.[45] As will be seen, patriarchal language is challenged in incest narratives; by casting a 'reflective credibility backward' and 'remembering what you can't imagine', the male-authored story is reclaimed and rewritten, implanted with alternative perspectives (and indeed, even in *King Lear*, Cordelia rephrases her father's speech: 'So young and so untender?'; 'So young, my Lord, and true').[46] However, as the critical responses to *A Thousand Acres*, *Exposure*, and *Beautiful Kate* demonstrate, telling incest remains entangled in a conflict between expression and evasion. 'Waking in the dark', those who have experienced incest are both subject to a new knowledge and entrapped by it, their freshly gained perspicuity shadowed by continued prejudice, doubt, and inexpressibility.[47]

A Thousand Acres (1991)

Just as Smiley struggles to define her responses to *King Lear* – 'Without being able to articulate why, I thought Goneril and Regan got the short end of the stick' – Ginny is plagued by inexpressibility, as what 'was never given utterance eventually becomes too nebulous to recall'.[48] Speech and silence are gendered, controlled by man's monopoly of expression; Caroline 'had simply spoken as a woman rather than as a daughter. That was something … that Rose and I were pretty careful never to do'. Tellingly, Larry's first direct speech is dictatorial – 'That's the plan' – and his presence deadening: 'Now the glare was for me … I couldn't think of anything to say'.[49]

Indeed, anticipating the criticism against *A Thousand Acres*, speaking is constricting and 'dangerous'; Ginny's 'conversation made [her] *breathless*' [my italics], a difficulty that is presented as particularly feminine: 'as if I were wearing a girdle with tight stays'.[50] Following the disclosure of incest, Ginny's public voice remains stifled: ' "that constitutes evidence that he was – ". Still staring at her, I jumped over this part'.[51] As Ginny 'floundered to a halt', she is unable to express her memory directly.[52] Instead, she displaces her voice, just as she is displaced from her abused body: 'It happened like you said'.[53] As she reflects, 'it was easy … to see it his way … When he talked, he had this effect on me. Of course it was silly to talk about "my point of view". When my father asserted his point of view, mine vanished. Not even I could remember it'.[54]

However, in the 'power of telling rather than being told', Smiley's novel challenges Herman's theory that abused daughters align their perspectives with their fathers'.[55] Crucially, just as Larry's 'thousand acres' present a disrupted natural order that mirrors the disturbed relationship between father and daughter (Rose's cancer, 'the child of her union with Daddy', is echoed by fertilisers causing infertility, for example), Ginny's retrospective language assumes a duality of meaning that challenges her father's 'way of making unanswerable remarks'.[56] In this, Smiley evokes and reworks the very notion of False Memory Syndrome, as her portrait of farm life 'plants' Ginny's remembrances over both Larry's story and, by poisoning the mythologised connection between man and the land, the (male) canonical American narrative; Ginny rewrites 'this grand history' through 'blows'.[57]

Ying-Chiao Lin argues that 'Ginny is forced to silence her individual voice so that her own subjectivity becomes deformed and detached. She remains defined as the daughter of the father, not herself'.[58] However, as a retrospective narrator, Ginny manipulates language in order to 'stand up to [Larry]', diminishing the 'monolith that he seemed to be'.[59] This is epitomised by her use of the words 'Daddy' and 'Father' in her memories. Although Herman maintains that it is common for abused women to refer to their fathers as 'Daddy', Ginny's lexical choices reassert her agency, privileging her in the hierarchy of their relationship.[60] While 'Father' presents Larry as a figure-head, 'never dwarfed by the landscape', its formality provides Ginny with a distance denied to her in rape (a similar mechanism is seen in *Beautiful Kate*, as Ned calls his father 'Bruce'); tellingly, 'Father' is most often used in her private, internal recollections.[61] Likewise, while 'Daddy' figures Ginny as a child, it also curtails his stature. Revealingly, his daughter defines him in such terms in public.

Ultimately, 'Daddy ... is what he is and can't be labeled'.[62] However, Ginny's narrative erases his patriarchal hold over 'the immensity of the piece of land [he] owned', the 'biggest farm farmed by the biggest farmer'; in her very opening line – 'At sixty miles an hour, you could pass our farm in a minute' – Larry's thousand acres are forgotten in their fleetingness.[63] Similarly, as will be seen in *Exposure*, tense is used to deliberate effect, enabling Ginny to 'bury' her father linguistically. ' "[A]fraid of anything having to do with Daddy' ", her fear is embodied by the immediacy of her language: 'The flesh of his lower jaw tightens as he grits his teeth. ... His face reddens, his eyes seek yours'.[64] However, the switch to the past tense – 'That *was* Daddy' [my italics] – deadens his presence, his direct voice finally edited out and silenced. Significantly, Ginny 'forgot to take a last look at the farm'.[65] In this, forgetting becomes a form of empowerment; recalling the farm's insubstantiality in the opening passage, the novel is encircled by the elision of patriarchal power.

Ginny's narrative invests her with 'a feeling of being drenched with insight ... Rather than feeling 'not myself', I felt intensely, newly, more myself than ever before'.[66] Confronting ' "Laurence Cook – the great I AM" ', Ginny 'plants' herself back into the text: 'One thing Daddy took from *me* when he came to *me* in *my* room at night was the memory of *my* body'; 'And so *my* father came to *me* and had intercourse with *me*' [my italics].[67] Just as 'the water in the soil' and Ginny's unburied nightdress symbolise the resurfacing of memory, her linguistic foreshadowing provides her own 'undercurrents', denying the 'solid ground' of patriarchal, public narratives of family.[68] Anticipating the distorted sound effects and 'grittiness' of Moorhouse's adaptation of *A Thousand Acres* and Ward's *Beautiful Kate*, Ginny's voice associates domesticity with violence; 'the screen door *slapped*'; Caroline's kisses '*smack* [Larry] on the lips'; the 'sight of [Larry] stopped me ... so that Rose ... ran *smack* into me' [my italics]. Although this can be read as an internalisation of Larry's abuse, Ginny questions her (publicly) regulated voice and, consequently, exposes her father: Caroline 'could have opened the door and come in, even after Daddy closed it (slammed it?)'.[69]

Smiley's motivations in writing *A Thousand Acres* frame the novel with rewritten memory, as she challenges the 'Generations of silence' that followed Shakespeare's text (and that of Nahum Tate, whose 1681 adaptation of *King Lear* closed the play within a reinstated patriarchal order).[70] However, the novel itself engages with the ambiguity of memory; while Ginny's voice appropriates Larry's 'motto ... what you get is what you deserve', and 'plants' her own story over her father's, Rose directs Ginny's recollections: 'It was incredible to me to hear Rose speak like this, but it was intoxicating, too, as sweet and forbidden as anything I had ever done. I couldn't resist her'.[71] As Ginny tries 'to remember [her] father', she both controls, and is controlled by, memory; although she constructs her narrative, 'phrasing and rephrasing ... sentences in [her] mind', she also admits 'It may be true ... I did hear a truck'; 'it may be that it ... inserted itself into those memories'.[72]

Indeed, memory is shaped within the course of the narrative. Ginny revisits the recollection of her mother's funeral, but edits and expands it: 'I watched the parrot, then went home and to bed. Rose stole the flashlight'.[73] Above all, Ginny engages with the struggle to express and comprehend traumatic memory as outlined by Caruth and Rodi-Risberg, her narrative itself becoming part of her 'gleaming obsidian shard'; a dark mirror reflecting darkly, it conflicts both with the past and with Ginny:

> What I remembered of Daddy did not gel into a full figure, but always remained fragments of sound and smell and presence. That capacity Rose had, of remembering, knowing, judging, as if continually viewing our father through the cross hairs of a bombsight, was her special talent, and didn't extend to me.[74]

The rage that eludes Ginny, however, finds voice in the critical backlash against *A Thousand Acres*, as her observation – 'The one thing that ... maybe no family could tolerate, was things coming into the open' – is realised by certain reviewers' uneasiness with the novel's 'dredging-up' of 'horrors from the past'.[75] Tellingly, although the novel was generally praised, its uncovering of incest prompted some calls for its re-concealment. Just as Rose exclaims '"It's like he's going to smother me, just cover me over as if I were always his, never my own – "', her 'voice *strangled to a halt*' [my italics], *A Thousand Acres* was suppressed in 1994 by a Washington high school.[76] Significantly, the treatment of incest was seen to conflict with 'art', the school's principal deriding Smiley's novel as holding 'no literary value'.[77] Likewise, as Hortense Spillers contends, 'whether or not father–daughter incest actually happens ... is not a problem for *literary* interpretation'.[78] This cultural amnesia was reinforced by enraged supporters of 'the Bard', the embodiment of the male literary canon, who expostulated that Smiley's text 'insults [Lear] retroactively and robs him of majesty'.[79] Certainly, Smiley's own response to *A Thousand Acres* exemplifies the distorted familial relationships and controversy that it explores; 'despite all the success the novel has had, I still feel alienated from it. My monster child'.[80] In 1995, however, such ambivalence became vitriolic in 'Making the Incest Scene', Katie Roiphe's notorious critique of *A Thousand Acres*: 'the ancient theme of *Oedipus Rex* is accompanied by the clattering breakfast plates of twentieth-century realism and the tragic, shimmering myth becomes an actual event described in pornographic detail'.[81]

Exposure (1993)

It is the relationship between obscenity and art that is interrogated in *Exposure*, as Harrison's intricate narrative, shifting between past and present, father and daughter, both upholds and fragments 'culture'. Whereas critics of *A Thousand Acres* perceived a dichotomy between the incest narrative and 'art', in *Exposure* 'culture' forms a (seemingly) protective screen, concealing and excusing male voyeurism: the 'professor jumped up from the print he was examining with a magnifying lens, his eyebrows just inches above the image of Ann's face, her bare chest'; 'Mr Elliott looked at Mariette witheringly. "This is *art*", he said, uselessly'.[82]

However, recalling *A Thousand Acres*, the patriarchal story is rewritten through Edgar's exposure, as Harrison interrogates the line between photography and pornography, complicity and control, and, in doing so, unveils the possessiveness of the male gaze and the predatoriness of the voyeur. Responding to Rodi-Risberg's concern over the literary struggle to represent trauma, *Exposure*'s multifaceted narrative, simultaneously interlocking and divided, embodies and expresses Ann's splintered self. Torn between the public and the private, there 'were two Anns': 'I found myself referring to the girl in the pictures as "she", "her"'.[83] At the same time, it presents the tensions between remembering and forgetting that are central to the 'Memory Wars', just as the ambiguity of the pictures, and the controversy they generate, embody the uneasy interplay between truth and suggestion. Indeed, photographs both construct, and are constructed by, 'reality'; as the novel's inscription asserts, 'A photograph is a secret about a secret. The more it tells you, the less you know'.[84]

Whereas Ginny's memories are verbalised – and arguably controlled and possessed – through her own retrospective voice, Ann's past is visualised for her through Edgar's photographs; in the fixity of the portraits, she is forever framed by her father. Caught in the 'quagmire of the past', pictures of Ann echo those of her mother, as the father replaces the wife with the daughter (following both Herman's theory of abuse and the pattern of incest established by tales such as 'Thousandfurs'[85], in which the king seeks a union with the girl born to him by his queen): the 'first good photographs Edgar took were of Virginia', 'her milky white legs in the air'.[86] Ann's disintegration is therefore born within her mother; deprived of maternal protection, she has merely 'pictures of parts of her mother's body, hands, knees, shoulders, spine', 'disorganised fragments', and 'not one picture of the whole woman'.[87]

Just as 'the shutter's instant theft' steals Ann's body, this lack of 'wholeness' is mirrored by Harrison's use of the third person throughout much of the novel.[88] Dispossessed of the autonomy of first-person perspective, the narrative style forms an omniscient gaze, itself becoming, like the photographs, an 'unhappy document of her past hanging on a stranger's wall. Posed as if dead. Naked'.[89] Participating in the externalisation of Ann, the narrative reinforces the fact that she is 'so looked at. Judged'.[90] This fragmentation is further asserted by the imposition of other narratives (just as the photographic record of Ann is set against *Exposure*). The first introduction of the Retrospective show (and Ann's past) is via the public, male-authored newspaper article, which reinforces a voyeuristic fascination with the female (mutilated) body: 'Woman Sets Self on Fire', 'Doused Hair with Kerosene'. Depriving the nameless woman of the autonomy of '*herself*', '*her* hair', the linguistic diminishment of female individuality is echoed by Sullivan's objectification of Ann; as he stalks her, she becomes, simply, '[t]he girl'.[91]

Significantly, the first image of Ann is of her undressing, as she 'hurries to free the heel of her black satin pump'.[92] As 'past tangles' prefigure 'the present world', Harrison's language intimates Ann's continued self-imprisonment; tellingly, just as she 'hurries to *free*' her shoe, she '*struggles* into the *narrow skirt*', a 'perfect fit that leaves *no room* for lingerie' [my italics].[93] Recalling the importance of clothing in fairy tales concerning or connected with incest ('Cinderella' and 'Thousandfurs', for instance), her constant undressing chains her to the past, the exposure of her body linked with an exposure of memory.[94] Crucially, her theft of garments defines the concealment of her body as forbidden, just as she is literally exposed when fleeing from her mirror image: 'The longer her stride, the higher it forced the skirt'.[95]

By externalising Ann, the narrative therefore positions the *reader* as a scopophiliac (recalling also 'the gallery goer', 'forced ... emphatically into the position of a voyeur'). In focusing upon her physicality through Edgar's camera (itself framed by that of his ancestor) and through language, Ann is doubly gazed upon: 'He ... composed a shot. Her slender legs ... their fair skin ... Her blond hair in the dirt. One hand to her mouth, the thumb just grazing her bottom lip'.[96]

Just as Edgar's first picture of Ann shows her sleeping passively, his 'will seem[s] to paralyse her'.[97] Tellingly, his voice overrides the omniscient narrator and directs the first line of the childhood narrative; rather than presenting Ann's memory, it is a past controlled by her father. Consequently, Ann, the 'sole keeper of her history ... cannot remember even half of it'; her first recollection is couched in terms of doubt: ' "I've realised I don't remember it at all, nothing" '.[98] In many ways, her father's opening line: ' "Forget it" ' – therefore reverberates throughout the text as a whole.[99]

Indeed, alongside the pictures' inherent ambiguity, the ambivalence of recollection tempers condemnation of Edgar's work as 'offensive and misogynist'.[100]

Ann herself creates memories, reconstructing reality. It 'is up to Ann to render what she has recorded into a happy, if inexact, memory', implanted into her clients' minds; even 'a disappointing wedding ... is transformed ... into a happy memory', making 'what she imagines the bride fantasised it would be'.[101] Ann is constantly late, out-of-time, just as her memories are displaced. Vitally, 'whatever she remembers threatens to recede, evaporate, when she contemplates articulating it for someone else'; even 'as she tried ... to tell Carl about posing for her father's camera, it was as if she were trying to recount a dream: what she remembered seemed absurd, and parts of what she thought was a coherent story were suddenly missing'.[102] Tellingly, although the 'present' sections contain specific dates the 'past' narratives are less defined, with instances alluding to a whole year rather than a particular month or day, clouded by memory's uncertainties.

As in *A Thousand Acres*, however, Harrison's novel exhibits a duality of meaning that 'plants' the female perspective over that of the male. This is embodied by the very title, as the physical exposure of Ann is interlinked with the moral exposure of Edgar. Consequently, his first words: ' "Forget it. It *isn't right*" ' [my italics] – assume darker connotations; the father's speech is worked against him, just as he is framed throughout the novel by public and private questions: 'Edgar's work has long been the focus of debate over the definitions of art and obscenity'; ' "I don't think your father should take pictures like that. I don't think it's right" '.[103]

Certainly, Ann's past, chained to her father's, is memorialised according to a regulated narrative, defined by (implicitly male) art critics; whilst the pictures multiply and commodify Ann (stressed by the passages that record the plate details, in which she is titled simply as a numeral), *Ann: Fifty Photographs* constructs her according to a public gaze. Indeed, Harrison's narrative structure emulates the consequent tensions in the interplay between speech and suppression inherent to incest narratives; the expressiveness of Ann's first-person recollections is silenced by the opening of the following chapter, re-burying her memory: ' "Please, let's not talk" '.[104]

Nevertheless, the 'exposures' (photographs) of Ann are male-authored texts that are written over; as the pictures become palimpsests, the 'reality' behind the art is revealed. Plate 'Ann CCX, 1973', for example, in which the bruised-covered 'subject is apparently awake: at least her eyes are open, but their unfocused state is that of a trance', follows the detailing of Ann's hospitalisation during the composition of the portrait.[105] Edgar's defensive plea – ' "It doesn't mean anything. It's just a picture" ' – is undermined.[106]

Ann's repossession of the past is instead gradually revealed, as she inscribes herself over patriarchal public discourses regarding the Retrospective. The male reviewer declares that the 'show poses questions it cannot answer'.[107] Just as Edgar 'hides' behind the elusiveness of 'art' – 'photography is such a mystery that even I am not sure what I have taken' – the exhibition is placed beyond criticism: the

> newly released works make it clear that if Rogers understood anything as an artist, it is the profound and ironical effect of offensive subject matter exquisitely crafted .... [It] will be a surprise to many that it is the newly released photographs that offer relief in that they are the most lighthearted of the works, a sort of a Peeping Tom's record ... [All] that remains clear is the intensity of Rogers's feeling for his subject, Ann. One could not define that emotion as either love or hate, pride or pity. In view of the photographs' power other questions recede, especially those seeking to define and thus limit art.[108]

However, by repossessing the portraits – in 'the photograph was a girl, herself'; this '"is me. Mine"' – Ann reclaims her past. This is emulated by structural shifts in the childhood passages.[109] Initially, Ann's interiority is absent in these sections, overwhelmed by Edgar's omniscience: 'Her father looked at her – she could have told you this even without seeing it'.[110] Gradually, her perspective asserts itself against her father's gaze – '"I don't always look like myself in pictures"' – and is realised fully in the first-person narrative sections, which, tellingly, are heralded by Edgar's death.[111] Although, arguably, Ann's voice can only be expressed once she is released from her father (thereby asserting his hegemonic possessiveness), as in *A Thousand Acres* the traditional silence surrounding incest is reworked, as language is manipulated in order to castigate the male. In his early photographic career, for example, Rogers is named as Edgar; once Ann becomes his model, however, he is defined as a father, thereby stressing and exposing his tense relationship with his daughter. Crucially, Ann's first-person narrative commences with a desire to remove and forget: 'As soon as it happened [Edgar's death], I rehearsed the sound of it as if it were something long ago in the past'.[112] Beyond the complexity of her tie to her 'Papi', and the simultaneous truth and constructedness of recollected and pictorial memory, Ann's regained mind and body are emblematised by her power over her father's corpse: 'I abolished [you], had you burned up'.[113]

Nevertheless, just as the Retrospective enables Edgar to speak beyond death – Ann 'expected [him] to disappear. And for a while [he] did. But now [he's] back' – *Exposure* remains framed by patriarchal discourse.[114] As Harrison asserts, 'to novelize [sic] a story of incest is to participate in the societal imperative to always lie about it, to say it's not happening, or that you made it up'.[115] Certainly, *Exposure* is 'a revelation not only of one artist's work but of our culture, which ... encourages exploitation even as it punishes those who chronicle it'.[116] Showing that 'it's the nearly silent whir of tape through a camcorder that ensures the experience is real', the novel exposes the commonality of voyeurism.[117] Nonetheless, the critical responses to Harrison's work realise her concerns about the novel as incest narrative. Whereas her three incest *fictions* (*Thicker than Water* (1992), *Exposure* (1993) and *Poison* (1995), received praise, her *memoir* – *The Kiss* – was castigated by many; aligned with Roiphe's hostility towards 'twentieth-century realism',[118] Harrison was condemned for telling her own story (she herself experienced incest with her father).[119] Ironically mirroring Edgar's excuses, *Exposure* is socially 'acceptable' through its status as art, as a fabrication.

A Thousand Acres (dir. Jocelyn Moorhouse, 1997)

Presenting a picture of incest that is too 'real' is especially pertinent to film, as the medium has the potential to realise Roiphe's aversion to 'pornographic detail'.[120] Jocelyn Moorhouse's adaptation of *A Thousand Acres* therefore holds a complex, and often problematic, relationship with Smiley's novel, coloured by perceived difficulties in screening 'what is below the level of the visible' and constricted by 'the exigencies of Hollywood film-making'.[121] Crucially, although the screenplay offers intricate analyses of the literary text, its compression and simplification of the novel's themes mirror the essential silencing of incest in the production's promotional material.[122]

As Sharon O'Dair notes, whilst Smiley's narrative challenges 'the validity of appearance', it is possible to question whether film is 'a good medium … for capturing what is beyond … the visible'.[123] However, although voiceover is used ostensibly to represent the divide between the internal and external, Moorhouse's camerawork does provide subtle visualisations of Ginny's dual interiority and objectification. Close-ups of Ginny, for instance, illustrate the oppressive effects of remembered trauma, imprisoning her within her memory, and the juxtaposition of scenes intimates her perspective.

Mirrors are a significant motif in Moorhouse's adaptation, literally framing the characters and emblematising the relationship between self-truth and self-construction. In the clothes shop, for instance, Ginny sees Larry, not herself, in the mirror; as her 'father's daughter', she is surrounded and obliterated by his presence. As in *Exposure*, the unveiling of the body is intertwined with the unveiling of memory. Tellingly, her recollections occur 'standing in "women's underwear"', as increasing close-ups of Ginny, intercut with images of Larry, portray her inescapable ties to her father; although her memory shows an open window, Larry's shadow – his 'face … a black ocean' – looms across it, as distorted sounds replace the musical soundtrack (recalling Smiley's use of violent language to describe 'ordinary' domesticity).[124] As Larry's image blackens the screen – presenting a visual 'silencing' – Ginny's memory remains incomplete, its fragmentation upholding Caruth's notion of the essential incomprehensibility and inexpressibility of trauma.

The first shot of the Father's Day celebration is likewise filmed as a mirror image, literalising the lack of substance and the performativity inherent to the

Cook family. Vitally, the mirror distorts and reverses the characters, whilst the heavy frame cuts through Ginny's and Rose's heads; physically fragmented and marginalised, the image of the daughters is implicitly through Larry's gaze. However, just as the sisters' perspectives are reasserted through shifting camerawork (the camera draws away – recoils – from a close-up of Larry's face), the word 'Father' on the banner is reversed in the mirror's reflection. As in the novel, patriarchal language is evoked to be rewritten.

Whereas Smiley's novel manipulates language to imply Ginny's perspective, Moorhouse's film employs visual techniques in order to suggest that, in the Cook family, there is 'more to it than meets the eye'.[125] The novel's deliberate use of paternal titles, for instance, is recalled on screen, as Ginny's cry – 'Daddy?' – cuts to a forbidding image of his darkened silhouette.[126] The tension in Larry's paternal status is exposed, as the use of distancing long shot undermines the intimacy of the word 'Daddy' (tellingly, the initial view of Larry shows only his silhouetted *body*, anticipating his suffocating shadow in Ginny's flashback; the first shot of his face is low-angled, looming, and, in extreme close-up, violates the screen).[127] Indeed, Larry is frequently foregrounded in shots (with Ginny in the background), and often presented in close-up; visually, he is inescapable, just as 'in [Ginny's] recollections, Daddy's presence in any scene had the effect of dimming the surroundings'.[128]

Whilst distorted flashbacks illustrate Ginny's suffocating self-imprisonment (echoing Caruth's concept of trauma's latency and responding to Rodi-Risberg's call to find ways to represent the incomprehensibility of past abuse), she is also frequently filmed through the perspectives of others. The adaptation consequently raises the recovered memory debate, as her remembrances are framed by Rose's (and Jess's) gaze. As Laura Mulvey (1975) argues, film promotes a 'male gaze'; recalling the photography in *Exposure*, filmic representations of incest are further complicated by inherent notions of the male framing the female (and, in the case of *A Thousand Acres* and *Beautiful Kate*, heightened by *adaptation's* intrinsic possession and reconstruction of a text).[129] This is explored in Moorhouse's production at times, as shots privilege male perspectives and endow them with directorial control. Following Larry's accident, Ginny reworks his words (remembered from childhood) – 'Daddy, this is your warning!'[130] However, an immediate cut is made to an exasperated Ty; subsequently, Ginny is shown in medium long shot, diminished as a mirror-image, her head cut off slightly by the frame. Although she asserts 'I mean it about the driving', she remains filmed through the car rear-view mirror, taken from an implied male perspective (she is seated behind Ty and Larry) and denied direct screen presence; her containment within a male view is then compounded by a dominating close-up of Larry's face.[131]

Consequently, Jess's comment to Ginny – 'You're just oblivious' – assumes 'treacherous undercurrents', as recurring scenes in which she is objectified by his perspective highlight male voyeurism (in Smiley's novel, such tensions are implied linguistically: 'Jess Clark was standing right beside me ... I *bumped* against him, and he *gripped* my arm' [my italics]).[132] Equally, however, Ginny is often defined by Rose's gaze, lending ambiguity to her recollections of abuse. Just as, in the novel, Ginny is 'a captive of [Rose's] stare, staring back', Moorhouse engages with False Memory Syndrome.[133] Rose's revelation commences with her *fiction* about her mother's alternative life. Against the backdrop of the storm blackout, the sisters are literally 'waking in the dark'.[134] with Rose physically privileged as she sits over Ginny (who, tellingly, is lying passively on a (therapist's) couch), filling the frame; the viewer's vision, like Ginny's, is dominated by Rose. Following her recollection, the scene cuts to a looming shadow, an assumed representation of Larry; the *audience* therefore implants the image with meaning. In contrast to Rose's visual dominance, the shot of Ginny, as she exclaims 'I don't know what you want me to say', is blurred (a device used extensively in *Beautiful Kate*).[135] Visually obliterated by her sister, Ginny's voice, as it constructs her memory, is directed: 'Say it'; 'Say what?' ... 'It happened like you said'.[136] As her speech diminishes to a whisper, her figure blurred and pushed out of the frame, she is displaced by Rose: 'Say the words, Ginny – If he hadn't beaten us...'[137]

As O'Dair notes, however, 'Hollywood requires a happy ... conclusion'.[138] The film ultimately refuses to 'Say the words' and evades 'the category of the unmentionable', upholding Bluestone's observation that the power of the 'businessman and audience' shapes a need for an inoffensive product.[139] Romantic, sweeping music and idyllic, bucolic imagery undermine the tense notion that 'there's always some mystery', as the sisters' conflict, the poisoning of nature and the consequent corruption of the American Dream (the celebration of the land and its associated freedom, propagated in US literature from Fenimore-Cooper to Cather, Twain to Kerouac) are 'forgotten'.[140] Instead, the 'male' texts of idealised domesticity and man's mythical connection with the soil are written back into Smiley's story.

Although O'Dair argues that 'only the incest receives serious attention in the film', the adaptation's paratexts conceal its intricacies, just as condemnatory reviews of Smiley's novel and Harrison's memoir sought to subdue their advocacy.[141] Posters and the DVD cover depict Ginny and Rose embracing with uncomplicated affection and, just as the DVD box description omits any mention of incest, the Title Menu's pictorial backdrop implies an idealised American family.

Beautiful Kate *(dir. Rachel Ward, 2009; adapted from Newton Thornburg's* Beautiful Kate, *1982)*

The need to silence such exposure likewise constricted *Beautiful Kate* initially. As Rachel Ward comments, after the film rights were first purchased,

'Waking in the dark'

production remained inhibited for many years 'because of its ... confrontational material and taboo subject'.[142] However, a decade after Moorhouse's *A Thousand Acres*, Ward's adaptation presents 'a ballsy but kind of beautiful exploration of incest'.[143] In opposition to the backlash against incest narratives in the 1990s, which questioned their status as 'art', critics of *Beautiful Kate* applauded an 'intricate, painful drama' that 'beguiles almost to the last frame'.[144]

Even the trailer for *Beautiful Kate* intimates incest, pro-actively placing the film within a controversial and challenging framework. The trailer opens with Kate's voice and image, shot, tellingly, through the bars of a black screen as she kisses her brother. In her command – 'Come here – *closer*' – she both entices Ned (she is subsequently conflated with his girlfriend in the trailer) and invites scrutiny of her incestuous relationship, her voice and memory reverberating beyond the grave and acting as a directive for the film as a whole.[145] At the same time, the trailer highlights the ruptures caused by remembering; although she is memorialised in the photograph album as 'Beautiful Kate' (recalling *Exposure*'s study of the self mediated through pictures), the image is darkened by the abrupt cut to her shooting kangaroos. As the film illustrates, the past is deadly.

In the bonus footage to the DVD of *Beautiful Kate* Leah Churchill-Brown (Producer) notes, this is a 'story of a family in disarray', and yet, as Sophie Lowe ('Kate') responds, it 'is about love'.[146] As in *A Thousand Acres* and *Exposure*, however, familial relationships are disturbed and imprisoned within the past. The film's 'tag-line' – 'the past is always present' – is interrogated through intricately constructed flashbacks, whilst visual motifs intimate a suffocating memory that is gradually confronted.[147] Ned's incarceration within 'the black well of time' is indeed embodied in the opening sequence as he runs over a kangaroo.[148] His return home, intertwined with the confrontation of memory, is linked inextricably with his sister, both in her own shooting of the animals and in the manner of her death: 'They swerved to avoid a roo. Kate's killed'.[149] Viewed from the front passenger seat, Ned is filmed through his car windscreen, obscured by the kangaroo's blood; implying Kate's perspective in her own fatal accident, she is a constant presence, lingering 'seductively on the palate as the human embodiment of the film's enigmatic core'.[150]

This ambiguity, lying at the heart of Ned's conflicted recollections, is epitomised by the characterisation of incest as a game. Their precocious 'play' highlights in itself the merging of old and young selves that memory creates, and recalls the uneasy boundary between childhood and adulthood explored in *Exposure*. Significantly, Kate's first invitation to Ned – 'Tickle?' – is posited as a question; as in *A Thousand Acres*, there is 'more to it than meets the eye' (following their argument, Kate's offer to 'Kiss and make up?' is likewise both a game and a challenge).[151] As they play 'this is Nelson's nose', Kate pulls Ned's hand over her body, her intimacy unsettling her innocence; her cry – 'Don't look!' – implies both childish indignation at the spoilt game and a forbidden voyeurism. Lolita-like, Kate's response after her union with Ned is to sing 'If you're happy and you know it clap your hands'.[152] Filmed in long shot, the distancing camerawork presents brother and sister as both voyeured and vilified through a public gaze. However, as is later revealed, the scene is directed by the perspective of younger sister Sally; her memories (and involvement through association) provide another complex framework which foregrounds, rather than conceals, incest.

Significantly, characters are often shot in extreme close-up (recalling Edgar's portraits of Virginia in *Exposure*), from obscure angles. They are depicted simultaneously as fragmented and confined within themselves, their self-division heightened through Ward's camerawork, as she switches from first-person to external shots. Moreover, like Harrison's multiple narratives, the shifts in visual perspective and the disruptive 'invasion' of flashbacks emulate the splintering of self and memory, as recollections cut in abruptly, distorted through intensified sound and rapid, unfocused camera movement. In returning to the present, the camera pans around Ned each time, encircling and entrapping him within remembered incest.

Crucially, first-person shots are often slightly blurred, pointing both to the inaccessibility of memory and to the notion that 'looking' is forbidden. As in *A Thousand Acres*, mirrors are prominent, merging the tensions of voyeurism with self-reflection and confrontation. The mirror intertwines past and present, brother and sister; as Ned regards his image, he is led back to his memory of Kate. Tellingly, the subsequent introduction of Kate and Ned together revolves around possession. Ned discovers his sister's belongings, kept as relics. As Kate's voice exclaims 'That's mine, Neddy', her hand reaches for it and the scene moves seamlessly into the past.[153]

In its interconnections with, and shaping of, the present, the incestuous past is inescapable. Above all, the shifting perspectives that drive the recollections posit memory as a source of challenge and conflict, both within Ned and in terms of his relationship with Kate. The first memory embodies the complex power dynamic between the siblings. In close-up, Kate is seen from Ned's perspective, but, although he 'directs' the shot, it is she who overwhelms the frame. Using 'breathing camera' (therefore emulating the 'presentness' of the past), the initial memories are shown through Ned's eyes; contrasting with his external adult self, he comes 'alive' in recollected youth. However, his voice echoes and remembered images are blurred; the past can never be regained. His physical absence from the early memories intimates the disassociation experienced by Ginny, a 'self-conscious distance from [the] body' as his recollection is coloured by a troubled awareness of the trajectory of his relationship with Kate (as he later exclaims to Sally, 'Don't look at me. Don't touch me').[154]

As in Smiley's and Harrison's texts, *Beautiful Kate* examines how memory is mediated, written, and rewritten, the potential ambiguity of Ned's recollections of incest embodied by his status as an author of 'filthy' novels; whereas Rose and Ginny wake in the dark, Ned writes in the dark of his shadowed study. Tellingly, the opening of his 'fictional' diary about 'that last summer' displaces Kate and therefore eludes his relationship with her: 'I've been back all of two days, back in my father's house, so where else would I find myself but in the old schoolroom, picking at my brother's suicide like an old scab and following a trail of wounds that leads inexorably to the bastard dying next door'.[155] The conflation of Toni and Kate arguably highlights the tense boundary between the 'real' and the reconstructed, as intercut scenes merge past and present; images of Ned and Toni in his childhood bed follow those of brother and sister, the former planting meaning into the latter. Ultimately, however, Bruce's cry ('Have you any idea how much we needed you here?'), as he fragments and scatters Ned's 'stories' across the floor, privileges truth over fiction; although Ned states 'Cliff accidentally killed his sister ... That's the end of the story', this public memory is scrutinised.[156] In contrast to Buckmaster's critique of *Beautiful Kate* as 'wishy-washy-film-as-quasi-poetry', in which 'there isn't much to get excited about', Ward's production both expands understandings of incest (in her focus upon *male* victimhood) and, through marrying explicitness and artistry, confronts the silencing that faced *The Kiss*.[157]

As Smiley asserts, 'you don't write a novel to salve a wound, but to bear witness'.[158] Caught between remembering and recoiling, the proliferation of incest narratives in the 1990s, and the subsequent backlash against the genre, embodies the tensions at the very heart of bearing witness. The divide between confession and concealment, silence and speech, haunts Smiley's and Harrison's work; in remembering incest, their writing became subject to censure and censorship, a desire to keep their awakened challenges to patriarchal dictates 'in the dark'. More than a decade later, however, Ward's highly applauded and commercially successful film allows victims of incest, finally, to '[S]peak what' they 'feel, not what' they 'ought to say'.

Notes

1 Jane Smiley, *A Thousand Acres* (Flamingo, 1992), p. 370.
2 William Shakespeare, Jay L. Halio (ed.), *The Tragedy of King Lear* (Cambridge University Press, 1992), p. 120 (1.3.3).
3 *Ibid.*, p. 117 (1.2.108).
4 *Ibid.*, p. 101 (1.1.108).
5 *Ibid.*, p. 260 (5.3.246–7).
6 *Ibid.*, p. 142 (2.1.47).

7 *Ibid.*, p. 100 (1.1. 87).
8 *Ibid.*, p. 171 (2.4.271).
9 Alfar, Christine León, *Fantasies of Female Evil: The Dynamics of Gender and Power in Shakespearean Tragedy* (University of Delaware Press, 2003; Associated University Presses, 2003), p. 18.
10 Kathryn Harrison, *Exposure* (Fourth Estate, 1995), p. 210.
11 Jane Smiley, 'Shakespeare in Iceland', in Marianne Novy (ed.), *Transforming Shakespeare* (Macmillan, 1999), pp. 172–3.
12 Smiley, *A Thousand Acres*, p. 94.
13 Shakespeare, *King Lear*, p. 177 (3.2.50).
14 *Ibid.*, p. 168 (2.4.215).
15 *Ibid.*, p. 177 (3.2.53).
16 *Ibid.*, p. 120 (1.3.6).
17 *Ibid.*, p. 223 (4.5.120, 124–5).
18 Smiley, *A Thousand Acres*, p. 22.
19 Shakespeare, *King Lear*, p, 120 (1.3.5).
20 Doane and Hodges discuss African American incest narratives in detail, see, for example, 'Signifying Incest: African-American Revision', in Janice Doane and Devon Hodges, *Telling Incest: Narratives of Dangerous Remembering from Stein to Sapphire* (University of Michigan Press, 2001), pp. 3–46.
21 Mako E. Yoshikawa, *Riddles and Revelations* (PhD dissertation, University of Michigan, 2008), p. 108, https://deepblue.lib.umich.edu/handle/2027.42/60839 (accessed 11 April 2017).
22 Vikki Bell, *Interrogating Incest* (Routledge, 1993), p. 3.
23 John C. Norcross et al., *Self-Help That Works* 4th edn (Oxford University Press, 2013), pp. 14–16).
24 E. Loftus and J. Pickrell, 'The formation of false memories', *Psychiatric Annals*, 25 (1995), pp. 723, 720.
25 Fiona E. Raitt and M. Suzanne Zeedyk, *The Implicit Relation of Psychology and Law* (Routledge; Taylor & Francis e-library, 2000), pp. 138–9.
26 Richard Webster, *Why Freud Was Wrong* (Basic Books, 1995).
27 Sigmund Freud, *Introductory Lectures of Psychoanalysis* (1933), Vintage Classics; new edition (20 September 2001).
28 Rosaria Champagne, *The Politics of Survivorship* (New York University Press, 1996), pp. 167, 169.
29 Katha Pollitt quoted in S. Chira, 'The nation; sex abuse: The coil of truth and memory', *New York Times*, 12 May 1993, www.nytimes.com/1993/12/05/weekinreview/the-nation-sex-abuse-the-coil-of-truth-and-memory.html (accessed 9 September 2013).
30 Doane and Hodges, *Telling Incest*, p. 29.
31 For reference to Wigmore, see: Judith Herman, *Father-Daughter Incest* (Harvard University Press, 1982), p. 11.
32 Smiley, 'Shakespeare in Iceland', pp. 172–3.
33 Shakespeare, *King Lear*, p. 101 (1.1. 103).

34 Smiley, 'Shakespeare in Iceland', pp. 172–3.
35 Doane and Hodges, *Telling Incest*, p. 72.
36 Smiley, *A Thousand Acres*, p. 256.
37 Cathy Caruth, 'Introduction', in Cathy Caruth (ed.), *Trauma* (Johns Hopkins University Press, 1995), p. 6.
38 Smiley, *A Thousand Acres*, p. 153.
39 Marinella Rodi-Risberg, 'Writing Trauma, Writing Time and Space: Jane Smiley's *A Thousand Acres* and the *Lear* Group of Father-Daughter Incest Narratives' (PhD dissertation, Universitas Wasaensis, 2010), pp. 11, 2.
40 Rodi-Risberg, 'Writing Trauma', p. 2; Karen De Witt, 'Incest as a selling point', *New York Times*, 30 March 1997, www.nytimes.com/1997/03/30/weekinreview/incest-as-a-selling-point.html (accessed 11 November 2013).
41 Laura Shapiro, 'They're Daddy's little girls', *Newsweek* (1994), as cited in Susan Elizabeth Farrell, *Jane Smiley's* A Thousand Acres (Continuum, 2001), p. 68.
42 Smiley, *A Thousand Acres*, p. 191.
43 Linda Kelsey, 'Degrading, disgusting, and demeaning: I'm ashamed of modern women's magazines says a former Cosmo editor', *Daily Mail Online*, 21 February 2009, www.dailymail.co.uk/femail/article-1151404/Degrading-disgusting-demeaning-Im-ashamed-modern-womens-magazines-says-Cosmo-editor.html (accessed 27 October 2013).
44 Janet Todd, 'A dysfunctional portrait', *Mail on Sunday* (1 March 1998), as cited in Rodi-Risberg, 'Writing Trauma', p. 212; Farrell, *A Reader's Guide*, p. 68.
45 Herman, *Father-Daughter Incest*, p. 153.
46 Smiley, *A Thousand Acres*, pp. 212, 370; Shakespeare, *King Lear*, p. 101 (1.1. 101–2).
47 Smiley *A Thousand Acres*, p. 370.
48 Ying Chiao Lin, 'Father's farmland, daughter's innerland: Retelling and recovery in Jane Smiley's *A Thousand Acres*', *Concentric* 29:1 (2003), p. 96; Smiley, *A Thousand Acres*, p. 304.
49 Smiley, *A Thousand Acres*, pp. 21, 18, 103.
50 *Ibid.*, p. 173.
51 *Ibid.*, p. 189.
52 *Ibid.*, p. 245.
53 *Ibid.*, p. 274.
54 *Ibid.*, p. 176.
55 *Ibid.*, p. 173; Herman, *Father-Daughter Incest*, p. 81.
56 Smiley, *A Thousand Acres*, pp. 323, 66.
57 *Ibid.*, p. 342. In Smiley's inscription – 'the body repeats the landscape' – the rape of Ginny is echoed in intensive agriculture's 'rape' of the earth.
58 Lin, 'Father's farmland', p. 98.
59 Smiley, *A Thousand Acres*, pp. 92, 115.
60 Herman, *Father-Daughter Incest*, p. 114.
61 Smiley, *A Thousand Acres*, p. 20.
62 *Ibid.*, p. 369.

63 *Ibid.*, pp. 3–4, 20, 3.
64 *Ibid.*, pp. 211, 306.
65 *Ibid.*, pp. 306, 366.
66 *Ibid.*, p. 305.
67 *Ibid.*, pp. 211, 280.
68 *Ibid.*, pp. 16, 104.
69 *Ibid.*, pp. 150, 64, 213, 100.
70 *Ibid.*, p. 9.
71 Smiley, *A Thousand Acres*, pp. 35, 216.
72 *Ibid.*, pp. 105, 115, 178.
73 *Ibid.*, p. 292.
74 *Ibid.*, pp. 371, 280.
75 *Ibid.*, pp. 251–2, 191.
76 *Ibid.*, p. 238.
77 Rodi-Risberg, 'Writing Trauma', p. 200.
78 Hortense Spillers, '"The permanent obliquity of an in[pha]llibly straight": In the time of the daughters and the fathers', in Lynda Boose and Betty S. Flowers (eds), *Daughters and Fathers* (Johns Hopkins University Press, 1989), p. 158.
79 Christopher Lehmann-Haupt, 'Books of our times; On an Iowa farm, a tragedy with echoes of *Lear*', *New York Times*, 31 October 1991, www.nytimes.com/1991/10/31/books/books-of-the-times-on-an-iowa-farm-a-tragedy-with-echoes-of-lear.html (accessed 11 November 2013).
80 Jane Smiley, 'Sharper than the serpent's tooth', *Observer* (25 October 1992), p. 1.
81 Katie Roiphe, 'Making the incest scene' (1995), quoted in Lin, 'Father's farmland', p. 97.
82 Harrison, *Exposure*, pp. 119, 159.
83 Harrison, *Exposure*, pp. 32, 112.
84 Diane Arbus, quoted in Harrison, *Exposure*, n.p. The quotation is credited to Arbus in: Peter Schjedldahl, 'Looking Back', *The New Yorker*, 21 March 2005, www.newyorker.com/magazine/2005/03/21/looking-back-8 (accessed 20 March 2017).
85 See Emma V. Miller's discussion in Chapter 6 of this volume.
86 Harrison, *Exposure*, pp. 108, 27.
87 *Ibid.*, pp. 26, 28, 26.
88 *Ibid.*, p. 65.
89 *Ibid.*, p. 56.
90 *Ibid.*, p. 204.
91 *Ibid.*, pp. 19, 131.
92 *Ibid.*, p. 3.
93 Smiley, *A Thousand Acres*, p. 248; Harrison, *Exposure*, p. 3.
94 The pattern of illness in *A Thousand Acres*, *Exposure*, and *Beautiful Kate* likewise recalls Sophoclean punishment.
95 Harrison, *Exposure*, p. 38.
96 *Ibid.*, pp. 191, 23.

97 *Ibid.*, p. 24.
98 *Ibid.*, p. 111.
99 *Ibid.*, p. 4.
100 *Ibid.*, p. 18.
101 *Ibid.*, pp. 6, 13.
102 *Ibid.*, p. 41.
103 *Ibid.*, pp. 4, 19, 135.
104 *Ibid.*, p. 61.
105 *Ibid.*, p. 50.
106 *Ibid.*, p. 136.
107 *Ibid.*, p. 189.
108 *Ibid.*, pp. 138, 190–1.
109 *Ibid.*, pp. 158–9.
110 *Ibid.*, p. 25.
111 *Ibid.*, p. 29.
112 *Ibid.*, p. 30.
113 *Ibid.*, p. 31.
114 *Ibid.*, p. 31.
115 Kathryn Harrison, as cited in Yoshikawa, *Riddles and Revelations*, p. 112.
116 Harrison, *Exposure*, p. 191.
117 *Ibid.*, p. 12.
118 Roiphe, 'Making the incest scene' (1995), as cited in Lin, 'Father's farmland', p. 97.
119 Yoshikawa outlines the significant differences in telling incest as a novel and as a memoir (Yoshikawa, *Riddles and Revelations*, p. 113).
120 Roiphe, 'Making the incest scene' (1995), as cited in Lin, 'Father's farmland', p. 97.
121 Smiley, *A Thousand Acres*, p. 9. Sharon O'Dair, 'Horror or realism? Filming "toxic discourse" in Jane Smiley's *A Thousand Acres*', *Textual Practice* 19:2 (2005), p. 267.
122 Moorhouse's film is generally perceived negatively with an IMDb rating of 5.9 (October 2013).
123 O'Dair, 'Horror or realism?', pp. 265, 272.
124 Smiley, *A Thousand Acres*, pp. 271, 216.
125 *Ibid.*, p. 195.
126 *A Thousand Acres* (writ. Jane Smiley (novel), Laura Jones (screenplay); dir. Jocelyn Moorhouse, 1997).
127 *Ibid.*
128 Smiley, *A Thousand Acres*, p. 48.
129 Laura Mulvey, 'Visual pleasure and narrative cinema', *Screen*, 16:3 (1975), pp. 6–18.
130 *A Thousand Acres* (writ. Jane Smiley (novel), Laura Jones (screenplay); dir. Jocelyn Moorhouse, 1997).
131 *Ibid.*
132 *Ibid.*; Smiley, *A Thousand Acres*, pp. 104, 21.

133 Smiley, *A Thousand Acres*, p. 189.
134 *Ibid.*, p. 370.
135 *A Thousand Acres* (writ. Smiley (novel), Jones (screenplay); dir. Jocelyn Moorhouse, 1997).
136 *Ibid.*
137 *Ibid.*
138 O'Dair, 'Horror or realism?', p. 269.
139 Smiley, *A Thousand Acres*, p. 6; George Bluestone, *Novels into Film* (University of California Press, 1966), p. 42.
140 Smiley, *A Thousand Acres*, p. 104.
141 O'Dair, 'Horror or realism?', p. 268.
142 Rachel Ward, *Beautiful Kate* (writ. Newton Thornburg (novel), Rachel Ward (screenplay); dir. Rachel Ward, producer, Leah Churchill-Brown, Beautiful Kate Productions, Doll Australia, New Town Films, Screen Australia, 2009) DVD Bonus Interview, Matchbox Films, 2009. All quotations are printed with kind permission of © Rachel Ward, New Town Films, Screen Australia and Doll henceforth.
143 Luke Buckmaster, '*Beautiful Kate* Film review: Handsomely ho-hum', *Cinetology*, 28 July 2009, http://blogs.crikey.com.au/cinetology/2009/07/28/beautiful-kate-film-review-handsomely-ho-hum/ (accessed 22 October 2013).
144 Anthony Quinn, '*Beautiful Kate*', *Independent* (30 July 2010). Available at: www.independent.co.uk/arts-entertainment/films/reviews/beautiful-kate-15-2038788.html (accessed 22 October 2013.
145 *Beautiful Kate*, 2009.
146 Leah Churchill-Brown and Sophie Lowe, *Beautiful Kate*, DVD Bonus Interview, Matchbox Films, 2009.
147 The 'tag-line' is presented on the DVD box (Matchbox Films, 2009).
148 Smiley, *A Thousand Acres*, p. 47.
149 *Beautiful Kate*, 2009.
150 Buckmaster, '*Beautiful Kate* Film Review: Handsomely ho-hum'.
151 *Beautiful Kate*, 2009; Smiley, *A Thousand Acres*, p. 195.
152 *Beautiful Kate*, 2009.
153 *Ibid.*
154 Smiley, *A Thousand Acres*, p. 227.
155 *Ibid.*
156 *Ibid.*
157 Buckmaster, '*Beautiful Kate* Film Review: Handsomely ho-hum'.
158 Jane Smiley, *Thirteen Ways of Looking at the Novel* (Faber & Faber, 2006), p. 8.

Bibliography

Fiction

Basile, Giambattista 'L'Orsa' – trans. 'The Bear', in Jack Zipes (ed.), *The Great Fairy Tale Tradition* (Norton, 2001) pp. 33–8

Grimm, Jacob and Wilhelm Grimm, 'All Fur', in Jack Zipes (ed.), *The Great Fairy Tale Tradition* (Norton, 2001), pp. 47–50
Harrison, Kathryn, *Exposure* (Fourth Estate, 1995)
Morrison, Toni, *The Bluest Eye* (Vintage, 2016)
Perrault, Charles, 'Cinderella; or, The Glass Slipper', in Jack Zipes (ed. and trans.), *The Great Fairy Tale Tradition From Straparola and Basile to the Brothers Grimm* (Norton, 2001), pp. 468–73
Shakespeare, William, John Russell Brown (ed.), *The Merchant of Venice* (Arden Shakespeare, 2006)
——., Jay L. Halio (ed.), *The Tragedy of King Lear* (Cambridge University Press, 1992)
Smiley, Jane, *A Thousand Acres* (Flamingo, 1992)
Thornburg, Newton, *Beautiful Kate* (Diversion Books, 2015)
Walker, Alice, *The Color Purple* (Phoenix, 1992)

Non-fiction

Alfar, Christine León, *Fantasies of Female Evil: The Dynamics of Gender and Power in Shakespearean Tragedy* (University of Delaware Press, 2003; Associated University Presses, 2003)
Arens, William, *The Original Sin: Incest and its Meaning* (Oxford University Press, 1986)
Barnes, Elizabeth (ed.), *Incest and the Literary Imagination* (University Press of Florida, 2002)
Bell, Vikki, *Interrogating Incest: Feminism, Foucault and the Law* (Routledge, 1993)
Bluestone, George, *Novels into Film* (University of California Press, 1966)
Caruth, Cathy (ed.), *Trauma: Explorations in Memory* (Johns Hopkins University Press, 1995)
Champagne, Rosaria, *The Politics of Survivorship: Incest, Women's Literature and Feminist Theory* (New York University Press, 1996)
Daly, Brenda, 'When the daughter tells her story', in Carol L. Winkelmann and Christine Shearer-Cremean (eds), *Survivor Rhetoric: Negotiations and Narrativity in Abused Women's Language* (University of Toronto Press, 2004) pp. 139–65
Doane, Janice and Devon Hodges, *Telling Incest: Narratives of Dangerous Remembering from Stein to Sapphire* (University of Michigan Press, 2001)
Farrell, Susan Elizabeth. *Jane Smiley's* A Thousand Acres: *A Reader's Guide* (Continuum, 2001)
Hacking, Ian, *Rewriting the Soul: Multiple Personality and the Science of Memory* (Princeton University Press, 1995)
Harrison, Kathryn, *The Kiss* (Avon, 1998)
Herman, Judith, *Father-Daughter Incest* (Harvard University Press, 1982)
Lin, Ying-Chiao, 'Father's farmland, daughter's innerland: Retelling and recovery in Jane Smiley's *A Thousand Acres*', *Concentric: Studies in English Literature and Linguistics*, 29:1 (2003), pp. 95–118
Lindhé, Anna, 'Interpersonal complications and intertextual relations: *A Thousand Acres* and *King Lear*', *NJES: Nordic Journal of English Studies* 4:1 (2005), pp. 55–78

Loftus, Elizabeth, F., 'When a lie becomes memory's truth: Memory distortion after exposure to misinformation', *Current Directions in Psychological Science* 1:4 (1992), pp. 121–3

——., and Katherine Ketcham. *The Myth of Repressed Memory* (St. Martin's Press, 1994)

——., and Jacqueline Pickrell, 'The formation of false memories'. *Psychiatric Annals.* 25 (1995), pp. 720–5

Luckhurst, Roger and Peter Marks (eds), *Literature and the Contemporary: Fictions and Theories of the Present* (Pearson, 1999)

Mollon, Phil, *Freud and False Memory Syndrome* (Icon, 2000)

Mulvey, Laura, 'Visual pleasure and narrative cinema', *Screen* 16:3 (1975), pp. 6–18

Nakadate, Neil, *Understanding Jane Smiley* (University of South Carolina Press, 1999)

Norcross, John C., Linda F. Campbell, John M. Grohol, John W. Santrock, Florin Selagea and Robert Sommer, *Self-Help That Works: Resources to Improve Emotional Health and Strengthen Relationships*, 4th edn (Oxford University Press, 2013)

O'Dair, Sharon, 'Horror or realism? Filming "Toxic Discourse" in Jane Smiley's *A Thousand Acres*', *Textual Practice* 19:2 (2005), pp. 263–82

Ofshe, Richard and Ethan Watters, *Making Monsters: False Memories, Psychotherapy and Sexual Hysteria* (University of California Press, 1996)

Pendergast, Mark, *Victims of Memory: Incest Accusations and Shattered Lives* (Upper Access Books, 1996)

Raitt, Fiona E. and M. Suzanne Zeedyk, *The Implicit Relation of Psychology and Law: Women and Syndrome Evidence* (Routledge; Taylor & Francis e-library, 2000)

Reid, Stephen, 'In defense of Goneril and Regan', *American Imago* 27 (1970), pp. 226–44

Rodi-Risberg, Marinella, 'Writing Trauma, Writing Time and Space: Jane Smiley's *A Thousand Acres* and the *Lear* Group of Father-Daughter Incest Narratives' (PhD dissertation, Universitas Wasaensis, 2010)

Sacco, Lynn, *Unspeakable: Father-Daughter Incest in American History* (Johns Hopkins University Press, 2009)

Smiley, Jane, 'Shakespeare in Iceland', in Marianne Novy (ed.), *Transforming Shakespeare: Contemporary Women's Re-Visions in Literature and Performance* (Macmillan, 1999), pp. 159–79

——., 'Not a pretty picture', in M. Carnes (ed.), *Novel History: Historians and Novelists Confront America's Past (and Each Other)* (Simon & Schuster, 2001), pp. 160–3

——., *Thirteen Ways of Looking at the Novel* (Faber & Faber, 2006)

Spillers, Hortense, '"The permanent obliquity of an in[pha]llibly straight": In the time of the daughters and the fathers', in Lynda Boose and Betty S. Flowers (eds), *Daughters and Fathers* (Johns Hopkins University Press, 1989), pp. 157–77

Underwager, Ralph and Hollida Wakefield, *The Return of the Furies: Analysis of Recovered Memory Therapy* (Open Court, 1994)

Webster, Richard, *Why Freud Was Wrong: Sin Science and Psychoanalysis* (Basic Books, 1995)

Wigmore, John Henry, *A Treatise on the Anglo-American System of Evidence in Trials at Common Law*, vol. 3A, rev. James H. Chadbourn (Little Brown, 1970)

Yoshikawa, Mako E., *Riddles and Revelations: Forms of Incest Telling in Twentieth-Century America* (PhD dissertation, University of Michigan, 2008), https://deepblue.lib.umich.edu/handle/2027.42/60839 (accessed 11 April 2017)

Filmography

A Thousand Acres (writ. Jane Smiley (novel), Laura Jones (screenplay); dir. Jocelyn Moorhouse, 1997)

Beautiful Kate (writ. Newton Thornburg (novel), Rachel Ward (screenplay); dir. Rachel Ward, producer, Leah Churchill-Brown, Beautiful Kate Productions, Doll Australia, New Town Films, Screen Australia, 2009) and DVD Bonus Interview (Matchbox Films, 2009)

Websites

Anon., 'Sins of the Father', Oprah.com, From 'Shattering the Secrecy of Incest: Mackenzie Phillips' Follow-Up', 15 October 2009, www.oprah.com/relationships/incest-survivor-kathryn-harrisons-the-kiss (accessed 11 April 2017)

Anon., 'The Kiss: A Memoir', *Publishers Weekly*, 3 March 1997, www.publishersweekly.com/978-0-679-44999-7 (accessed 11 April 2017)

Bass, Ellen and Laura Davis, Reply by Frederick C. Crews, 'Thanks for the Memories', *New York Review of Books*, 16 February 1995, www.nybooks.com/articles/1995/02/16/thanks-for-the-memories/ (accessed 9 April 2017)

Buckmaster, Luke, '*Beautiful Kate* Film review: Handsomely ho-hum', *Cinetology*. 28 July 2009, http://blogs.crikey.com.au/cinetology/2009/07/28/beautiful-kate-film-review-handsomely-ho-hum/ (accessed 22 October 2013)

Burne, Jerome 'Kathryn Harrison's account of an affair with her father is being called tasteless, cynical and irresponsible. But there's one thing her tale is not: unique', *Independent*, 16 April 1997, www.independent.co.uk/life-style/the-lust-that-dare-not-speak-its-name-1267565.html (accessed 11 April 2017)

Chira, Susan, 'The nation; Sex abuse: The coil of truth and memory', *New York Times*, 12 May 1993, www.nytimes.com/1993/12/05/weekinreview/the-nation-sex-abuse-the-coil-of-truth-and-memory.html (accessed 9/ September 2013)

Crews, Frederick C., 'The revenge of the repressed: Part II', *New York Review of Books*, 1 December 1994, www.nybooks.com/articles/1994/12/01/the-revenge-of-the-repressed-part-ii/ (accessed 9 April 2017)

De Witt, Karen, 'Incest as a selling point', *New York Times*, 30 March 1997, www.nytimes.com/1997/03/30/weekinreview/incest-as-a-selling-point.html (accessed 11 November 2013)

Goleman, Daniel, 'Childhood trauma: Memory or invention?', *New York Times*. 21 July 1992, www.nytimes.com/1992/07/21/science/childhood-trauma-memory-or-invention.html (accessed 7 September 2013)

Kelsey, Linda, 'Degrading, disgusting, and demeaning: I'm ashamed of modern women's magazines says a former Cosmo editor', *Daily Mail Online*, 21 February 2009, www.dailymail.co.uk/femail/article-1151404/Degrading-disgusting-demeaning-Im-ashamed-modern-womens-magazines-says-Cosmo-editor.html (accessed 27 October 2013)

Lehmann-Haupt, Christopher, 'Books of our times; On an Iowa farm, a tragedy with echoes of *Lear*', *New York Times*, 31 October 1991, www.nytimes.com/1991/10/31/books/books-of-the-times-on-an-iowa-farm-a-tragedy-with-echoes-of-lear.html (accessed 11 November 2013)

———., 'Life with father: Incestuous and soul-deadening', *New York Times*, 27 February 1997, 97/02/27/books/life-with-father-incestuous-and-soul-deadening.html (accessed 11 April 2017)

Quinn, Anthony, '*Beautiful Kate*', *Independent*, 30 July 2010, www.independent.co.uk/arts-entertainment/films/reviews/beautiful-kate-15-2038788.html (accessed 22 October 2013)

Schjedldahl, Peter, 'Looking back', *The New Yorker*, 21 March 2005, www.newyorker.com/magazine/2005/03/21/looking-back-8 (accessed 20 March 2017)

Wolcott, James, 'The 20-year-old who dated her dad – and then wrote a book about it', *New Republic*, 31 March 1997, https://newrepublic.com/article/119008/james-wolcott-reviews-kiss (accessed 11 April 2017)

Yardley, Jonathan, 'Daddy's girl cashes in', *Washington Post*, 5 March 1997, www.washingtonpost.com/archive/lifestyle/1997/03/05/daddys-girl-cashes-in/50dd8efc-2a36-4395-9246-fec57565e677/?utm_term=.824a48eb52ed (accessed 11 April 2017)

Part II

Incest and the child protagonist

4

'The word is incest':[1] Narrative, affect and judgement in and across the *Lolitas*

Matthew Pateman

Incest in *Lolita* is manifested in two different forms. The first is, within the fictional world, what may be deemed incest by marriage. Humbert Humbert marries Charlotte Haze and begins a sexual affair with her daughter, now his step-daughter. That this is paedophilic as well as legally incestuous is something made very clear in both film versions (Stanley Kubrick's, released in 1962, set in 1957[2] and Adrian Lyne's, released 1997 and set in 1947).[3] It is also a strong feature of the novel (published in 1955 and set in 1947). The novel, however, also has a different form of incestuous relationship. This one we may call a formal incest in which the narrator creates (gives birth to) his desired object, an object that is a libidinal-lexical construct which he can manipulate and abuse. The novel can allow both these forms of incest to exist and mutually complicate and unsettle each other; the film and screenplay can only engage in the former. This chapter will assess the different ways in which the legal and the formal presentations of incest influence possible responses to the different versions of the story.

I will make reference to the screenplay[4] and the two films in relation to the main object of the essay, which is the literary *Lolita*. The portrayal of incest in *Lolita*, the novel, is necessarily different than in the screenplay or the films, and this difference, which is in some measure a question of point of view and therefore also a question of affective ontology, is crucial in understanding the novel's desperate power, its horror.

Nabokov, entomological polyglot, and literary glutton, plays with words. His novels abound with knowing references, insights, puns, anagrams, lexical puzzles, translational quizzes and patterns. To highlight the word (" '[t]he *word* is incest' "[5]) as forcefully as he does through Humbert's reporting of Lolita's expression is to foreground it, to encourage a reader to think beyond the obvious. It is Lolita's word (if we are to believe Humbert, who ascribes it to her in a seemingly playful scene in a hotel where she and he are staying) a word both commonplace and sensational in its claim. The juvenile vulgarity associated with Lolita as a character here (as elsewhere) is tied to a realisation that the vulgar, the everyday, the normal (the word is normal, casual, easily understood) can carry too the weight and power of the most esoteric of Humbert's refined European tongue (the word is aberrant, strenuous, incomprehensible).[6]

But the word can only exist with this level of figural force because it occurs in the novel. This is not because the novel is about words – though that is clearly a part – and nor is it because the films are not about words – that is clearly false – but because of how Lolita as a character is presented and understood in the novel, as opposed to how she is presented and understood in the films and the screenplay. Lolita is a name, and her name is distorted, broken, made and remade at Humbert's whim; the name (and the character who is in many ways in Humbert's narration, nothing more than the name) is mutated, made monstrous.

Nabokov is well versed in nominal distortion. Even working with only Nabokov's name this would take us from *Lolita*'s Vivian Darkbloom to *Speak, Memory*'s Vivian Bloodmark[7] who both derive from Vivian Calmbrood whose supposed play *The Wanderers* was eventually translated out of its original Russian into English by V. Sirin, the name used by Nabokov for his entire Russian oeuvre.[8] In addition to this, one may wish to trace the anagrammatic magic into his poetry, where the question of names and metafictional praise and punishment is discussed by, among others, Boris Katz and, from a different perspective, Omry Ronen.[9]

Eschewing the specifically Nabokovian, one may choose to employ a different theoretical approach. Indeed, it seems almost essential to do so, as Humbert's use of names (and Nabokov's, therefore) poses a deeply ethical set of questions. These ethical questions can be arrived at from a number of positions. One such would be that which is given in the extraordinary introduction to *Bleak House* (1985), by J. Hillis Miller which provides a number of ways of thinking about naming that have a peculiar resonance for *Lolita*. A general point he makes about names is that all 'proper names ... are metaphors. They alienate the person named from his unspeakable individuality and assimilate him into a system of language'[10]. The claim made by Hillis Miller is one that is central to a strand in contemporary continental philosophy, which, in its turn, is continuing a questioning that goes back to the Ancient Greeks, if not beyond. As Jacques Derrida wonders in the unbound *Prière d'insérer* included in each of the three booklets that were later collected together in 1995 in English under the name, *On the Name*, 'The name: What does one call thus? What does one understand under the name of name?'[11] He continues, 'What happens, above all, when it is necessary to sur-name, renaming there where, precisely, the name comes to be found lacking? What makes the proper name into a sort of sur-name, pseudonym, or cryptonym at once singular and singularly untranslatable?'[12] Jean-François Lyotard asks a related question in his extraordinary work, *Libidinal Economy* where naming is seen as an aspect of a broader set of questions regarding signification, and this will be addressed shortly.

All novels ask their readers to help create the characters. The novels offer the words, the reader takes them in and uses them to imagine the scene, the people, the interaction. Once understood as an aspect of phenomenology as in Wolfgang Iser's too frequently overlooked contributions in essays such as: 'The reading process: a phenomenological approach', the significance of the reader in the construction of character is paramount in an understanding of *Lolita*'s relationship to incest.[13] An insight that Iser provides that will become increasingly important to my reading of Lolita is as follows:

> It is a common enough experience for a person to say that on a second reading he noticed things he had missed when he read the book for the first time, but this is scarcely surprising in view of the fact that the second time he is looking at the text from a different perspective. The time sequence that he realized on his first reading cannot possibly be repeated on a second reading, and this unrepeatability is bound to result in modifications of his reading experience. This is not to say that the second reading is "truer" than the first – they are, quite simply, different: the reader establishes the virtual dimension of the text by realizing a new time sequence. Thus even on repeated viewings a text allows and, indeed, induces innovative reading.[14]

In his wide-ranging and careful consideration of the interplay between text (sentences in sequence, read through time) and the reader's desire/need/ability to create a meaningful world out of this, Iser, asserts, among other things:

> In reading, this obliges the reader to seek continually for consistency, because only then can he close up situations and comprehend the unfamiliar. But consistency-building is itself a living process in which one is constantly forced to make selective decisions – and these decisions in their turn give a reality to the possibilities which they exclude, insofar as they may take effect as a latent disturbance of the consistency established. This is what causes the reader to be entangled in the text – "gestalt" that he himself has produced. Through this entanglement the reader is bound to open himself up.[15]

I would add to Iser's suggestion the insistence that what the reader creates is a 'thing', but a 'thing' that is immaterial. Its immateriality is not to say that we do not 'know' it or 'recognise' it. The thing – in this case Lolita – has colour, and texture, and scent, and heft, and sound. This immaterially present thing also gives rise to, and is produced through, the emotional cues offered by the writing, and the subsequent sets of feelings that circulate as the immaterial object responds to and interacts both with the other immaterial presences created by the text, and the mind of the person they reside in. This complex interaction of immaterial presences, their various emotional resonances, and the further effect of these on the reader, I am defining as affective ontology.

Humbert Humbert in the novel is our only conduit to Lolita the character. Like all first-person narrators, he is unreliable, but he elevates unreliability to an art.[16] Whether through his celebration of the purposefully baroque and occasionally opaque 'fancy prose style';[17] the simply impossible feats of memory we are asked to believe such as transcribing word for word, diacritic for diacritic the page from *Who's who in the Limelight*[18] or the entirety of the secret diary he kept before it was destroyed by Charlotte; the apostrophised declamations to his imagined audience and/or declarations of mistake, insanity; or the very clear sense of himself as a wordsmith ('Oh, my Lolita, I have only words to play with'[19]), Humbert revels in the wordiness of his tale. And of especial importance here, beyond the jokes and puns, puzzles and misleads, the most significant factor is the construction of Lolita.

Humbert is brutally clear in respect of his ownership of Lolita: not simply in terms of some kind of assumed romantic-erotic monogamy but, more forcibly, as an actual person-creature-character. Much of the early part of the novel offers us Humbert's theory of the 'nymphet'[20] who is a natural force from which Humbert professes to be unable to escape ('the little deadly demon among the wholesome children'[21]). She is a mixture of the magical and material – irresistible as a force; elusive to the 'normal'[22] eye. For the 'madman'[23], 'the monster'[24], the 'ape'[25] (which Humbert self-identifies as), she is 'shifty', 'soul-shattering', 'insidious', 'mysterious'[26]. Located in fairy tale and myth, personal history (his initial pubescent love, Annabel Leigh who died being the 'precursor'[27] to Lolita) and literary intertext (Annabel is also Poe's Annabel Lee from which we get Humbert's 'princedom by the sea'[28], the nymph is the figure that Humbert argues, has determined his erotic experience. When he first sees Lolita, all the discursive networks that have preoccupied the early part of his narrative, all of the rhetorical devices that he has deployed to this point to explain-describe his fascination for very young girls come into his writerly armoury. He sees not Lolita, but Annabel. Lolita is the reincarnation of Annabel, the living link to his juvenile libido. He is the 'ape', the 'fairy tale nurse'; she is the 'dead bride' and she is the 'fatal consequence of that "princedom by the sea"'[29]. She is fantasm and fantasy; he is the morbid monster – the creator-destroyer; father and fatal lover.[30]

What Humbert sees is not Lolita, it is the palimpsest of his twenty-five year search for the recovery of his pubescent passion. Lolita is '*this* Lolita, *my* Lolita'[31]. She is, literally, his construct. She says what he says she said;

she acts, dresses, reads, listens to exactly what Humbert says. Such a level of scepticism towards a narrator makes it difficult to construct the character he describes. But the great achievement of Nabokov is that for many readers, the initial read will not have induced the levels of scepticism that subsequent readings do. Forgetful, perhaps, of John Ray Jr's warning in the foreword to be suspicious of 'old-fashioned' reading practices, and a desire to believe that the people in the fiction are 'real'[32], a first reading of Humbert's narrative can produce the character of Lolita with an affective ontology in the reader's mind as real as any other fictional character. However, this construct has to begin to unravel once the games, quizzes, puns and intertexts become clearer and '*my* Lolita'[33] is seen to be precisely that – Humbert's invention, his creation. His child abuse and rape, his incestuous relationship is not the only way he steals her innocence and affects her being – in his recounting of his story, through the very confession that is meant as a kind of expiation, a peculiar catharsis, he destroys her identity by making her entirely in his own nymphic image. And it begins, and continues, and ends with her name.

Lolita in the novel is a scrapbook, an amalgamation of names, diminutives, intertexts, biographies, tales, figments, phantasms, desires and traces. The reader constructs her with difficulty from Humbert's histories and histrionics. The more times we read, the less like a traditional character she appears, and the less like a traditional character she appears, the greater, I would contend, are the affects produced. Less and less unified, more and more a linguistic construct, a textual being: Lolita is the name given to Humbert's delirium. This peculiar, problematic, ontology is affectively powerful and intense: the destruction of the little girl through rape and incest is replicated through narration and naming.

Even if we were to view the literary Lolita as a realist construction, the intermediary fact of Humbert makes her always once removed, and makes her construction, the reader's bringing-into-being of her (the affective ontology) highly problematic. If there is an assumption that we can 'know' a singular, realist, if oblique, Lolita, that singular Lolita is Humbert's. The playful, worldly, amused little girl may be a true *version* of the girl he knew, but we have to be attentive to the self-serving nature of his tale. While he appears to be honest about what he did, and comes to realise the horror of it, the characterisations (of himself, as well as of others) have to be queried. In the film, this cannot be the case because the medium lends itself to singular versions of characters and to a conceptually simplified idea of naming. The character Lolita in Lyne's film version is embodied by Dominique Swain and that embodied character is singular and develops in a more or less linear unfolding. The viewer does not see her (cannot see her) as the partial, invented, constructed, palimpsest of the novel, because she is not the partial, invented, constructed palimpsest of the novel: she is the unified, singular character of the film. She giggles at her own rape and we have to believe that this is the true response of the character. We then respond to this as we will, with whatever affects, and subsequent judgements. But the response is to an embodied character. The analogous character in literature (the Iserian phenomenological account assumes that the reader 'embodies' a character in his or her mind) is also singular and unified. This is not Lolita in the novel.

Lolita is not her name. Neither is Dolores Haze, where the family name is merely a shimmering homophone. Mrs Richard F Schiller is equally false, so that all we have are the variations and versions of a nickname. Hillis Miller's general observations regarding nicknames mentioned above assume a very precise and emphatic power: The ethical impact of naming (whether as 'real' name or a nickname) places the namer in a structure of power with the namee. This is obviously true of Humbert's efforts with Dolores's name, the transmutations of which all serve to locate her as being linguistically tied to him. The various nicknames, which shall be discussed further and in a different context later, are also used by Charlotte Haze, Dolores's mother. To that extent, Lolita's name and the different usages of it by Humbert, Charlotte and others, is not just tied to Humbert though it is with Humbert that the names attain a particular type of resonance, especially as they also operate within other types of linguistic containment through the different categories into which Lolita is drawn. These, as has been noted by Alfred Appel Jr., revolve around groupings relating to nymphs and other fairy creatures, the various manifestations of Carmen, and the combinations of words whose phonic or semantic ties link them to her surname, 'Haze', among which are the words 'grey' and 'daze'.[34] It is, however, important to be continually attentive to the fact that all of the names in Lolita are invented, or have been changed in one way or another – and they have been changed by Humbert.

Humbert creates the world and gives names to the people in it. We see his world, and learn about his people. There is no vantage point other than that of Humbert. He is our point of view. The screenplay's most significant shift is that all the characters who we know only through Humbert's mediation in the novel are seen through the neutral eye, and heard though the flattened ear of their 'own' naming. Humbert is immediately relegated from the role of world-creator to that of world sharer; the other characters are no longer his linguistic constructs; rather they exist equally. And as such the abuse, rape and incest of Lolita is no longer located within the wider structures of linguistic-libidinal self-justification and self-hatred. Instead of the (as we shall see) nominal corporeal, affective, sexual and emotional contortions that Humbert puts Lolita through and which the reader sees only through Humbert's confession, the screenplay necessarily has to make Lolita complicit. The horror of Humbert's narration is that we see the attempt, and failure, to justify his actions in relation to the girl only through his eyes – he makes Lolita as he needs her to be (bold, forward, vulgar, sexual, seductive) and we see the terror and frozen anguish of him as he understands the suffering he has caused – both in terms of the abuse, and in terms of the denial of her even as a character. His excuse to Charlotte when she discovers his diary is that 'the notes you found were fragments of a novel'[35]. In many ways this is true. Lolita, Dolores, Lo, Dolly is only ever a character, written, rewritten, retranscribed and reinscribed by Humbert to serve the purpose of expressing his desire, his regret, his need, his pain, his monstrousness. She is even less real than John Ray Jr. might think. The screenplay, and the films, have to make her real, give her her own voice, offer her the consolation of being, an ontology beyond Humbert's fictionalising.

Yet, by virtue of being a character in a novel (both Nabokov's and Humbert's) Lolita is given the power and force, the emotional resonance that comes with affective ontology which is to say with the imagined character the reader creates from the words given: who is felt, understood, 'seen' or at least perceived in a fashion 'richer' than this specific filmic embodiment can allow.[36]

Unlike Iser, I am not claiming a general truth about literature *contra* film. The embodied character in a film is clearly capable of producing extraordinary emotional responses in a viewer, but in *Lolita*, the doubly distanced Lolita – a character in a novel effectively created by a character in a novel – is produced with an especially powerful affective ontology for the very reason that constructing her via Humbert's fancies, perversions and mutations is so hard. The reader's investment in Lolita is so great because she/he has to work so hard to see through Humbert. The same is not and cannot be true of the films. The linguistic mutations that mean that each instantiation of Lolita is potentially different from the previous one, is not possible when the character is physically embodied by an actor. The same is true of all the characters in this novel, of course, as our only access to them is through Humbert's narration (with the important exception of John Ray Jr.'s Foreword). While the films show us the later Lolita as Mrs Richard F. Schiller, and we see (more so in Lyne's than in Kubrick's) the difference of two years, and pregnancy, on the young girl (she is still only sixteen in the novel), this is a physically presented alteration that does not fundamentally make us challenge the identity of her. Humbert's narration in the novel, which is partially replicated in the opening to Lyne's film, offers us a Lolita whose name and identity is constantly in flux. The desire he feels for 'her' is also the desire he expresses in constructing 'her' '*my* Lolita'.[37]

Humbert's abuse of Lolita which is turned into a kind of mocking seduction in Kubrick, and is presented as a devastating entropy in Lyne, is a baroque memorialisation in the novel: Humbert's contortions, his effort to deflect blame, to assign culpability to Lolita all fail as the full weight of his own guilt, the appalling realisation of what he has done breaks through the fancy prose, the cute games. He has raped her, now he remakes her in his own image, an image constantly in excess of his ability to control and one that finally breaks free of his control – literally and biographically (she runs away with Quilty, then runs away again to Dick; and Humbert finally has to allow her the textual freedom in which to see the abuse, the crime, the rape, the incest are figured, understood, admitted to and repented of). He expresses his dislike of capital punishment 'for reasons that may appear more obvious than they really are'[38], but suggests he be sentenced to 'thirty-five years for rape'[39] while no charges be brought for the murder of Quilty.

The centrality of Quilty as clown in Kubrick's version undermines significantly his function as double, spectre or trap in the novel; and also means that the additional rapes endured by Lolita are either ignored or trivialised. Again, it is the novel's ability to imply a character, to hide that character and then have him explode into the story at the end which allows the reader the confusion, the vertigo of unknowing that in a different way afflicts Humbert. We feel Humbert's self-loathing and self-hatred. He creates and obfuscates in equal measure. And his greatest creation is the obfuscation of Dolores in the vulgar dispersal of Lolita.

'Lolita ... Lolita'.[40] Between these two designations is the rest of the whole of Humbert Humbert's narration. Is this, then, a comfortable circularity, the safe return to the same, a motion that arrives at pure equivalence? Phillip Schweighauser suggests something similar in his compelling argument.[41] However, this assumes that the repeated term is identical in both instances. For this to be so, the two designators, 'Lolita' would have to have attached to them the same value with regard to the thing designated, which is to say that the character of Lolita would be the same in each case. And this is patently not so. The opening designation, 'Lolita'[42] designates an abstraction unfilled by any concept except the one that further designates the need for a character who is not yet present. The cumulative effect of the narrative, Humbert's desire that the reader should discover Lolita gradually is made explicit in relation to the discovery of Quilty. Humbert says of his design and patterning that it has been arranged 'with the express purpose of having the ripe fruit fall at the right moment'.[43] We are meant to recognise Lolita differently in the last enunciation of her name than in the first.

The last designation, 'Lolita',[44] suffers from a superabundance of concepts, an overwhelming affluence of regimes. She is massively over-invested with character. Does this then allow us to imagine the second 'Lolita' as full signifier, as the completion of the earlier 'Lolita', as the eschatological promised land that will bring to Humbert the remission of evil? This would imply that the 'moral apotheosis'[45] identified by John Ray Jr, finds its semantic equivalent in the totality of Lolita's signifying practice. It is questionable whether such an apotheosis is present at all, and it is certainly not the case that the final Lolita is so conveniently categorised.

What has Humbert written, then? The answers to this are, of course, multiple, but one of the things he has written is a paean to the productive eroticism of naming, as an attempted salve for his recognition of the destructive obscenity of raping, and incest. He has written a text whose name is 'Lolita': not the novel that also bears the same name, but the object to which his whole aching body is directed. 'Lolita, light of my life, fire of my loins. My sin, my soul. Lo-lee-ta: the tip of the tongue taking a trip of three steps down the palate to tap, at three, on the teeth. Lo. Lee. Ta.'[46] The name is initially intact, inviolable, impregnable: 'Lolita'. Though it is also, as we soon discover, a derivation of a derivation – an extended nickname invented from the middle of the 'real' name Dolores. Humbert's narration begins with a name he has invented from his initial invention's invented contraction: already doubly alienated from its supposed object, the name 'Lolita' *signifies* nothing except its own signification: not empty, but tensorial already (like all signs, but explicitly so). The name greets us in its totality (which is to say, in its designation of total abstraction), and is then added to. The proper name needs its object, desires (perhaps) its object. Where is she? Who is she? She is, whatever else may happen, the predicate of a sweet symmetry, of a genitive illumination and heating-up, of an assertion of life-giving and libidinal prowess: she is 'light' and 'fire' of 'life' and 'loins'.[47] And she is, so far, perfectly proportioned. She is the possessor-creator of damnation and salvation. And then she falls apart. The seductive power of Humbert's words obscure, but cannot hide, the inevitable destruction of the object he creates, even as that construction is intended to occlude the real girl already torn apart by his abuse and obsession.

The name is not inviolable at all. 'Lolita' is, if nothing else, as Humbert's linguistic toy and sexual plaything, easily spread. 'Lo-lee-ta'.[48] Our palatal journey, our physical introduction, our tonguely tour of her literary body in all its divisibility, takes us to her complete sundering: the phonemes have become, as indeed they ought to be as the true bearers of signification, whole in themselves. They no longer need her. 'Lo. Lee. Ta.'[49] The mention (hidden, deceptive, totally Humbertian) of Poe's Annabel Lee shows how from the very beginning she is a collage of Humbert's desires and hopes: his palimpsestually perverse creation.[50]

Each mention of her, of Lolita, takes us further and further away from any idea of her as a character. Instead, she becomes a lexical object to be used and rearranged in the frenetic linguistic excess, the wordy violence, of Humbert's desire. This desire is manifested in naming, through naming. He thinks he controls Lolita's destiny because he controls the execution of her name. But even as he seeks to overpower her by creating her, and to create her via the histories and desires of his own reading and excess, he falls prey to those histories' own excess, their uncontrollable, tensorial energy.

The final naming of Lolita is the last word of the book, and is part of the small adjectival phrase 'my Lolita'.[51] The possessive pronoun also acts as a descriptor, which is important here as it demonstrates the very real way in which Humbert has attempted to construct Lolita for himself, through the array of different discursive intersections. While Humbert tries to assuage his own tremors of unease at his treatment of the girl, he cannot avoid certain moments of recognition: 'What I had madly possessed was not she, but my own creation, another fanciful Lolita – perhaps more real than Lolita; overlapping, encasing her; floating between me and her, and having no will, no consciousness – indeed, no life of her own.'[52] The empty designation of the first Lolita is rapidly filled in by Humbert, and it begins to overflow. Dolores grows and leaves him, has an affair with Quilty, marries Richard and dies in childbirth. Lolita simply exceeds his own creation. He invests so much in her in his libidinal-lexical desire that his discourse of her is constantly blocked by the irruption of her name.

Jean-François Lyotard discusses the importance of naming in *Libidinal Economy*. For the purposes of this chapter, I am going to concentrate on the section of Lyotard's text subtitled 'Intensity, the Name'. Here the writer of *Libidinal Economy* poses a common problem which is that the name 'refers in principle to a single reference and does not appear to be exchangeable against other terms in the logico-linguistic structure: there is no intra-systemic equivalent of the proper name, it points towards the outside like a deictic, it has no connotations, or it is interminable.'[53] Arguing against logicians whom he unifies under the proper names Frege and Russell as if there were no problem with this, Lyotard insists that the predicate of existence postulated by the philosophers cannot be the 'anchoring'[54] that he claims they claim it is. Using the example of Daniel Paul Schreber's *Memoirs of my Nervous Illness*, Lyotard asks questions of the proper name Fleschig, who was Schreber's analyst. For Lyotard, the name Fleschig, under the influence of Schreber's delirium is subject to a '*dividuation*'.[55] This means that propositions that ought to be incompossible in relation to the 'subject' Fleschig are rendered compatible. This, in turn, means that one name can refer to a number of different possibilities for the same 'subject'. Lyotard is keen to assert that this is not simply polysemia, as this would amount to saying only that there were a multiple number of exchanges available within the structure of language. For Lyotard, this would keep the name safely within the semiotic structure or set-up, the primacy of which would then be asserted and maintained. Rather, he wishes to insist that in the proper name (here of Klossowski's 'Roberte') there are two incompossible 'orders' that meet and that are no longer two but, rather, 'indiscernible'.[56] This incompossible admixture is the site of a shock to the system, to the set-up. It cannot, within its own rules, allow for this to happen, yet it is also a necessary condition of the set-up in the first place. The libidinal energy disrupts the supposed conformity of the system. Put differently, the name 'Roberte' becomes an event that disrupts the discourse, which moves in excess of the discourse: it is a testament to singularity, a rejection of homogeneity. It is clear that Lyotard valorises the libidinal influx over the calm of the set-up. This fluxion, and the libidinal intensities attendant upon it are presented by Lyotard with, at times, a sort of Humbertian delight-horror. The opening page of *Libidinal Economy* provides a wonderful repudiation of totalised systems of knowledge through the gleeful and sadistic description of a body being cut open and spread apart. Among other injunctions, Lyotard tells us, 'dilate the diaphragm of the anal sphincter, longitudinally cut and flatten out the black conduit of the rectum, then the colon, then the caecum, now a ribbon with its surface all striated and polluted with shit'.[57] This general sadism, and its refusal of the homogenous body, of the ordered, 'economical' body, becomes more imbued with Humbertian overtones.

Invoking the German artist Hans Bellmer (though only by surname, and with no context – Lyotard's naming has its own complicated ethics), he disavows the substitutionality of body parts, or rather their metonymic 'stand in' capacity. It is not enough, says Lyotard, to say 'like Bellmer, that the fold in the armpit of the child, dreamily intent, her elbow on the table and chin in her hand, could *count as* [*valoir pour*] the folds of her groin, or even as juncture of the lips of her sex'.[58] Lyotard's invocation of the child dolls made by Bellmer, and his refusal to allow Bellmer's desired substitution of one part for another, leads us in two directions. First, the caustic rejoinder against 'counting as' is a ferocious injunction against substitionality, semiological being, the homogenous body: 'It is not a part of the body, of what body? – the organic body, organised with survival as its goal against what excites it to death, assured against riot and agitation – not a part which comes to be *substituted* for another part, like, for example, in the case of this little girl, the fleshiness of the arm for that of the thighs and its faint fold for the vaginal slit.'[59] The 'organic body' is also the body of '*political economy*', and such a body presupposes a bodily 'unity' which is of no interest to Lyotard who will rather 'go immediately to the very limits of cruelty, perform the dissection of polymorphous perversion'.[60] It is such a dissection that Humbert performs on Lolita, not on her body as such, but on her creation, a creation that is, after all, his; she is his lexical toy, his wordy plaything, his incestuous desire. And this takes us in the second direction invited by Lyotard's use of Bellmer.

In his discussion of Bellmer, Andrew Brink makes a comparison between the German artist whose distorted, disfigured adolescent dolls appeared in photographic form anonymously in 1934, and Humbert Humbert whose object of fascination, Lolita, is born in 1935. Though he does not mention the chronological coincidence relating to the 'birth' and subsequent deformation and distortion of Bellmer's dolls, and Humbert's 'doll' (Dolores), Brink makes the following observations about their creators. Brink writes:

> Bellmer's sly and winning sadism suggests an obsessive character pathology that enlists the viewer, or reader – a tactic brilliantly used by Nabokov when presenting the pedophile Humbert Humbert. But Bellmer's dolls are uncompromisingly forlorn and damaged when compared to Nabokov's idealized inveigling child-woman Lolita who excited Humbert into frantic pursuit.[61]

Neither Nabokov nor Lyotard would have approved of Brink's 'psychobiographical with attachment theory'[62] approach, but the temptation to see a direct link from *Libidinal Economy* to *Lolita* which is already strong in terms of a certain experimentation, a particular sadism, an attention to the singular, and the focus on the perverse and the cruel is made stronger by Lyotard's use of Bellmer and Bellmer's relationship to Humbert, or more properly the contiguity of time, place and violence heaped upon their dolls (despite Brink's assertion, Lolita is clearly forlorn and damaged, well before her early death on Christmas day 1952, aged seventeen years). Humbert's perversion is not just his paedophilic desire and his incestuous fulfilment of that desire: it is also that he seeks to control the girl through nominally atomising her. As Bellmer's limbs become specific and individuated fetish tokens of the possible whole doll-child, so Lolita's many names and dispersals by Humbert have the effect of producing a monstrous cavalcade of fetishised Lolitas

The name 'Lolita' has already been stretched, sundered, torn apart; and in its tearing other names inhabit it, dissimulate each other, become indiscernible bursting its signifying potential and even destabilising its already unstable designatory power. Most immediate, both in terms of its location in the narrative, and in terms of Humbert's own pre-history is the 'Lee' of 'Lo. Lee. Ta.'[63] This, as mentioned above, is an echo of Annabel Lee, the eponymous character in Edgar Allan Poe's poem of childhood love, desire and death. This instigates a subset of intensities that swirl in Lolita's name. Already Lolita is inhabited by the immediate discourse of the poem, and the additional one of Poe's sexual biography. Lee, however, is also homonymic with Annabel Leigh, Humbert's tragic typhus-catching trauma-explaining first love.[64]

Lolita then is inhabited by Poe, by the two Annabels, and is seen by Humbert here as a sort of metaphor for the initial, the 'real' signified which is his first

Annabel. Later, the dissimulation of signs is made graphically evident when Humbert mutates and stretches the names into 'Annabel Haze, alias Dolores Lee, alias Loleeta' (p. 167) where each mutation stands as an intensification of the succeeding mutated sign in an endless deferral of non-signifying terms, but ones which nevertheless designate. This then, is less a translation than a transmutation. To translate implies some notion of equivalence between the initial term and its translated stand-in. What these terms designate, is the intensity of Humbert's lexical-libidinal desire, of his attempt to decant the horror of the incest and rapes he has made Lolita suffer into the repository of his language. This intensity is marked by the libidinal investments in the name from the four different discourses: the libidinal investment of the narrator of the poem for his Annabel; Humbert's investment in his Annabel; Poe's investment in his child bride Virginia;[65] and Humbert's investment in his Lolita.

Humbert's invention, the name that designates his libidinal, his literary and his linguistic delirium, is subjected to a frantic, promiscuous eclecticism. The design of Humbert's narrative, its seemingly constraining symmetry, suggests that the careful interweaving of allusive antecedents and apologies is an effort to constrain the name, to keep it within discursive bondage. The attempted constraints, however, operate as discourses to be dissimulated as much as they do as cuffs. The name 'Lolita' is penetrated and passed through by, in no special order, the discourses attached to the (predominantly masculine) names Joyce, Mérimée, Shakespeare, Doyle, Christie, Leblanc, Blake, Beardsley, Eliot, Marat, de Sade and many others. Each of these names is used differently and their resultant intensities, likewise, can be read in a variety of ways.

The use of de Sade is interesting because it brings together a number of elements in the novel and provides a certain narrative consistency while imbuing 'Lolita' with an even greater sense of energetic influxes that push her further beyond the restrictions of that discourse. Lolita is telling Humbert of the time she spent with Quilty. Quilty, like Humbert, is a paedophile, but his is a general desire – any young child being equivalent to any other young child so long as they will perform acts for him to film. Quilty's desired objects are transferable and exchangeable within a closed system. Humbert has no system; there can be no exchange: only the singular Lolita will do (except, of course, the 'singular' Lolita is monstrously multiple in Humbert's perverse polymorphous invention). Lolita tells Humbert that she was kicked out by Quilty when she refused to be filmed having oral sex with another child. This, the text suggests, is not so much out of repulsion at the act, but because (in a bizarre inversion of Humbert) she only wants Quilty, and refuses to exchange him for someone or be exchanged by him for someone. When hearing of the "'weird, filthy, fancy things'" demanded of Lolita by Quilty,[66] Humbert parenthetically exclaims '(Sade's *Justine* was twelve at the start)'.[67] Here there is an equivalence postulated. The young Lolita is in a similar position to Justine. Later, Quilty boasts about having made several films of eighteenth-century 'sexcapades', including *Justine*.[68] The circulation of names (Lolita and Justine) operates as a struggle for ownership, not of Lolita but of the moral right to express and feel indignation and shame. If Humbert can equate Lolita with Justine he can also equate Quilty with de Sade.

Kubrick's Quilty dominates the film. Peter Sellers's often improvised portrayal offers us a clown creature, a master of disguise whom we always recognise: playful, caustic, mischievous, amusing. The novel's barely present ghost of a character is for Kubrick, the film's centre, but a centre who makes little sense. Because of the restrictions on what could be shown, Humbert's decision to shoot Quilty, and Lolita's relationship with him, seem much more conventional. Lolita is presented as simply a seduced young woman, beguiled by this chancer; Humbert a poor dupe of the pair of them. The fact of the incest is barely registered; the fact of the child rape is refigured as a pseudo-comic seduction. Humbert's horror at his own actions in the novel, and the necessary displacement of the extremity of the crimes he has committed onto the hazy figure of Quilty is entirely lacking. While the affective ontology in relation to Lolita is a significant factor in the different responses to her incest and rape in the novel and the Kubrick film, Quilty is figured as such an entirely different character that it is not really possible to make a comparison. The Lyne film is different. Quilty is, inevitably, embodied and much more physically present than is possible (or desirable) in the novel. However, he is also enigmatic, half-hidden, presented in partial presence – a hand, an obscured face, a shoe, a voice. And when we do meet him, the languidly enervated dipsomania, the sated impotence of the man, offer us a figure much more akin to the novel's and to the novel's requirements. Quilty is a ruined man, a predator, bereft of compassion or empathy, and Humbert can project onto him the self-loathing he feels. He feels jealousy, rage and betrayal as well of course, and Quilty's inability to feel at all provides us in the Lyne film, with the movie analogue of literary Humbert's recounting of their meeting and fight: Lyne employed Stephen Schiff to write the screenplay, and Schiff used more of the novel's text than Kubrick's film had done, and here that pays off with a neat filmic representation of Humbert's unheroic account:

> We fell to wrestling again. We rolled all over the floor, in each other's arms, like two huge helpless children. He was naked and goatish under his robe, and I felt suffocated as he rolled over me. I rolled over him. We rolled over me. They rolled over him. We rolled over us…[69]

Humbert and Quilty (like Lolita and Annabel Lee) become embroiled, coterminous synonymous. The characters share in each other's contempt, their guilt, their disease. Lyne's film presents this commingling, and as a consequence, presents a version of Humbert's self-disgust at his actions, which serves to heighten the realisation of his abuse, his violence and rape of the little girl who became his daughter.

While the film has to present Lolita as embodied, and therefore, in some sense always represented as somehow complicit in and responsible for her own despoliation, Lyne – as in the novel – gives us a Humbert who is aware of his depredations.[70] While in the final pages of the novel Humbert muses, 'What I heard was but the melody of children at play, nothing but that ... and then I knew that the hopelessly poignant thing was not Lolita's absence from my side, but the absence of her voice from that concord.'[71] The film ends with Jeremy Irons's Humbert standing by a hillside hearing the sound of children from a school in the valley below.[72] As the police who have been involved in the low-speed car chase negotiate the cows and hillocks to move towards and arrest him, a voice over from Humbert expresses his knowledge of the harm done to Lolita by echoing, with very few differences, the prose quoted above.[73]

The final scene of the film before the post-script mention of both Humbert's and Lolita's deaths in 1950, is of Lolita, younger and still under Humbert's thrall, leaning back on her bed, vacant of expression and doll-like. This brief image, juxtaposed with Humbert's standing on the hillside, and contained within the same score, is the closest the film can come to the kind of unembodied affective ontology of the novel as the girl is unvoiced, juxtapositional, analeptic. The largely realist aesthetic of the film is here passed over in favour of a very brief, but affectively vital sense of montage – and while montage cannot be said to be the same as the scrapbook Lolita of the novel which I mentioned earlier, it is much nearer to that than any of the previous moments.

Nabokov's novel is so powerful in its portrayal of incest, rape and abuse because the affective onotolgies required by the reader demand a disquieting sympathetic recognition of Humbert's rapture, delirium, remorse and madness; as well as an understanding that seemingly 'realist' Lolita is a Humbertian construct, a justification, an alibi; but that moreover, the 'realism' cannot sustain itself beyond a first reading, and the character of Lolita is even more removed from the real, even more violate by virtue of being a figment, a palimpsest, an expression of a desire that does not even offer the respect to the 'real' Lolita it might pretend to.

The screenplay and films cannot offer this dual distancing, this articulated and obscured abuse. By virtue of having to embody the characters in real bodies, the constructed nature of Humbert's world disappears, and along with it the horror of his rhetorical as well as actual rapes. Kubrick's decision to make Quilty a trickster clown figure means that the film keeps much of the bleak, grim humour of the novel, none of its force for repugnance is offered. Lyne tries harder to marry the twin poles of Humbert's 'fancy prose style'[74] (humour and horror), and achieves this in greater measure by making Quilty as he does.

Nabokov's novel is rightly celebrated from a literary perspective, for its linguistic energy, the power and wit of Humbert's narration. However, this wit, power and energy is also harnessed to evince horror at Humbert's abuses, his incest-rape and despoliation of Lolita, as well as to recognise the further abuse done to her in occluding the 'real' girl through the games, stratagems and self-justificatory rhetorics. The word is 'incest'[75] and the Lolita is a palimpsest: together they offer us a terrifying pretence at a confession; and a tragic story of corruption, abuse and death made all the more real by virtue of its artifice.

Notes

1 Vladimir Nabokov, Alfred Appel Jr. (ed., pref., introd. and notes), *The Annotated Lolita* (Penguin, 2000), p. 119.
2 *Lolita* (writ. Vladimir Nabokov, dir. Stanley Kubrick, Metro-Goldwyn-Mayer, Seven Arts Pictures, A.A. Productions Ltd., Anya, Harris-Kubrick Productions, Transworld Pictures, 1962).
3 *Lolita* (writ. Vladimir Nabokov (novel), Stephen Schiff (screenplay), dir. Adrian Lyne, Guild, Lolita Productions and Pathé, 1997).
4 Vladimir Nabokov, *Lolita: A Screenplay* (Vintage Books, 1997).
5 Nabokov, *The Annotated Lolita*, p. 119 [emphasis mine].
6 Eric Goldman. ' "Knowing" Lolita: Sexual deviance and normality in Nabokov's *Lolita*', *Nabokov Studies* 8 (2004), pp. 87–104.
7 Vladimir Nabokov, *Speak, Memory* (Penguin Books, 2000).
8 For a full description of this topic see note 4/9 in Alfred Appel, Notes, in *The Annotated Lolita*, pp. 323–4.
9 Boris Katz, 'My name or any such-like phantom', *The Russian Review* 58 (1999), pp. 565–73. Ronen Omry, 'Emulation, anti-parody, intertextuality, and annotation', *Nabokov Studies* 5 (1998/1999), pp. 63–70.
10 J. Hillis Miller, 'Dickens's *Bleak House*', in Steven Connor (ed.), *Charles Dickens* (Routledge, 2013), p. 68.
11 Jacques Derrida, Thomas Dutoit (ed.), David Wood, John P Leavy and Ian McLeod (trans.), *On the Name* (Stanford University Press, 1995), p. xiv.
12 Derrida, *On the Name*, p. xiv.
13 Wolfgang Iser, 'The reading process: A phenomenological approach' in David Lodge and Nigel Wood (eds), *Modern Criticism and Theory* (Taylor and Francis, 2000), pp. 189–206.

14 *Ibid.*, p. 196.
15 *Ibid.*, p. 201.
16 See, for instance: Anthony R. Moore, 'How unreliable is Humbert in *Lolita*?' *Journal of Modern Literature* 25:1 (Autumn, 2000), pp. 71–80.
17 Nabokov, *The Annotated Lolita*, p. 9.
18 An exceptionally enlightening discussion of this core moment is to be found in George Ferger, 'Who's who in the sublimelight: "Suave John Ray" and Lolita's "Secret Points"', *Nabokov Studies* 8 (2004), pp. 137–98.
19 Nabokov, *The Annotated Lolita*, p. 32.
20 See for example: *Ibid.*, pp. 16–22.
21 *Ibid.*, p. 16.
22 *Ibid.*, p. 17.
23 *Ibid.*, p. 17.
24 For examples of Humbert making allusions to being a 'monster', see: *Ibid.*, pp. 44, 124, 284.
25 For examples of Humbert referring to being ape-like see: *Ibid.*, pp. 39, 48, 258. Also see Appel, 'Introduction', *The Annotated Lolita*, pp. lx–lxi, and notes 42/5 and 48/2, pp. 357–60.
26 *Ibid,.* p. 17.
27 *Ibid.*, p. 9.
28 *Ibid.*, p. 9. Also see Appel, in *The Annotated Lolita*, notes 9/1 and 9/2, pp. 328–32.
29 *Ibid.*, pp. 39–40.
30 The relationship between monstrosity and paedophilia in *Lolita* is engaged with in Frederick Whiting, '"The strange particularity of the lover's preference": Paedophilia, pornography and the anatomy of monstrosity in *Lolita*', in *American Literature* 70 (1998), pp. 833–62.
31 Nabokov, *The Annotated Lolita*, p. 40.
32 *Ibid.*, p. 4.
33 *Ibid.*, p. 40.
34 See: Appel, in *The Annotated Lolita*, pp. 338–40 (16/6). Humbert uses the word daze on multiple occasions, see for example pp. 69, 210, 255, 293.
35 *Ibid.*, p. 96.
36 Iser, 'The reading process', p. 203.
37 Nabokov, *The Annotated Lolita*, p. 40.
38 *Ibid.*, p. 308.
39 *Ibid.*, p. 308.
40 *Ibid.*, pp. 9–309.
41 Phillip Schweighauser, 'Metafiction, transcendence, and death in Nabokov's *Lolita*', *Nabokov Studies* (1998/99), pp. 99–116.
42 Nabokov, *The Annotated Lolita*, p. 9.
43 *Ibid.*, p. 272.
44 *Ibid.*, p. 309.

45 *Ibid.*, p. 5.
46 *Ibid.*, p. 9.
47 *Ibid.*, p. 9.
48 *Ibid.*, p. 9.
49 *Ibid.*, p. 9.
50 See Peter Coviello. 'Poe in love: Pedophilia, morbidity, and the logic of slavery', *English Literary History* 70:3 (2003), pp. 875–901.
51 *Ibid.*, p. 309.
52 *Ibid.*, p. 62.
53 Jean-Francois Lyotard, Iain Hamilton Grant (trans.), *Libidinal Economy* (The Athlone Press, 1993), p. 55.
54 *Ibid.*, p. 55.
55 *Ibid.*, p. 55.
56 *Ibid.*, p. 56.
57 *Ibid.*, p. 1.
58 *Ibid.*, p. 2 [italics in original].
59 *Ibid.*, p. 2 [italics in original].
60 *Ibid.*, p. 2 [italics in original].
61 Andrew Brink, *Desire and Avoidance in Art* (Peter Lang, 2007), p. 78.
62 *Ibid.*, p. 72.
63 Nabokov, *The Annotated Lolita*, p. 9.
64 For a discussion of the 'Lee' of 'Lo. Lee. Ta.' referencing Poe's Annabel Lee see: Appel, *The Annotated Lolita*, notes 9/1 and 9/7 pp. 328–34.
65 Poe was twenty-seven years old and Virginia just thirteen when they married, although '[a] witness swore that she was twenty-one'. See: Jeffrey Meyers, *Edgar Allan Poe* (John Murray, 1992), p. 85.
66 Nabokov, *The Annotated Lolita*, p. 276.
67 *Ibid.*, p. 276.
68 *Ibid.*, p. 298.
69 *Ibid.*, pp. 298–9.
70 It is of course possible to provide different points of view to the same embodied character in film, and to offer something akin to the palimpsest we find in Nabokov's novel – but neither Kubrick nor Lyne choose to adopt techniques that would make this manifest.
71 Nabokov, *The Annotated Lolita*, p. 308.
72 The importance of the detail provided by Nabokov to the different parts of America that Humbert drives to both with Lolita and in order to find her are discussed by David Castronovo, 'Humbert's America', *New England Review* 23:2 (2002), pp. 33–41.
73 *Lolita* (writ. Vladimir Nabokov (novel), Stephen Schiff (screenplay), dir. Adrian Lyne, Guild, Lolita Productions © 1998 PATHÉ PRODUCTION).
74 Nabokov, *The Annotated Lolita*, p. 9.
75 *Ibid.*, p. 119.

Bibliography

Fiction

Nabokov, Vladimir, *Lolita: A Screenplay* (Vintage Books, 1997)
Nabokov, Vladimir, Alfred Appel Jr. (ed., pref., introd. and notes), *The Annotated Lolita* (Penguin, 2000)

Non-fiction

Appel Jr., Alfred, 'Preface', 'Introduction' and 'Notes', *The Annotated Lolita* (Penguin, 2000)
Brink, Andrew, *Desire and Avoidance in Art: Pablo Picasso, Hans Bellmer, Balthus, and Joseph Cornell Psychobiographical Studies with Attachment Theory* (Peter Lang, 2007)
Castronovo, David, 'Humbert's America', *New England Review* 23:2 (2002), pp. 33–41
Coviello, Peter, 'Poe in love: Pedophilia, morbidity, and the logic of slavery', *English Literary History* 70:3 (2003), pp. 875–901
Derrida, Jacques, Thomas Dutoit (ed.), David Wood, John P. Leavy and Ian McLeod (trans.), *On the Name* (Stanford University Press, 1995)
Ferger, George, 'Who's who in the sublimelight: "Suave John Ray" and Lolita's "Secret Points"', *Nabokov Studies* 8 (2004), pp. 137–98
Goldman, Eric, '"Knowing" Lolita: Sexual deviance and normality in Nabokov's *Lolita*', *Nabokov Studies* 8 (2004), pp. 87–104
Hillis Miller, J., 'Dickens's *Bleak House*', in Steven Connor (ed.), *Charles Dickens* (Routledge), pp. 59–75. Reprinted from 'Introduction', in Dickens, Charles, Norman Page (ed.), *Bleak House* (Harmondsworth: Penguin, 1971), pp. 11, 13–30
Iser, Wolfgang, 'The reading process: A phenomenological approach' in David Lodge and Nigel Wood (eds), *Modern Criticism and Theory: A Reader* (Taylor and Francis, 2000), pp. 189–206
Katz, Boris, 'My name or any such-like phantom', *The Russian Review* 58 (1999), pp. 565–73
Lyotard, Jean-Francois, Iain Hamilton Grant (trans.), *Libidinal Economy* (The Athlone Press, 1993)
Meyers, Jeffrey, *Edgar Allan Poe: His Life and Legacy* (John Murray, 1992)
Moore, Anthony R., 'How unreliable is Humbert in *Lolita*? *Journal of Modern Literature* 25:1 (Autumn, 2000), pp. 71–80
Nabokov, Vladimir, 'On a book entitled Lolita', in Vladimir Nabokov, *The Annotated Lolita* (Penguin, 2000), pp. 311–17
Omry, Ronen, 'Emulation, anti-parody, intertextuality, and annotation', *Nabokov Studies* 5 (1998/1999), pp. 63–70
Schweighauser, Phillip, 'Metafiction, transcendence, and death in Nabokov's *Lolita*', *Nabokov Studies* (1998/1999), pp. 99–116

Whiting, Frederick, ' "The strange particularity of the lover's preference": Paedophilia, pornography and the anatomy of monstrosity in *Lolita*', *American Literature* 70 (1998), pp. 833–62

Film and television

Lolita (writ. Vladimir Nabokov, dir. Stanley Kubrick, Metro-Goldwyn-Mayer, Seven Arts Pictures, A.A. Productions Ltd., Anya, Harris-Kubrick Productions, Transworld Pictures, 1962)

Lolita (writ. Vladimir Nabokov (novel), Stephen Schiff (screenplay), dir. Adrian Lyne, Guild, Lolita Productions © 1998 PATHÉ PRODUCTION)

5

Appropriate or anathema? The representation of incest in children's literature

Alice Mills

The history of children's literature in the English-speaking world over the past seventy years could be encapsulated within two sets of bookshop shelves. For the first sixty years of the twentieth century, children's literature occupied a smallish set of shelves in the average non-specialist bookshop, barely (if at all) differentiated by genre or reading age; when I was growing up in the north of England in the 1950s, I was lucky to find 300 books for children in a bookshop. By the turn of the millennium, children's literature occupied a far larger proportion of the bookshop space, and was differentiated into non-fiction; picture story books; chapter books, also known as books for beginner readers or younger readers; and books for young adults (formerly termed teenagers or adolescents), this last category sometimes separated into fantasy and realist fiction in countries such as the United Kingdom, Canada, Australia and the USA.[1] There have been attempts by some publishers and librarians to introduce a further category, that of 'tween' fiction for the pre-teens, generally girls.[2] These shelf-space divisions offer little or no acknowledgement of the legal definitions of the child, the Piagetian understanding of child development, the psychoanalytic child in all its variations, or the religious child (in Christianity, either born in sin and requiring adult intervention in order to be saved or born innocent and prone to corruption in the bleak world of adult experience), to say nothing of the postmodern child, the queer child, or the postcolonial child. They pay no attention to the reading abilities or psychological maturity of individual children. Nevertheless, they offer a set of definitions of the contemporary child as understood by the marketplace, and it is in these terms that I shall work through my examination of the (very small) field of children's literature concerned with incest.

The division between young adult fiction and the rest of children's literature was forced on the market by the phenomenal popularity of books setting out to smash taboos, beginning in the 1960s and at its height in the 1970s.

Suddenly young adult fiction became almost entirely focussed on themes largely unspeakable in the earlier part of the twentieth century, such as extreme poverty, homelessness, alcoholism, drug addiction, teen pregnancy, homosexuality, menstruation, abortion and mental illness. All of these were deemed problems, suitable topics for a novel of adolescent anguish that most often ended badly; Robert Cormier's books are a prime set of examples[3]. Eating disorders became prominent with the rise in public awareness of anorexia, then bulimia. The category of 'young adult' from the late 1960s on has served both as a warning to cautious adult buyers of content considered unsuitable for younger readers, and as a marketing tool to attract teen buyers to previously forbidden literary territory.[4] What is barely present, in all this profusion of formerly taboo topics, is incest, arguably the last taboo in children's literature.

While there are young adult problem novels that touch on incestuous advances from a parent as a compelling reason for a child to leave home, or a family to collapse, very few treat the issue in any depth, and they almost universally cast the father (or those safer substitutes, the step-father and uncle) in the role of incestuous adult and the daughter in the role of victim. Among the more impressive of these books are Margo Lanagan's *Tender Morsels* (2008), Chris Crutcher's *Chinese Handcuffs* (1989) and Heather Waldorf's *Leftovers* (2009). Still almost unspeakable, even in the progressively more extreme situations depicted by many writers of young adult problem novels, are other incestuous possibilities such as father's advances towards son, mother's towards child of either gender, child's towards parent or siblings' towards one another. In his 1999 study of 'incestuous sexual themes in contemporary novels for adolescence', W. Bernard Lukenbill found only ten books to explore, excluding one fantasy novel as outside his field. As he notes:

> The incestuous acts portrayed in these novels were exclusively male–female contacts. Of these, the most widely presented sexual acts occurred between fathers (including stepfathers), and their daughters (7 cases), followed by contacts between uncles and nieces (2 cases).[5]

Interestingly, although the 'sexual abuse' title of his article ought to exclude it, he includes in his study Sonya Hartnett's *Sleeping Dogs* (1995), an Australian novel which presents incest as consensual between an adolescent brother and his sister.

In the context of the young adult problem novel, perhaps the most unusual aspect of this incestuous relationship in *Sleeping Dogs* is that it is not understood – at least by the sister – as a lifelong commitment. She does not define herself in terms of incest, while other problem novels tend to define the perpetrator as irrevocably driven by incestuous urges. In Hartnett's novel, it is the violently abusive father who speaks in terms of moral outrage when he discovers the relationship, judging his children to be no better than animals, assuming the right to murder his son. The extremeness of his response at the point of revelation functions to mitigate any moral outrage that a reader might bring to bear on the children. On the other hand, the relationship between the siblings is not presented as idyllic; the daughter does have qualms about whether it is morally wrong and it is stated that the isolation from other families, enforced on these children, has caused them to seek comfort and intimacy from each other.

> It is not something they often talk of: they know what they do is said to be wrong and yet certainly it appears to hurt no one ... Griffin [the father] hitting Jordan [the son] provides the penalty they don't want but know they probably deserve despite everything they endure, the monotony, the seclusion, the occasional misery of the farm. Denied the chance to do so as children, they are now both incapable of making outside friends: their closeness brings solace and companionship and seems only just.[6]

As Joanne McPherson argues,

> Their justification for what they both recognise as 'sinful' acts, evident in their expectation that something may 'come down from the sky to blight them', is the belief that their relationship is just reward for suffering the domineering and abusive tendencies of their father. Yet, there is no clear prohibition, no statement of taboo against incest within the limited social, familial and institutional frameworks that comprise the lives of the Willow children.[7]

It is a rare achievement, for an author for this readership, to do as Hartnett does and offer her readers space in which to form their own judgement on the siblings' incest, rather than resorting to easy labels.

Robin McKinley's *Deerskin* (1993) is unusual in a different way. Its early episodes of incestuous sexual abuse follow the standard pattern of father–daughter incest as laid out by Lukenbill. In this instance the father is grieving for his wife's death and chooses as her replacement his horrified daughter, as a result of her close physical resemblance to her mother. While her father's desires are explained thus, his surrender to them is in no way justified. Onlookers comment:

> That is probably the girl's doing. Every girl wants her father to herself. Look at her now, pretending to be so bashful, so shy that she cannot open her eyes, as if she did not like being the centre of attention. Look at her, half-swooning, making sure by her weakness that her father will stand close, will hold her, protect her, not take his eyes off her. She probably has a hundred little petting, luring ways with him when they're alone together.[8]

These comments, blaming the victim, are demonstrably wrong. Lissar's long-enduring distress at her father's brutal attentions is powerfully evoked, as is their physical cost in terms of bodily hurt and eventual miscarriage.

In Donkeyskin, *Deerskin*, Allerleirauh: The reality of the fairy tale,[9] Helen Pilinovsky argues that the queen, Lissar's mother, was abused by her own father, since he sought to repel her suitors and died of a broken heart once she married. Such material is strong fare even in young adult problem realist fiction. I am counting *Deerskin* as a work of fiction for both adults and young adults. It was originally marketed for adults but has been reviewed in a variety of school library journals and *The Booklist* as young adult fiction; Amelia Rutledge offers a brief discussion of its readership, saying, 'the novel demands mature empathy (but not beyond the scope of some readers in this group.)'[10]

It is not, however, the psychological and emotional depth of this book, disturbing though it is, that renders it unusual; indeed, its concern for exposing a patriarchal sexual economy is much the same as that of contemporary feminist scholars such as Stoltenberg. Rather, what distinguishes this novel is McKinley's choice to retell a fairy tale, sometimes known as 'Catskin', which has been almost entirely censored in the latter half of the twentieth century and beyond. In brief, it tells the story of a widowed king who selects his daughter to be his next wife. She agrees to the marriage on condition she receive several splendid dresses and a coat of many furs (or the hide of a gold-producing donkey in Perrault's version).[11] Then she flees, disguised in her coat, to take a lowly position as kitchen maid at the court of another king where, Cinderella-like, she eventually becomes his bride. As Tatar comments in *The Hard Facts of the Grimms' Fairy Tales*, among these tales 'Thousandfurs' is the only one which does not 'mask incestuous desire … Only in 'Thousandfurs' was a father permitted to stand as the active source of evil at home, with the consequence that the theme of incest was broached and pushed to its limits'.[12] For most retellers of the tales, such a theme was to be censored out of existence. A new literary category of full-length novels retelling fairy tales for young adults developed during the 1980s and 1990s.[13] Tales of incest have generally been avoided here also, in favour of a glut of amplifications and modernisations of 'Cinderella' and 'Beauty and the Beast'. Perhaps because her story would be unfamiliar to most of her readers, McKinley does not modernise her tale but retains the hierarchy of a royal court where the king's decree is law. The simple framework of a fairy tale gives all the more strength to her evocation of her heroine's psychological and physical distress.

Since the Second World War, fairy tales have been incessantly republished in the form of anthologies, picture story books and single-story illustrated books for younger readers. These tales most often derive from Perrault, the Grimm brothers and Andersen. Amongst this source material are two incest stories, Perrault's 'Peau d'Ane' (Donkeyskin) and the equivalent Grimm brothers' tale, 'Allerleirauh' (sometimes translated as 'Catskin', or the 'Coat of Many Furs', or similar terms). There are, to my knowledge, no collections of fairy tales for children published since the 1970s which contain either of these stories. There is one bowdlerised picture story book version, *Princess Furball*, in which the incestuous king is replaced by an ogre, not part of the family.

The Puffin Classics collection of *Grimms' Fairy Tales*, first published in Puffin Books for the child reader in 1948, contains a 'Cat-Skin', and Lore Segal and Randall Jarrell's 1973 collection, *The Juniper Tree*, contains a 'Many-Fur'. Apart from these, there is a censored version of 'Allerleirauh' available in the Dover facsimile edition of Andrew Lang's (c. 1892) *Green Fairy Book*. Here the king's desire to marry his daughter is transformed into respectable parental concern:

> he said to his councillors, 'I will marry my daughter to one of you, and she shall be queen, for she is exactly like her dead mother, and when I die her husband shall be king.'[14]

No contemporary collection of fairy tales for the child reader goes even this far. I can speak from personal experience, as the editor of several anthologies of literature for children, including the *Random House Children's Treasury* (1998). The publisher with whom I worked on all these books gave me instructions as to what could not be included in them; to my regret, 'Bluebeard', for instance, was ruled inadmissible by him because of its serial bride murders. Suitability for young children, in my publisher's opinion, meant minimal sexual reference of any kind apart from the obligatory courtship and happy-ever-after marriages that end a number of these tales. Incest was utterly inadmissible as a topic.

It was partly in reaction to censored collections like these that feminists produced such books as *The Virago Book of Fairy Tales*, including 'The Princess in the Suit of Leather', and *The Second Virago Book of Fairy Tales*, including 'Diirawic and her Incestuous Brother', a Sudanese story. These stories, edited by Angela Carter, for all their liveliness were not marketed for children. As its title indicates, nor was Terri Windling's 1995 anthology of fairy tales about child abuse, *The Armless Maiden: and Other Tales for Childhood's Survivors*. This collection includes Windling's own intertwining of 'Catskin' with a contemporary realist tale and Jane Yolen's brilliant and terrible variant on the same incest theme. Pilinovsky offers an extended discussion of these, along with McKinley's book, in her 'Donkeyskin, *Deerskin*, Allerleirauh: The reality of the fairy tale', commenting that all 'focus upon the reality of a number of issues which had been brushed over in previous versions, even those that most closely approached the taboo aspects'.[15]

Stories with a theme of incest are unlikely to be found within 'tween' fiction, since these books are marketed as dealing with far less controversial themes than young adult problem novels; but there is a cluster of picture story books and illustrated books for beginner readers that specifically address the topic of sexual abuse for didactic purposes. It is understandable that books on stranger danger should be made available to children at a time of transition from the (presumed) protection of the family to more independent life at and around a school, in contact with unfamiliar people in unfamiliar places. Such books, whether fiction or non-fiction, aim to define the rights of the young child, make clear what kinds of touch are inappropriate and set out strategies for the child to avoid situations of potential abuse and put an end to abuse that is occurring. There is no similar cluster of books dealing with incestuous abuse of the young child within the immediate family. To my knowledge, only two such picture story books have been published, both dealing with father–child incest, Barbara Behm and Ellen Anderson's 1999, *Tears of Joy* and Shannon Riggs and Jaime Zollar's *Not In Room 204* (2007).

It is easy to find reasons for this paucity of texts. For this age group, books are not going to be bought by the child but by older family members, teachers and librarians on their behalf. Incest is an emotionally charged subject and false accusations of incest can be hugely damaging to all concerned. Such considerations may have weighed with Wendy Smith-D'Arezzo and Susan Thompson when, having listed one book on incest in their survey of picture story books on 'topics of stress and abuse', they classify this, and only this, text as useful in the clinic but not in the classroom. Despite all these issues, such books can give incestuously abused children the knowledge that their situation is not unique, nor are they wicked. Reading about other abused children may give them the courage to speak out. As such, the fewness of such texts is regrettable.

So too is their handling of the problem. Smith-D'Arezzo and Thompson comment on *Tears of Joy*:

> [The young girl] tells her teacher at school and because she tells her teacher, she is relieved and happy again knowing that her teacher will help her. The happy ending is unrealistic and can offer false hope for children.[16]

Much the same could be said about *Not In Room 204*. The bulk of this picture story book's pages are devoted to establishing the classroom as a safe place with rules which the teacher easily and consistently enforces. The teacher's claim to her pupils that 'I know *exactly* what to do to help'[17] in cases of incest, suggests in this context that inappropriate touching by a family member can be dealt with as easily and promptly as a classroom fight or the theft of a chocolate. It takes no account of what a child is likely to endure in the way of police questioning, medical investigation, court proceedings, possible accusations of lying, probable family breakdown. Instead, it implies that only the teacher needs to take action ('I know exactly what to do' to resolve the problem), which is a promise all too frequently very distant from the truth. The choice made by author and illustrator to leave the issue at this point is understandable in that dealing with such likely outcomes as family disruption, disbelief on the part of the other parent and attempts to discredit the child might discourage any child reader who also suffers incestuous abuse from mentioning it. There is no obvious optimal path for a picture story book for younger readers to take with regard to this serious ethical issue.

So far in this discussion of post-war children's literature, I have been discussing books whose overt theme is incest as generally understood in Western culture. It is in the field of picture story books and illustrated books for younger readers that more complex treatments of incest can be found and where the boundaries of incest, as commonly understood, are challenged. A miniature example of this complexity can be located in Maurice Sendak's illustration to *The Juniper Tree*'s version of 'Catskin', 'Many-Fur'. From its placement at the end of the story, this illustration could be read as depicting the courtship dance of the young king with Many-Fur, dressed in her Cinderella-style finery, prior to discovering her identity and marrying her. Yet the king's intent glare, his hand across her belly and his grizzled beard all suggest that this illustration depicts a scene early in the tale where the incestuous father clutches at his reluctant daughter during their dance. The ambiguity as to which king is dancing with the princess points to a joyless interpretation of the story in which marriage is a manifestation of abusive patriarchal power, all bridegrooms taking on the role of the father as they take possession of the bride.

'Catskin' or 'Peau d'Ane' is an obvious choice for a contemporary writer or illustrator wishing to explore the theme of incest via the reworking of a traditional fairy tale. Much less obvious is the choice of 'Bluebeard', a tale which exists in many variants in English literature, as explored in Casie Hermansson's *Bluebeard: A Reader's Guide to the English Tradition* (2009). Hermansson's work does not include any contemporary reworkings of Bluebeard for a child audience, but one such work arguably exists, Gary Crew's *In My Father's Room* (2000). Bluebeard variants (apart from those which confuse the serial killer with Blackbeard the pirate) centre upon the discovery by Bluebeard's latest wife of her predecessors' bodies in her husband's secret chamber. A key figures significantly in the story, given to the wife with instructions not to use it, magically resistant to being cleaned once it has become stained with the dead wives' blood. It is a story that resonates, since Perrault's moralising version, with Eve's eating of the forbidden apple and Pandora's opening of the forbidden box. Combined with an incest theme, as in Crew and Scott's work, it raises the taboo topic of the child's participation in sexual intimacy with the father.

The complexities of *In My Father's Room* require close reading. At first glance, this Australian picture story book appears to carry a slight story-line about a child whose father never sticks to any of the hobbies that he enthusiastically takes up, until he begins to be very secretive about what he is doing in his room. The child explores the room while her parents are away and discovers that the father has been writing a story for her to receive as a birthday present. This story is quite bland in summary and may appear at first reading to be reassuring even to the point of sentimentality. It ends with a promise that the finished book will appear for the child's tenth birthday as a marker of the father's love for her and of his achievement in actually finishing a project. The pictures can be read as corresponding straightforwardly to the verbal text. Everything is explained, the father's secret work at night is disclosed as a harmless, loving activity and a confident prediction is made by the child narrator about a happy future. All of this is subverted, once the allusions to Bluebeard are recognised.

The child's name, 'Too Good', raises questions of interpretation. It is no ordinary, everyday name, but has the fairy-tale characteristic of impersonality, a name like 'Sleeping Beauty' or 'Snow White'. 'Too Good' implies the phrase, 'too good to be true', and raises the question of exactly what this child is too good for, especially as she does not seem to be extraordinarily virtuous. She takes advantage of her parents' absence to break into the secret room and spy on her father's secrets. This suggests a reading of her name as 'too good to be true', meaning 'not good at all'.

It appears that the father's secrecy is a recent phenomenon. Previously, it was well known that his downstairs room was the place where he stored his abandoned equipment, his telescope and train set and lacquer screen and beehives. Now, quite suddenly, 'he locked the door. I was watching from beneath the stairs and saw where he put the key'.[18] This locked room of the father's is reminiscent of Bluebeard's secret room. The secret in this case turns out to be a manuscript, not multiple murders, but the depiction of the manuscript is ominous. According to the verbal text, it is kept in a folder as a 'stack of cream paper, thick and stiff.'[19] The accompanying illustration shows not a cream sheet but a page of multi-coloured paper stained in black (presumably an ink splatter) and smeared rust-red, the colour of dried blood. The father's secret is thus simultaneously innocuous (a story for his daughter) and terrible (a secret involving the shedding of blood).

Allusions to the 'Bluebeard' story begin when the child becomes curious about what is hidden in her father's room to the point of stealing the key and opening the forbidden door. The account of her descent of the dark stairs and the squeak of the door opening invoke the conventions of horror, and though the illustrations reassure with their brightly lit stairs and room full of junk, there is a disconcerting element amidst the clutter, the two enormous items that common sense identifies as the father's gloves, discarded from some abandoned hobby, but that also bear an uncanny resemblance to severed hands, cut off well above the wrist. The room, then, may be a chamber of horrors masquerading as innocent.

Incestuous possibilities are hinted at in the depictions of the family house. The child lies in bed every night listening to her father walk along the hall and down the nineteen steps to his room after he has visited her bedroom and told her it is time to sleep. His secret room is directly under his daughter's bedroom. The layout of the house is quite odd. The child's bedroom is somewhat detached from the main body of the house, with its door and window opening onto an outside veranda whose steps lead down to the father's room. The book is quite clear that the father's secret night-time activities do not concern his wife, who is an insignificant figure in a narrative concerned with a father labouring secretly at night just under his daughter's bedroom in order to give her pleasure. Incest is strongly implied in the first visual representation of the girl's bed, with a wrinkled brownish bedspread, some of whose markings resemble naked human torsos lying across the bed. In the second illustration of this bed, with the child lying under the sheets, the wrinkled bedspread takes the form of a gigantic hand with fingers outstretched as if to grab her.

Several more details of this bedroom as depicted throughout the picture story book deserve scrutiny. The closed purse, massive torch and serpentine lamp-cord by the girl's bed, and the rocket ship design on one of her bedroom curtains, can be seen as sexually suggestive. The little purse is reminiscent of the little curved handle that fingers must enter and push at in order to discover the father's secret; the illustrations show fingers at work in this handle twice, little fingers for the daughter and big fingers for the father. The phallic implications of torch and lamp-cord, and the vaginal suggestions of purse and handle, make for a text saturated in sexual innuendo.

The mother also plays a part in this story, although she tends to be an onlooker rather than a participant. She is said to love her husband because he keeps replacing one half-finished project with another ('Variety is the spice of life,' was all my mother said. 'You can't help but love him for it.'[20]) The 'Bluebeard' connotations of the forbidden room render this a far from reassuring comment. The mother likes reading: 'She reads True Romance every chance she can get.'[21] 'True Romance' is as ambiguous a term as the child's name, Too Good. 'True' here really means 'lie' in the form of made-up romantic fiction with a guaranteed happy ending (another case of 'too good to be true'). This strong reading preference can be understood as compensation in the pages of a book for the romance that she does not share with her husband who is always turning his attention away to another project. If there is any 'romance' in this picture story book, it is arguably to be found in the implications of incestuous attraction between father and daughter.

What is most disturbing about such a reading is the child's eagerness to open the forbidden door and find out the father's secrets, placing her fingers just where her father's fingers have been (opening his desk drawer). This can be construed as a story of a powerful older male forcing his attentions on a reluctant child, not directly, by physical violence, but through the subtler coercion of parental inattentiveness. Of course, the child's discovery of her father's story, dedicated to her, reveals that her father is in reality far from inattentive to her. Hiding his story away in a drawer, in a locked room, functions in psychoanalytic terms as a metaphor for repression of his feelings; in a Freudian context, the choice of a desk drawer opened by two sets of fingers, those of father and daughter, is (so to speak) pregnant with the sexual implications of 'drawers' in their other meaning, as underwear.[22]

Too Good's first effort within the story to gain her father's attention is to mimic him by taking up a hobby of her own, creating a *papier-maché* head of her father, making creative use of the scraps left over from his unfinished projects. Suddenly, at the end of the book, the completed head loses its homemade, improvised quality and appears much more lifelike, with shiny brown eyes replacing the postage stamps that the child used as improvised eyes. This transformed head can be seen to function as a surrogate Dad, one who is never absent, always watching, always attentive. The head is constructed in Too Good's bedroom; it is unclear where it ends up, possibly on the mantelpiece of the living room, possibly presiding over the bedroom with its suggestively rumpled coverings.

The presence of this head raises the question of just who holds power at the end of the book. The *papier-maché* head dominates the space in which it is set, but it can be understood as representing the daughter's power, her ability to shape her father, to complete a project. Or is ultimate power in the hands of the father who, Too Good believes, will have finished his book in time to read it to her on her tenth birthday? Or is this another instance of something too good to be true? Perhaps the father's final power over his daughter is to disappoint her again with yet another unfinished project, for the story's last words are the child's voicing of a fervent hope that 'he'll cuddle up to me and begin. I just know that. I know that for sure.'[23] This insistence can be read as covering doubt. In such a reading, the Bluebeard-father's room contains no literally murdered bodies but evidence of a multitude of dead projects and the possibility of a murdered hope for his expectant daughter. 'Cuddling up' is a problematic act of intimacy whether the father is understood as hope-murderer or daughter-penetrator with those busy fingers of his.

The phrase, 'cuddling up', encapsulates the difficulty of differentiating clearly between loving, appropriate touch between family members and the incestuous touch of sexual desire. It is on this issue that psychoanalytic theory offers some of its most disquieting and controversial insights. Freud's essays on the child's psychosexual development, and in particular his proposal of the Oedipus complex (slightly different for the girl from the boy), has been justly criticised for laying all its emphasis on the child's psyche and disregarding the role of the parent. For Freud, the incestuous pull towards the opposite-gender parent is a normal and necessary part of the child's development towards being able to look beyond the family for a sexual partner.[24] The post-Freudian psychoanalytic theorist, Julia Kristeva, makes even larger claims than these. According to Kristeva's essay on *Romeo and Juliet* in *Tales of Love*, children never outgrow incestuous leanings towards their parents, predilections that date back to long before the Oedipus complex, to that oceanic blissful union with the mother in the womb, that loving bond with the ideal father in infancy:

> The child, male or female, hallucinates its merging with a nourishing-mother-and-ideal-father, in short a conglomeration that already condenses two into one … Man or woman, when he or she aspires to be a couple, the lover goes through the mirage of being the 'husband' or 'wife' or an ideal father … One soon notices, however, in the last instance (that is, if the couple truly becomes one, if it lasts), that each of the protagonists, he and she, has married, through the other, his or her mother.[25]

Incest in this sense is not a desire proper only to a defined period in a child's growing up; nor is it a prohibited set of sexual relationships with other family members. Instead, incest is always being practised psychologically whenever two people form a loving relationship. Also, it does not, as in the Freudian understanding of incest, require the child to choose the opposite-gender parent as object of desire.

From a Kristevan perspective, several well-loved picture story books take on quite a different meaning from the straightforward celebration of a parent's love for his or her child. Margaret Wise Brown and Clement Hurd's (1970) *The Runaway Bunny* is my earliest example. Here the simple, repetitive narrative tells of a young rabbit who imagines running away from his mother. She responds to each scenario with the promise that she will pursue him, whether by climbing a mountain or swinging from a trapeze or gardening. In Kristevan terms, this is an incestuous set of exchanges between mother and son, one in which the blissful safety of the womb is echoed in her promises that she will always find him. The story can also be read more harshly as a set of maternal threats to the small child daring to seek independence, if only in his imagination, as Claudia Pearson points out in her book, *Have A Carrot*. The double spread illustration following the crocus-gardener exchange shows mother rabbit in overalls and hat, bucket and hoe in her paws – but surely baskets are for collecting cut flowers and hoes for eradicating weeds and digging plants up by the roots. The safety she offers is thus the other face of death (a connection between womb and tomb that Freud points out in his essay on the uncanny and that Kristeva reiterates in her essay on *Romeo and Juliet*). A Freudian reading would go on to discuss castration at this point, but in the Kristevan context mother is seen as the inescapable power who ensures that, whatever the child's exploits in the world may turn out to be, he will always return to the womb-lair and to her ambiguous protection.

A second example of the Kristevan form of incestuous love, Sam McBratney and Anita Jeram's (1994) *Guess How Much I Love You*, uses two anthropomorphised hares to stand for human father and son. Here love is expressed in terms of quantity, again in a simple, repetitive pattern of exchanges (as is common in books to be read aloud to pre-literate children). Each time Little Nutbrown Hare makes a claim about the bigness of his love, Big Nutbrown Hare effortlessly caps it. Big Hare's arms can reach wider and higher, he can hop higher and his love reaches not only to the moon but also back again. As with *The Runaway Bunny*, all of this can be read somewhat sentimentally as an outpouring of love between parent and child. A less pleasant reading would note the regrettable moves to quantify love and the equally regrettable tendency for Big Hare to put down Little Hare as a lesser being, never able to love as much as the parent. As with *The Runaway Bunny*, if understood in Kristevan terms, the text suffocates: in the entire universe, there is no place beyond Big Hare's all-encompassing love. Little Hare's gestures of power and accomplishment are forever contained and judged in Big Hare's huge embrace. (Incidentally, the innocent pleasure so many take in these books depends on totally anthropomorphising the protagonists, not allowing any thoughts of the actual leporine mating and breeding behaviours.) As a model of ideal love, *Guess How Much I Love You* proposes another version of the all-encompassing, stifling, blissful womb where one partner is always the small child and one the powerful parent.

Equally equivocal is Robert Munsch and Sheila McGraw's 1986 *Love You Forever*. Like *The Runaway Bunny* and *Guess How Much I Love You*, this story has a patterned, repetitive narrative, going through the passage of time from a mother's giving birth to her son, to the son's wife giving birth to their daughter. At the start of the book, the mother sings to her new-born son:

> I'll love you forever,
> I'll like you for always,
> As long as I'm living
> my baby you'll be.

She creeps into the son's bedroom and sings the same song to him as he sleeps when he is two, nine, an adult. This extraordinary (and creepy) creeping cannot be motivated by the desire not to awaken her son for, in the illustration that accompanies the two-year-old version, the light from the passageway streams from the open door directly onto the child's face. Mother and son thus both claim the space of beloved infant and loving parent in the bedroom, no matter what their respective ages happen to be (though he does not appear to be a crawler), and the cycle is perpetuated when he sings the same song to his new-born daughter. The incestuous nature of this relationship, in a Kristevan reading, becomes very clear if its pattern is extrapolated to the point where an aging father climbs up the ladder and through the bedroom window of his adult, sleeping daughter. In her analysis of *Romeo and Juliet*, Kristeva generalises the nature of romantic love as always containing merger with both mother and ideal father:

> Whether heterosexual or homosexual, the couple is the utopic wager that paradise lost can be made lasting – but perhaps it is merely desired and truly never known? – the paradise of loving understanding between the child and its parents. The child, male or female, hallucinates its merging with a nourishing-mother-and-ideal-father, in short a conglomeration that already condenses two into one.[26]

For Kristeva, in this chapter, intimacy between two subjects always implicates four and entails incest. The dandled, sung-to person in Munsch's book may not have subject status due to their age or state of unconsciousness at the time, but the adult dandler and singer can be understood in the Kristevan sense as expressing incestuous desires on each occasion, the general flavour of creepiness becoming more obvious as the beloved becomes older.

Post-war depictions of incest in literature for children may be sparse, if incest is understood as prohibited sexual relations between family members; writers of didactic tales concerning sexual abuse may turn to the easier topic of stranger danger; but from a Kristevan viewpoint, a subtler form of incest pervades all literature that deals with loving relationships which involve at least one subject, from seemingly simple picture story books for pre-literature child listeners to the sublimities of Shakespeare. More generally, literature for children brings up in sharpest focus the difficult issues of suitability for the target audience and censorship. Given that individual children display great differences in maturity and that some child readers will have experienced or witnessed incest, it appears impossible to mount any all-encompassing argument in terms of suitability for the child reader. In my view, being informed and having some means of at least stating the problem to those duty-bound to intervene is preferable to suffering through ignorance, and the best of children's books on the topic of incest can help prevent and put an end to individual cases of incestuous abuse. On the other hand, those that blame the victim or those that offer false hope (however laudable their intentions) deserve to be censored. Finding an ethically just and compassionate way to treat this most difficult topic is a task that all writers and illustrators for children, dealing with the issue of incest, should take most seriously.

Notes

1. Brozo, William, *To Be A Boy, To Be A Reader* (International Reading Association, 2010).
2. See, for example, Chapter 2 of D. Halverson's *Writing Young Adult Fiction for Dummies* (Wiley Publishing, 2011).
3. See Kenneth Donelson and Alleen Nilsen, *Literature for Today's Young Adults* (Scott, Foresman and Co., 1980).
4. For the ongoing debate around 'Young adult' fiction see Jen Doll 'What does young adult mean?', *The Atlantic*, 19 April 2012, www.theatlantic.com/entertainment/archive/2012/04/what-does-young-adult-mean/329105/ (accessed 20 June 2017).
5. Bernard W. Lukenbill, 'Incestuous sexual abuse themes in contemporary adolescence: A cultural study', *New Review of Children's Literature and Librarianship* 5:1 (1999), p. 157.
6. Sonya Hartnett, *Sleeping Dogs* (Viking, 1995), p. 58.
7. Joanne McPherson, 'The abject and the Oedipal in Sonya Hartnett's *Sleeping Dogs*', *Papers* 9:3 (1999), p. 19.
8. Robin McKinley, *Deerskin* (Ace Books, 1993), p. 69.
9. See http://endicottstudio.typepad.com/articleslist/donkeyskin-deerskin-allerleirauh-the-reality-of-the-fairy-tale-by-helen-pilinovsky.html (accessed 19 June 2017).
10. Amelia Rutledge, 'Robin McKinley's *Deerskin*: Challenging narcissisms', *Marvels & Tales* 15:2 (2001), p. 170.
11. Charles Perrault, *Classic Fairy Tales of Charles Perrault* (Gill and Macmillan, 2012), p. 48.
12. Maria Tatar, *The Hard Fact of the Grimms' Fairy Tales* (Princeton University Press, 1987), p. 152.
13. Vanessa Joosen, *Critical and Creative Perspectives on Fairy Tales* (Wayne State Univeristy Press, 2011), p. 65.
14. Andrew Lang (ed.), *The Green Fairy Book* (Dover, 1965), p. 276.
15. Helen Pilinovsky, 'Donkeyskin, *Deerskin*, Allerleirauh: The reality of the fairy tale', *Journal of Mythic Arts* (2007), p. 2.
16. Wendy Smith-D'Arezzo and Susan Thompson, 'Topics of stress and abuse in picture books for children', *Children's Literature in Education* (2006), p. 340.
17. Shannon Riggs, *Not In Room 204* (Albert Whitman & Co., 2007).
18. Gary Crew, *In My Father's Room* (Hodder, 2000), p. 4.
19. *Ibid.*, p. 4.
20. *Ibid.*, p. 6.
21. *Ibid.*, p. 7.
22. https://en.oxforddictionaries.com/definition/drawer (accessed 17 July 2015).
23. Gary Crew, *In My Father's Room*, p. 31.
24. Freud formulated this view of the child's psychosexual development, which became known as the Oedipus complex, after rejecting the Seduction Theory which asserted a very different interpretation of incestuous desire.

25 Julia Kristeva, Leon Roudie, (trans.) *Tales of Love*, (Columbia University Press, 1987), p. 222.
26 *Ibid.*, pp. 222–3.

Bibliography

Fiction

Behm, Barbara, *Tears of Joy* (WayWord Publishing, 1999)
Brown, Margaret Wise, *The Runaway Bunny* (Harper and Row, 1970)
Carter, Angela (ed.), *The Virago Book of Fairy Tales* (Virago, 1991)
———. (ed.), *The Second Virago Book of Fairy Tales* (Virago, 1992)
Crew, Gary, *In My Father's Room* (Hodder, 2000)
Crutcher, Chris, *Chinese Handcuffs* (Greenwillow Press, 1989)
Grimm Brothers, *Grimms' Fairy Tales* (1823; Penguin, 1948)
Hartnett, Sonya, *Sleeping Dogs* (Viking, 1995)
Huck, Charlotte, *Princess Furball* (Mulberry Books, 1994)
Lanagan, Margo, *Tender Morsels* (Allen & Unwin, 2008)
Lang, Andrew (ed.), *The Green Fairy Book* (Dover, 1965)
McBratney, Sam, *Guess How Much I Love You* (Walker Books, 1994)
McKinley, Robin, *Deerskin* (Ace Books, 1993)
Munsch, Robert, *Love You Forever* (Firefly Books, 1986)
Perrault, Charles, *Classic Fairy Tales of Charles Perrault* (Gill and Macmillan, 2012)
Riggs, Shannon, *Not In Room 204* (Albert Whitman & Co., 2007)
Segal, Lore and Jarrell Randall, *The Juniper Tree and Other Tales from Grimm* (The Bodley Head, 1973)
Waldorf, Heather, *Leftovers* (Orca Publishing, 2009)

Non-fiction

Brozo, William, *To Be A Boy, To Be A Reader: Engaging Teen and Preteen Boys in Active Literacy.* (International Reading Association, 2010)
Donelson, Kenneth, and Alleen Nilsen, *Literature for Today's Young Adults* (Scott, Foresman and Co., 1980)
Halverson, D., *Writing Young Adult Fiction For Dummies* (Wiley Publishing, 2011)
Hermansson, Casie, *Bluebeard: A Reader's Guide to the English Tradition* (University Press of Mississippi, 2009)
Joosen, Vanessa, *Critical and Creative Perspectives on Fairy Tales: An Intertextual Dialogue between Fairy-Tale Scholarship and Postmodern Retellings* (Wayne State University Press, 2011)
Kristeva, Julia, Leon Roudiez (trans.) *Tales of Love*, (Columbia University Press, 1987)
Lukenbill, W. Bernard, 'Incestuous sexual abuse themes in contemporary adolescence: A cultural study', *New Review of Children's Literature and Librarianship* 5:1 (1999), pp. 151–67

McPherson, Joanne, 'The abject and the Oedipal in Sonya Hartnett's *Sleeping Dogs*', *Papers* 9:3 (1999), pp. 15–22

Masson, Jeffery, *The Assault on Truth: Freud's Suppression of the Seduction Theory* (Penguin, 1985)

Mills, Alice, *The Random House Children's Treasury* (Colour Library Direct, 1998)

Pearson, Claudia, *Have A Carrot: Oedipal Theory and Symbolism in Margaret Wise Brown's Runaway Bunny Trilogy* (Look Again Press, 2010)

Pilinovsky, Helen, 'Donkeyskin, *Deerskin*, Allerleirauh: The reality of the fairy tale', *Journal of Mythic Arts* (2007) http://endicottstudio.typepad.com/articleslist/donkeyskin-deerskin-allerleirauh-the-reality-of-the-fairy-tale-by-helen-pilinovsky.html (accessed 22 January 2018)

Rutledge, Amelia, 'Robin McKinley's *Deerskin*: Challenging narcissisms', *Marvels & Tales* 15:2 (2001), pp. 168–82

Smith-D'Arezzo, Wendy and Susan Thompson, 'Topics of stress and abuse in picture books for children', *Children's Literature in Education* 37 (2006), pp. 335–47

Stoltenberg, John, Christine Stark and Rebecca Whisnant (eds), *Pornography and International Human Rights* (Spinifex, 2004), pp. 400–9

Tatar, Maria, *The Hard Fact of the Grimms' Fairy Tales* (Princeton University Press, 1987)

Website

Doll, Jen, 'What does young adult mean?', *The Atlantic*, 19 April (2012), www.theatlantic.com/entertainment/archive/2012/04/what-does-young-adult-mean/329105/ (accessed 22 January 2018)

6

'[B]orn to make a real life, however it cracks your heart':[1] Creative women and daydreaming in Margo Lanagan's *Tender Morsels* (2008)

Emma V. Miller

Margo Lanagan's *Tender Morsels* has attracted equal amounts of praise and censure. In 2008 it was a finalist for the Shirley Jackson Award;[2] and in 2009 it was the winner of a World Fantasy Award for best novel, and a Michael L. Printz Honor Award for excellence,[3] as well as being a finalist for the Locus Award for Best Young Adult Book.[4] Yet, as a text marketed toward the category of reader known as Young Adult (YA) – which can mean a readership of as young as ten years old and upwards[5] – it has been severely criticised for containing circumstances too challenging and traumatic for child readers; and with incestuous sexual abuse and gang rape in the first few pages it is easy to see why that has been the case.[6] However, although Lanagan is well known as an author of books for children, she has always pushed against the boundaries of the definition of *acceptable* content for her readers. Interestingly though, this novel in particular has received an unprecedented degree of negative attention, with children's author, Anne Fine saying: 'If you look at online reviews, nearly all the parents think it is quite unsuitable. Many of the children loved the book but among the girls, a lot of them found it frightening or even repulsive.'[7] Yet criticism has not just come from worried parents and young readers. Feminist website, *Bitch Media* listed *Tender Morsels* as one of their one-hundred recommended 'Young Adult Books for the Feminist Reader' in January 2011, but by 1 February in the same year, the title had been removed. The reason for taking *Tender Morsels* off the list was given as: 'because of the way that the book validates (by failing to critique or discuss) characters who use rape as an act of vengeance'.[8] So it appears that it was not so much that the book contained these incidents, even for such a young readership, but the means of narrating them with which the website took exception. Yet not all of the attention was so negative, with Philip Pullman added his voice to the escalating debate saying, 'I don't think there should be areas that children's books can't deal with. Why should there be, given that children are likely to encounter much stronger subjects in real life …?'[9]

The novel, considered on its own literary merit, without the marketing tags, is shocking, certainly, but not prurient nor sensationalist, and, although no doubt challenging for many young readers, its consideration of fairy-tale themes and many of the ways it uses parallel universes, time travel and magic lend themselves to a strong feminist message. Indeed, the strengths of this text are built around the confrontation of civilisation, through Freudian and Lacanian psychoanalytic interpretations of female sexuality, expression, language and creativity. It consistently challenges what it means to be real – both in terms of a sexualised and gendered personal identity – but also within the discourses of a gendered universe. In this novel, the only entirely safe place for women is a dream world that exists through the heroine's imagination. Through magical intervention Liga – who conceived her eldest child after years of abuse at the hands of her own father, and her youngest after a gang rape by local boys – gains the privilege of living in this world for a number of years with her two children. Conversely, the reality is an environment where women cannot move freely without fear of, at the very least censure, and at the most, horrific sexual humiliation. By juxtaposing dominant psychoanalytic theories of literary criticism, with the fairy-tale retellings by feminist authors from the 1970s to the present time, as well as key second-wave feminist texts like Simone de Beauvoir's *The Second Sex* (1949) and Susan Brownmiller's *Against Our Will* (1975), this novel can be seen not only to challenge the prevalence of a 'real' feminism in our literary criticism, but also in the Western world at large.

Which craft?

This is not the first time that Lanagan has addressed such disturbing sexual material. *Touching Earth Lightly*, which was published by Allen and Unwin's children's imprint, Little Arc in 1995, depicts Janey, who throughout her adolescence is sexually abused by both her father and her brother. She goes on to repeatedly engage in casual sexual encounters with strangers, and when she finally leaves home she is eventually attacked and murdered by a group of boys in a disused parking lot. Yet despite its challenging content, *Touching Earth Lightly* has not received the kind of critical attention that *Tender Morsels* has, and this may be precisely because *Tender Morsels* has also attracted a much greater positive response. Therefore, it may simply be that the later book's content is perceived as more dangerous *because* it is more widely known, and will therefore affect more readers. Yet, and the reasoning of *Bitch Media* suggests that this may be the way it is viewed by a number of its critics, it could be viewed as *both* more popular and more dangerous *because* of the way it is narrated.

Touching Earth Lightly is set in a contemporary city in the known world; *Tender Morsels*, however, is a retelling of the fairy tale of 'Snow White and Rose Red', and is set in a fantasy locale, out of time, using magic realism. The former is told through the eyes of Janey's best friend who suspects the extent of the abuse Janey suffers but struggles to face the reality of it. Conversely, *Tender Morsels* may be located in a fantasy world, but the abuse is described from the viewpoint of the sufferer, Liga, and although Lanagan makes some concessions to the age of her readers by not naming rape, abortion or miscarriage, the disturbing events Liga experiences are all there in the text if you know how to interpret them.

Tender Morsels therefore, reads more like the genre of trauma fiction, as described by Anne Whitehead with reference to Geoffrey Hartman's essay, 'On Traumatic Studies and Literary Studies' (1995):

> trauma fiction problematises its own formal properties, at the levels of reference (what relation does the narrative bear to reality?), subjectivity (can the traumatised subject still say 'I' in a way that has meaning?) and story (does the character control the 'plot', or is he or she controlled by it?). Trauma fiction often demands of the reader a suspension of disbelief and novelists frequently draw on the supernatural ... Alternatively, the realist novel is troubled by coincidences and fantastic elements which lurk just beneath the surface ... These disruptions of the real signal to the reader that there has been a rupture of the symbolic order. The real can no longer appear directly or be expressed in a conventional realist mode.[10]

Yet, there are layers of what is real, and what reality constitutes. Whitehead and Hartman are referring to 'the real' here to mean reality, i.e. the known physical world, but Whitehead also discusses Michael Rothberg's theory of 'traumatic realism',[11] which focuses on literature as a means to explore responses to and understandings of the Holocaust. While the topic of Rothberg's discussion is clearly distinct from the subject of this chapter, his assessment of trauma as something that exists within the realms of the known world and yet is simultaneously in extremis to it, resonates with this argument. Rothberg writes that: 'Beyond this deadlock between the "abyss" and the banality of evil, it is in the nonreductive articulation of the extreme and the everyday that I find the possibility for a reworking of realism under the sign of trauma.'[12] The real may also incorporate the powerful nature of fantasy in so far as it affects the lived experience, and it may also refer to the dread of the Lacanian '*real*',[13] 'the essential object which isn't an object any longer, but this something faced with which all words cease and all categories fail, the object of anxiety *par excellence*'.[14] It is the 'unassimilable' nature of the *real* which is for Lacan what renders it traumatic.[15] Lanagan plays with these concepts in an intelligent way, and by the definition given by Whitehead above, *Tender Morsels* is a work of trauma fiction, but it does not read like some of the more well-known examples of this genre. For instance Lanagan does not attempt to investigate and reflect the psyche of trauma sufferers in the way that a writer like Toni Morrison does in the very adult, *Beloved* (1981).[16] For Lanagan's readership something quite different is required, making allowances for not only different stages of reading ability, but of emotional intelligence, and many would say, as *Bitch Media* have done, that YA authors should avoid anything of a potentially 'triggering nature'; and perhaps even guide their readers over how to react to the horrific events portrayed.[17] Lanagan does make some concessions to her readership's special circumstances, but at no point does she tell them how to react.

This is not a dogmatic text, and it is educational only insofar as any work of art with a social dimension may be educational. It does, as Whitehead describes, 'problematise its own formal properties', including the very nature of reality, and fictional reality, the Lacanian *real*, and realism versus the known world. Nothing is safe in this text, it is generically unstable and neither the reader nor the central protagonists know the limits of their own personhood or their context (geographically or historically). Like many other trauma narrators she uses the supernatural to speak about events that are still largely unspeakable. However, unlike Morrison's ghost baby in *Beloved* – which is specific to the world of *her* fiction – Lanagan rewrites a fairy tale that is popularly viewed as a children's story, that of 'Snow White and Rose Red', a circumstance that causes further complications.

Lanagan builds upon the bones of the tale in its well-known form as collected by the Grimm Brothers and translated as *Children's and Household Tales* (first published 1812 as *Kinder und Hausmärchen* and thereafter revised and republished numerous times). She not only suggests a critical reading of the Grimms' tale in *Tender Morsels*, but expands it in new and surprising ways. She introduces human violence exacted on other innocent individuals, something that is not evidenced in the Grimms' version, whilst imbuing the tale with the kind of emotional intensity that makes both the existing events of the tale, and the additional ones, more affecting than they were in the simplistic episodic prose of the fairy tale. The violence, however, should perhaps not come as such a shock. Until the Brothers Grimm began to collect and amend a collection of fairy tales for a child readership, fairy tales, which derive from the oral folk-tale tradition, were not intended for an age-specific readership, and many earlier variants contain brutal and disturbing events.[18] Indeed, while Lanagan's novel uses the story of 'Snow White and Rose Red', its narrative discourse draws upon the fairy-tale tradition much more broadly. Many of these earlier folk tales contained crude humour and overt sexual content,[19] and while they may have served as warnings to adults and children alike, of child abuse, rape, cannibalistic husbands and violent wives, they did not universally aspire to what the Grimms described rather hopefully as, 'an education manual'.[20] 'Snow White and Rose Red' is not the only tale that is evidenced throughout Lanagan's novel, but rather she has drawn upon other less familiar variants of the now largely anaesthetised fairy-tale tradition.

The men that accidentally stumble into Liga's heaven are transformed into bears, and although they never revert to their human form whilst they are in her heaven, Liga and her daughters nevertheless recognise a difference between these bears and those that they are used to seeing in the surrounding woodland. First Liga, and then her eldest daughter, Branza, when she reaches her teenage years, recognise that these men-bears require different treatment too. Liga develops a romantic attachment to the first bear, which is strong enough in its intensity to stay with her many years later when she meets the man, Davit Ramstrong, in reality. Liga is also concerned when her quickly maturing daughters play with the second bear, known in his human form as Teasel Wurledge, worrying that he 'luxuriate[s] too much in the game' and that it is '[i]mproper'.[21]

Branza's experience with the second man-bear is different because he has a more promiscuous and unkind character both in his bear form and his human state. Although he never succeeds in having intercourse with her he does attempt to undress her and after he has seen her witness his 'coupling' with a female bear, '[h]e plunged towards her – the ridiculous pipe-thing, the nozzle of him waggling under his belly, and there was no mistaking that he desired to have of Branza in just the manner he had of the she-bear'.[22] It is Teasel though, not Davit that also at one point assumes the role of rescuer when, in a parallel of the event in 'Snow White and Rose Red', he devours the greedy and bad mannered, 'little man',[23] Mister Dought. In the fairy tale the bear secures the hand of one of the daughters by this act, but in *Tender Morsels* it is the first bear, kind, Davit, who in his human form eventually marries Branza, and despite aspiring to the role of rescuer, Teasel Wurledge is a sexual threat in both forms. As a man, alone with the unworldly Branza, he threatens: "'you will have me, Branza Cotting'".[24] The romantic lead of the original fairy tale then appears to have been split into two, as many things in this narrative are: the world in this novel is divided into an almost heavenly dream and an earthly reality, in other words, between fantasy and reality; and the extremes of traditional female heroism are split between the two girls (Branza is for the most part of the narrative associated with peace and docility, Urdda, with intelligence and adventurous bravery). Yet these divisions are not as straightforward as they first seem.

The first bear, Davit, is not entirely unthreatening, although he is presented as a better man to Teasel. Because of the time difference between the heaven and reality, when Branza and Liga re-enter reality they are ten years older than they ought to be, and instead of Davit Ramstrong proposing marriage to the mother whom he fell in love with as a bear, he proposes to her daughter, who treated him almost like a father. The incest motif then is repeated, but in a more subtle and socially acceptable way. That both men are depicted as bears suggests that they are *both* potentially dangerous, but appreciating the many faces of danger is necessarily convoluted and these hybrid creatures represent both the wild strength and instinctual desire present in every man, as well as the potential for kindness and intelligence in the unfamiliar or the apparently uncivilised.

According to Marina Warner, in medieval times, the bear was 'the strongest and heaviest of animals in the Western forests' and 'an emblem of feudal heraldry'.[25] The feudal system in Europe was a patriarchal hierarchical arrangement whereby the majority of the population were dependent upon a relatively small number of wealthy landowners; a structure often maintained through brute force.[26] Warner states that Saint Augustine had 'likened both the bear and the lion to the Devil', and 'the bear figures as the totem of the wild man, the dweller in the untamed forest, all natural appetite and ferocity … The bear was called "the beast that walks like a man". Tales of women ravished by bears continued until the present century, possibly contributing to the identification of the fairy tale Beast with bears above all.'[27] W.J. Thomas Mitchell writes that, 'Animals stand for all forms of social otherness: race, class and gender, are frequently figured in images of subhuman brutishness, bestial appetite, and mechanical servility'.[28] The bear then simultaneously represents the power of the patriarchal feudal system but also perversely, the perceived threat of the Other to that very social order. By depicting a man-bear, Lanagan implies that there is no difference between the two – one being can be both familiar and Other, a consideration further highlighted by the fact that the men are dressed in bear costumes in their own town before they pass accidentally through into Liga's heaven and become actual bears. Interestingly, it is an honour to be selected to wear these costumes, as part of an ancient feast day where the chosen men perform the part of an aggressive animal for the women of the town.

However, it is not just the men in this novel, nor those in the folk and fairy-tale tradition, who display bestial traits. The bear in a tale of incest, such as this, also refers to a group of tales, which include partial or complete metamorphoses by the heroine to escape a sexual threat or to fight back against one.[29] Examples include: Charles Perrault's 'Donkey-Skin', the Grimms' 'Allerleirauh' ('All Fur') and 'L'Orsa' ('The Bear') by Giambattista Basile. 'The Bear' is the closest parallel to Lanagan's tale, which tells of a father determined to take his daughter, Preziosa, as his wife, saying to her: "'Lower your voice, and keep your tongue quiet! We shall tie the marriage knot this very night. Otherwise, your ear will be the biggest piece left of you!'"[30] In desperation she accepts the assistance of an old woman who offers her a stick to put in her mouth whenever her father approaches her. The stick transforms her into a bear and enables her escape. The similarities between 'The She-Bear' and *Tender Morsels* are evident. Liga's father refers to her as a 'wife',[31] and although the witch or 'mudwife',[32] Annie, does not initially help her, but provides her father with potions to terminate her pregnancies, it is Annie's anger at his treatment of Liga that, it is indicated, causes his death. Magical intervention, either from Annie or from the still unborn magical child Urdda, also finally secures Liga's escape from reality and into her heaven after she has been raped by the group of local boys. In a later incident Branza escapes the imminent threat of a similar group of boys in the actual world by behaving in an animal-like fashion. Interestingly, considering that Perrault's 'Donkey-Skin' is also a tale of attempted sexual abuse, Branza is trying to defend a donkey that is being whipped when the boys descend on her:

> When she tried to see her way, the rows of their teeth and eyes bobbed below the roofs and the window-shutters ... Their noises swam in her head: bumpings of bodies and cooing voices and slapping feet. If only Wolf were beside her now, his growl bubbled in her throat ... Branza bared her teeth ... She barked, sudden and deep. She bit at the air, right close to the ones in front of her ... She was full of wolf-teeth, wolf love of herself, wolf-rage on her behalf. She took the boy's head in hands in her two hands and bent to him among the others' hoots and whistles, and she bit his cheek hard.[33]

Up until this point Branza has always been the gentler and more submissive of the two sisters, her relationship with the world is described thus: 'Branza sat in her patience, like a rock lodged in a stream-bed, and the frail animals came to her. It was gratifying that there were creatures smaller and frailer and quieter than herself, the quietest and most timid of all her family.'[34] Both sisters struggle to learn how they are expected to act differently when away from Liga's heaven, but Branza, who is a woman in her twenties before she leaves the heaven, and who is the least adventurous of the siblings, finds it particularly difficult to comprehend what the Ramstrong family mean when they caution her, "'you must go out with at least another girl, if not a grown woman is better'".[35] Mrs Ramstrong states that if they leave the house alone, they will be subject to taunts of "'bold and a trollop. You might get things thrown at you, you know'", she says, before going on to explain: "'You would be asking for that.'"[36]

The Ramstrongs' description represents what Lacan calls 'the symbolic order', the social and cultural expectations which modify the behaviour of the individual, and are expressed both through language and action.[37] Once Liga's family have left her heaven, they are obliged to accept that they are subject to the gaze of Lacan's Other, which is the constant awareness of this cultural and social order. As such the movement from heaven to reality seems to mimic the process of the child as it moves past Lacan's mirror stage. This theory details how the human infant initially sees the reflection of itself as a whole and unified image (a '*Gestalt*'),[38] and then it eventually becomes aware of its place in the symbolic order, as someone viewed by the Other and therefore subject to the Other's gaze, as Merleau-Ponty elaborates:

> Thus for him, it is a problem first of understanding that the visual image of his body which he sees over there in the mirror is not himself since he is not in the mirror but here, where he feels himself; and second, he must understand that, not being located there in the mirror, but rather where he feels himself introceptively, he can nonetheless be seen by an external witness *at the very place at which he feels himself to be* with the same visual appearance that he has from the mirror.[39]

In his seminar, *The Psychoses*, Lacan writes: 'While the image equally plays a capital role in our domain [a role dominant, although not absolute, during the mirror stage], this role is completely taken up and caught up within, remoulded and reanimated by the symbolic order. The image is always more or less integrated into this order'.[40] The child appears to move from the imaginary to the symbolic, from images and daydreams of unity to the awareness of language, structure and law. This is similar to what appears to happen to Branza and Urdda who move from a place with no apparent external social jurisdiction, except that imagined by Liga, to one where they are obliged to become aware of the symbolic. Yet, although this is partly true, Liga's heaven is not entirely separate from the symbolic order, it is a response to it and therefore, although Branza does not know how to conduct herself in the actual world, she is not entirely ignorant of the symbolic order. She has been exposed to both language and narrative through the years by listening to her mother's stories, and crucially, because of Liga's pre-heaven experiences, she is brought up aware of some of the discourses pertaining to a patriarchal society.

Branza, however, is resistant to acknowledging her part in the ideological framework until the incident when she is confronted by the gang of boys. The description shows how, threatened by human beings who are behaving as animals, their humanity fragmented in Branza's vision, she responds in kind, fighting violently and attempting to destroy the symbolic structure that allows her to be assaulted. Branza recognises these men as primitive beings capable of committing atrocities that are not civilised, but are nevertheless known to occur, and are thus part of the actual but unspoken symbolic order. She is constantly being reminded that it is risky in this world for women to be without male protection, although the nature of the danger is never made explicit, with her sister saying, '[i]t isn't safe, a woman alone'.[41] The nature of the symbolic order is enforced by the fairy-tale realm of which Branza is a part, and Lanagan has commented that in rewriting 'Snow White and Rose Red', she was affected by how the Grimms' version suggested that, 'women will be rewarded for putting up with men's unrelentingly appalling behaviour ... Great harm, I wanted to assert, can come to women when they're isolated from society and not taught to stand up for themselves'.[42]

This novel draws upon a distinctly second wave feminist discourse and echoes of Lanagan's purpose can be identified in Simone de Beauvoir's polemic, *The Second Sex* (1949) as well as Susan Brownmiller's *Against Our Will* (1975). Beauvoir writes of the young female:

> She learns that to be happy she must be loved; to be loved, she must await love's coming. Woman is the Sleeping Beauty, Cinderella, Snow White, she who receives and submits. In song and story, the young man is seen departing adventurously in search of woman; he slays the dragon, he battles giants; she is locked up in a tower, a palace, a garden, a cave, she is chained to a rock, a captive, sound asleep: she waits.[43]

From thirteen years of age to fifteen Liga is forbidden by her father from going into town and so she lives in isolation, fearing that 'she must smell of Da's handling somehow, or betray it in the way she moved, in her face; it must leak out of her eyes. That was why, she thought, Da had kept her from the town lately'.[44] He tricks her into having agonising abortions and when she experiences a stillbirth he says, "'don't imagine this is anything more than you bleed out every month'", and he is described as 'clawing for it, the child held like waste meat'.[45] Nobody interrupts their existence, even though Liga's father is well known in the town, and the woman that sells him the concoctions that cause Liga to go into premature labour, Annie Bywell, is sure he is 'filling up' his 'daughter with unwanted kin'.[46] As an adult, Liga will still not seek criminal and social justice because she fears she will not be believed as the victim of her father's assault, but rather that people will view her as complicit, saying:

> But what if people should recognize her? What if true-world people – a stab of sick horror shook her – should recognize in Branza and Urdda not only their mam but their different fathers? Liga might be unworldly, but she knew, by Da's anxiety for concealment all that time ago as well as by the wrongness written deep in her body that a bab got by one's da was not a thing the true world would forgive.[47]

Susan Brownmiller whose groundbreaking text, *Against Our Will* was published in 1975 and described rape as a crime of power not sex, challenges Liga's father's cry that '*I cannot help myself ... A man must do it* [have sex] *or he will go mad*' [italics in the original].[48] Brownmiller describes: 'The unholy silence that shrouds the interfamily sexual abuse of children and prevents a realistic appraisal of its true incidence', as well as identifying the foundation of such abuse as, 'rooted in the same patriarchal philosophy of sexual private property that shaped and determined historic male attitudes toward rape. For if woman was man's original corporeal property, then children were, and are, a wholly owned subsidiary'.[49] Liga's father clearly views her as his to do as he pleases with, and the children that are born as a result of his sexual appetite are nothing more than unavoidable and irritating 'waste' by-products that must be destroyed.[50]

However, by recognising that the threat of sexual violence is part of the symbolic order, Branza, unlike her mother, escapes the ideology that attempts to ensnare her by expecting her to respond as a victim and succumb to the advances of the gang of boys. Instead she aims to realise her own desire by fighting back and regaining control. That Branza is later arrested indicates just how deeply embedded in the symbolic realm of law and social order are the gendered roles of victim and aggressor in this novel. Liga's other daughter, Urdda, who has, unknown to her, strong magical powers, inadvertently avenges her mother, by creating cloth men who, it is suggested, abuse Liga's attackers in a similar manner to that which they chose to originally hurt Liga. Urdda, unlike Branza, is not obviously associated with the attack, as she is not directly threatened by these men and nor is she aware of the extent of her abilities when enraged. Her actions are consequently not subjected to the socially agreed system of punishment. Yet, like Branza, she shows the men that she will not meekly accept their behaviour and she too becomes animal-like in her anger, using violence instinctively. 'This was too great a pain, too monstrous a series of injuries. It lumped in the past like … like a bear on a hearthrug, impossible to ignore. But the lump was not as big as a bear; it was only as big as an Urdda.'[51] Urdda, 'practical, true-worldly Urdda',[52] is shown throughout the novel to be have a greater awareness of the symbolic order within which she exists than her family, a symbolic order that empowers the strong to use sex as a weapon, and it is this awareness – so deeply ingrained in her psyche that she does not fully appreciate her own culpability until it is too late – that inspires her revenge.

Through her actions at this point she is shown to be just as dangerous as the original offenders were, similarly exacting terrible crimes and avoiding social censure. The boys who raped her mother have since become accepted men of the community, who 'moved and lived, entirely free'.[53] Urdda's actions and their lack of immediate repercussions when compared with the response to her sister's wolfish defence, expose a hidden system unacknowledged by the governing law, a primitive 'survival of the fittest'[54] regime, that enables the strong and the powerful to dominate others, but disadvantages the majority of women and children who have no recourse to magic to redress the balance of power. Liga receives no legal justice for the sexual attacks she experiences both at the hands of her father and the townsmen, and at fifteen she considers suicide and infanticide as a consequence. When Urdda commits her crimes though, she is not yet an adult and is depicted by Lanagan as still vulnerable even in the midst of this new horror, her anger operating through her magic while she sleeps, not aware of what she is capable of until she sees the evidence, and '[s]hakingly' acknowledges, "'I don't know what I did.'"[55]

The masculine 'wild' identity of the trope of the bear, and its association with 'ravishing' women,[56] similarly suggests that Basile's Preziosa may not just look like a beast, but that she also has the capacity to act like one. The stick she puts in her mouth can be read as a phallus, destabilising the gendering of expectations of behaviour in the tale and suggesting that like Urdda, she has the potential to be just as much a sexual threat to her father as he may become to her. Unlike the Classical metamorphoses of Ovid's protagonists Daphne and Philomela, who are subjected to unwanted sexual attentions and are subsequently transformed indefinitely, these temporary fairy-tale transformations make the women stronger and better able to cope with their banishment, even if they appear to be degraded by their a bestial form. When she loses her baby Liga is described as 'an animal in the snow, tearing herself to pieces with the wrongness of everything'. She reasons that 'she had fallen as low as she could from the life she had before Mam died ... out of town, out of safety', and indicates that her animal-like state is a result of being exiled from society, but it is also this metamorphosis that seems to help her. As '[a]t first her knees would not unbend, so she tipped herself forward onto her front ... paws, they felt like, her front claws'.[57] It is these 'paws' and 'claws' that aid her to extract herself from the snow and survive.

Like Liga who determines to 'sleep in a forest place where he [her father] could not find her',[58] the Grimms' Allerleirauh also seeks refuge from the threat of her father's attentions by hiding in the forest in a hollow tree, and in 'Donkey-Skin' the princess, whose 'face was made ugly by dirt', is described in her disguise as 'a creature' who 'smelled'. As Maria Tatar writes: '[t]hese fairy tale outcasts live like animals, sleeping in woodland sanctuaries and foraging for food'.[59] Yet, it is these very transformations that mean they can escape, but only for a finite amount of time. If they want to be re-assimilated into society they must embrace the confinements of civilisation. Preziosa maintains her bear-form when she lives in the forest, only removing the 'stick' and being transformed into a human female, when she is treated kindly by a prince whom she believes, will "'[t]ake care of my honour'",[60] and she thus consents to be his wife, an act that sees her once again re-assimilated into the gendered expectations of the court. Similarly, Liga must assume a new identity with a false name, a fiction of a deceased husband and a marketable (and traditionally female) skill as a fine seamstress before she can once again be subsumed into the society she was at first refused access to by her father, and later bullied by a gang of men into leaving.

The Real

As for Liga the experience of abuse removes these fairy-tale characters from the known symbolic realm, and they are consequently doubly threatened: by the possibility of a repetition of the trauma already experienced, and also of falling altogether outside of the discourses they know into the abyss of nothing that is Jacques Lacan's theory of 'The *Real*'. As Sean Homer argues, 'For Lacan, our reality consists of symbols and the process of signification. Therefore, what we call reality is associated with the symbolic order or "social reality." The *real* is the unknown that persists at the limit of this socio-symbolic universe and is in constant tension with it' [italics mine].[61] Lacan came to believe that the *real* 'does not exist, as existence is a product of thought and language and the real precedes language. The *real* is "that which resists symbolization absolutely"'. It is though, 'opposed to both the imaginary and the symbolic'.[62] Homer describes how:

> Psychic trauma arises from the confrontation between external stimulus and the subjects' inability to understand and master these excitations …
>
> The idea of trauma implies that there is a certain blockage or fixation in the process of signification … What Lacan adds to the Freudian conception is the notion that trauma is *real* insofar as it remains unsymbolizable and is a permanent dislocation at the heart of the subject. The experience of trauma also reveals how the real can never be completely absorbed into the symbolic, into social reality.[63]

This is the threat implicit in Shakespeare's *King Lear*, a play which Alan Dundes and Maria Tatar have described as a retelling of 'Love Like Salt',[64] a tale which, like 'All Fur' and 'Donkey-Skin', 'belongs to a major form of the Cinderella cycle, a folk tale whose normal form contains an overt paternal demand for an incestuous relationship with a daughter'.[65] In 'Love Like Salt' a king presents a love test to his daughter,[66] when she, like Cordelia, does not meet his verbal or emotional expectations, but states she loves him as much as salt, he casts her out of his kingdom.[67] Similarly, Cordelia answers Lear's demand for a description of her devotion with the word, 'Nothing', choosing to love her father, 'according to her bond, no more, no less',[68] and in doing so she also, perhaps unwittingly, chooses her exile. By saying, 'Nothing' she indicates the impossibility of articulating her experience. Her words, 'Unhappy that I am, I cannot heave/my heart into my mouth', may be read as either that she is unhappy she cannot articulate her devotion or that she cannot articulate her unhappiness.[69] Indeed, many have speculated whether the incest Lear refers to when raving upon the heath in Act 3, Scene

3 might refer to incest within the royal family.[70] In the same speech he refers to 'undivulged crimes, / Unwhipped of justice' and acknowledges his own capacity for 'sinning'.[71] Indeed, Dundes has drawn attention to Lear's hope that he will 'die bravely, like a smug bridegroom' when finally reunited with Cordelia.[72] *King Lear* has also been likened to other variants of this group of fairy tales and parallels can be seen between Cordelia and their female protagonists. These heroines, like Liga, rely upon their fathers for social inclusion and the constant threat of expulsion from the family unit if they disobey or displease means that they continue to teeter on the edge of the *real*. The difficulty in articulating their stories, partly because they fear they will not be believed, compounds the danger. Liga describes how her father refused to allow her into society, and how she has internalised the guilt of being involved in incest however innocently, to believe that she will also be despised if the truth should be revealed.

This is why it is imperative that the novel is narrated with the focus on female experience – first Liga's and later that of her daughters – to make it believable through their telling. Yet, historically, storytellers in general have been viewed as untrustworthy, with the female storyteller in particular being associated with a frivolous tale devoid of truth. As Elaine Showalter argues, regarding the Victorian period, the connection of realism with literary ability was claimed by a male-dominated literary profession in a time where the up-and-coming female writers generally had a very different, and ultimately inferior, education to their male rivals, both in terms of formal education and in terms of life experience.

> [T]he doctrine of realism made accuracy of detail essential for any novelist; Kenneth Graham, in *English Criticism of the Novel (1865–1900)*, says that during this period "critics are always at their most scathing when they discover a factual error. Detailed verisimilitude is demanded, and any offenses against it are considered fatal to the work: reviews abound with triumphant discoveries of minute inaccuracies."… Thus aspiring women writers struggled to educate themselves against tremendous financial odds.[73]

Angela Carter comments on the gender distinction made between believable and non-believable tales with reference to the fairy tale and the fable, saying, 'there exists a European convention of an archetypal female storyteller … an old woman sitting by the fireside, spinning – literally "spinning a yarn"'.[74] However, when this cultural appraisal of the female storyteller as, at best creative with the truth, and at worst, guilty of deceit is associated with tales of rape and incest it becomes an increasingly disturbing phenomenon. Lanagan draws these considerations together in Liga, who becomes both a skilled seamstress and a fine storyteller, but who feels unable to tell her own tale. Carter's description of 'spinning a yarn' is here pertinent, when we think of the tale of Ovid's Philomela in *The Metamorphoses*, who is abducted by her brother-in-law, Tereus, with the express intention of raping her, and when she threatens to expose his crime, he cuts out her tongue so she cannot verbalise her testimony. Instead, she chooses to weave a pictorial depiction of her story and sends it secretly to her sister.

The connections here between Philomela's circumstances and that of Liga's are highlighted when we consider that Tereus is aroused by his sister-in-law's affection for her father and he thinks: 'would he were / Himself her father! Nor would his sin be less!'[75] Furthermore, Philomela's father, says to Tereus, "'I beseech you … To guard her with a father's love'",[76] and the abuse eventually takes place as Liga's does, in 'a cabin in the woods, remote / And hidden away among dark ancient trees'.[77] Once again, as in the fairy tales considered in this chapter, both victim and attacker are likened to animals at the point of the sexual abuse (although in Ovid's tale their eventual transformation is of a different kind). Philomela, we are told, 'shivered like a little frightened lamb, / Mauled by a grizzled wolf'".[78] Interestingly, when her sister, Procne, receives the woven testimony, she too is unable to speak of it, this time because 'anguish locked / Her lips' and 'Her tongue could find no speech to match / Her outraged anger'.[79] Here the tale, passed from woman to woman *is* believed, just as Liga's story is eventually given credence by Urdda and the Mudwife, Annie. Yet once again, the women seek violent revenge, and as Urdda exacted a like-for-like vengeance on her mother's attackers, so Procne desires to "'pluck his tongue out, cut away those parts / That stole your honour'",[80] although ultimately she does what Liga is saved from doing, and commits infanticide.

Once upon a time…

Yet, despite the many connections between Lanagan's novel and these older tales, it is the way she weaves the tales together, juxtaposing them, and presenting them in narrative, in short, the artistry of storytelling, that Lanagan adopts which makes her approach new, and the manipulation of time is an essential component of her approach. Time is a central concern because it has been stated that traumatic events can have a disruptive temporal effect on an individual. As Irene Kacandes explains: 'Severe or prolonged stress can affect the hippocampal localisation system (which normally allows memories to be placed in their proper context in time and place)'.[81] The familiar beginning, middle and end that Aristotle indicated a preference for in his *Poetics*,[82] and which seems to reflect the human journey from birth to death, is not the psychological experience of those with post-traumatic stress disorders (PTSDs). Furthermore as Bessel van der Kolk and Onno van der Hart assert: 'Traumatic memory is not adaptive; comes unbidden, is often accompanied by overwhelming affect, and is not addressed to anybody'.[83] Yet, as Kacandes writes: '[b]ecause PTSD appears to be caused by an inability of the individual to integrate atrocities into consciousness, there is almost universal agreement that in order for the traumatised individual to go on with life more smoothly, some kind of transformation of the initial imprinting of the experience has to take place' there is what she describes as 'a need' to form a narrative of the trauma 'that can truly be heard'.[84] The true temporal experience of trauma and the impact of narrative are then important issues to consider together, whether that be in a fictional or a non-fictional setting. Laurie Vickroy in *Trauma and Survival in Contemporary Fiction* has described how trauma narratives 'internalize the rhythms, processes and uncertainties of traumatic experience within their underlying sensibilities and structures'.[85] And although fictional descriptions of trauma may problematise the necessity of being heard and believed in life, the artistry of the fictional trauma narrative may more closely reflect the temporal dislocation of sufferers than the traditional linear timeline.

Nicola King has commented on this topic, regarding trauma fiction that depicts the Holocaust, saying that it 'has come to represent a rupture in historical continuity, problematising the relationship between past and present';[86] and Anne Whitehead explains how this is conveyed in the literary treatment of this topic, saying that:

> In the face of this 'rupture', trauma fiction shares trauma theory's epistemological belief that the Holocaust is not knowable through traditional frameworks of knowledge and that it cannot be represented by conventional historical, cultural and autobiographical narratives. The Holocaust past, that is to say, cannot be narrated in an objective mode without omitting all that is most significant to understanding its power over the present … If trauma fiction is effective, it cannot avoid registering the shocking and unassimilable nature of its subject matter in formal terms.[87]

While they clearly focus on a distinct area of trauma literature, King's and Whitehead's discussions are nevertheless pertinent to the broader concerns of trauma narratology, including that of incest abuse, as the personal and individual trauma of child abuse creates a personal 'rupture' in the 'historical continuity'[88] of an individual. The order of life as it is expected to be lived, through childish innocence to eventual adult experience has been destroyed, and another order of events must be considered as the trauma cannot easily be explored through conventional chronological formats.

Fairy tales, myths and fables are a useful basis for such a narrative because they exist 'out of time', as Angela Carter asserts: 'The history, sociology and psychology transmitted to us by fairy tales is unofficial – they pay even less attention to national and international affairs than do the novels of Jane

Austen.' She continues to say, that '[t]hey are also anonymous and genderless' because 'we can never know the name of the person who invented' a 'story in the first place'.[89] The huge numbers of variants of most tales means that there is no one definitive edition and as much as they generally lack the psychological realism of contemporary fiction, their unfixed location in time means that horrific events can be considered without their being associated to a particular person or historical place. Their temporal fluidity also means that the extremes of innocence and experience, good and evil, can be explored more easily without specific cultural or temporal complications.

Lanagan uses the 'out-of-time' characteristic of the fairy-tale narrative to present Liga's experience of sexual trauma. From saying that her father's 'scorn as usual made her doubt her word, made her doubt her memory',[90] Liga forges a new world specifically *because she believes in it*. In this place, time also moves at a different speed, so that when she is forced to return to the real world she has lost ten years of her life and is now, it is indicated, too old to do the things that she wants to do, such as marry and have more children. Liga's removal from the chronology of the known world can be read as a means of explaining the damaging effects of this particular type of trauma, where she is prematurely aged in terms of sexual experience by her father's interference but is also simultaneously kept ignorant of the world at large. When she returns to reality this confusion of time is expressed by Liga through her own interpretation of her appearance: 'this face – older than she recalled, but younger by far than it ought to be'.[91] Liga does not benefit in the long term from her escape from the real world, because while she is safe, she is also depicted as numbed, incapable of strong feelings or of remembering clearly, and all that remains is a sense of fear directed towards masculinity. Her return to the town she grew up adjacent to, is overwhelmingly sensory, not only in terms of her dread at being similarly abused but also by the strength of her feelings of love towards her daughters, who have also grown up out of time, maintaining their innocence and ignorance for so long that the real world terrifies.

Creative women and daydreaming

Freud argued in *The Creative Writer and Daydreaming* (1907) that: 'The motive forces of fantasies are unsatisfied wishes, and every single fantasy is the fulfilment of a wish, a correction of unsatisfying reality'.[92] For Freud, as Ellie Ragland-Sullivan explains with reference to the work of Herbert Marcuse, fantasy was about freedom from and opposition to reality, 'the imagination uses fantasy to return its commitment to the id, or to a psychic structure as it was prior to the social reality principle, which is characterized by reason and repression'.[93] However, Lacan asserts in Seminar XX, that 'everything we are allowed to approach by way of reality remains rooted in fantasy'.[94] Fantasy then, which plays out desire, does not constitute true freedom but is part of the organised society of which we are a part, a symptom of the civilised condition. In this novel, where fantasy is a location in which to live, it is tempting to see Liga's safe place, her heaven, as an escape from reality but instead it is *a response to it*, and therefore not separate from it. Liga creates a place to be the submissive female, engaged in traditional female pursuits, a role that society has encouraged her to view as ideal, and here she can perform this role in safety. What Liga seeks to avoid here is the threatening presence of the *real*, the possibility of being rejected entirely by her fellow creatures, whose acceptance and approval she associates with her continued existence. Even her father's domineering views establish a means within which she can structure her self, so that her psyche does not disintegrate.

As Lacan asserts in his *Four Fundamental Concepts of Psychoanalysis*, 'What determines me at the most profound level, in the visible is the gaze that is outside.'[95] By this he refers to the gaze of the Other, and it is the early awareness of this that gives the child's psyche a sense of wholeness from fragmentation, when during the mirror stage the child sees its reflection as whole and complete, and understands that the symbolic necessarily supports this conclusion: 'the child, grasping himself in the inaugural experience of recognition in the mirror, comes to terms with himself as a totality functioning as such in his specular image ... turns towards the adult as if to call upon his assent, and then back to the image, he seems to be asking the one supporting him, and who here represents the big Other, to ratify the value of this image.'[96] To refuse the Other, who represents the symbolic order, would be to fall into fragmentation and the real. Therefore, freedom from her father's tyranny, her only link to the outside world, at first threatens Liga with the real, and she does not know how to make her own decisions, 'everything up to now had been constructed on her father's purposes – her whole life and, she assumed, the world around it'.[97] When Liga's attempt to live independently is interrupted so horrifically by the townsmen, it appears as if her assumption that her father's views are reflected by the world at large is correct. When given the opportunity then, Liga seeks to create a dream world entirely of her own, which is opposed to reality, the 'fantasy' in Freudian terms, but she has no experience upon which to draw of what such a world might consist of, so instead she imagines a partial blueprint of the symbolic, without the pain and, necessarily, as she knows very little of them, without many of the rewards.

Although she would rather die than continue to exist in the actual world with all of its dangers, she remains desirous of being part of the symbolic order, which once she associated with her father and now she can only create based on the fragments of knowledge she has of the outside world away from evil. The heaven is therefore an example of a thin but recognisable patriarchal civilisation and she is, in Lacanian terms, still performing her socially dictated role, trapped in the ideology of that culture. Liga, like her daughters, can only realise her self as individual and free, when as Evelyn Jaffe Schreiber suggests, 'this irrational desire – the cultural symbolic structure – is understood to be the irrational desire of one's culture'. Scheiber goes on to argue that 'Lacan suggests that individuals enact change when they become what I call "subjects of knowledge"; that is they recognize that they are meaningless links in the signifying chain'.[98] As Lacan explains, when the subject can finally name his or her desire, 'the subject creates, brings forth, a new presence in the world';[99] and although it could be argued that this occurs when Liga names her desire for a husband in Davit Ramstrong, this is not an entirely independent desire, but one which will also secure her place in the symbolic civilised realm, as a wife, with a husband to define her as her father once did.

This book is problematic because its narrative is complex, it seeks to examine the intricacies and boundaries of human nature but it also aims to test the limitations of what literature can do, particularly for an age specific readership. Lanagan herself suggested the novel explores at what point it is sensible to keep children innocent, i.e. to stop time, and at what point that becomes dangerous in itself. She commented on the criticism the text received that while for some 'reading is an escape from real-life difficulties … but this book isn't comfort reading except in the most roundabout way.'[100] This novel is not just about real life but also about fantasy, daydreams, and the real, it is in other words about everything that constitutes reality, and how the worlds we create can also be dangerous. The debate over whether novels for YA readers can deal with such controversial and sensitive subject matter as sexual abuse and PTSD, and whether there is a preferable manner in which to do this, continues. This is not a safe book, and it is not an easy read, but considered as a work of art, of trauma fiction that explores literature's relationship with growing up and negotiating the impact of domestic abuse and rape, it is narratologically innovative, intellectually complex, and confronts Western society's attitudes in literature and the wider world to women, children, and the right to possess one's self both physically and mentally.

Notes

1 Margot Lanagan, *Tender Morsels* (Random House, 2012), Digital Edition, p. 400.
2 The Shirley Jackson Awards are for 'outstanding achievement in the literature of psychological suspense, horror, and the dark fantastic.' 'The Shirley Jackson Awards', www.shirleyjacksonawards.org/ (accessed 25 March 2017).

3 'Margo Langan', Allen & Unwin Book Publishers, www.allenandunwin.com/authors/l/margo-lanagan (accessed 25 March 2017).

The Micheal L. Printz Award is awarded by the Young Adult Library Association 'based entirely on ... literary merit'. 'Printz Award', Young Adult Library Services Association, A Division of the American Library Association, 1996–2017, www.ala.org/yalsa/printz-award#previous (accessed 25 March 2017).

4 '2009 Locus Award Finalists', 27 April 2009, www.locusmag.com/News/2009/04/2009-locus-award-finalists.html (accessed 25 March 17).

5 There is no definitive definition of the young adult reader, and it varies between different countries and social groups.

6 Danuta Kean, 'Rape, abortion, incest. Is this what CHILDREN should read? *Daily Mail*, 9 July 2009, www.dailymail.co.uk/femail/article-1198485/Rape-abortion-incest-Is-CHILDREN-read.html (accessed 25 March 2017).

7 Anne Fine quoted in Vanessa Thorpe, 'Parents alarmed over sex assault in children's novel', *Observer*, 25 July 2009, www.guardian.co.uk/books/2009/jul/05/tender-morsels-childrens-novel-sex (accessed 01 February 2013).

8 Ashley McAllister, 'Revisions to the list', *Bitch Media*, bitchmedia.org/post/from-the-library-100-young-adult-books-for-the-feminist-reader (accessed 1 March 2013).

9 Philip Pullman, quoted in Thorpe, 'Parents alarmed over sex assault in children's novel'.

10 Anne Whitehead, *Trauma Fiction* (Edinburgh University Press, 2004), pp. 83–4.

11 *Ibid.*, p. 84.

12 Michael Rothberg, *Traumatic Realism* (University of Minnesota Press, 2000), p. 118.

13 I have chosen to italicise every mention of the Lacanian concept of 'the *real*' to avoid confusion with the use of the word 'real' in common parlance.

14 Jacques Lacan, Jacques Alain-Miller (ed.), Sylvana Tomaselli (trans.), John Forrester (notes), *The Ego in Freud's Theory* (Norton, 1991).

15 Jacques Lacan, Jacques-Alain Miller (ed.), Alan Sheridan (trans.), *The Four Fundamental Concepts of Psychoanalysis* (Norton, 1998), p. 55.

16 Although *Beloved* is not unequivocally classed as trauma fiction by all critics, many do give it this title. See Anne Whitehead, *Trauma Fiction*, pp. 5–6.

17 See the reviews and associated comments in notes 6, 7 and 8.

18 Maria Tatar, *The Hard Facts of the Grimms' Fairy Tales* (Princeton University Press, 1987), p. 33.

19 Maria Tatar, *'Off with their Heads!': Fairy Tales and the Culture of Childhood* (Princeton University Press, 1992), pp. 3–21.

20 Brothers Grimm, quoted in Tatar, *'Off with their Heads!'*, p. 16.

21 Lanagan, *Tender Morsels*, p. 195.

22 *Ibid.*, p. 211.

23 *Ibid.*, p. 184.

24 *Ibid.*, p. 372.

25 Marina Warner, *From the Beast to the Blonde* (Vintage, 1995), p. 300.

26 Barbara Whitmer, *The Violence Mythos* (State University of New York Press, 1997), pp. 78ff.
27 Warner, *From the Beast to the Blonde*, pp. 300–2.
28 W.J. Thomas Mitchell, 'Looking at animals looking: Art, illusion, and power', in Frederick Burwick and Walter Pape (eds), *Aesthetic Illusion* (Walter de Gruyter, 1990), p. 69.
29 To avoid unnecessary digression and complication I have omitted an explanation of the history of the categorisation of these folk tales according to their related themes.
30 Giambattista Basile, 'L'Orsa' trans. 'The Bear', in Jack Zipes (ed. and trans.), *The Great Fairy Tale Tradition* (Norton, 2001), p. 35.
31 Lanagan, *Tender Morsels*, p. 21.
32 *Ibid.*, p. 27.
33 *Ibid.*, p. 376.
34 *Ibid.*, p. 99.
35 *Ibid.*, p. 230.
36 *Ibid.*, p. 230.
37 Jacques Lacan, Russell Grigg (trans. and notes), Jacques-Alain Miller (ed.), *The Psychoses, The Seminar of Jacques Lacan Book III* (Norton, 1997), p. 9.
38 *Ibid.*, pp. 164–5.
39 Maurice Merleau-Ponty, (trans.) William Cobb, 'The child's relations with others', in James M. Edie (ed.), *The Primacy of Perception* (Northwestern University Press, 1964), p. 129.
40 Lacan, *Psychoses*, p. 9.
41 Lanagan, *Tender Morsels*, p. 372.
42 Margo Lanagan, 'How I wrote *Tender Morsels*', *Guardian*, 24 August 2012 www.guardian.co.uk/childrens-books-site/2012/aug/24/margo-lanagan-tender-morsels (accessed 1 February 2013).
43 Simone de Beauvoir, H.M. Parshley (trans.), *The Second Sex*. Orig. *Le Deuxieme Sex* (Vintage, 1997), p. 318.
44 Lanagan, *Tender Morsels*, p. 34.
45 *Ibid.*, p. 19.
46 *Ibid.*, p. 28.
47 *Ibid.*, p. 331.
48 *Ibid.*, p. 40.
49 Brownmiller, Susan, *Against Our Will* (Penguin, 1976), p. 281.
50 Lanagan, *Tender Morsels*, p. 19.
51 *Ibid.*, p. 436.
52 *Ibid.*, p. 438.
53 *Ibid.*, p. 431.
54 Herbert Spencer, *Principles of Biology*, vol. 1. (Williams & Norgate, 1864), p. 453.
55 Lanagan, *Tender Morsels*, p. 455.

56 Warner, *From the Beast to the Blonde*, pp. 300–2.
57 *Ibid.*, p. 11.
58 *Ibid.*, p. 31.
59 Tatar, '*Off with their Heads!*', p. 133.
60 Basile, 'The Bear', p. 38.
61 Sean Homer, *Jacques Lacan* (Routledge, 2005) p. 81.
62 Homer, *Jacques Lacan*, p. 83. Homer quotes Lacan from: Jacques Lacan, John Forrester (trans. and notes), Jacques Alain-Miller (ed.), *Freud's Papers on Technique 1953–1954* (Norton, 1991), p. 66.
63 Homer, *Jacques Lacan*, p. 83.
64 Alan Dundes, "'To love my father all': A psychanalytic study in the folktale source of *King Lear*', in Dundes (ed.), *Cinderella: A Casebook* (University of Wisconsin Press, 1988), pp. 229–44.
   Tatar, '*Off with their Heads!*', pp. 131–2.
65 Dundes, *Cinderella*, p. 220.
66 See Ernest Jones, 'The symbolic significance of salt in folklore and superstition', in Ernest Jones (ed.), *Essays in Applied Psychoanalysis* (Hogarth Press, 1951), pp. 22–109.
67 Tatar, '*Off with their Heads!*', p. 131–2.
68 Shakespeare, William, Cedric Watts (introd. and notes), *King Lear* (Wordsworth, 2004), p. 35 (1.1. 88, 90–1).
69 *Ibid.*, p. 35 (1.1. 90–1).
70 See Dundes, *Cinderella*, pp. 229–44.
71 Shakespeare, *King Lear*, p. 81 (3.3.51–9).
72 Shakespeare, *King Lear*, p. 112 (4.6.198).
   Dundes, *Cinderella*, pp. 235, 244.
73 Elaine Showalter, *A Literature of Their Own* (Virago, 1999), p. 43.
74 Angela Carter, 'Introduction', *Angela Carter's Book of Fairy Tales* (Virago, 2005), p. xiii.
75 Ovid, A.D. Melville (trans.), E.J. Kenney (introd. and notes), 'Tereus, Procne and Philomela', *Metamorphoses* (Oxford University Press, 2008), p. 136 (l.484–5).
76 *Ibid.*, p. 136 (l.497–9).
77 *Ibid.*, p. 137, l.525–6.
78 *Ibid.*, p. 137, l.533–4.
79 *Ibid.*, p. 139 (l.589–93).
80 *Ibid.*, p. 140 (l.623–4).
81 Irene Kacandes, 'Trauma theory', in David Herman, Manfred Jahn and Marie-Laure Ryan (eds), *Routledge Encyclopedia of Narrative Theory* (Routledge, 2005), p. 616.
82 Aristotle, Anthony Kenny (trans.), *Poetics* (Oxford University Press, 2013), p. 26.
83 B.A. van der Kolk and Onno van der Hart, 'The intrusive past: The flexibility of memory and the engraving of trauma' (1991), in Cathy Caruth (ed.), *Trauma: Explorations in Memory* (Johns Hopkins University Press, 1995) quoted in Kacandes, 'Trauma theory', p. 616.
84 Kacandes, 'Trauma theory', p. 616.

85 Laurie Vickroy, *Trauma and Survival in Contemporary Fiction* (University of Virginia Press, 2002), p. 3.
86 Nicola King, '"We come after": Remembering the Holocaust,' in Roger Luckhurst and Peter Marks (eds), *Literature and the Contemporary* (Longman, 1999), p. 94.
87 Whitehead, *Trauma Fiction*, p. 83.
88 *Ibid.*, p. 83.
89 Carter, *Book of Fairy Tales*, p. xii.
90 Lanagan, *Tender Morsels*, p. 11.
91 *Ibid.*, p. 324.
92 Sigmund Freud, 'The creative writer and daydreaming', *The Uncanny* (Penguin, 2003), p. 28.
93 Ellie Ragland-Sullivan, *Jacques Lacan and the Philosophy of Psychoanalysis* (Croom Helm, 1986), p. 139. Herbert Marcuse, *Eros and Civilisation* (Vintage, 1962), pp. 127–8.
94 Jacques Lacan, Jacques-Alain Miller (ed.), Bruce Fink (trans. and notes), *On Feminine Sexuality* (Norton, 1999), p. 95.
95 Lacan. *The Four Fundamental Concepts of Psychoanalysis*, p. 106.
96 Jacques Lacan, Jacques-Alain Miller (ed.), A. R. Price (trans.), *Anxiety* (Polity Press, 2016), p. 32.
97 Lanagan, *Tender Morsels*, p. 41.
98 Evelyn Jaffe Shreiber, *Race, Trauma and Home in the Novels of Toni Morrison* (Louisiana State University Press, 2010), p. 21.
99 Jacques Lacan, *The Ego in Freud's Theory*, p. 229.
100 Lanagan, 'How I wrote *Tender Morsels*'.

Bibliography

Fiction

Basile, Giambattista 'L'Orsa' (trans.) 'The Bear', in Jack Zipes (trans., ed. and selected), *The Great Fairy Tale Tradition* (Norton, 2001) pp. 33–8
Grimm, Jacob and Wilhelm Grimm, A.S. Byatt (introd.), 'Snow White and Rose Red', in Maria Tatar (ed. and annotations), *The Annotated Brothers Grimm* (Norton, 2012), pp. 341–52
——, 'All Fur', in Jack Zipes (ed.), *The Great Fairy Tale Tradition: From Straparola and Basile to the Brothers Grimm* (Norton, 2001), pp. 47–50
Lanagan, Margo, *Tender Morsels* (David Fickling, 2010), Digital Edition
——., *Touching Earth Lightly* (Little Arc, 1995), Digital Edition
Morrison, Toni, *Beloved* (Vintage, 2005)
Ovid, A.D. Melville (trans.), E.J. Kenney (introd. and notes), 'Tereus, Procne and Philomela', *Metamorphoses* (Oxford University Press, 2008), pp. 134–42
Perrault, Charles, 'Cinderella; or, The Glass Slipper', in Jack Zipes (ed. and trans.), *The Great Fairy Tale Tradition From Straparola and Basile to the Brothers Grimm* (Norton, 2001), pp. 468–73

———., 'Donkey-Skin', in Jack Zipes (ed.), *The Great Fairy Tale Tradition From Straparola and Basile to the Brothers Grimm* (Norton, 2001), pp. 38–46

Non-fiction

Aristotle, Anthony Kenny (trans.), *Poetics* (Oxford University Press, 2013)
Beauvoir, Simone de, H.M. Parshley (trans.), *The Second Sex* (Vintage, 1997)
Boose, Linda E., 'The family in Shakespeare studies', *Renaissance Quarterly* 40 (1987), pp. 713–42
Brownmiller, Susan, *Against Our Will: Men, Women and Rape.* (Penguin, 1976)
Carter, Angela, 'Introduction', *Angela Carter's Book of Fairy Tales* (Virago, 2005), pp. xi–xxiv
Dundes, Alan, " "To love my father all": A psychanalytic study in the folktale source of King Lear', in Alan Dundes (ed.), *Cinderella: A Casebook* (University of Wisconsin Press, 1988), pp. 229–44
Fox-Genovese, Elizabeth, 'Unspeakable things unspoken: Ghosts and memories in *Beloved*', in Harold Bloom (ed.), *Modern Critical Interpretations: Beloved* (Bloom's Literary Criticism, 1999), pp. 97–114
Freud, Sigmund, 'The creative writer and daydreaming', in *The Uncanny* (Penguin, 2003), pp. 23–34
Graham, Kenneth, *English Criticism of the Novel (1865–1900)* (Clarendon, 1965)
Hartman, Geoffrey, 'On traumatic studies and literary studies', *New Literary History* 26:3 (1995), pp. 537–63
Homer, Sean, *Jacques Lacan* (Routledge, 2005)
Jones, Ernest, 'The symbolic significance of salt in folklore and superstition', in Ernest Jones (ed.), *Essays in Applied Psychoanalysis, Vol. 2, Essays in Folklore, Anthropology and Religion* (Hogarth Press, 1951), pp. 22–109
Kacandes, Irene, 'Trauma theory', in David Herman, Manfred Jahn and Marie-Laure Ryan (eds), *Routledge Encyclopedia of Narrative Theory* (Routledge, 2005), pp. 615–19
Kahn, Coppélia, 'The absent mother in King Lear,' in Maureen W. Ferguson, Maureen Quilligan and Nancy J. Vickers (eds), *Rewriting the Renaissance: The Discourses of Sexual Difference in Early Modern Europe* (University of Chicago Press, 1986), pp. 33–6
King, Nicola, " "We come after": Remembering the Holocaust', in Roger Luckhurst and Peter Marks (eds), *Literature and the Contemporary: Fictions and Theories of the Present* (Longman, 1999), pp. 94–108
Lacan, Jacques, Jacques-Alain Miller (ed.), John Forrester (trans. and notes), *Freud's Papers on Technique 1953–1954, The Seminar of Jacques Lacan: Book I* (Norton, 1991)
———., Jacques-Alain Miller (ed.), Russell Grigg (trans. and notes) *The Psychoses 1955–1956, The Seminar of Jacques Lacan: Book III* (Norton, 1997)
———., Jacques-Alain Miller (ed.), Sylvana Tomaselli (trans.), John Forrester (notes), *The Ego in Freud's Theory and in the Technique of Psychoanalysis, 1954–1955, The Seminar of Jacques Lacan: Book II* (Norton, 1991)

———., Jacques-Alain Miller (ed.), A.R. Price (trans.), *Anxiety: The Seminar of Jacques Lacan: Book X* (Polity Press, 2016)
———., Jacques-Alain Miller (ed.), Alan Sheridan (trans.), *The Four Fundamental Concepts of Psychoanalysis, The Seminar of Jacques Lacan: Book XI* (Norton, 1998)
———., Jacques-Alain Miller (ed.), Bruce Fink (trans. and notes), *On Feminine Sexuality: The Limits of Love and Knowledge, 1972–3, Encore, The Seminar of Jacques Lacan: Book XX* (Norton, 1999)
Marcuse, Herbert, *Eros and Civilisation: A Philosophical Inquiry into Freud* (Vintage, 1962)
Merleau-Ponty, Maurice, 'The child's relations with others', in James M. Edie (ed.), trans. William Cobb, *The Primacy of Perception: And Other Essays on Phenomenological Perception* (Northwestern University Press, 1964), pp. 99–156
Peterson, Christopher, 'Beloved's claim', in Harold Bloom (ed.), *Modern Critical Interpretations: Beloved* (Bloom's Literary Criticism, 2009), pp. 151–72
Plato, Robin Waterfield (trans.), *Republic* (Oxford University Press, 1993)
Quilligan, Maureen, *Incest and Agency in Elizabeth's England* (University of Pennsylvania Press, 2005)
Ragland-Sullivan, Ellie, *Jacques Lacan and the Philosophy of Psychoanalysis* (Croom Helm, 1986)
Rothberg, Michael, *Traumatic Realism: The Demands of Holocaust Representation* (University of Minnesota Press, 2000)
Shakespeare, William, Cedric Watts (introd. and notes), *King Lear* (Wordsworth, 2004)
Showalter, Elaine, *A Literature of Their Own: British Women Novelists from Brontë to Lessing* (Virago, 1999)
Shreiber, Evelyn Jaffe, *Race, Trauma and Home in the Novels of Toni Morrison* (Louisiana State University Press, 2010)
Spencer, Herbert, *Principles of Biology*, vol. 1. (Williams & Norgate, 1864)
Tatar, Maria, *'Off with their Heads!': Fairy Tales and the Culture of Childhood* (Princeton University Press, 1992)
———., *The Hard Fact of the Grimms' Fairy Tales* (Princeton University Press, 1987)
Thomas Mitchell, W.J., 'Looking at animals looking: Arty, illusion, and power', in Frederick Burwick and Walter Pape (eds), *Aesthetic Illusion: Theoretical and Historical Approaches* (Walter de Gruyter, 1990), pp. 65–78
Thompson, Stith, *Motif-Index of Folk-Literature: A Classification of Narrative Elements in Folktales, Ballads, Myths, Fables, Mediaeval Romances, Exempla Fabliaux, Jest-Books, and Local Legends*, rev. 6 vols., 1955–1958 (Indiana University Press, 1975)
Uther, Hans Jörg, *The Types of International Folktales: A Classification and Bibliography Based on the System of Antti Aarnne and Stith Thompson*, 3 vols. (Academia Scientiarum Fennica, 2004)
Vickroy, Laurie, *Trauma and Survival in Contemporary Fiction* (University of Virginia Press, 2002)
Warner, Marina, *From the Beast to the Blonde* (Vintage, 1995)
Whitehead, Anne, *Trauma Fiction* (Edinburgh University Press, 2004)

Whitmer, Barbara, *The Violence Mythos* (State University of New York Press, 1997)
Zak, William F., *Sovereign Shame: A Study of King Lear* (Associated University Presses, 1984)

Websites

'2009 Locus Award finalists', 27 April 2009, www.locusmag.com/News/2009/04/2009-locus-award-finalists.html (accessed 25 March 2017)

Cart, Michael, 'The value of young adult literature,' YALSA, American Library Association, 1996–2017, www.ala.org/yalsa/guidelines/whitepapers/yalit (accessed 28 March 2013)

Clinton, Jane, 'When children's books offer adult action between the covers', *Express*, 19 July 2009, www.express.co.uk/expressyourself/114885/When-children-s-books-offer-adult-action-between-the-covers (accessed 25 March 2017)

Kean, Danuta, 'Rape, abortion, incest. Is this what CHILDREN should read?', *Daily Mail*, 9 July 2009, www.dailymail.co.uk/femail/article-1198485/Rape-abortion-incest-Is-CHILDREN-read.html (accessed 25 March 2017)

Lanagan, Margo, 'How I wrote *Tender Morsels*', *Guardian*, 24 August 2012, www.guardian.co.uk/childrens-books-site/2012/aug/24/margo-lanagan-tender-morsels (accessed 1 February 2013)

McAllister, Ashley, 'Revisions to the List', https://bitchmedia.org/post/from-the-library-100-young-adult-books-for-the-feminist-reader (accessed 1 March 2013)

'Margo Lanagan', Allen & Unwin Book Publishers, www.allenandunwin.com/authors/l/margo-lanagan (accessed 25 March 2017)

'The Michael L. Printz Award Policies and Procedures' (Last revised March 2013), YALSA, American Library Association'. 1996–2017, www.ala.org/yalsa/booklistsawards/bookawards/printzaward/aboutprintz/criteria (accessed 25 March 2017)

'Printz Award', YALSA, American Library Association, 1996–2017, www.ala.org/yalsa/printz-award#previous (accessed 25 March 2017)

'The Shirley Jackson Awards', www.shirleyjacksonawards.org/ (accessed 25 March 2017)

Thorpe, Vanessa, 'Parents alarmed over sex assault in children's novel', *Observer*, 25 July 2009, www.guardian.co.uk/books/2009/jul/05/tender-morsels-childrens-novel-sex (accessed 1 February 2013)

Part III

Incest as a political conceit

7

The desire for power and the power of desire: The case of Pier Paolo Pasolini

Michael Mack

> 'I'll never be able to forget that Italian society condemned me in its courtrooms'
> Pasolino, *Il Giorno*, 17 February 1966

As the quotation opening this chapter indicates, Pasolini's life and death were characterised by scandal and outrage. He was summoned to court more than thirty times and scandal was an important theme in his literary and cinematic work.[1] Indeed, as Enzo Siciliano states: 'It is the scandal that bursts forth from confessions, from the projection into words of what our bodies and sensibilities unconsciously contain. This was the scandal that boomeranged on the heart and passion of Pasolini.'[2] Even Pasolini's death was controversial, and his murder on a derelict field on the outskirts of Rome has been the subject matter for debate over the last four decades.[3] It is not therefore surprising that he chose the topic of incest to play a central role in his work. This chapter will first introduce the reader to Pasolini's ethics and aesthetics of scandal and contamination, through a brief discussion of his early films *Accatone*, *Mamma Roma* (both released in the early 1960s) and his later works *Oedipe Re* and *Teorema*.

Pasolini's notion of contamination is at once political and scientific. The term scientific here denotes a broadening of our horizon of knowledge and understanding about cognitive operations that do not fit into accounts of what is normative. Pasolini's idiosyncratic usage of the word scandal precisely describes a departure from what has become accepted as common knowledge. The discovery of new, or indeed, little discussed, knowledge about human nature is scandalous – an affront to social structures or political order and cultural conceptions of morality. Pasolini does not differentiate between art and science, between interpretation and perception. Strikingly, his approach is backed up by recent neuroscientific findings that show that the acquisition of knowledge never goes without interpretation. There is no such thing as immediate or 'pure' empirical perception of facts and data. Pasolini refers to the notion of contamination in order to highlight the diverse nature of human minds, experiences and perceptions.[4]

As Daniel C. Dennett has put it: 'What we actually experience is a product of many processes of interpretation – editorial processes, in effect. They take in relatively raw and one-sided representations, and yield collated, revised enhanced representations, and they take place in the streams of activity occurring in various parts of the brain.'[5] 'In other words, discrimination does not lead to a *representation* of the already discriminated feature for the benefit of the audience in the Cartesian Theatre – for there is no Cartesian Theatre.'[6] Pasolini's presentation of scandalous knowledge enriches the multi-layered stream of consciousness that constitutes knowledge. Our acquisition of knowledge resembles 'a narrative stream or sequence, which can be thought of as subject to continual editing'.[7] By contaminating our consciousness with what has been deleted from 'multiple "drafts" of narrative fragments',[8] Pasolini illuminates that which has been suppressed not perhaps so much by the working of our minds but by the rules and commands of a politics which attempts to put an end to the heterogeneity through and by which our brains work.

This cognitive-scientific questioning of what has become accepted as normative knowledge is also political: bringing into public discussion voices that have been silenced. The chapter will then discuss what I call the cognitive-affective role of the mother, in his infamous poem to his mother, '*Supplica a mia madre*', which appears in *Oedipe Re*, in his last (posthumously published) novel *Petrolio* and in his play *Affabulacione*. The latter is concerned with a father who has a sexual relationship with his son and is consequently so possessive that he murders the boy. This can be seen as a new take on the plot of *Oedipus Rex* and, as we shall see, Sophocles's ghost is a key character in the play. Thus, *Affublacione* problematises the Oedipus complex, presenting a homosexual actual event of incest rather than the fantasy of heterosexual incest that Freud proposed.[9] Yet, Pasolini's play *Affabulacione* is Oedipal too: it is premised on the desire for power and the power of desire.

This chapter focuses on Pasolini's creation of a form of new politics. This novel form of politics interrupts the violence which governs the desire for power that has come to coincide with the power of desire. This coincidence of sexuality, domination and violence characterises what Freud presented when he first discussed the Oedipus complex in his *The Interpretation of Dreams* (1899). The work of Pier Paulo Pasolini looms large in reflections about this topic: in different but related ways his cinematic and literary *oeuvre* pivots around the sexual politics of father–son as well as mother–son relationships. These relationships govern the structure of politics and history. In order to find ways out of this violent arrangement, we therefore need to inquire into the ambiguities of love-hate encounters between fathers and their sons. Psychoanalysis and art here meet politics.

Introduction to Pasolini's subjectivity

The political aspect of mental life and its deceptive representations are themes that permeate Pasolini's approach not only towards the father–son relationship but also towards that between mother and son. The assumption of a central, homogenous control centre gives rise to deceptive representations, which Pasolini attempts to disrupt through his cinematic and poetic presentation of scandalous knowledge. In doing so he adumbrates an understanding of selfhood which is truly diverse and which turns false when it appears as homogenous. As Dennett has argued the self is indeed a heterogeneous assembly:

> In our brains there is a cobble-together collection of specialist brain circuits, which, thanks to a family of habits inculcated partly by culture and partly by individual self-exploration, conspire together to produce a more or less effective, more or less well-designed virtual machine, the *Joycean machine*. By yoking these independently evolved specialist organs together in common causes, and thereby giving their union vastly enhanced powers, this virtual machine, this software of the brain, performs a sort of internal political miracle: It creates a *virtual captain* of the crew, without elevating any one of them to dictatorial power.[10]

This chapter highlights the cognitive-scientific basis of Pasolini's political critique of homogeneity. Pasolini employs allegory in a way that is close to Walter Benjamin's understanding of this term: images that are filled to the brim with a multiplicity of meanings and so do justice to a cognitive reality that is multi-layered rather than homogenous.

The chapter will first focus on mother–son relationships in Pasolini's work. Even though it does not explicitly allude to Oedipus, his early film *Mamma Roma* (1962) has an Oedipal subtext or subplot: the violent, deceitful and exploitative father who – like *Accatone* (1961), his first film produced in the early 1960s – is a pimp; with the important difference, however, that Pasolini depicts Accatone as a Christ-like figure due to his social decline and total exclusion.[11]

Accatone performs contamination: the film commingles the profane with the sacred, social abjection with the saintly. At the centre of the film is a fight in the slums of Rome. The frame of the profane fight scene draws upon sacred allusions: long shots accompanied by Bach's religious music from the St. Matthew Passion. The voices of Bach's music sing of eternal peace whereas the reality of the scene in *Accatone* is a seemingly endless fight to drive away the crooked outcast, the loser, and the mean exploiter and pimp Accatone. At one point the father of Accatone's wife even draws a knife threatening to intervene with deadly force in the hand-to-hand fisting and wrestling. What brings about this scandalous contamination is the allegorical, highly self-conscious and artistic superimposition of one language (sacred and highly intelligent, refined language of Bach) onto a radically different one. What is style in *Accatone* is a critique of *petit-bourgeois* aspirations in *Mamma Roma*.

As Pasolini puts it: 'The element that distinguishes this film from *Accatone* is the moral question not to be found in *Accatone*.'[12] Most importantly, the stylistic and the ethical operate on the same level: both are scandalous and diverge radically from the *status quo*.

As has repeatedly been pointed out from Enzo Siciliano (1978) to, more recently, Armando Maggi (2009) the word *scandalo* permeates Pasolini's oeuvre.[13] What then is scandalous? On a popular, tabloid newspaper level, scandal is what brings about the fall or the vilification of public figures. Indeed, as celebrity Pasolini was the subject of many scandals, which, often instigated by the Italian press, ended up in tedious and hurtful condemnations in over thirty different court hearings. Pasolini arguably came to embody scandal for the Italian and international public at large. In contrast to more recent public misdoings and outrages associated with the former Prime Minister Berlusconi, Pasolini was clearly an outsider (a gay intellectual who was expelled from the communist party on account of his sexual orientation).[14]

Pasolini's science of difference grows out of the artistic discovery which reveals the sacred and the profane in their mutual contamination.[15] This is precisely what scandal does – it connects the sacred with the profane: 'I am scandalous. I am so to the extent to which I stretch a cord, an umbilical cord, in fact, between the sacred and the profane.'[16] Pasolini here highlights our non-homogenous constitution: at birth the profane and the sacred, the corporeal and the mental already are contaminating each other.

As the neuroscientist Antonio Damasio has recently argued the concept of contamination goes along with the social emotion of disgust: 'Humans can be disgusted not just by seeing spoiled food and the foul smell and taste that accompany it but by a variety of situations in which the purity of objects or behaviour is compromised and there is "contamination".'[17] Our society accustoms us to feel disgust at what we perceive to be contaminating. The contamination in question concerns the meeting point between purity and danger, selfhood and the other – the latter here appears as a threat. Contamination could be defined in terms of the gaze. Pasolini's aesthetic and ethical notion of scandal makes us see the profane, the threatening other, the abject and or poisonous from a new perspective. Pasolini's site of scandal is first of all his selfhood, his autobiographical self. It is important not to equate the artistic presentation of Pasolini with Pasolini himself. The author and director Pasolini often uses his subjectivity for various scientific experiments. He does so from the important poem '*Supplica*' (1962) to his last, posthumously published novel *Petrolio* (1992). In a letter to his friend, the poet Alberto Moravia, Pasolini highlights the novelty of the reader's shocking confrontation with the author's subjectivity. Whereas in traditional novels the author's selfhood recedes, making place for the objectivity of the main characters, Pasolini stages the subjective front and centre:

> In a novel the narrator usually disappears, giving way to a conventional figure who alone can have a real relationship with the reader – real precisely because of conventional ... [In *Petrolio*] I have spoken to the reader myself, in flesh and bone, as I write you this letter ... I have made the novel an object between the reader and me (and I have discussed it as one can do by oneself when writing).[18]

Clearly, here Pasolini distances himself from John Keats's 'negative capability'[19] as well as from other poetic and narrative techniques which are premised on the identification with different, 'objective' characters.

Pasolini's cognitive poetics, contrasts with what Keats has called 'pleasures of not knowing'.[20] 'Negative' denotes the not knowing. The 'capability' in question is that of identification. Pasolini's poetic voice, however, knows or wants to know. As will be discussed at the end of the following section, his cinematic version of Sophocles' *Oedipus Rex* interprets the cause of the tragedy not in a quest for knowledge but in its avoidance through mindless acts which resemble the violence in action movies: Pasolini's Oedipus does not even listen to the sphinx and far from solving her riddle; he with brute force pushes her into the abyss.

Knowledge here, however, does not refer to the biographical facts of Pasolini himself. As Maggi writes: 'Some critics have hailed the novelty of Pasolini's direct voice in his last novel, ignoring or forgetting the distinction between author (the person who has written the book and whose name is printed on the cover) and the extradiegetic/intradiegetic narrator, that is, the character of the writer who narrates in the "I" form and, even when he is external to the events, speaks from within the narrative space.'[21] There is still, however, a capability at work in Pasolini's foregrounding of subjectivity: it is the capability to identify with a self that transcends the boundaries of selfhood.

The identification at work here is a knowing or cognisant one which also maps the scientific scope of knowledge beyond the limits which patriarchal society places on matters considered scandalous. Rather than revealing private subject matters, Pasolini highlights the self in order to discover universal forms of knowledge whose uncovering has been interdicted by the authority of the father – the figure of the father yet again does not coincide with the father of Pasolini's biography. Violating the laws of the father (which from a Lacanian perspective are the statutes of society)[22] Pasolini embarks on a cognitive inquiry into the psycho-physical foundations of his life. His autobiographical self has its foundation in the paradigm established by Freud and Kafka. The precise philological or textual location of Freud's paradigm is not relevant here, because as Nicola Petkovic has pointed out, 'Freud's work exists in bourgeois Europe as a kind of common cultural usage, whether or not that usage refers explicitly to any of Freud's writings.'[23] In this paradigm the father embodies the interdiction of the scientific quest for self-discovery. The father is an allegory for political repression, which proscribes a cognitive encounter with reality.

The patriarchal figure represses cognition of different realities and he reduces human experience to an instrumental exploitative level. Contrasting with the character of Accatone, in *Mamma Roma* the father figure lacks association with the sacred: his modus vivendi is pure instrumentality, he is a pimp; an exploiter of women. The father's role contrasts with the mother who loves her son and does everything for him only to find out that she has sacrificed their lives to *petit bourgeois* aspirations. She is the victim of deceptions. There does not seem to be such a thing as innocence of 'love' in Pasolini's work. Love needs to be exposed to the contamination of knowledge in order to avoid being taken in by deceptions. Pasolini's cognitive rule of contamination, however, allows for the discovery of complex realities. Crucially the disclosure of such disavowed actualities falsifies both our fears (of the abject or poisonous) and our hopes (of innocent desire freed from power). The principle of contamination commingles our fears with our hopes. Conversely, Pasolini associates certain figures, locations and affiliations with exploitation, instrumental reason and manipulation, while at the same time putting such associative distortions into perspective.

The point of Pasolini's science of difference is precisely to disrupt homogeneity and conformism. The art and ethics of such science consists in what Pasolini calls scandal and, his idiosyncratic understanding of scandal, as we have seen above, amounts to the performance of contamination. The figure of the father attempts to render void the possibility of more than one actuality. The father reduces the past to the present, the virtual to the actual, the exuberant to the profitable and each entity to that which conforms to its nomenclature.

In this way Pasolini embodies his allegories of power around the figure of the Father. The darkness of his cinematic and literary creations arises from the absence of a clearly delineated alternative to power. Where such an alternative appears, as in his light-hearted *Trilogy of Life* (i.e. the films *Decameron*, 1971, *Canterbury Tales*, 1972 and *Arabian Nights*, 1974), the innocence of desire portrayed in these films (*Decameron*, 1971, *Canterbury Tales*, 1972 and *Arabian Nights*, 1974) turns out to be delusory and deceptive. Hence Pasolini's 'Repudiation of the *Trilogy of Life*' which finds its cinematic equivalent in the one-dimensional horror of sadistic and criminal domination, torture and murder in his last film *Salò* (1975). *Salò* presents the simultaneity between the contemporary conformism of consumerist and permissive 'freedom' and the systematic genocide of what is perceived to be different in fascist violence.

The *Trilogy of Life*, by contrast, celebrates desire beyond power or domination and in doing so it has already been co-opted or manipulated by the powers of permissive consumerism. As a result, Pasolini renounces his three highly popular films because of their deceptive and manipulated depiction of desire's innocence. Rather than being innocent, desire has already been controlled by power: 'one must realize how much one has been manipulated by the power structure'.[24] In Pasolini's work, love is always already contaminated by power and violence. As has been intimated above, Mamma Roma is obsessed with social advancement – which she attempts to accomplish by working as a prostitute. Her social and economic ambitions ironically prepare for the death of her beloved son. It is advancement not towards well-being but brutality.

Mother–sons: Mamma Roma, 'Supplica a mia madre' and Oedipe Re

Violence lies at the core of Pasolini's early novels *Vita Violenta* (1959) and *Raggaci di Vita* (Streetboys, 1955). Everyone falls prey to violence. Someone is bound to be killed whether it is the son or the father, and one parent is bound to be a partner to incest. Pasolini's Oedipus film emphasises this point. Later in this chapter I will illustrate how the escape from Pasolini's apocalyptical assessment of our private as well as social lives is potentially what could be called *the disruptive or contaminative moment*. Examples of such a disruptive or contaminative scenario can be found in the ending of almost all of Pasolini's films. In the closing scene of *Mamma Roma*, this is exemplified when Anna Magnani's manic stare of recognition prompts the spectator to realise that the view from her middle-class apartment actually coincides with the feared-for morbidity of a cemetery – the view of her previous working-class flat. The ending of *Oedipus* also demonstrates this scenario, as it is the absolute exclusion from society that contaminates Oedipus' incest-induced impurity, with the purity of the outcast and the blind. Perhaps the prime instance of contamination is in *Teorema* (1968) where the sudden appearance and consequent absence of the divine boy – with whom everyone has become obsessed – causes complete disintegration. This disintegration is illustrated by the catatonic madness of the daughter, the wild promiscuity of the wife, and by the husband's giving away of cherished possessions disposing of his factory and his clothes at Milan's train station.

Pasolini wrote the poem '*Supplica a mia madre*' in the same year in which he filmed *Mamma Roma* (1962). As we have seen, the mother figure is ambiguous, even though she is clearly presented in terms that seek the audience's sympathies. Conversely, she represents Pasolini's abhorrent view of the *petite bourgeoisie* as a social group intent upon socio-economic advancement. The film reveals such advancement to result in the catastrophic breakdown of all human relations. Pasolini confronts what he sees as false aspiration with the bitter reality of affect or desire-ridden politics. As his biographer Enzo Siciliano has astutely put it: 'He was a utopian – but he did not hesitate to rend this utopianism for the inescapable demands of Eros. From there sprung his originality – he was not afraid of his own demon.'[25]

In contrast to other pleas for the survival of a parent, Pasolini's poem does not exclude horrendous aspects of the affective relationship which binds parent and child. Whereas a comparable poem – Dylan Thomas's 'Do not go Gentle into that Good Night'[26]– revolves around humanity's struggle against death. Pasolini's '*Supplica*' opens and ends with the subjective position of the poet. The focus of Thomas's famous poem is clearly the confrontation with mortality on a level beyond the singular fate of the poet's father. Pasolini's 'Supplica' revolves not only about the poet's subjective position but also about power/domination and desire. Hence the poet's torment: it is indeed a horrendous, terrible subject-matter, which is of course also that of Kafka (his *Letter to my Father*).[27] Similar to Kafka's Letter Pasolini's poem pivots around power relationships as the foundation of family life.[28]

The poem dramatises its seeming subjectivity and reaches a crisis point. Through its repetition of the *schiav* root, the middle or centre of the poem formally inscribes a sense or feeling of being enslaved. This impetus moves the already emotionally intense situation into a larger socio-political context. The whole poem vibrates in the tension between innocence and corruption, 'love' and domination. The halting opening doubles or mirrors its oxymoronic force towards the opening of its penultimate strophe, when the poet invokes survival after the previous line has already spelled out the end of a certain life or relationship between mother and son: which they nevertheless somehow exist beyond. This is a most curious survival which takes place after everything is over. Yet this paradox is of course an important theological *topos* – especially within the New Testament where, according to the Gospel of John, Jesus restores Lazarus of Bethany to life four days after Lazarus had died.[29]

Pasolini's poem evokes the theological horizon of resurrection while immediately withdrawing from such belief-based context. In keeping with the cognitive approach that permeates the poem in its entirety, the poetic voice characterises the paradox of life after the end as irrational. This precarious survival faces yet another end in the last stanza of the poem, which only then fulfils what its title promises: it only then turns into a prayer. The title already anticipates the invocation of and withdrawal from the theological, which the poem as a whole performs. The poetic voice here too foregrounds selfhood: the mother's life in a future April involves the otherwise isolated self of the poet. In Thomas's poem, by contrast, we do not find the subjectivity of the speaker foregrounded. On the contrary, the poem invokes general terms that are the subject matter of each strophe, except for the first and last one. The poet refers to 'men' that are 'wise' then 'good', then 'wild', and then 'grave'.[30] A variety of general types of which exemplify how to rebel against the mortal journey. At the end the poem the persona apparently returns to the singular figure of the male parent but here too the language is broad rather than particular, evoking a range of possible characteristics encompassing the extremities of cursing and blessing.

Striking an entirely different note, Pasolini's '*Supplica*' avoids reference to the general or to what we are accustomed to – the traditional forms of cursing and blessing which figure prominently in Thomas's poem. Even before evoking the mortality theme of Thomas's poem, Pasolini introduces us to a demise which is not that of life, but of a specific relationship. The poem takes pains to do justice to the specific and the singular. This may be the poem's main theme around which it revolves both in terms of its form and content – and this from the very opening. The poem gives form to the difficulty of finding equivalence in the generality of words for the singularity of events, feelings, happenings both in the subjective and the objective sphere. Its opening almost takes back what it has just begun to unfold: the words of the child are not adequate enough to do justice to what is actually taking place in heart of the self, profiled here. The first two lines are a rhyming couplet, but the rhyme associates a coincidence called into question by the strophe itself: the 'son' does not coincide with its representation or likeness established through the generality of the 'word'. Representation disrupts itself here. This disruption constitutes the form of the poem, which creates a new space wherein we enter a world to which are not accustomed: one wherein we are capable of discovering so far invisible or entirely new forms of life. The poem witnesses the discovery of the infinitely mixed nature of life, of which the maternal figure is of course the giver or originator. The opening strophe announces and performs this hybridity in its evocation of words that are then almost withheld or withdrawn. Vocabulary shrinks to little signs or to silences which could do justice to the life of the heart – the subjectivity of the speaker.

In the following strophe the emotion no longer belongs to the subject. The mother knows more about the beginnings of affection than the one who carries the 'heart'. The words of the son are inadequate not least because the subject is always already displaced by what preceded subjectivity. Here the cognitive theme of the poem first introduces the mother in cognitive terms as a vessel of and for knowledge. The relationship between mother and son covers the intersection of affect and cognition. The poem traces the itinerary of a cognitive trajectory in which the son becomes the discoverer of a terrible recognition. Here we witness a second birth, which is one of cognition. It is the recognition of the hybrid reality of life. Most importantly thought and life here contaminate each other. We behold the discovery of a new form of birth in which one phenomenon or characteristic (grace) gives life to its opposite (distress). This is exactly what Pasolini understands by scandal: that there are no such things as pure entities but the contamination of such entities with each other. The adjective '*orrendo*' evokes the scandal of such discovery. As Maggi has recently pointed out Pasolini's central notion of a second birth describes 'the acquisition of a cultural consciousness.'[31] Cultural consciousness introduces the subject to the symbolic order.

As Claude Levi-Strauss has maintained, the prohibition of incest is the foundation of all kinds of symbolic orders that constitute all human societies.[32] Following Levi-Strauss, Julia Kristeva has argued that the universal prohibition of incest depends on *the social conditioning of an affect*: that of abjection or disgust when faced with the maternal body. According to Kristeva, affect combines the biological or physical with cognition and science.

If it be true, as Claude Lévi-Strauss has demonstrated, that the prohibition of incest has the logical import of founding, by means of that very prohibition, the discreteness of interchangeable units, thus establishing social order and the symbolic, I shall maintain that such a logical operation is carried out owing to a subjective benefit derived from it on the level of libidinal economy.[33] As Winfried Menninghaus has recently put it, Kristeva's notion of the abject:

> is universally and biologically grounded (in the maternal body); likewise, the constitution of the speaking subject through the repudiation of the pre-objectival *corps maternal* and its pleasure belongs, for Kristeva, to the fundamental, unchangeable givens of subject formation and of the symbolic order in general.[34]

Prohibition of incest is, of course, normative. It is a social norm and partakes of the social order.[35] Feeling and intellection are, however, intimately bound up with each other: a feeling of the abject accompanies the normative avoidance of incest. Pasolini's second birth includes Levi-Strauss's universal prohibition of incest. The second birth of cognition, however, brings about what I call the *disruptive moment of contamination*. Pasolini introduces an interruptive or contaminating moment to both Kristeva's and Levi-Strauss's accounts of the universal homogeneity of prohibiting incest.

This moment is creative and nascent: it validates life from a cognitive perspective, by bringing together dangerous or disgusting elements with beneficial ones. Neither one exists without the other. In contrast to Kristeva's account the mother is here not solely the object of rejection and abjection. Rather Pasolini's science of difference allows for hybridity and fluidity in natural and social entities. His language interrupts itself and in doing so it precludes the consumption of solid and ready-made cognitive statements of truth. Truth here emerges as fractured and highly nuanced. Revulsion is not so much affiliated with the body of the mother (as in Kristeva) but with the symbolic order as whole. Disgust with the social order, however, does not mean a rejection of it. On the contrary disgust may include beauty, as the abject contaminates the beauty of grace.

In a repressive society entities may be reduced to one single point of denomination (a striking example is Kristeva's distinct notion of the *abject*). This custom of isolation and compartmentalisation turns our lives into lies. Pasolini's poem attempts to counter such lies of the instrumental, reductive and exploitative by scandalously bringing together what we have been trained to separate. From its opening stanza onwards, '*Supplica*', takes one step in one direction while simultaneously taking another one in the opposite direction: it evokes words while at the same time highlighting their potential inadequacy. During the course of the poem we discover that the distortion of words resides in their isolation: in the separation of 'grace' from its contaminating opposite, in the separation of the affect (love) from domination. The work of art (whether cinema, the novel or the poem) offers a new space to which we have not become accustomed otherwise: a space wherein we discover the hybridity of our world.

Under the aegis of this hybridity the form of the poem connects what it ostensibly separates. The most glaring point of such separation is the love of bodies without soul. The hybrid form of the poem, which, as we have seen, instructs us to read words not in isolation, refers the sequestered expression 'senza anima' back to its deceptive opposite – to the soul that resides in the mother. This connection between the chastity of the maternal and promiscuity, which characterises Pasolini's understanding of homosexuality – 'For Pasolini, the male homosexual pursues sexual encounters only with 'real' men, heterosexual men who use the homosexual as woman'[36] – finds a striking point of culmination in the notorious note 55 of his last novel *Petrolio*. This is the novel's most extensive part and it describes how a man (Carlo 2) who has been transformed into a woman is penetrated by twenty young heterosexual men from Rome's sub-proletariat. Carlo's humiliation – where he is compared to a prostitute who is paid for her services – of course affronts bourgeois values of pride, success and conformity. The field in which it takes place 'evokes [in the context of Pasolini's films and novels] humiliation, suspension of social norms, poverty, and violence.'[37] Within this violent suspension of social norms, the maternal manifests itself in the seemingly 'soulless bodies' of the young men:

> He was perhaps barely sixteen and in fact in his eyes sparkled the smile not only of a boy but of a boy who practises the good manners his mother has taught him: a mother from the people, for whom a good upbringing is naturally an instinctive, deep-rooted politeness. This maternal politeness was betrayed in all of Sandro's gestures and movements. It had remained attached to him like a smell. Moreover, his clothes, too, the simple pants and plain shirt, had the appearance of having been bought at some market stall by him and his mother together, with money from the family.[38]

Whereas the heterosexual man, Carlo 2, violates his mother, grandmother and his sisters in acts of incest, once he has turned into a woman/man he avoids acts of defilement. 'Carlo 2 brings to the fore (gives life to) a revenant, the image of a maternal home that is gone forever. This home ruled by the mother is natural and divine.'[39] Pasolini frames the maternal in terms of the sacred.

One of the most striking instances of such framing emerges at the opening of his film *Oedipe Re* where Pasolini stages a mother–baby scene on green grass surrounded by idyllic trees. The camera switches from the baby to the face of the mother and lingers there. We are confronted with an unsettling close up which traces maternal affects from the peaceful to the foreboding of anguish to come. In *Cinema 1* (1983) Giles Deleuze characterises close-ups as affection-images. Deleuze goes so far as to claim that on a general and universal level close-ups have to do with nothing else but affects: 'But, in all these cases, the close-up retains the same power to tear the image away from spatio-temporal co-ordinates in order to call forth the pure affect of the expressed.'[40] Deleuze argues that the affection-image removes us from the action-image. Whereas action takes place in time and space, the close-up expresses affect.

Why does Pasolini detach the audience from the sphere of action right at the beginning of the movie? Pasolini is of course well known for the contemplative nature of his films. Nevertheless, the length (over two minutes) and the position (at the beginning of a movie) of this affection-image highlights its significance. The face of the mother reveals truthful affects, because the foreboding feeling of anguish will prove to be true in acts of violence and incest. The baby we see will literally violate his mother.

With a Kafkaesque sensibility Pasolini combines the affective with the truth or factuality of the action-image. As Deleuze has pointed out, Kafka was the first to connect two types of modern technologies of transport:

> Kafka distinguished two equally modern technological pedigrees: on the one hand the means of communication-translation, which ensure our insertion and our conquests in space and time (boat, car, train, aeroplane...); and on the other hand the means of communication-expression which summon up phantoms on our route and turn us off course towards affects which are uncoordinated, outside co-ordinates (letters, the telephone, the radio, all imaginable 'gramophones' and cinematographs...).[41]

Ironically in the close up of the mother at the opening of *Oedipe Re* communication-translation does not summon up phantoms but the action to come.

Hence its central position at the beginning of the movie. Here the affect-image in a sense anticipates the action-image. How does it do so? Similar to the operation of the poem '*Supplica*' Pasolini's work in entirety explores the affects not to detach us from factual reality but, on the contrary, to make us recognise truths that we would otherwise not uncover. Feelings partake of cognitive processes. As Damasio states, 'emotion and core consciousness are clearly associated'.[42] The close-up of the mother's face in the opening section of *Oedipe Re* depicts consciousness. We do not hear and read words but are faced with an image which in turn re-enacts the workings of the mind. As Damasio has shown:

> *core consciousness occurs when the brain's representation devices generate an imaged, non-verbal account of how the organism's own state is affected by the organism's processing of an object, and when this process enhances the image of the causative object, thus placing it saliently in a spatial and temporal context* [italicised in the original].[43]

Crucially what we see in the affect-image of the mother's close-up is not the spatial and temporal context – as discussed above, this would be an action-image – but how her facial expressions anticipate (as affective states) the violence and anguish to come in the action scenes of Oedipus' fratricide and incest.

Whereas the affective work of the mother reveals truth, her son Oedipus falls prey to emotions that blind his cognition. The maternal sphere is both sacred and truthful. The son, however, violates the mother through his lethal commingling of affect and action. In striking contrast to Sophocles, Pasolini's Oedipus does not solve the riddle of the Sphinx. Instead of solving a cognitive problem, Oedipus here simply shouts and pushes the Sphinx into the abyss. Before dying the Sphinx quickly admonishes Oedipus to search for knowledge in his interior sphere rather than blindly rushing into action. Oedipus, the adult son has abandoned the contemplative sphere that his mother inhabits in the close-up discussed above. The maternal is the sacred where we encounter the affective as cognitive force which sees the truth. The action scenes of *Oedipe Re* show the work of affects which are no longer contemplated or thought through. They are blind acts of violence or incest.

In his poem '*Supplica*', Pasolini associates the maternal *with both the affective and the cognitive* – with the emotions of the soul. Like anguish or the abject, the soul, however, is not a pure entity. Pasolini's cinematic and poetic and novelistic forms uncover purity as scientific illusion which turns out to be pseudo-scientific. Impurity is a fallacious concept too. At the point of Oedipus' recognition of his impure actions, he blinds himself and becomes as outcast of his native city. As outcast Oedipus, however, is no longer one-dimensionally impure. On the contrary, Pasolini has the blind Oedipus with his young partner Angelo wander dissatisfied through both modern Italian bourgeois and working-class society. He only reaches peace when he finds himself on the spot on which the close-up of the maternal face took place at the opening section of the movie. Oedipus the impure, contaminates the purity of Oedipus the seer (blind like the seer Tiresias) and outcast. Within the poem '*Supplica*', apparently soulless bodies are contaminated with the soul. *Oedipus Re* ends where it began: on the green and tree-lined idyllic spot of the mother's affect-image. The form of the poem and the film allow for the flowing together of otherwise compartmentalised spheres of purity and impurity, of falsehood and truth.

In doing so Pasolini's cinematic and poetic work changes the meaning of words as we encounter them in their instrumentalist and reductive isolation. Far from saying that the love for bodies without souls is soulless, '*Supplica*' connects this affect with the attachment to the soul that is the mother. The flow of the poem's form thus disrupts the order of separated entities, which is the work of reduction. The confusion outside or beyond the realm of reason may not be irrational. It could give rise to a new constellation. As Armando

Maggi has recently postulated, Pasolini diagnosed modernity in terms of confusion and mental illness (schizophrenia):

> His interviewer Jean Duffot remarks that, according to Herbert Marcuse, our modern values require a new language. Nowadays, it is impossible to conceive of a morality based on the concept of beauty. Pasolini responds by saying that this is because 'we are entering the moment of variants,' by which he means a time of variations and confusion, a sort of modern tower of Babel whose builders await divine punishment.[44]

The image of the tower of Babel evokes the sin of hubris and its consequent divine punishment. This moralistic aspect is, however, absent from Pasolini's diagnosis of modernity. As Maggi points out later on, 'the "form" invoked by Pasolini is a statement, a "something" that exposes itself as neither good nor bad, neither progressive or regressive, but only existent'.[45] The notion of confusion refers back to '*Supplica*', but also alludes to Pasolini's film *Oedipe Re* and his last novel *Petrolio*. The two latter works profile the scandal of incest which Pasolini's poem of 1962 evokes but eventually avoids; hovering ambiguously in the confusing hybridity of soulless bodies and the soul of the mother. Crucially neither the main protagonist of *Oedipe Re* nor Carlo 2 of *Petrolio* find a defining moment of identity in the act of incest, because Pasolini's aesthetics and ethics have done away with points of beginning and end which would define a distinct identity or entity.

Pasolini's last novel creates a new form that has overcome the compartmentalisation or isolation of specific subjects and substances. The novel unfolds not so much the vertical line of a building such as the tower of Babel but the horizontal growth of infinite birth: 'The concept of giving birth to a form is crucial for a correct understanding of *Petrolio*. The 'initial form of thought' is a thought that is in a perennial state of birth'.[46] Strikingly, the novel begins with the repudiation of a beginning: 'This novel does not begin.'[47] Having neither beginning nor end Pasolini's last novel grows laterally rather than in terms of linearity. It practises as form what Giles Deleuze and Félix Guattari have confined to a thought-image: that of the rhizome which is non-hierarchical and allows for multiplicity and diversity.

Multiple narrators compose *Petrolio* and its main character is not a single subject but splits into two: Carlo 1 and Carlo 2. Carlo 1 desires power and wealth by trying to climb the hierarchical ladder of the state-owned Italian petroleum company Eni. Power is, however, not pure but corrupted. Corruption does its work through Carlo 1 and Eni's as well as various political parties' affiliation with the Mafia. The other side of impurity is the splitting of Carlo 1 (who, as an Eni executive, belongs to the ruling class) into Carlo 2 (who is a middle-class heterosexual engineer). Carlo 2 is driven by incestuous desires: he has sexual intercourse with his mother, grandmother and his

The desire for power and the power of desire

sisters. The identity of the man Carlo 1 and Carlo 2 completely breaks down when they both undergo a sex-change from male to female.

The stories of Carlo 1 and Carlo 2 are, however, not the subject matter of the novel, as Pasolini repeatedly emphasises:

> Well, these printed but illegible pages are intended to announce my decision in a way that is extreme – but is then established symbolically for the rest of the book; that is, not to write a story but to construct a form (as will become clearer later on): a form consisting simply of 'something written'. I do not deny that certainly the best thing would be to invent an alphabet, perhaps of ideographs or hieroglyphics, and to print the entire book that way.[48]

Pasolini goes on to refer to Henri Michaux's *Idéogrammes en Chine* (1975) – a book constituting 'the patient invention of non-alphabetic signs'.[49] Rather than working with non-alphabetic signs Pasolini reconstructs modern allegories which are illegible, which refuse to turn into linear and understandable narrative. The form that Pasolini creates not only in *Petrolio* but also in various films (*Accatone* to *Oedipe Re* to *Teorma* and *Salò*) is that of allegory – an allegory which bursts with a multiplicity of meanings so as to render 'meaning' or 'narrative' into multiple and contaminating constellations. As we shall see in the following section, Pasolini's notion of allegory comes close to Walter Benjamin's. The relationship between Pasolini and Benjamin has, however, not yet been investigated. Regardless of whether Pasolini was deeply familiar with Benjamin's work, their mutual emphasis on a modern form of allegory is crucial for better understanding of their critique of regressive or brutalising elements within modernity, of which incest is a most striking example. Central to both Benjamin's and Pasolini's interpretation of allegory is the element of interruption.

Allegory is modernity's interruption of itself. A break of course constitutes the definition of the modern: it is the departure from the past, from tradition or the beginning of the new (modernity is *Neuzeit* in German). Why does the break with the past require a second break – a breaking away from itself? This is due to the failure of the modern project to implement what it had promised in the first place: a better world where we live without the harm and violence that had characterised that which preceded it. From Pasolini's perspective incest increases rather than abates in the wake of neo-capitalism. The modern urgently needs renewal – a renewal that returns to pre-modern forms of cognition such as allegory. The birth of the modern requires a second cognitive birth which returns to the intellectual-spiritual realm of the contemplative mother which pre-dominates the opening sequence of |*Oedipus Re*. Pasolini describes this renewal out of the past as follows: 'Even if I had not determined it, willed it, this writing necessarily had to be a 'new game' – even if not, perhaps, lexically and formally; everything in it, in fact, is heavy allegory, almost medieval (that is, illegible).'⁵⁰ According to both Pasolini and Benjamin, modernity's second, more thoughtful birth coincides with the renaissance of a modern and pre-modern hybrid of contemplation: allegory.

Conclusion: Walter Benjamin's 'allegory' and Pasolini's Affabulazione

Pasolini's *Affabulazione* (*Fabrications*) stages incest as a neo-capitalist form of globalisation. Here incest is no longer heterosexual but homosexual. As in almost all of Pasolini's works, the play *Affublazione* revolves around family life. The setting is the home of a wealthy industrialist of Milan. We do not know his first name or his surname. He simply appears as 'Father', his wife as 'Mother' and his son as 'Son'. The absence of specific names turns the characters into representatives of their role. They act out a specific role. In this way they are allegories. As allegories, the actors purport to represent some form of truth in a symbolic way.

Walter Benjamin has established a salient account of allegory which relates the term to the radically secularised world of bourgeois modernity. As a secularised literary device Benjamin's modern and postmodern allegory may have become stripped of its theological context but it nevertheless relates to theology whose content it empties of spiritual as well as intellectual meaning (what the unique German term *Geist* denotes). Signs are now valid without carrying any spiritual or intellectual significance. The prospect of transcendent redemption has disappeared but what remains is the now secularised version of guilt – Augustine's original sin – that encompasses nature and our embodied life on an all-encompassing scale. The contempt with nature, with the body, with the profane, furthers the desire to read the world allegorically. Allegory performs the destruction of the natural and the corporeal. According to Benjamin, it is the literary trope for the destruction of an immanence that cannot be salvaged by a now defunct transcendence.⁵¹ The command to destroy the profane, motivates allegorical readings of the world (here these readings of course go without any reference to a spiritual realm). Instead of reaching towards a redemptive beyond, allegory immanently destroys the immanent to the point of annihilating it.

Only in their annihilation natural bodies come close to a signification that would be transferred to them in their redeemed, resurrected state: 'The human body could not be an exception to the commandment which ordered the destruction of the organic so that the true meaning, as it was written and ordained, might be picked up from its fragments.'⁵² According to Benjamin, this allegorical destruction of the body gains in force with the progress of capitalism. Benjamin does not abandon the theological. Indeed the profane rediscovers and thereby re-establishes its spiritual or intellectual significance at the point where it bursts into fragments, into shards which could form the basis of a new life and a new form of politics. The creative and destructive works of the arts are the basis for this novel polis.⁵³ Intellectual critique is therefore always already part of

The desire for power and the power of desire   177

the constructive work towards a less violent body politics. My understanding of literature, the humanities and the arts as the ground for new and less harmful ways of social, economic, medical and political interaction requires a departure from traditional understanding of what politics is.[54]

Notes

1. Ian Thomson, 'Pier Paolo Pasolini: No saint', *Guardian*, 22 February 2013. www.theguardian.com/film/2013/feb/22/pier-paolo-pasolini (accessed 25 April 2017).
2. Enzo Siciliano, John Shepley (trans.), *Pasolini: A Biography* (Random House, 1982), p. 359.
3. Ed Vulliamy, 'Who really killed Pier Paolo Pasolini?', *Guardian*, 24 August 2014. www.theguardian.com/world/2014/aug/24/who-really-killed-pier-paolo-pasolini-venice-film-festival-biennale-abel-ferrara (accessed 26 April 2017).
4. See Daniel Dennett *Consciousness Explained* (Penguin, 1991), pp. 225–6.
5. Dennett, *Consciousness Explained*, p. 112.
6. *Ibid.*, p. 113.
7. *Ibid.*, p. 113.
8. *Ibid.*, p. 113.
9. Sigmund Freud, James Strachey (trans.), *Totem and Taboo* (Routledge, 2004), p. 149.
10. Dennett, *Consciousness Explained*, p. 228.
11. See Siciliano *Pasolini*, p. 247.
12. *Ibid.*, p. 250.
13. Armando Maggi, *The Resurrection of the Body* (University of Chicago Press, 2009), p. 314.
14. Siciliano, *Pasolini*.
15. See Patrick A. Rumble, *Allegories of Contamination* (University of Toronto Press, 1997).
16. Siciliano, *Pasolini*, p. 359.
17. Antonio Damasio, *Self Comes to Mind* (Vintage, 2010), p. 117.
18. Pier Paolo Pasolini, Ann Goldstein (trans.), *Petrolio* (Pantheon Books, 1997), pp. xi–xii.
19. For a discussion of Keats's term 'negative capability see Robert Gittings, *John Keats* (Penguin, 1979), p. 262.
20. Gittings, *John Keats*, p. 262.
21. Maggi, *Resurrection of the Body*, p. 169.
22. Jacques Lacan, Jacques-Alain Miller (ed.) *The Psychoses: The Seminar of Jacques Lacan; Book III 1955–56* (Routledge, 2000), p. 268.
23. Nikola Petkovic, 'Re-writing the myth, rereading the life: The universalizing game in Pier Paolo Pasolini's *Edipe Re*', *American Imago* 54:1 (1997), p. 42.
24. Pier Pasolini, 'Repudiation of the *Trilogy of Life*', in Pier Pasolini, Ben Lawton and Louise K. Barnett (eds), *Heretical Empiricism* (New Academic Publishing, 2005), pp. xvii–xx.

25 Siciliano, *Pasolini*, p. 398.
26 Dylan Thomas, J. Goodby (ed.), *The Collected Poetry of Dylan Thomas* (W&N, 2016), p. 193.
27 Franz Kafka, *Letter to his Father* (Schocken, 2015).
28 See Elias Canetti's *Kafka's Other Trial: The Letters to Felice* (Schocken Books, 1989).
29 See G.W. Most, *Doubting Thomas* (Harvard University Press, 2005).
30 Thomas, *Collected Poetry of Dylan Thomas*. p. 193.
31 Maggi, *Resurrection of the Body*, p. 186.
32 See Michael Mack, *Anthropology as Memory: Elias Canetti's and Franz Baermann Steiner's Responses to the Holocaust* (Niemeyer, 2001), pp. 40–8.
33 Julia Kristeva, Leon S. Roudie (trans.), *Powers of Horror* (Columbia University Press, 1982), p. 63.
34 Winfried Menninghaus, Howard Eiland and Joel Golb (trans.), *Disgust* (State University of New York, 2003), p. 392.
35 For a discussion of this point see Mack, *Anthropology as Memory*, pp. 40–8.
36 Maggi, *Resurrection of the Body*, p. 201.
37 *Ibid.*, p. 202.
38 Pasolini, *Petrolio*, p. 168.
39 Maggi, *Resurrection of the Body*, p. 216.
40 Gilles Deleuze, Hugh Tomlinson and Barbara Haberjam (trans.) *Cinema 1* (Continuum, 1997), p. 99.
41 Deleuze, *Cinema 1: The Movement Image*, p. 103.
42 Antonio Damasio, *The Feeling of what Happens* (Vintage, 2000), p. 122.
43 Damasio, *The Feeling of what Happens*, p. 169.
44 Maggi, *Resurrection of the Body*, p. 159.
45 *Ibid.*, p. 159.
46 *Ibid.*, p. 160.
47 Pasolini, *Petrolio*, p. 3.
48 *Ibid.*, p. 129.
49 *Ibid.*, p. 129.
50 *Ibid.*, p. 37.
51 See M. Mack *German Idealism and the Jew: The Inner Anti-Semitism of Philosophy and German Jewish Responses* (University of Chicago Press, 2003), pp. 155–70.
52 Walter Benjamin, John Osborne (trans.) *The Origin of the German Baroque Tragic Drama* (NLB, 1977), pp. 216–17.
53 The term polis is appropriate here because Benjamin's politics of art sharply contrast with Plato's exclusion of the arts from his conception of an ideal republic.
54 See Michael Mack *How Literature Changes the Way we Think* (Continuum, 2011).

Bibliography

Fiction

Kafka, Franz, *Letter to his Father* (Schocken, 2015)
Pasolini, Pier, Ann Goldstein (trans.), *Petrolio* (Pantheon Books, 1997)

Pasolini, Pier, Jamie McKendrick (trans.), *Fabrication (Affabulazione)* (Oberon Books, 2010)
Thomas, Dylan, J. Goodby (ed.), *The Collected Poetry of Dylan Thomas: The Centenary Edition* (W&N, 2016)

Non-fiction

Benjamin, Walter, John Osborne (trans.), *The Origin of the German Baroque Tragic Drama* (NLB, 1977)
Canetti, Elias, *Kafka's Other Trial: The Letters to Felice* (Schocken Books, 1989)
Damasio, Antonio, *The Feeling of what Happens: Body, Emotion and the Making of Consciousness* (Vintage, 2000)
——., *Self Comes to Mind: Constructing the Conscious Brain* (Vintage, 2010)
Deleuze, Gilles, Hugh Tomlinson and Barbara Haberjam (trans.), *Cinema 1: The Movement Image* (Continuum, 1997)
Dennett, Daniel, *Consciousness Explained* (Penguin, 1993)
Freud, Sigmund, *Totem and Taboo* (Routledge, 2004)
——., *The Interpretation of Dreams* (Penguin, 1991)
Geuss, Raymond, *Politics and the Imagination* (Princeton University Press, 2010)
Gittings, Robert, *John Keats* (Penguin, 1979)
Kristeva, Julia, *Powers of Horror: An Essay on Abjection* (Columbia University Press, 1982)
Lacan, Jacques, Jacques-Alain Miller (ed.), Russell Grigg (trans.), *The Psychoses: The Seminars of Jacques Lacan; Book III 1955–56* (Routledge, 2000)
Mack, Michael, *Anthropology as Memory: Elias Canetti's and Franz Baermann Steiner's Responses to the Holocaust* (Niemeyer, 2001)
——., *German Idealism and the Jew: The Inner Anti-Semitism of Philosophy and German Jewish Responses* (University of Chicago Press, 2003)
——., *How Literature Changes the Way We Think* (Continuum, 2011)
Maggi, Armando, *The Resurrection of the Body: Pier Paolo Pasolini* (University of Chicago Press, 2009)
Menninghaus, Winfried, Howard Eiland and Joel Golb (trans.), *Disgust: Theory and History of a Strong Sensation* (State University of New York, 2003)
Most, G. W., *Doubting Thomas* (Harvard University Press, 2005)
Pasolini, Pier, Ben Lawton and Louise K. Barnett (trans.), 'Repudiation of the Trilogy of Life,' in Pier Pasolini, *Heretical Empiricism* (New Academic Publishing, 2005)
Petkovic, Nikola, 'Re-writing the myth, rereading the life: The universalizing game in Pier Paolo Pasolini's *Edipo Re*,' *American Imago* 54:1 (1997)
Rumble, Patrick A., *Allegories of Contamination: Pier Paolo Pasolini's Trilogy of Life* (University of Toronto Press, 1997)
Siciliano, Enzo, John Shepley (trans.), *Pasolini: A Biography* (Random House, 1982)
Sophocles, Hannah Wilson (ed.), *Oedipus Rex* (CreateSpace, 2014)

8

'Our close but prohibited union': Sibling incest, class and national identity in Iain Banks's *The Steep Approach to Garbadale* (2007)

Robert Duggan

The work of Iain Banks has been prominent in exploring the crossings of different kinds of borders: national, aesthetic and generic, ontological, gender and class to name but a few. Banks has also been part of a wider preoccupation in contemporary Scottish writing to do with inhabiting border zones, where the border ceases to be an idealised geometric line with almost no width or physical extension, and instead broadens to become a site that one can reside in, the ground against which the figure emerges.[1] The clearest example of this in Banks's work is probably *The Bridge* (1986), in which the unnamed hero (Alexander Lennox as we later learn) is injured in a car crash on the Forth Road Bridge and in his coma is transported as an amnesiac into the fantasy world of the Bridge, a huge structure which stretches across water in both directions as far as the eye can see and which is home for thousands of inhabitants.[2] *The Bridge*, along with another Banks book set in contemporary Scotland *The Crow Road* (1992)[3] will form the background to my analysis of Banks's novel *The Steep Approach to Garbadale*.[4] This essay will illuminate how *The Steep Approach to Garbadale*'s continuation of, and departure from, the border explorations and reflections on national identity of his earlier books is rendered through the crucial deployment of the motif of sibling incest in the novel.

Before exploring in detail the profound significance of sibling incest within the novel, it is worth considering where *The Steep Approach to Garbadale* fits into Banks's *oeuvre*. Grouping it together with *The Bridge* and *The Crow Road*, one is struck by how even the books' titles signal an interest in travel and connection. Unlike novel titles typical of nineteenth-century fiction that identify a person or a town or house (*The Mayor of Casterbridge*,

Wuthering Heights, Oliver Twist), the titles of these novels by Banks offer no reference to people and suggest liminal places on the road between different locations rather than a single geographical site. *The Bridge* denotes the Forth rail and road bridges and also the fantasy world of the Bridge, while *The Crow Road* signals both a road to the west of Glasgow and the passage between life and death, 'away the Crow Road' serving as a euphemism for death in the novel. However in Banks's work these in-between places themselves become important locations that define the characters that populate them, and that embody complex networks of affiliations and pressures. His novels feature many episodes of characters travelling from the cities to the highlands, often at the wheel of powerful vehicles. As Cristie March notes, Banks often uses the geography of Scotland to both delineate and connect a jet-setting and cosmopolitan lifestyle on the one hand with a more down-to-earth rural one on the other[5] and *The Steep Approach to Garbadale* is no exception, beginning as it does with a touch of misdirection as the reader follows the wealthy Fielding Wopuld driving his Mercedes into a Perth housing estate so down-at-heel that even the graffiti is 'poor quality'.[6] It is not Fielding that is to be the novel's protagonist however, but his cousin Alban who despite his wealthy background is a guest in a council house there. Alban's journey will be to return to Garbadale, the grand Wopuld family home in the Scottish countryside, and to discover the secret of incest hidden within his wealthy family. The unearthing of incest will transform Alban's sense of his own identity and throw into question the Wopuld's problematic status as family/nation.

In its playful opening migration between different points of view, from Fielding's snobbery, to Alban's laconic enigma to his host Tango's working-class domestic scene, *Garbadale* echoes *The Bridge*'s play with downward class mobility on the part of its often disaffected protagonist, as the ambitious and accomplished Lennox of the real world who has left his West Coast roots to become wealthy and middle class is transmuted, in the fantasy world of the Bridge, into the bourgeois Orr, who then proceeds to slide down the hierarchy of the bridge society until he ends up in a cramped room on a small allowance. Alban McGill has spent a period away from the Wopuld family firm literally in the wilderness working as a forester and after developing a long-term work-related injury has moved into Tango's house spending his money on alcohol and drugs. Both books project sensitivity to class within a Scottish context and the plots of both novels act to intertwine the lives of middle-class and working-class characters, while the narrative also intertwines Standard English with non-standard Scots. The Scots-speaking Barbarian who haunts *The Bridge* shares certain similarities with Tango, the uneducated character whose first-person narrative (full of misplaced apostrophes) begins and ends *Garbadale*, bookending the adventures of the middle-class protagonist and perhaps broadening the context and import of Alban's decisions beyond the scope of the bourgeois and incestuous Wopuld clan. In this sense, Tango is also reminiscent of *The Bridge*'s Lynchy, a working-class neighbour who helps down-on-his-luck Orr when almost all of Orr's former friends have shunned him. Of course, the linguistic differentiation also has a national resonance: as Thom Nairn has pointed out in relation to *The Bridge*, the fact that the semi-literate Scots-speaking Barbarian is shackled to his RP-speaking familiar has as much to do with that state of the Union as it does with the inside of Lennox's head.[7]

The Steep Approach to Garbadale is perhaps closest to *The Crow Road*, published fifteen years earlier, in its portrayal of large families and their various disputes and secrets. The Wopuld family of *Garbadale* and the McHoans of *The Crow Road* both have skeletons in their cupboards, and Alban's mother's mysterious suicide by drowning in a loch recalls the disappearance of Prentice's uncle Rory in *The Crow Road*, who has been murdered and his body dumped. Both Prentice and Alban are drawn to the enigma of the missing body in the lake, a scenario heavy with mythic resonance, and both protagonists struggle to find out why their relatives are gone, and also very significantly, why they wanted to leave their life behind. Prentice and Alban are disaffected, youthful characters, who seem at least initially uninterested in their family's aspirations for them 'to get on' and both are drawn to relations (Rory, Alban's mother) who were themselves disaffected, and dropouts of a kind. The troubled heroes of *The Crow Road* and *Garbadale* are both poised between different worlds and are struggling to find their place, while simultaneously trying to discover the truth about the fates of their precursors, contributing to the strong bildungsroman aspects that have been a feature of Banks's work since *The Wasp Factory*.[8]

While the perception of a profound duality within Scottish literature and culture, the so-called Caledonian antisyzygy, has continued to be both an important focus and a site of strong disagreement, there seems to be more consensus within scholarly discussions on the importance of being between to Scottish literature and culture. This has been articulated widely within critical circles, most influentially by Cairns Craig whose *Out of History* has a chapter entitled 'Being between': 'The condition of "being between" is not the degeneration of a culture but the essential means of its generation ... Culture is not an organism, nor a totality, nor a unity: it is the site of a dialogue, it is a dialectic, a dialect. It is being between.'[9] Eleanor Bell, although pursuing an approach that is apparently antipathetic to Craig's, concurs with him on the importance of betweeness for Scottish literature, claiming that 'it is imperative that we view Scotland comparatively, as existing *between* cultures rather than as an isolated unit'.[10] While academics have been wary of applying postcolonial theory to Scottish literature, the essays collected in *Scottish Literature and Postcolonial Literature* marks a closer connection between these domains than has perhaps previously been admitted.[11] The heated revisionism debates that took place within Irish Studies in the 1990s[12] are a good indicator of the difficulties of regarding contemporary Scottish literature as postcolonial, so it is not surprising that a cautious approach to these issues has been prevalent. Nonetheless it is clear that there are significant connections between the Scottish between-ness of Craig and Bell and important areas of postcolonial theory, especially in work on cultural hybridity and on rhizomic structures. While Banks's previous novels are bursting with the crossing and re-crossing of borders and divisions between nations, regions, classes, dialects, realities and genders, *The Steep Approach to Garbadale* is distinct in its attempt to situate this Scottish sensibility of between-ness within a new national and global context and marks a significant exploration of Scotland's post-devolution political and economic choices through its ambivalent treatment of family and business connections.

Garbadale tells the story of Alban McGill, a member of the wealthy Wopuld family that has made its fortune from a board game that involves conquest and trade. The plot involves Alban participating in the debate over whether the family shareholders should sell their firm to the American company Spraint Inc, and coming to terms with his feelings for his cousin Sophie, with whom he conducted an adolescent romance, and for his current girlfriend Verushka, a professor of mathematics and game theory. Alban is also haunted by his mother's suicide when he was just a baby and one enigma that the novel sets out to resolve is why she took her own life, a resolution that has profound consequences for Alban's sense of identity. The boardgame the Wopulds own is called *Empire!* and involves several players competing to conquer the world. Banks has some fun with how the game has been renamed over the Twentieth Century, from *Empire!* to *Commonwealth* and finally to its American incarnation *Liberty!* As this makes clear, there is a strong sense of national allegory at work here, with the British (royal) family that brought the world Empire guided by an ageing matriarch in the person of Grandma Win now ceding global control to the American corporation who is bringing the world Liberty. The names of Grandma Win and her deceased husband Bert signal how closely the spectres of the widowed Queen Victoria (Victory) and Prince Albert hang over the fictional proceedings, encouraging the kind of political reading frequently solicited both by Banks's mainstream output and by his science fiction published under his Iain M. Banks imprimatur.[13]

Alban, whose name's closeness to Alba (the ancient name for Scotland) is another strong nod towards national allegory, is, despite his age, similar to the university student Prentice in *The Crow Road* in being 'between', experiencing arrested development and being suspended between adult and pre-adult status. As Craig has observed, temporal suspension and suspended animation are important motifs in much contemporary Scottish literature:

> Such suspended animation [in ref to Alasdair Gray's *Lanark*] will become a regular image of the changeless and paralysed condition of modern Scotland ... in Iain Banks's *The Bridge*, as in Irvine Welsh's *Marabou Stork Nightmares*, the narrator is immobilised in his hospital bed.[14]

Alban exhibits the same of kind of stasis that we see in the realist strands of *Lanark*, *The Bridge* and *Marabou Stork Nightmare* where the young Scotsman struggles with the task of defining his goals and ambitions.[15] Part of the reason for Alban's 'suspension' may have to do with his predicament about how he should regard the sale of the family firm, and here we come to the central, politically resonant conundrum of the novel. Alban is caught between a matriarchal, hidebound, secretive, semi-feudal, incestuous clan on the one hand and an American-dominated, Middle-East meddling, global capitalist system on the other. He must try to balance his loyalty to his family members with his distrust of their motives and methods while being faced with the imminent demise of their status as share-owning decision makers at the hands of an American corporation.

Banks emphasises this political aspect of the Wopuld family's situation in Alban's attempt to describe it to his half-Czech and very cosmopolitan girlfriend Verushka Graef: 'I feel like a UN Observer or something', he tells her. 'I'm going to watch them tear themselves apart, for money. Or stay shackled together, in some dubious spirit of solidarity. Which we are not, frankly, very good at.'[16] The supposedly neutral United Nations observer status that Alban describes does not quite do justice to his own sense of involvement and identification with the participants, signalled by his switch from 'them' to 'we'[17] in describing his family and its shortcomings and this extract neatly expresses scepticism about both options the family face: whether to sell up and start arguing about the price or to remain locked in 'dubious' solidarity within a secretive and incestuous clan.

In describing the Wopulds as an incestuous clan, I am being literal in that Alban discovers at the end of the novel that he is the product of a brother and sister sexual union. His biological father is his uncle Blake who has been exiled to Hong Kong for having sex with his sister Irene (Alban's mother), who committed suicide as a result. Alban's liminal status explains why his grandmother was so keen to put a stop to the burgeoning romance with his cousin Sophie, given the probability of birth defects if they were to have children.[18] The revelation of paternity is important for *Garbadale*'s plot in that it acts to resolve a number of the novel's mysteries but it is this introduction of the sibling-incest theme that I think is especially significant in shedding light on Banks's treatment of trade and family, and by extension of post-devolution Scotland's status and future. The title of this essay 'our close but prohibited union' comes from Banks's novel *A Song of Stone* and is the narrator Abel describing his incestuous relationship with his sister Morgan.[19] *A Song of Stone* takes place in the confused aftermath of a civil war in an unnamed place and details the humiliations experienced by the aristocrats Abel and Morgan at the hands of a female Lieutenant who, with her gang of outlaws, takes over their castle as a military base. Banks had earlier used sibling incest in *Walking on Glass* and in one of his Culture series of science fiction novels *Use of Weapons*.[20]

Approaches to sibling incest have generally been dominated by psychoanalysis on the one hand and sociological or anthropological work on the other, the former represented in most detail by Otto Rank, Freud's disciple, and the latter by Edward Westermarck. For psychoanalysts like Rank, author of the encyclopaedic *The Incest Theme in Literature and Legend* first published in 1912, the patriarchal taboo against both maternal and sibling incest was the necessary control against something we all (unconsciously) desire, and which contributes to the subject's growth into the post-Oedipal phase of development:

> Despite all these taboos, restrictions, and threats of punishment, the tendency for sexual intercourse with one's closest relatives, deep-seated in human nature and barely kept in check by education and culture, not only appears in our dreams, in the creations of literary fantasy, and in neurosis, but also expresses itself in forbidden acts still frequent to this day.[21]

Westermarck by contrast claimed the exact opposite, that the incest-taboo was merely an expression of something we naturally found repellent. He coined the so-called Westermarck effect, where those who grow up in close proximity to each other are naturally disinclined to be sexually attracted to one another, whether they are genetically related or not. The Westermarck effect, elsewhere called natural avoidance, posits that people who grow up as siblings, even if they are not related, will not grow to regard each other with sexual interest. Westermarck's work possibly supplies some support for Genetic Sexual Attraction (GSA) that emerged as a term in the 1980s and is probably the converse of the Westermarck effect, where people who are related grow up apart, but when they meet, they find themselves sexually attracted to one another.[22] There have been recent cases in America and Scotland and media interest has ranged from the predictably prurient 'Siblings' Sick Fling Not a First' headlines to more sympathetic accounts.[23]

For Claude Lévi-Strauss, the incest taboo is so fundamental to human society that it almost defies analysis:

> The prohibition of incest is in origin neither purely cultural nor purely natural, nor is it a composite mixture of elements from both nature and culture. It is the fundamental step because of which, by which, but above all in which, the transition from nature to culture is accomplished.[24]

Here Lévi-Strauss almost struggles to articulate the importance of the incest taboo and positions it as the simplest building block of human society. According to this analysis the need for exogamy is crucial to human development and so for the structuralist anthropologists, the incest taboo enforces the patriarchal exchange of women as a means of developing social networks and affiliations without which the community cannot develop and thrive and the move from nature into culture cannot be achieved. What if the family does not need these economic and social ties however? What if the family is aristocratic and wishes to conserve its wealth? This is part of the long association of sibling incest with the aristocracy, from the Ptolemy dynasty in Egypt to the Hapsburgs of Europe.[25] Elizabethan and Jacobean drama registered sibling incest as fed by pressure within noble families not to mix their blood with families of lesser status and this is the scenario in Webster's *The Duchess of Malfi* where Ferdinand's incestuous desire for his sister the Duchess is encouraged by her marriage to her steward, a marriage beneath her according to Ferdinand. In fact so common was the sibling incest motif in English Renaissance drama that even the energetic and meticulous scholar of incest Otto Rank was forced to concede its 'tiring monotony'[26] in the works of Beaumont and Fletcher.

This connection between sibling incest and nobility is a particularly strong one in the work of Iain Banks, and in *A Song of Stone* Abel and Morgan's incestuous sexual relationship is a sign of their feudal aristocratic status, rather than any putative backwoods immorality. Having been disgusted by the democratic 'equality' of the sexual act, Abel addresses Morgan and vows to render himself distinguished by his sexual deviance as much as by conventional markers of social distinction:

> [T]o be worth anything at all I – we – must evade such mundane pursuits and set ourselves apart as much in the staging of that customary act as in our dress, habitation, speech or subsidiary manners. Thus have I degraded both of us in order to set us equally as far apart from the lowly as my imagination can devise, hoping – by these indiscretions – to make us both discrete.[27]

The hesitation between 'I' and 'we' in Abel's account anticipates Alban's move from 'them' and 'we' discussed above and strengthens the sense of families engendering a somewhat confused dual perspective in their members, both distinct from and part of a collective. As Abel's willingness here to act on behalf of the silent Morgan shows, social supremacy and marked reluctance to mix with others goes to the heart of Banks's use of sibling incest. When by the end of the novel the female Lieutenant has succeeded in taking Morgan as a lover, it is clear that the secluded and privileged dyad Abel tried to preserve has come crashing down among the lowly outlaws who now run the castle.

While the early English novel abounds with sibling incest, in works including Daniel Defoe's *Moll Flanders* (1722), Henry Fielding's *Joseph Andrews* (1742), Fanny Burney's *Evelina* (1778), and Horace Walpole's *The Mysterious Mother* (1791), the incest involved is often 'unwitting', as the characters only find out they are related after the fact. There are also frequent cases of 'near misses' where the couple think they are related but turn out not to be. In the Romantic era things change significantly, as sibling incest in literature is now read not as a perversion but as an extension and amplification of sibling love. Sibling love becomes arguably the highest form of love and devotion and in many respects forms the paradigm for Romantic love, being based on sentiment and mutual respect, and lying outside patriarchal and capitalist systems of exchange. For Romantics, sibling incest is often part of a general rebellion against patriarchal and divine law, and is connected to atheism and political radicalism, particularly in the work of Percy Shelley (*The Revolt of Islam*) and Byron (*Manfred*). Paternal incest, so common in gothic fiction, is evil and tyrannical, whereas sibling incest here speaks of equality and mutual devotion. Editorial changes to key Romantic works also show the sensitivity to sibling incest: Laon and Cythna in Percy Shelley's *The Revolt of Islam* were originally brother and sister but Cythna then became a foster sibling. In Mary Shelley's *Frankenstein*, the narrative of which is framed by letters from Walton to his sister, Elizabeth is famously described by Victor as 'my more than sister' and was Victor's cousin in the 1818 edition before becoming a foster sibling in the 1831 edition. The ambivalence of poetic treatments of incest, and incest's capacity to embody diametrically opposed values clearly fascinated Percy Shelley:

> [Incest is] like many other incorrect things, a very poetical circumstance. It may be the excess of love or hate. It may be the defiance of everything for the sake of another, which clothes itself in the glory of the highest heroism, or it may be that cynical rage which, confounding the good and the bad in existing opinions, breaks through them for the purpose of rioting in selfishness and antipathy.[28]

The 'poetical circumstance' attributed by Shelley indicates the importance of context for our understanding of incest, and this dual definition of the nature of incest may be broken down along paternal and sibling lines, with paternal incest issuing from an excess of hate while sibling love issues from an excess of love. Certainly Percy Shelley's treatment of paternal incest in his play *The Cenci* is one of horror and tyranny.

In contrast to these Romantic treatments of sibling incest, American literature has tended to focus on the destructive consequences of such relations, most notably in Edgar Allan Poe's 'The Fall of the House of Usher' (1839) that describes a family collapsing in on itself due to sibling incest. For James

Twitchell, this marks out the American presentations of the motif as significantly different in tone and outcome to Romantic projections:

> [T]he centrifugal forces placed in a usually motherless family as the male sexual violation of daughter/sister is no longer threatened, but often realised, caused a catastrophe so complete that finally nothing of the family remains. Let the English mythologize incest as did Byron, or metaphysicalize it as did Shelley, the Nineteenth Century American experience is uniformly horrible, irrepressibly gothic, maybe even characteristically pragmatic.[29]

Twitchell here however seems to be underplaying the extent to which Romantic plots involving incest also tend to end horribly for the characters involved. As Alan Richardson points out, while the Romantics may have gone out of their way to valorise sibling incest and see it as a special intensification of sentimental sibling attachment, they did not go out of their way to supply the characters with a happy ending in *Manfred* or *The Revolt of Islam*, thus preserving the association of sibling incest with destruction.[30]

As Twitchell notes above, the absence of the mother seems a common feature of sibling incest narratives and *Garbadale* is no exception. Some psychoanalytic approaches suggest that sibling incest proceeds from the same source as maternal incest, and may be a strategy for the brother to preserve the mother and vicariously experience Oedipal fulfilment. That sibling incest might stem from a desire to 'preserve' the family in absence of the mother is something that Richard McCabe hints at in his comments on John Ford's *'Tis Pity She's a Whore* claiming that 'psychologists have long regarded relationships with siblings as substitutes or replacements for relationships with parents'[31] and certainly Ian McEwan's treatment of brother and sister incest in *The Cement Garden* (1978) follows this pattern.[32] Having said that, the absent mother is not an ostensible factor in Blake Wopuld's incestuous desire for his sister Irene in *The Steep Approach to Garbadale* so we are drawn back to Blake's significance as a greedy criminal, who is originally believed by Alban to have defrauded the Wopuld company only for him to discover later that Blake's crime was more moral than financial. This linking of financial and moral deviance in the figure of Blake attests to the ways in which *Garbadale* both draws from and contributes to a literary tradition of sibling incest that has been notable for its emphasis on both social class and sibling incest's destructive outcomes, anti-patriarchal potential notwithstanding. The link between sibling incest and social privilege is clearly important for Banks's fiction but *Garbadale* develops this further in exploring the connection to trade. If the social structure of so many patriarchal societies has been historically defined by the exchange of women, by a 'trade'[33] between families, then sibling incest might be read as the biggest resistance to trade. Viewed from this perspective the refusal of exogamy or marrying outside the family is the refusal to interact with others for mutual benefit, not to enter into social alliances and extended family networks of interdependence but to keep everything for oneself. Sibling incest might therefore signal the arrogant refusal of the need to trade, and a disavowal of the need to become involved in exchange.

As Sander Gilman has shown, anti-Semitic thought in the nineteenth century often conflated sibling incest and economic consolidation:

> The Jews, in their refusal to marry beyond the 'inner group', were understood as incestuous or inbred, and their practice of perpetual endogamy, or marriage within specified segments of a society, was harshly condemned by conservatives as well as liberals. If the Jews are an incestuous people, it is because they demand that their children marry one another and the reason for that was assumed to be to perpetuate their economic power.[34]

Garbadale does not seem to code any of its characters as Jewish, and as discussed above the novel, through its pattern of character names, offers some strong pointers to national resonance. What Banks's novel does adopt and adapt from the literary tradition of sibling incest is the conjunction of economic, status and sexual issues within a family scenario. If we read *The Steep Approach to Garbadale* as at least partly about the choices facing post-devolution Scotland, then while the national 'family' of the UK may offer shelter from an existence exposed to the pitiless actions of the free market, it may also, like the Wopuld family, be a place of conflict, deception and potentially sinister secrets. Banks's careful treatment of the mechanics and politics of shareholder voting and financial negotiation in the novel also signals the extent to which economic interests may be heavily imbricated within the fabric of a democratic voting system. Alban as a (Scottish) subject attempting to navigate his way through complex relationships is placed in a position often found in Banks's novels, that of the game player, and *Garbadale* shows his continued fascination with games and how they are played.

Alban gradually realises that he has been a pawn in his grandmother's game: by fomenting resistance to the sale of the family company among its shareholders, he has been driving up the selling price to be extracted from Sprint Inc. while not being allowed to ever threaten the sale taking place. Once he has accomplished this, Grandma Win takes steps to prevent Alban disrupting the shareholder meeting by arranging for his boat to be sabotaged. Having used him to drive up the asking price, she no longer needs him. As Craig has asserted in relation to previous novels by Banks: 'For many of Banks's characters, the solution to the discovery that they have been trapped in such a game is to accept, themselves, the very role scripted for them – to play consciously and better the game which they did not realise they had been playing.'[35] Craig's description perfectly anticipates *Garbadale*, as once Alban has realised his grandmother has been playing a game with him he decides to trick her into revealing the truth behind his mother's death and ultimately the secret of his paternity. So the 'dupe' of the game learns from his experience and becomes a better games player, playing the game to his advantage. This movement deeper into the structure of the game is however not an unalloyed triumph. True, one can play the game better, but should one accept that the rules of the game cannot be changed? *The Steep Approach to Garbadale*, while following the pattern of increasingly sophisticated game-playing on the part of its characters, also meditates on the extent to which the framing of human beings as self-interested game players may have undesirable consequences particularly for collectives, whether national or familial. Game theory both in relation to the board game *Empire!* and to economics looms large in the novel. Alban meets Verushka at a game theory conference and she exhibits strong signs of pursuing her professional and romantic goals in single-minded, game-playing mode. When his uncle Blake tells Alban ' "Remember, Alban; always look out for number one. Be selfish. Every other bugger is" ' this is a classic summary of game theory applied to social situations, that by everyone behaving selfishly, the market will even things out and equilibrium will be established, recalling Adam Smith's 'invisible hand' metaphor where society as a whole benefits from each individual trying to do the best for himself or herself.[36]

Money's status as a fetish, as being on the one hand a set of mathematical signs and on the other access to tangible goods, finds its way into Banks's treatment of the negotiations at Garbadale. Having been told by his uncle Blake that measuring oneself against others in terms of wealth is unrewarding when you discover richer people are often unlikeable, Alban is later informed by Larry Feaguing, Spraint Inc.'s chief negotiator, that money is only part of the picture:

> 'You know,' Larry said, sitting back, frowning, 'this might sound like a strange thing to say, but in a way money is kind of irrelevant.'
> Alban widened his eyes. 'Really?'
> 'What I mean is, it's just how you keep score. Like a ball game. The scoreboard, the numbers on it; they're just things. It's what those numbers buy you, what they get you that matters; not the numbers themselves.'[37]

Feaguing offers a rather strange account of how 'the numbers' are both part of and not part of a game. His emphasis on money as buying power is met with some scepticism by Alban because Feaguing's account of money as a way of 'keeping score' ostensibly signals the triviality of its pursuit while simultaneously outlining a games-playing approach to the acquisition of wealth that can be found elsewhere in the Wopuld clan, not least in the destructive and self-destructive Blake. Feaguing's suggestion that because 'the numbers' are part of a game they can consequently be read as insignificant is a proposition that the novel works to undermine by its treatment of people as goal-oriented game-players who must learn to play the game more effectively in order to survive. The fact that Alban stands to make very little money from the sale of his small amount of shares reinforces his status as both a family insider and an outsider who does not share his relatives' financial concerns but whose opposition to the firm's proposed sale proceeds from a rather obscure desire for family solidarity in the face of an American corporate takeover.

At the Wopuld family meeting, only Alban votes against the sale of the company, everyone else voting in favour of a price significantly higher than Spraint's first offer, much to the dismay of Feaguing. Grandma Win's plan of increasing the asking price of the company has worked and Feaguing's perception of the family as unsophisticated has led to him being outmanoeuvred. Alban had already hinted at his family's capacity to make hardnosed business decisions in a revealing passage toward the end of the novel:

> 'Maybe we're both getting this the wrong way round,' Alban suggested. 'Perhaps you're right about the character and morals of Spraint Corp, but you're giving the Wopuld clan way too much respect for their beliefs and collective character. Maybe all *we're* interested in is money.'
> 'Do you really believe that, Alban?' Feaguing asked quietly.
> Alban looked around the room at all his many, many relations, this widespread but, for now – briefly – concentrated family, which he had loved and hated and served and exiled himself from and longed for and come to an accommodation with and still half loved and half hated sometimes, and then he looked back at Feaguing with a small smile. 'I don't know,' he said. 'But if I were you I'd treat it as a decent working hypothesis.'[38]

As a picture of a national family, half-loved and half-hated, this is filled with disappointment: the only thing to be decided is how much the members want to sell up for. Alban's complicated feelings about his family are shot through with a degree of cynicism regarding their capacity for acting only in their individual economic self-interest and the democratic exercise of shareholder voting becomes a rather hollow event. While the Wopuld clan are 'winners' as far as Feaguing's ball-game of numbers goes, family sentiment has been revealed as a very weak force without the potential to withstand integration into global capital. The family that brought the world *Empire!* has not lost its game-playing skills or capacity for subterfuge.

The novel ends surprisingly with Alban inheriting lots of money from Blake and starting an adventure centre for disadvantaged urban youth with the help of Tango, whose friendship with a victim of domestic abuse at the start of the book has become a romantic relationship by the end. Having benefited from help and hospitality from his working-class friend when he was down on his luck, Alban sets out to be a generous benefactor and changes his surname to Wopuld, acknowledging his true heritage and forsaking the good Scottish name of McGill to Tango's mystified disapproval. The turn to altruism and community action echoes the end of Banks's earlier novel *The Business* (1999) where the heroine Kate Telman leaves behind an important role in a powerful global conglomerate to work for the improvement of the lives of the subjects of a remote Himalayan monarchy.[39] Alban has profited from the fruits of *Empire!* but chooses to share his new-found wealth with those less fortunate.

Alban's path to the truth behind his mother's death and to a wealthy bequest follows Prentice's progress in *The Crow Road*. As Duncan Petrie describes 'in retracing Rory's footsteps, Prentice also functions as a kind of double for his uncle, revealing then confronting the guilty Fergus and ultimately driving him to suicide.'[40] This is the same path followed by Alban, whose investigations into his mother's death lead to the discovery of his true paternity and his villainous 'uncle's' subsequent suicide. Incest's association with the production of 'monstrous' offspring positions Alban as the monster at the centre of the labyrinth. *The Crow Road*'s treatment of game-playing also anticipates *Garbadale*'s interest in board-games, with Prentice as a boy playing a board-game based on trade created by his father called the River Game. Prentice and his brother however soon developed their own version called the Black River Game, which involved warships, much to the displeasure of their father. While playing at trade may not be as exciting as playing at military conquest (to little boys at least), trade is no doubt far preferable in the real world. One key question however is the degree to which trade is inevitable. In these novels the characters who do not 'trade', the incestuous Blake, Irene (even Rory from *The Crow Road*) end up dead, permanently, as Jean Baudrillard would say, outside exchange.

Ray Ryan in the introduction to his study *Ireland and Scotland: Literature and Culture, Nation and State* discusses comments by Alex Salmond, made when he was leader of the Scottish National Party (SNP), about Ireland and its economic success during the 1990s. Salmond's argument that Ireland's prosperity issued from its political independence acts to support the SNP's ultimate goal of Scottish independence and in this analysis the Republic of Ireland unconstrained by British hegemony is free to pursue its economic national interest (if we're game theorists we might say self-interest) in a European and global context.[41] The significance in post-devolution Scotland of the economic argument in favour of full independence forms the sociohistorical context of *Garbadale* and the novel continues Banks's explorations of class and national identity in *The Bridge* and *The Crow Road*, combining them with a more globally oriented focus. The (Scottish) subject must now negotiate both national and class structures in Scotland/Britain *and* Scotland/Britain's relations with the wider world, especially the United States. This is the difficult path to tread between paternalistic power and vested and inherited interests on the one hand and USA-led international capitalism on the other. The protagonist is trying to leave behind the inbred and incestuous world of sheltered privilege and stagnation while seeking to remain particular and distinctive by resisting complete assimilation into the neo-liberal machinery of international finance. However *Garbadale*'s exploration of relationships that are not primarily defined by money, often associated with family and national affiliations, tends to show how deeply wealth can affect these systems of supposedly non-economic relation. Although Alban's predicament may at first look like a balanced dilemma, the novel irresistibly moves towards the necessity of trade and the qualified rejection of the family in favour of new class and national connections between people, most clearly represented by Verushka and the children Tango brings to Alban's large house at the end of the novel. This movement towards exposing the dangers of narrow national and family identification is helped in no small part by the sibling incest motif, and in fact the importance of this motif in the novel is that it acts to stigmatise the (national) family by rendering it incestuous, offering an alternative to global exchange that is not an alternative as it only leads to inbreeding and monstrosity. Sibling incest therefore serves to underline the unavoidability of trade and exchange, by coding the refusal to trade as an act of abusive and self-destructive aristocratic perversity.

Stefanie Lehner concludes her discussion of the work of A.L. Kennedy and James Kelman by claiming that both Scottish writers exemplify a 'subaltern aesthetic' that sensitively registers the local action of global capital:

> By mapping their characters' specific experiences of subjugation and oppression onto the socio-political and economic processes that implicate Scotland's devolution within a global capitalist network designated as the 'end of history', both writers [Kennedy and Kelman] produce what I would like to term a 'subaltern aesthetic'.[42]

The Steep Approach to Garbadale can be read as partaking to a degree in this 'subaltern aesthetic' given its allegorical presentation of Scottish devolution within a globalised economic context and the challenges this creates. The novel's turn away from the incestuous world of the (national) family however is shot through with feelings of profound ambivalence, particularly in relation to the apparent 'end-of-history' inevitability of international capitalist trade, a future Alban reluctantly accepts principally it would seem due to the monstrosity of the alternative. The narrative's culmination in

Alban's embracing of cosmopolitan and cross-class Scottishness from his privileged social position offers a counterweight to the world of Spraint Inc. The charitable impulse to run a scheme for disadvantaged children however is something of a throwback to the plot resolutions of the 'industrial novels' of the nineteenth century so memorably and perceptively critiqued by Raymond Williams.[43] The challenge of modelling relations 'outside' systems of exchange is perhaps a recurrent feature of both Banks's mainstream work and science fiction, although as this essay has shown the novel's treatment of sibling incest projects the independent subject as better off outside the national family and integrated into globalised systems of exchange and circulation, despite the possible/probable injustices such systems may generate. The perverse preservation of the family, however attractive, always seems to lead to stagnation, stasis and entropy.

Notes

1 See Robert Duggan, 'The geopolitics of inner space in contemporary British fiction', *Textual Practice* 27:5 (2013), pp. 899–920.
2 Iain Banks, *The Bridge* (Little Brown, 1986).
3 Iain Banks, *The Crow Road* (Little Brown, 1992).
4 Iain Banks, *The Steep Approach to Garbadale* (Little Brown, 2007).
5 Cristie March, *Rewriting Scotland* (Manchester University Press, 2002), p. 103.
6 Banks, *Garbadale*, p. 2.
7 Thom Nairn, 'Iain Banks and the fiction factory', in Gavin Wallace and Randall Stevenson (eds), *The Scottish Novel since the Seventies* (Edinburgh University Press, 1993), p. 133.
8 See Robert Duggan, *The Grotesque in Contemporary British Fiction* (Manchester University Press, 2013).
9 Craig Cairns, *Out of History* (Polygon, 1996), pp. 205–6.
10 Eleanor Bell, *Questioning Scotland* (Palgrave, 2004), p. 47.
11 Michael Gardiner and Graeme MacDonald (eds), *Scottish Literature and Postcolonial Literature* (Edinburgh University Press, 2011).
12 Irish studies came to be a place of conflict in the 1990s as the term 'Irishness' and 'the Irish diaspora' were strongly debated.
13 For more on the significance of the Gulf War for Banks's science fiction, see Robert Duggan, 'Iain M. Banks, postmodernism and the Gulf War,' *Extrapolation* 48:3 (2007), pp. 558–77.
14 Cairns Craig, *The Modern Scottish Novel* (Edinburgh University Press, 1999), p. 132.
15 Alasdair Gray, *Lanark* (Canongate, 1981). Irvine Welsh, *Marabou Stork Nightmares* (Jonathan Cape, 1995).
16 Banks, *Garbadale*, p. 253.

17 *Ibid.*, p. 256.
18 Alan H. Bittles and James V. Neel, 'The costs of human inbreeding and their implications for variations at the DNA level', *Nature Genetics* 8 (1994), pp. 117–21.
19 Iain Banks, *A Song of Stone* (Little Brown, 1997), p. 232.
20 Iain Banks, *Walking on Glass* (Macmillan, 1985). Iain M. Banks, *Use of Weapons* (London: Orbit, 1990).
21 Otto Rank, Gregory Richter (trans.) *The Incest Theme in Literature and Legend* ([1912] Johns Hopkins University Press, 1992), p. 355.
22 Johanna Stiebert, *First-Degree Incest and the Hebrew Bible* (Bloomsbury, 2016), p. 22.
23 Kenny Angove, 'Siblings' sick fling not a first', The *Sun* 7 September 2011. www.thesun.co.uk/sol/homepage/news/scottishnews/3799322/Siblings-sick-fling-not-a-first.html (accessed 26 April 2013). Alix Kirsta, 'Genetic sexual attraction,' *Guardian* 17 May 2003. www.guardian.co.uk/theguardian/2003/may/17/weekend7.weekend2 (accessed 26 April 2013).
24 Claude Lévi-Strauss, *The Elementary Structures of Kinship* (Beacon, 1969), p. 24.
25 Sheila L. Ager, 'The power of excess: Royal incest and the Ptolemaic Dynasty', *Anthropologica* 48:2 (2006), pp. 165–86.
26 Otto Rank, *The Incest Theme*.
27 Banks, *A Song of Stone*, pp. 71–2.
28 Percy Shelley quoted in Richard McCabe, *Incest, Drama and Nature's Law 1550–1700* (Cambridge University Press, 1993), p. 228.
29 James B. Twitchell, *Forbidden Partners* (Columbia University Press, 1987), p. 196.
30 Alan Richardson, 'Rethinking romantic incest: Human universals, literary representation, and the biology of mind', *New Literary History* 31:3 (2000), pp. 553–72.
31 McCabe, *Incest, Drama and Nature's Law*, p. 233.
32 Ian McEwan, *The Cement Garden* (Jonathan Cape, 1978).
33 Mary Murray, *The Law of the Father? Patriarchy in the Transition from Feudalism to Capitalism* (Routledge, 1995), p. 9.
34 Sander Gilman, 'Sibling incest, madness and the 'Jews', *Social Research* 65:2 (1998), p. 404.
35 Cairns Craig, *Complicity* (Continuum, 2002), p. 20.
36 Banks, *Garbadale*, p. 240.
37 *Ibid.*, p. 319.
38 *Ibid.*, pp. 320–1.
39 Iain Banks, *The Business* (Little Brown, 1999).
40 Duncan Petrie, *Contemporary Scottish Fictions* (Edinburgh University Press, 2004), p. 123.
41 Ray Ryan, *Ireland and Scotland: Literature and Culture, Nation and State* (Oxford University Press, 2002), p. 1–2.

42 Stefanie Lehner, 'Subaltern Scotland: Devolution and postcoloniality' in Berthold Schoene (ed.) *The Edinburgh Companion to Scottish Literature* (Edinburgh University Press, 2007), p. 300.
43 Raymond Williams, *Culture and Society 1780–1950* (Chatto and Windus, 1958).

Bibliography

Fiction

Banks, Iain, *Walking on Glass* (Macmillan, 1985)
——., *The Bridge* (Little Brown, 1986)
——., *Use of Weapons* (Orbit, 1990)
——., *The Crow Road* (Little Brown, 1992)
——., *A Song of Stone* (Little Brown, 1997)
——., *The Business* (Little Brown, 1999)
——., *The Steep Approach to Garbadale* (Little Brown, 2007)
Gray, Alasdair, *Lanark* (Canongate, 1981)
McEwan, Ian, *The Cement Garden* (Jonathan Cape, 1978)
Welsh, Irvine, *Marabou Stork Nightmares* (Jonathan Cape, 1995)

Non-fiction

Ager, Sheila L., 'The power of excess: Royal incest and the Ptolemaic Dynasty', *Anthropologica* 48:2 (2006), pp. 165–86
Angove, Kenny, 'Siblings' sick fling not a first', *The Sun* (7 September, 2011)
Bell, Eleanor, *Questioning Scotland: Literature, Nationalism, Postmodernism* (Palgrave, 2004)
Bittles, Alan H. and James V. Neel, 'The costs of human inbreeding and their implications for variations at the DNA level' in *Nature Genetics* 8 (1994), pp. 117–21
Cairns, Craig, *Out of History* (Polygon, 1996)
——., *Complicity: A Reader's Guide* (Continuum, 2002)
Duggan, Robert, 'Iain M. Banks, postmodernism and the Gulf War', *Extrapolation* 48:3 (2007), pp. 558–77
——., *The Grotesque in Contemporary British Fiction* (Manchester University Press, 2013)
Gardiner, Michael and Graeme Macdonald, (eds), *Scottish Literature and Postcolonial Literature* (Edinburgh University Press, 2011)
Gilman, Sander, 'Sibling incest, madness and the "Jews"', *Social Research* 65:2 (1998), pp. 157–79
Kirsta, Alix, 'Genetic sexual attraction', *Guardian* (17 May 2003)
Lehner, Stefanie, 'Subaltern Scotland: Devolution and postcoloniality', in Berthold Schoene (ed.), *The Edinburgh Companion to Scottish Literature* (Edinburgh University Press, 2007), pp. 292–301

Lévi-Strauss, Claude, *The Elementary Structures of Kinship* (Beacon, 1969)
McCabe, Richard, *Incest, Drama and Nature's Law 1550–1700* (Cambridge University Press, 1993)
March, Christie, *Rewriting Scotland* (Manchester University Press, 2002)
Murray, Mary, *The Law of the Father? Patriarchy in the Transition from Feudalism to Capitalism* (Routledge, 1995)
Nairn, Thom, 'Iain Banks and the fiction factory', in Gavin Wallace and Randall Stevenson (eds), *The Scottish Novel since the Seventies* (Edinburgh University Press, 1993), pp. 127–35
Petrie, Duncan, *Contemporary Scottish Fictions* (Edinburgh University Press, 2004)
Rank, Otto, Richter Gregory (trans.) *The Incest Theme in Literature and Legend*, ([1912] Johns Hopkins University Press, 1992)
Richardson, Alan, 'Rethinking romantic incest: Human universals, literary representation, and the biology of mind', *New Literary History* 31:3 (2000), pp. 553–72
Ryan, Ray, *Ireland and Scotland: Literature and Culture, Nation and State* (Oxford University Press, 2002)
Stiebert, Johanna, *First-Degree Incest and the Hebrew Bible: Sex in the Family* (Bloomsbury, 2016)
Twitchell, James B., *Forbidden Partners: The Incest Taboo in Modern Culture* (Columbia University Press, 1987)
Williams, Raymond, *Culture and Society 1780–1950* (Chatto and Windus, 1958)

9

Is posthuman incest possible? Science fiction and the futures of the body

Alistair Brown

Introduction: Posthuman bodies, postmodern values

As we become increasingly able to change our bodies through technologies, the human will transgress into the posthuman, a state in which – as the word's relationship to postmodernism implies – our cultural value systems will also change.[1]: the *Oxford English Dictionary* defines 'Posthuman' as 'The idea that humanity can be transformed, transcended, or eliminated either by technological advances or the evolutionary process; artistic, scientific, or philosophical practice which reflects this belief'.[2] Whether browsing social networks, wearing augmented reality devices such as the Microsoft Hololens, or genetically profiling our potential offspring, technologies seem destined to alter our deep-rooted behaviours: the work we do, the imaginative worlds we inhabit and, most significantly for the context of the present book, our familial and sexual relations.[3] This chapter looks towards the futures of incest through the lens of science fiction. By examining the depiction of incest in three narratives concerned with different posthuman technologies of reproduction and embodiment – androids (*Abiogenesis*), genetic cloning (*Plan for Chaos*), and artificial intelligence (*Neuromancer*) – it asks whether, although society may become posthuman, it will also become post-incestuous. As well as using science fiction to look forwards, however, these fictitious visions of posthumanism also testify to, and indeed serve to shape, our reactions to technologies in the present; thus this chapter also examines how fiction may intersect current debates as we stand on the cusp of the posthuman revolution, such as the changing ethics of familial relations brought about through IVF.

As the other chapters in this volume demonstrate, incest is a staple within popular culture, which invokes the taboo in order to transgress it, attracting readers or viewers who want to imagine what 'anarchy can do to the measured fears they have been carefully instructed to cherish'.[4] It is not a coincidence

Is posthuman incest possible?

that in the nineteenth century, when modern ideas about incest were confirmed through the rise of print culture, it was popular gothic that mediated them. It is therefore interesting that although across a broad range of fantasy novels incest is a recurring theme (witness Emma V. Miller's discussion of *Tender Morsels* elsewhere in this collection), incest features very rarely when it comes to mass-market science fiction works involving androids.[5] Perhaps this is because the cognitive estrangements demanded by this type of science fiction are in themselves sufficient to provide the sense of 'anarchy' that readers require.

The degree to which the incest taboo is a universal feature of humanity, rooted in the evolutionary need for genetic mixing, or a result of cultural and social ideologies which are continually changing, has been much discussed. Nature and culture (which are themselves contested terms) interplay in a complex and varying manner, such that it would be incorrect to see biological necessity as the sole factor in determining what counts as incest.[6] After all, in the current era of contraception the need to protect against genetic mutation is less relevant to human sexuality, yet incest remains on the statute books of most countries, and is defined not simply by genetic proximity and sexual risk, but by familial care (as between adults and their step-children) and psychological abuse. Nevertheless, biology does retain some vestigial influence over the ways in which we respond to incest. As Robin Fox suggests, biology explains why 'we are so easily made uneasy' by incest when it is perceived to occur, even if precisely what counts as an incestuous act may vary.[7]

In evaluating the interplay of biological and social interpretations of the incest taboo, most literary commentaries have used fiction to show how notions of incest have been changed historically by the variable of culture; in these accounts, the biological body remains a constant, whilst society adapts its parameters for what counts as incest and how it is punished.[8] However, science fiction introduces material embodiment as a variable, since fantasy bodies can be made (as in androids), radically altered (through genetics), or even removed entirely (through abstracting intelligence onto a computer). By examining three science fictions relating to these respective fields, we can assess how posthuman technologies will affect our embodied constitution, and thereby reshape social norms. In this sense, science fiction offers a popular mediation of postmodern theory which sees aspects of a person's identity, such as gender or the family, as fluid rather than biologically essential. Donna Haraway's feminist 'Cyborg manifesto' (1991), for example, suggests that in today's industrialised societies people are increasingly cyborgs, in that our human selfhood is bound up with the non-human technologies we use and integrate with our bodies.[9] As we no longer possess a singular embodiment, so the ways in which we should behave based on that embodiment are equally unfixed; we can no longer maintain essentialist beliefs about gender, sexuality, or race. For example, a video gamer (a cyborg hybrid of the physical player and his or her digital avatar) can role-play as a man or woman regardless of his or her own physical sex, and in online environments can perform acts that may or may not reflect how these genders conventionally behave in 'normal' society. According to Haraway's epistemology, 'normal' relationships – such as the old 'model of the organic family' – do not exist for the true cyborg. Following this trajectory, it would seem that abnormal relationships, including incestuous ones, are also potentially flexible. My readings of these science fictions affirm Haraway's assumption that the posthuman and postmodern subject will find the morality that governs his or her relationships is redefined by changing concepts of the body. However, careful reading of these novels reveals how important it is that society maintains relatively stable concepts of taboos such as incest at the present time, even while the technologies that are hypothesised may appear to undermine the biological predicate for such ethics in the future.

One reason for this is that science fiction does not only predict a future yet to come, but also affects perceptions of incest and sexuality in the present. Kaitlyn O'Connor's erotic novel *Abiogenesis* (2012) serves as useful evidence of the troublesome potential of popular culture as it reimagines incest through technological fantasy.[10] The novel represents close relationships between essentially identical androids, whose men are so similar that they can enjoy polygamous relations with a female heroine. Corresponding to Haraway's assumption, the novel revises the 'old model of the organic family' by presenting (and erotically enjoying) polygamy in an android context in which there are two factory-produced men to every woman. However, precisely because they have been designed to be near identical, and are described indeed as being like 'twins', there is also an undercurrent of incest in the relationships. *Abiogenesis* thus suggests that alternative familial and sexual relations are inevitable in posthuman societies. However, this approach may also normalise values in the reader's own context, in particular reinscribing a gender hierarchy in which the woman's ultimate aspiration and function is as childbearer, with the heroine being seen as a kind of Eve to a new race of androids. The novel celebrates a baby born of implied (but never overtly stated) incest as a reward for the female heroine's conformity to patriarchal values which have survived the transition from human to posthuman culture. The novel is not an innocent escapist fantasy for its implied female reader, but rather is problematically contradictory in celebrating the erotic potential of new family configurations that are facilitated by technology, whilst at the same time suggesting the most important identity of all, that of the female gender, remains innately that of willing mother, giving up her body to possibly incestuous relationships.

If O'Connor's work illustrates the dark side to Haraway's hope that cyborgism frees us from essentialist constraints, John Wyndham's *Plan for*

Chaos (c.1951) foresees how technologies such as cloning must alter the status of women, mothers, and incest simultaneously, in a semiotic web of relations where one term affects the other.[11] Within the context of genetic cloning, the forcefulness of the incest taboo is reduced relative to the more emphatic changes to the family that are wrought by the new science. Wyndham imagines a neo-Nazi clone where women are freed from the demands of childbearing, leading to a society modelled on the hive rather than the traditional nuclear family of the 1950s. Against this backdrop, incest between first cousins – the relationship of the novel's two protagonists – is presented as more acceptable than it might otherwise be. Indeed, mainstream society's attempt to prohibit non-abusive first-cousin relationships is represented as an analogous (and perhaps just as wrong) form of manipulation to the scientific tampering with nature carried out by the Nazis. Wyndham shows how the concept of incest is not a product of biology or culture alone, but varies according to the context in which it is framed and the different versions of 'unnatural' against which it is relativised. The novel thus resonates with Linda Nicolson's proposal that the definition of the 'traditional' family is variable, and appropriate family models should be judged according to instrumental criteria about whether that family provides emotional fulfilment, rather than absolute criteria of genetic affinity[12]. Projecting forwards to our own time, Wyndham's adaptive approach carries lessons for the new families that are possible through IVF. For example, on what epistemological basis can we continue stringently to invoke an incest taboo, if we as a society are creating children who genuinely cannot be sure who, genetically, their parents are? Both Wyndham and Nicolson suggest that imposing an absolute vision of the normal family is difficult when technology (for Wyndham) and society (for Nicolson) continually reshape that definition.

In exploring different aspects of posthumanism via androids and cloning, both *Abiogenesis* and *Plan for Chaos* reflect changing responses to incest as conventional human embodiment, and embodied birth, is transgressed through technology. However, what happens when the body is removed from the equation entirely? William Gibson's seminal cyberfiction, *Neuromancer* (1984),[13] suggests that whatever cultural perceptions we have of incest, kinship or sexuality in the human context today may be rendered irrelevant in a future in which individual (dis)embodiment is disconnected from the ethics of the body politic.[14] In the era of artificial intelligences, when minds occupy the ephemeral network rather than physical, shared, social space, it is indicated that incest will be just one of a suite of norms that will be eradicated. In accordance with Foucault's observation that 'relations of power are interwoven with other kinds of relations (production, kinship, family, sexuality),'[15] *Neuromancer* presents a corporation that has used incest to keep company ownership within a family. As that corporation collapses by the novel's end, which sees the rise of a true artificial intelligence, Gibson's work suggests that the risks of incest will be circumnavigated entirely as the embodied human subject, and the family predicated upon it, will no longer exist as such. The family will be replaced by the machine.

Progressively, then, my three novels show how technology may eventually effect such radical change upon human embodiment, sexuality and procreation that legislating for society's sexual or kinship relations in the future will be impossible. To worry about how literary fantasy – such as *Abiogenesis* – impacts upon readers today may be irrelevant: the prevailing force of change is technology rather than culture, and this will change the human body, from which incest concerns arise, beyond all recognition. Yet even as *Neuromancer* looks towards such a technologically determined future, this signifies the need to continue to theorise incest in a present when we are not yet truly cyborg. As I conclude with a discussion of how incest is legislated for in the virtual world of *Second Life*, there is a danger in perceiving that technology as it stands at present, or future technology as envisioned by science fiction, gives license for the abolition of current legal frameworks designed to protect people against incest. It is not permissible to enact non-physical abuse via online or social media simply because the perpetrators are virtualised and pseudonymous. Ultimately, all these novels remain hypothetical visions of a post-incestuous, posthuman future that inversely, through the fact that the future they envisage is not yet arrived, signifies our still human present.

Android incest: Kaitlyn O'Connor's Abiogenesis

The possibility that creatures such as androids might even be capable of emotions and relationships on any level is already a leap of the imagination; that android relationships might become so normalised as to be capable of becoming abnormal might seem to be a step too far. Yet when in the *Star Trek: The Next Generation* episode 'The Offspring' (1990) the android Data creates a daughter for himself, following the designs of his own creator Soong, there should, in principle, be something unsettling about a child who is, except for the appearance and sex that Data chooses for her, materially the same as her parent.[16] What is uncanny in this episode is not so much that Data is not human – he is so evidently not, with his pallid face – but that Data has created a daughter who looks very like himself. It is not the androids' otherness to the human, but their insufficient otherness to each other, that is most unnerving. Whilst science fiction often suggests the lines distinguishing humans from non-humans are blurry, it also implies that the lines separating one android from another are equally indistinct, because we are unsure of how they are made and therefore how similar they are to each other. Android replicants may be seen as the ontological equivalent of human twins, sharing a common parentage and moment of reproduction (on the assembly line or designer's template) – thus when they do have relationships, these could be construed as analogous to sibling incest.

However, whilst science fiction is fascinated by the uncomfortable relatedness of non-humans to humans, it rarely enquires explicitly as to whether the relationships between non-humans and non-humans are also uncomfortably close. As a self-published erotic novel that is part of a popular series, Kaitlyn O'Connor's *Abiogenesis* shows how ideas about posthumanism and cyborgism, theorised critically by the likes of Donna Haraway, have been incorporated by mass culture. By changing the ontology of the characters (they are androids that are made, not born) O'Connor projects into the seemingly distinctive space of fantasy, sibling desire that would normally be suppressed. As with pornography, however, it is dangerous to assume that by being fantasy rather than realism the genre relinquishes ethical responsibility, since fiction can still normalise values and ideologies that ought to be reflected on more critically. In this case, the novel glosses over the uncertainty about the androids' origins that might, ordinarily, make us wonder whether their sexual relations with one another are problematically incestuous.

The plot focuses on a one-time rebel hunter, Dalia, and group of rebel androids who are evading the company that created them in order to establish a new colony. Dalia turns out not to be human but android, whilst the antagonist, Reuel, is an android who initially appears to possess few emotions other than malevolence (he imprisons and dominates Dalia sexually), but who eventually reveals himself to have intensely human qualities, particularly the ability to love and empathise with another. The novel concludes with Dalia co-habiting with Pierce, a virtually identical android to Reuel, and having their twin babies through an unexplained process (abiogenesis) by which mechanical beings can beget living organisms.

Although reader reviews suggest that the novel was enjoyed as a science fiction as well as an erotic romance,[17] the main reason for the move into the fantastic is that its alternative sexual encounters such as bondage and polygamy can be enjoyed without this seeming like a manifesto for living in the real world. Additionally, the fact that they have been designed explains why they all seem possessed of athletic bodies, large phalluses, and great sexual intuition. Furthermore, they have been produced in a ratio of two men to every woman, so they must behave polygamously in order to reduce destructive male jealousy, thus enabling O'Connor to represent the *ménage à trois* that is her particular selling point.[18] Yet whilst the setting of the novel in the future elicits erotic affect, it also smoothes over the problematic relations between androids. Although there may not be a biological (that is, genetic) risk that stems from incest in a world of bio-mechanical beings, there is still something of the uncanny doppelganger about the androids, which stems from their manufactured origin. The fact that the narrative never expresses any anxiety about whether the androids who have sexual relations are also 'brothers' and 'sisters' because of their shared origin on the same production line shows how they are apparently no longer bound by the laws many consider to be innate, such as the incest taboo.[19]

To see how the novel subverts the incest taboo whilst also making aesthetic use of it, it is necessary to note the tension between O'Connor's emphasis on the androids' individuality, and their almost identikit similarity. At first, the novel suggests that each android is a unique individual rather than a reproduction from an assembly line template, as here when Dalia observes some of the rebels:

> There was no similarity between them beyond a general physical build, height and weight. Two were blond, two dark, but the shades varied drastically, as did their eye colour and facial features, but then she hadn't expected them to look as if they had come off an assembly line. They had arisen from a new generation of cyborg, and had been touted as 'each as uniquely different and natural as a real, live human being.'[20]

There is, however, an unconscious duplicity in the language used here. In having to deny their similarity, O'Connor admits that androids are most often perceived as duplicates of one another, whilst the same metaphor that seeks to assert their difference – they did not 'look as if they had come off an assembly line' – ironically reminds that they are in fact produced beings, identical except in those respects their manufacturers have sought to differentiate them, including their sex. On the face of it, androids might seem comparable to two animals from a different species: they are similar for the most part because of their common speciation, but sufficiently different to denote them as distinct individuals within that species. However, this metaphor only works so far. Individuals within a species are made individual because of a random mixing of certain genes at the tip of a pyramid – such as eye colour or body size – even though the majority of genes are the same since they code for species-level attributes. However, these androids are not differentiated as individuals on a random basis because their differences have been specifically designed in. Thus, although individual in this case, they might also in principle be made to be identical; this is in contrast to nature in which only the rare fluke of monozygotic twins leads to such close similarity. The production-line model of creation compromises the basic Enlightenment premise that each body contains a unique, autonomous, thinking subject who is different from every other autonomous subject, as is guaranteed by the randomness and fecundity of nature. It is the very need to allow nature to build in randomness to differentiate individual humans that accounts for the incest taboo in the first place, according to evolutionary interpretations.

However, when creatures are designed, and selectively differentiated, the old guarantee of autonomy no longer holds.

From the androids' own moral point of view we are supposed to see them as distinct individuals who happen to be of a different species but who have equivalent moral needs and rights to humans. However, readers are continually reminded of the fact that the androids have been made similarly, not born differently; this similarity is essential to the novel's desire to present polygamy in a positive way. Thus Dalia is a CO479 model, and Reuel and Pierce a CO478, a mere number apart; Dalia has simply been upgraded with simulated memories of childhood, thereby initially preventing her from realising that she is not human. All the females are named after flowers; all the men, with the exception of Reuel, after presidents. All the androids seem to be the same age. Since the men are essentially interchangeable – Reuel and Pierce have the same body type, both have equivalent personality and cognitive attributes as indicated by their being equally matched at chess – there are ultimately no wider relationship dilemmas that stem from their strategic decision to engage in polygamy. In his psychoanalytic study of doubling and incest, John Irwin has noted the preponderance of brotherly doubles in which one plays 'the role of the shadow – the dark self that is made to bear the consciously unacceptable desires' – specifically incest – that are 'repudiated by the bright half of the mind.'[21] At first, *Abiogenesis* seems to conform to this template. Reuel is aggressive and dominating, playing out sado-masochistic sex games on Dalia. Pierce seems more amenable. Yet rather than this good brother (the voice of social reason, or the superego) ultimately vanquishing Reuel (who represents pure sexual desire, or the id), instead there is an equalisation between them, so that both Reuel and Pierce become satisfying partners for Dalia, who participates increasingly willingly in submissive sex with them both. The equalisation of the three characters is marked by the fact that Dalia's twin babies belong to both men. By reminding us continually about their kinship, and the fact that each android is a double of the other (bar minor distinguishing features), neither man suffers as a consequence of Dalia's decision to sleep with both of them, whilst Dalia enjoys sexual partnership seemingly on her terms. The fantasy pursued here, then, is one of polygamy without consequences.

Yet this is not merely innocent escapism, in which because the androids are figured as not-human, the fiction does not need to honour humanist conventions of family and sexuality. In failing to draw attention to the incestuous implications upon which its polygamous eroticism depends, namely the fact that the androids are ontologically similar, *Abiogenesis* highlights the risks of science fiction that, as radical feminists have argued about male-authored pornography,[22] might unthinkingly normalise behaviours in the here and now of the reader. The one exception to the rule of android similarity is Dalia, the woman who alone can get pregnant, and who will gestate the new android society, free from the even more unnatural birth of the factory. Superficially, *Abiogenesis* seems to celebrate an empowered female future in which Dalia is the only truly unique individual in a world of male simulacra available to fulfil her sexual and procreative needs. This is, however, a naïve view given that it resorts to old models in which the woman is othered through her childbirthing capacity. Judith Herman reports of incest victims that they often 'seemed to feel that they deserved to be beaten'.[23] There is a sense in which the novel's, and Dalia's, relationships with two men, whose origins and likeness she (or the reader) never questions, makes her into a heroine whose new children constitute a reward she 'deserves', when in fact they might also stand for the unthinking exploitation of the mother's body by her two brothers.

This popular novel, appealing to the mass market as an ebook published under O'Connor's own imprint, thus serves as a useful benchmark of the degree to which changing embodiment in science fiction changes social norms in the present as well as simply imagining a future yet to come. For the reader of *Abiogenesis*, it seems that the translation to a fantasy context alleviates the ethical responsibilities of our own world, simply because the androids have been produced in a factory. In enquiring as to whether posthuman incest is possible, the novel seems to suggest that it is not, given that overtly polygamous and implicitly incestuous sexuality is here celebrated rather than challenged. However, looked at from another perspective, the fact that for the reader it requires the representation of android bodies to remove certain taboos (polygamy, incest) perhaps suggests the still pervasive significance of these ethics in our own humanly embodied culture in the here and now, from which fiction provides only temporary escape.

If this shows that we are still human rather than posthuman, and thus remain wedded to old taboos which it takes fantasy temporarily to transgress, then fiction bears a responsibility to deal with taboos with a similar degree of critical reflection to that which I have offered here. The danger of *Abiogenesis* is that it normalises gender and sexual stereotypes: male masochism as something to be enjoyed by a woman; pregnancy as the ultimate validation of female sexuality; polygamous relations with multiple men as the hallmark of a woman's ability to manipulate men, rather than (as is really the case) be exploited by them. In the same vein, by being latent within the novel, rather than being commented upon explicitly, *Abiogenesis* similarly suggests that we should not worry about sexual partners who may share our own ancestry. Whether this directly influences readers or not, it contributes to the sense that the uncertainty about another's identity that is brought about by technology licenses behaviours which we would ordinarily see as problematic. One example of this might be the way in which social media prompts people to be abusive, often sexually, in ways that they would not consider doing in real life. As I discuss at the end of this chapter, it is just such a naïve reading of posthuman ethics – in which technologies seem to decouple people from responsibility for their actions, because they decouple people from a traditional body – that needs to be challenged.

Cloning the family: John Wyndham's Plan For Chaos

While *Abiogenesis* needs to be read against the grain to show that incest and sexual care remain ethical imperatives for the reader, John Wyndham's novel is more explicit as to the interrelation of fantasy and reality. His work shows how imagining a speculative technology (cloning) in turn affects the semiotics of incest in the real-world present.[24] Wyndham weighs the unnaturalness of genetic modification against incest between first cousins, and perceives that whilst the former is genuinely threatening, taboos against the latter are based on flawed notions of what constitutes a proper family. He suggests that our negative attitudes to some degrees of incest (between first cousins) are ideological, similar to the Nazis' desire to manipulate the human species by breeding. At the same time, other degrees of incest (such as sibling incest) are taboo because of innate, biological imperatives. Presenting a spectrum of biological and cultural factors behind the taboo, Wyndham ultimately adopts an instrumental approach. He demands that we judge families according to whether they are emotionally satisfying, not according to absolute criteria about the degree of relatedness within them, since to impose such criteria may be structurally equivalent to fascist eugenics.

The story is centred on two betrothed first cousins, Freda Darl and Johnny Farthing. This relationship between two similar-looking cousins provides a context for the main plot of the novel. When a series of women who look peculiarly like Freda begin to go missing or suffer unfortunate deaths, Freda and Johnny begin to investigate; the mystery deepens when Johnny comes across men who look much like him who are implicated in the murders. It is only because of the familial resemblance between themselves and the victims that they are able to infiltrate what turns out to be a secretive Nazi order trying to establish a New Germany. New Germany is using the 'Eidermann process' of embryonic fission (a variant on the Bokanovsky process of *Brave New World*) to breed a virtually identical race of 512 sets of Aryan twins from the same parental sources. The leader of New Germany and mother of the clone-children is Marta Dahle, Johnny and Freda's aunt, which explains the likeness of the unnatural clones to the natural cousins. Wyndham implies that first-cousin relationships (which were legal in the UK at the time of the novel's composition although prohibited in much of the United States after the Civil War)[25] are of little worry compared to the implications of cloning, or to the political attempt to control what types of relationships are acceptable or beneficial to society.

In the longest monologue of the novel the narrator, Johnny, considers the implications of cloning for the family unit (as is common in Wyndham's fiction, the voice switches from that of a hard-boiled hero, to a more meditative mode that approximates his own).[26] The family, he observes, is institutionally designed to preserve and nurture life, which is always fragile and hard to reproduce. Once reproduction becomes possible on a mass scale, though, the family would naturally disintegrate: 'Once the symbol of the mother holding her child ceased to have universal significance for the race, anything might happen. There was not a standard, not a value that could not be changed.'[27] Like many of Wyndham's women, Marta, the original mother of New Germany, is unusually powerful, displaying what the novel codes as 'masculine' traits such as rationality and a lack of empathy. Her depiction, and the reflections on cloning, are consistent with Wyndham's fiction views that women are ultimately the stronger sex, having responsibility for the reproduction of the species. David Ketterer speculates that the plants of *Day of the Triffids* and the aliens in *The Kraken Wakes* can both be interpreted as symbolic 'manifestations of the fury of that female nature'.[28] In a more literal vein, Wyndham explores in *Plan for Chaos* how women might use a new mechanics of reproduction as a means of political empowerment, something that would have consequences on all family and social relations previously deemed essential.

Given this conservative depiction of women, it might be expected that the incestuous elements of the story would be used to provide further confirmation of the dangers of tampering with a perceived natural and gendered order. In fact, the opposite is the case. Chapter two, which takes its epigraph from Thomas Moore's 'Where I love I must not marry', sketches in the family history of Freda and Johnny. Uncle Nils, Freda's father and Marta's brother, is opposed to 'cousinly marriages'. Like many people, Nils has a 'thing in his nut' about them which Farthing is frustratingly unable to counter:

> You can Mendelize at them with nice patterns of X's and Y's; you can explain to them fully and patiently about dominants and recessives until the whole thing is as pellucid and tidy as Euclid, and you have a sore throat, but in the end it still turns out that several friends of theirs knew cousins who married and had offspring that weren't quite apple-pie. You can point out that they are statistically wrong and that only the failures get scored up, but there is still that know-better shake of the head.[29]

As the argument continues, Nils cuts it off by reminiscing, 'But ... but we gotta remember your Aunt Marta', who ostracised herself from the family when she joined the Nazi Party. Nils's concern is that 'There's a taint

Is posthuman incest possible?

somewhere that came out in your Aunt Marta. She was a fanatic – unbalanced. You two might perpetuate that taint.'[30] This concern is ironic, in that it unwittingly recapitulates those Nazi ideas about purity to which Nils otherwise objects. Just as the Nazis' anti-Semitic vision saw physical attributes as confirming the moral inferiority of the Jews, so Nils links Marta's personal behaviour and life choices, a product of nurture, to her genes, a biological determinant. Quite rightly Farthing observes that 'a mighty lot of people were lunatics in those times'. There cannot be any genetic 'taint' that predisposed Marta to fascism, which might then be propagated by Farthing and Freda's marriage. As Twitchell points out, there is no biological basis that justifies the first-cousin taboo, only a cultural one: 'Marry your cousin in our society and you risk unbalancing your family, not your progeny. In other words, the semiotics of incest – a social code – may be far more potent than the biology of inbreeding – a genetic code.'[31] Wyndham uses alleged first-cousin incest in connection with Nazi cloning to demonstrate that culture and biology are not easily separated in the popular imagination. In this case, biology *is* apparently used by Nils to suggest that the relationship between Freda and Farthing is illegitimate. Wyndham then inverts this logic to show how a change in the requirements of reproduction necessarily shifts cultural ideas about incest to be more accommodating, though never removing the taboo entirely.

Extending the thread of Farthing's quotation above, Wyndham implies that a total prohibition against incest, however well meaning, is potentially problematic because it could lead to a similar kind of effort to control sexual relations as that attempted by the Nazis, albeit with a different ideological justification. Farthing sardonically observes that 'Seeing that there is more empiric bunk talked about sex than pretty near anything else, you might think I'd not fall for my cousin.'[32] The fact that first-cousin consanguinity is only proscribed by false 'empiric bunk' rather than biological necessity is indicated by the relative perversion of artificial reproduction through cloning, which is genuinely threatening. Once sexual reproduction is not required, having been outsourced to a mechanical process, the institution of the 'family' will no longer exist, with individuals instead being drones serving the institution of the race. Sexual desire in New Germany is sublimated to the needs of the colony. However, one reason why the New Germany project collapses is because Marta has not accounted for the basic human urge for normal procreation with the opposite sex; reproduction is not simply a biological necessity, but a psychological one. The female clones become hysterical with anxiety about their ticking biological clocks, desires which they express towards the clone-brothers with whom they live, even if they do not actually act upon it. Caught between two instincts – the desire to procreate, and the incest taboo – the clone society self-destructs through repressed sexual energy.

Wyndham's assumption that the sibling incest prohibition is a biological imperative just like sexual desire, might be challenged, since some have argued that the taboo exists only because of the linguistic and cultural codes that construct it through prohibiting it.[33] Nevertheless, Wyndham also affirms, perhaps self-contradictorily, that more finely balanced prohibitions against incest, such as first-cousin relationships, are culturally constructed rather than biologically determined. In Wyndham's epistemology, as voiced through Farthing, nature is 'what makes the dandelion split the paving stone'.[34] Nature determines that sibling incest is forbidden, and that sexual desire is inevitably dangerous if repressed. The clone women suffer precisely because there is no way they can give vent to biological impulses. However, the marriage between two complementary first cousins seems reasonable, a safe outlet for inevitable feelings that would equally 'split the paving stone' if repressed because of arbitrary social mores against cousinly incest, which has no genetic justification. Farthing notes, in his typical dry tone, that Freda and he are:

> both tall, both fair, and ... shape-up according to our different natures, in a way that's pretty complementary. Most of the time our outlooks don't interlock so badly, either. I know that could sound dull to those who prefer to live in passionate misunderstanding amid a welter of sulter, but we happen to prefer it that way.[35]

The cousins' relationship, then, is represented as being as inevitable in the same way as the clones' lack of relationships inevitably forces them to a self-destructive repression. Drawing the logic of the novel's attitude towards cloning and the family together with its attitude towards cousinly relationships, Wyndham seems to adopt a laissez-faire approach, outsourcing ethical responsibility to nature. If incest between cousins were wrong, nature would work to prevent it, just as it does with the clone siblings.

Plan for Chaos therefore reminds us that perceptions of incest are defined by interrelated biological and cultural semiotics, and that this linkage remains even when the biology of reproduction alters. Twitchell proposes that the semiotics of incest are more potent than the biology of breeding, which explains why first-cousin marriages are frowned upon because they destabilise family norms despite carrying little biological risk. Wyndham flips this diagram around: the new biology of breeding – in this case, cloning – changes the semiotics of incest, turning certain degrees of incest from something unacceptable into something that is more normal than people like Nils make out, and that indeed should be permitted lest post-war society inadvertently sustains similar ideas to those of the Nazi racial purists. In this sense, the hypothesised use of cloning serves to destabilise the assumption, prominent in the 1950s, that we can absolutely distinguish between normal and abnormal families, and that we should celebrate the nuclear norm. As Linda Nicolson has shown, the belief that there is such a thing as a 'traditional' family was inculcated during this period, but in fact the concept of a 'traditional' family does not have any biological essence or stable ethical definition, but rather changes as families adapt to the economic and social realities in which they find themselves.[36] By using cloning to change the semiotics of incest, Wyndham affirms that the 'family' is a fluid category, changing depending on context (as when the family of the two cousins is superior to that of the clones) and biology (as when Wyndham hypothesises that a clone race would operate according to the hive rather than nuclear model). Nicolson has proposed that 'Whether a type of family provides economic and emotional sustenance to its members ... given the resources at its disposal and the demands it must face, should constitute the primary criteria by which it is evaluated.'[37] On this basis, Wyndham's evaluation is that Farthing and Freda do constitute an admirably supportive couple, whereas the cloned family of the new Nazis, which exploits them for military purposes rather than to provide emotional sustenance, should be perceived negatively.

As a corollary to this, the novel presciently speaks to legal issues surrounding familial relations in our own era of biotechnological interventions. Already, children at risk of certain inherited defects may be produced invitrously using the DNA of three parents: the nuclear DNA from the mother and father, and the mitochondrial DNA from a third woman. In the near future more radical innovations seem likely, with genes being selectively switched on or off, replaced and reengineered; in 2016 the first 'three-person' baby was born, with genes from two 'parents' plus a third donor.[38] A child might be parented by several adults yet share only a small proportion of each of their genes. Whose child does he or she then become? What is the status of this child compared to its siblings? If only partially genetically related, at what degree of genetic difference does 'sibling' incest become permissible? Legal statutes such as the UK's Human Fertilisation and Embryology Act 2008, which specifies that 'The woman who is carrying or has carried a child as a result of the placing in her of an embryo or of sperm and eggs, and no other woman, is to be treated as the mother of the child', seem likely to become increasingly stretched when determining at what degree of relatedness a sexual act counts as incestuous.[39] As these issues become increasingly subtle – with the mitochondrial mother case above representing a degree of genetic affinity similar to that between first cousins – the lesson of *Plan for Chaos* seems to be that we should not necessarily legislate against such relations, provided of course that such relationships are not emotionally or physically abusive. Indeed, concerning ourselves about incest in this new reproductive era may be to focus on the symptom rather than the real danger, which is that when a single identifiable mother is no longer central to childbirth, this may fundamentally change society's basic structural unit from the close-knit family to the hive. This, not incest *per se*, is the real danger of posthuman technology as Wyndham sees it.

Artificial intelligence and post-incest: William Gibson's Neuromancer

So far, the two fictions I have examined suggest that changing modes of reproduction (androids, clones) invite readers to treat the incest taboo in a more liberal way. Of the two, *Abiogenesis* is the more worrying work because it does not reflect upon the processes by which such relativism comes about, whereas *Plan for Chaos* is to a large extent about the semiotic field within which family and sexual conventions are constructed. Wyndham's anxiety about people trying to control nature sees incest as being relegated in significance against more holistic changes to the notion of the family brought about by new non-maternal means of procreation. William Gibson's *Neuromancer* (first published 1984) can be seen as extrapolating this same trend to a point where the risks of familial incest are eliminated entirely, since the body itself is made redundant through technology. Paradoxically, the incest taboo will vanish once the family itself is obliterated in a society in which the human is not embodied, but exists as a mind playing in the realm of cyberspace.

The chief antagonists of *Neuromancer* are the Tessier-Ashpool clan, a 'very quiet, very eccentric first-generation high-orbit family, run like a corporation'.[40] They are ensconced in a remote villa in the spacedock that Marie-France Tessier and Ashpool built, from which the family/corporation now derives its wealth. Their children are clones designated by a numeral, such as 8Jean and 3Jane. The clones, along with Ashpool himself, are cryogenically frozen, with different individuals being resurrected at intervals to assume control of the company. The family, indistinguishable from the business, is thus reconfigured as a kind of rotating boardroom of immortal executives cut off from wider society. As a school essay by 3Jane, one of the clone-daughters, comments, 'We have sealed ourselves away behind our money, growing inward, generating a seamless universe of self.'[41] In a theme that crosses with the New Germany of *Plan for Chaos*, Tessier-Ashpool can also be understood as a kind of hive mind, one in which individuals are less significant than the sum of the economic and informational network within which they are located. Case observes that 'The ziabatsus, the multinationals that shaped the course of human history, had transcended old barriers. Viewed as organisms, they had attained a kind of immortality.'[42] Each member or element of the company is interchangeable with another, whilst no individual has control over a self-sustaining organisation that has its own distributed intelligence.

The confused relationships in this 'universe of self' are confounded by the fact that the cryogenic process enables those of older generations to seem as youthful as those of younger generations and vice versa, a situation which creates new possibilities for incest.[43] The founder, Ashpool, has been asleep for thirty years, but is woken by the artificial intelligence program that organises the company. When he wakes he orders a Jane clone to be thawed. He comments that it is 'Strange, to lie every few decades with what legally amounts to one's own daughter.'[44] Although the Janes are described as clones, the implication is that they may originally have been or even still are produced by incest between Ashpool and his daughters: why else would Ashpool need to be awoken every ten years specifically to sleep with his daughter? Although Gibson does not clarify this point, cloning is symbolically equivalent to incest and vice versa: both are a means of maintaining patriarchal power and ensuring a company line is maintained within a family.

Such a link is metaphorically critical of the capitalism which causes it. As Michael Mack points out elsewhere in this volume, the desire for power has come to coincide with the power of desire – economic power being one specific locus. Gibson accordingly speculates about how sexual corruption signifies the contradictions of late capitalism, which threaten the entire economic system with collapse. Nicola Nixon observes that by representing the inward-looking nature of the corporation, whose hive mentality mimics the Yakuza of Japan, Gibson stages American anxieties about the different form of Japanese capitalism that was coming to prominence in the 1980s and 1990s.[45] Through fusing the 'tight familial bonds of the Italian-American mafia' with 'the equally tight employer–employee bonds of the frighteningly efficient Japanese industries',[46] Gibson presents the corporations of *Neuromancer* as engaging in shady business practices but in an economically effective manner. Once established, such corporations become antithetical to the American model of capitalism because they close down free enterprise, innovation and entrepreneurialism – all features valorised in the hacker. The cost of this model of capitalism is that the monolith can be maintained only through the in-bred industrialism seen in Tessier-Ashpool. Although Gibson's work is anxious about monopolistic companies which close down the competition on which free-market capitalism depends, the use of incest as a critique of such corporate structures shows how Gibson is also foreshadowing a greater technological danger that dispenses with capitalism altogether, and similarly with the need for a dynasty defined by the family.

In post-industrial capitalism, the most valuable commodity being traded is not material, but information. In *Neuromancer*, cyberspace – a visual representation of databases and communication exchanges – is in some ways more real and emotive than the cold reality depicted in the novel; certainly the novel's most lavish descriptions are of surfing the net. To some extent *Neuromancer* celebrates both the new form of capitalism and Baudrillard's hyperreal, when the simulation offers a more authentic experience than the original.[47] In this flipped situation, embodiment is decreasingly important. *Neuromancer*'s worldly goods and commodities are generally less significant than knowledge – and in such a context, the most powerful entities capable of commanding and running the economy are not people but computers, especially those with a degree of artificial intelligence. Consequently, despite the familial in-breeding designed to retain control of a company, it is the self-breeding of artificial intelligence which will finally come to dominate. The climax of *Neuromancer* depicts a Von Neumann-esque universal constructor,[48] a self-replicating machine capable of building successively better computers. This is the end point of the information economy: immaterial information is more efficiently reproduced and circulated by artificial intelligence programs than by people bound to material bodies. In this case, the ideologies and corporate memories of the Tessier-Ashpool company have come to reside within two artificial intelligences, Neuromancer and Wintermute. Marie-France Tessier, the company's founder, designed the two AIs to unite and destroy the 'sham immortality' of Ashpool's empire, sustained by the embodiment of incest and cloning. *Neuromancer* thus deviates from similar narratives, from *Frankenstein* to *Blade Runner*, in which the male scientist is punished for circumventing natural procreation. In this case, the creator is a female, whilst her agent of revenge, Wintermute, turns on the man whose own means of corporate procreation have been immoral. The two AIs are essentially twin versions of each other, which have since developed into a personality-focused artificial intelligence housed on a server in Brazil (Neuromancer) and a rational, 'decision maker' housed in Switzerland (Wintermute). Whilst *Abiogenesis* imagines the sexual union of originally identical androids leading to uncanny births, the eventual fusing of these two AIs leads to the propagation of something genuinely powerful if distinctly non-human: a fully intelligent AI with human qualities that is able to self-reproduce, realising Marie-France's dream of making her computer 'children' immortal, and thus in some senses herself vicariously through them. Marie-France, indeed, now resides within the fused AI construct that is the matrix, her soul having transcended her body, in stark contrast to Ashpool whose immoral 'soul' is indicated by his need to use his body incestuously with his daughters. *Neuromancer* punishes deviant patriarchal power relations, and invites its reader to connect its speculative fiction to moral codes surrounding gender and capitalism that pertain in our own world.

Neuromancer thus uses the theme of incest, and of mind–body dualism, to pose questions about what happens next to the human family, which has conventionally been seen as the microcosmic base from which human society is built. If an ever-more monopolistic capitalism entails the abuse – specifically incest – of the family in order to preserve that monopoly, this has consequences for society. However, when the human and economic world is based on the propagation of information, in order to propagate wealth money and the family, this has consequences for *all* of our cherished notions. Incest will no longer be necessary to sustain capitalism, or be a moral problem, because the body will be made redundant by artificial intelligences. The issue of incest, and of related institutions such as the family, gender, or the economy, may be elided entirely once the physically embodied basis of human society, or the body politic, is dissolved.

Conclusion: The second life of incest

In the three novels studied here, it is clear that various posthuman technologies will lead to increasing confusion as to what constitutes a family, as the family is no longer defined mainly by genetically or physically proximate relationships of biological selves. Whilst none of the technologies imagined in them have yet come to full fruition, as a literature of cognitive estrangement the value of science fiction is not simply in imagining the future, but raising our consciousness of the present by refracting it through a defamiliarising lens. Indeed, as N. Katherine Hayles observes, we do not have to be literal cyborgs, bodies affected directly by technology, in order to count as posthuman, since the very imagination of cyborgs is already changing our perceptions of what it is like to be human in the present. For Hayles, 'The defining characteristics [of posthumanism] involve the construction of subjectivity, not the presence of nonbiological components.'[49] Whatever technologies do is less significant than what they imply, and how their very possibility forces us to reimagine subjectivity in the here and now. We may not yet be clones or androids. However, the estrangement of the self and its link to a family through a single, biologically definable body is still characteristic of our times.

In this vein, there is something reassuring about the fact that all three fictions require readers to acknowledge that their technological premises involve some degree of transgression of the cultural norms of the present. Whether this transgression is naively celebrated for its erotic potential (as in *Abiogenesis*) or used critically (as when Ashpool's bodily abuse of his daughters is punished by a disembodied virtual intelligence), the fact that incest is still linked with the unnatural in a biological sense testifies that the taboo continues to exist in an ethical sense too. We may choose to cross the taboo willingly and temporarily, via erotica like *Abiogenesis*, but it is still there. Thus we still need to consider carefully how we police the distinction between appropriate and inappropriate sexual behaviour. The repressed desire of the clone brothers and sisters in *Plan for Chaos* highlights the nuance of this debate, since exercising absolute control over consensual incest (in this case between first cousins) might be as totalitarian as eugenics, or akin to manipulating nature through bio-engineering. Wyndham's lesson for our own time is that if we are prepared to reshape nature through the likes of IVF, we must also be prepared to think through the reshaping of ideologies that are attendant upon society's underlying means of reproduction. Wyndham's implicit claim that banning certain degrees of incest marks an attempt to manipulate nature that is as threatening as genetic modification or Nazi eugenics could certainly be challenged. Nevertheless, by showing how the biological body is no longer a constant, science fiction can contribute to the trajectory of postmodern theory that has similarly emphasised the inconstancy of presumed social norms, such as Robin Fox's revision of the idea of the traditional nuclear family or Haraway's denial that gender is fixed. In *Plan for Chaos*, as with the parents in the IVF scenario, the test of a 'good' family is not whether it is genetically approximate, but whether it provides mutual nurture, guided by instincts rather than dogma.

The value of *Plan for Chaos* in particular is to present a questionable ethics rather than naively succumbing to a technological determinism that sees science as eliding ethics entirely. Yet in the real world, amid the rapid development of social networks and virtual realities, a relinquishment of conventions is apparent. When I access the disembodied virtual world, such as on an internet chat forum or game, I may have no essential being: I can play at being a woman or a dwarf, be as old or young as my avatar or photograph presents me as being.[50] Because gender roles and sexual identities are not 'naturally' (i.e. biologically) rooted, there would appear to be no 'natural' (i.e. cultural) boundaries that can or cannot be transgressed. From revenge porn to twitter trolling, people carry out acts online that they would not perform in face-to-face reality. In terms of incest, there are online no bodily markers that straightforwardly distinguish acceptably distant from unacceptably close relationships. Thus on a discussion board about whether incest is permitted in *Second Life*, users seem almost unanimously to agree that because there is no biological risk, incestuous role-play is entirely allowed.[51] This seems naïve; it is the kind of wilful ignorance implicitly reinforced by a text such as *Abiogenesis*, which similarly implies that because the fictional characters are androids, all sexual, feminist and incestuous proprieties can be thrown away in the free play of speculative fantasy. To suggest that a cybersexual encounter is not incestuous purely because it is not embodied and thus does not risk genetic malformation is to adopt a pragmatic tone that does not respect the potential psychological trauma of the event from the perspective of the victim (or victims, since if both parties are unaware of the real identity of the virtual avatar they are courting the incest may be entirely unwitting). Inversely, in *Abiogenesis*, to celebrate the polygamy without jealousy that is facilitated by a world of android clones depends upon us overlooking the potentially incestuous basis on which such a world is predicated, and in celebrating rather than criticising the use of unnatural twin babies as a validation of Dalia's essentially conventional femininity, conforming to male desire and power.

In a posthuman context, genetic modification, virtual realities, and other technologies that affect the constitution of the human are unlikely to make incest any less harmful and self-destructive, even though they may make incest more possible. Indeed, the attitudes towards incest expressed on online forums perhaps lag behind or ignore the way the law works in actuality. The *Second Life* terms and conditions expressly forbid intimate engagement between adults and minors, whilst the UK's Defamation Act 2013 legislates against online acts of bullying, and sexual and racial abuse.[52] The *Second Life* community might want to permit incest, but the effects of such incest online – for abuse or manipulation – would likely still bring it under the rubric of the forbidden. Contrary to the fantasy pursued by *Abiogenesis*, or proponents of virtual worlds in which normal laws allegedly do not apply, we may be heading towards the posthuman, but we are not yet post-incestuous.

Notes

1 Nick Bostrom, 'The transhumanist FAQ: A general introduction', World Transhumanist Association, www.nickbostrom.com/views/transhumanist.pdf (accessed 31 March 2016).
2 Definition of 'Posthuman', https://en.oxforddictionaries.com/definition/posthumanism (accessed 27 June 2017).
3 In her work, the philosopher Francesca Ferrando contends that posthumanism is a term with at least seven definitions 'Posthumanism, transhumanism, antihumanism, metahumanism, and new materialisms: Differences and relations', *Existenz* 8:2 (Fall 2013), www.existenz.us/volumes/Vol.8-2Ferrando.pdf (accessed 27 June 2017).
4 James B. Twitchell, *Forbidden Partners* (Columbia University Press, 1986), p. 176.
5 Throughout this chapter, I use cyborg in its proper sense, originally established by Clynes and Kline, as a human being whose abilities have been extended by technological systems. Manfred E. Clynes and Nathan S. Kline, 'Cyborgs and space', *Astronautics* (September, 1960), pp. 26–76.
6 A. Paul and J. Kuester, 'The impact of kinship on mating and reproduction', in Bernard Chapais and Carol M. Berman (eds) *Kinship and Behaviour in Primates* (Oxford University Press, 2004), pp. 271–93; G.C. Leavitt, 'Disappearance of the incest taboo: A cross-cultural test of general evolutionary hypotheses', *American Anthropologist* 91:1 (1989): 116–31, www.jstor.org/stable/679741 (accessed 31 March 2016).
7 Robin Fox, *The Red Lamp of Incest* (Hutchinson, 1980), p. 2.
8 James B. Twitchell, *Forbidden Partners* (Columbia University Press, 1986).
9 Donna Haraway, 'A cyborg manifesto: Science, technology, and socialist-feminism in the late twentieth century', in Donna Haraway, *Simians, Cyborgs and Women* (Routledge, 1991), pp. 149–81.

10. Kaitlyn O'Connor, *Abiogenesis* (CreateSpace Independent Publishing Platform, 2012).
11. John Wyndham, David Ketterer and Andy Sawyer (eds), *Plan for Chaos* (Penguin, 2012).
12. Linda Nicolson, 'The myth of the traditional family', in Hilde Lindemann Nelson (ed.), *Feminism and Families* (Routledge, 1997), p. 33.
13. William Gibson, *Neuromancer* (Harper-Voyager, 2013).
14. David Tomas, 'The technophilic body: On technicity in William Gibson's cyborgculture', *New Formations* 8 (1989), p. 114.
15. Michel Foucault, *Power/Knowledge* (Harvester Wheatsheaf, 1980), p. 142.
16. 'The offspring', *Star Trek: The Next Generation* (dir. Jonathan Frakes, Paramount, 1990).
17. '*Abiogenesis* (Cyberevolution #3)', Goodreads, www.goodreads.com/book/show/2052174.Abiogenesis (accessed 30 March 2016).
18. Kaitlyn O'Connor, 'About Kaitlyn', http://kaitlynoconnor.com/about_kaitlyn (accessed 29 March 2016).
19. William H. Durham and Arthur P. Wolf, *Inbreeding, Incest, and the Incest Taboo* (Stanford University Press, 2004), p. 17.
20. O'Connor, *Abiogenesis*, p. 594
21. John T. Irwin, *Doubling and Incest/Repetition and Revenge* (Johns Hopkins University Press, 1975), p. 30.
22. Andrea Dworkin, *Pornography: Men Possessing Women* (Women's Press, 1981).
23. Judith Lewis Herman and Lisa Hirschman, *Father-Daughter Incest* (Harvard University Press, 2000), p. 101.
24. *Plan for Chaos* was written around 1951, but was published only in 2009, having failed to find a publisher when drafted during an interlude in the writing of *Day of the Triffids*.
25. Martin Oppenheimer, *Forbidden Relatives* (University of Illinois Press, 1996), pp. 19–41.
26. David Ketterer and Andy Sawyer (eds), 'The corrected and expanded Introduction to *Plan for Chaos*', in John Wyndham, David Ketterer and Andy Sawyer (eds), *Plan for Chaos* (Penguin, 2012).
27. Wyndham, *Plan for Chaos*, p. 154.
28. Ketterer and Sawyer, 'The corrected and expanded Introduction to *Plan for Chaos*'.
29. Wyndham, *Plan for Chaos*, p. 11.
30. *Ibid.*, p. 15.
31. Twitchell, *Forbidden Partners*, p. 9.
32. Wyndham, *Plan for chaos*, p. 9.
33. Ellen Pollak, *Incest and the English Novel, 1684–1814* (Johns Hopkins University Press, 2003), pp. 8–9.
34. Wyndham, *Plan for Chaos*, p. 143.
35. *Ibid.*, p. 9.
36. Nicolson, 'Myth of the Traditional Family', pp. 27–42.

37 *Ibid.*, p. 28.
38 Jessica Hamzelou, 'Exclusive: World's first baby born with new "3 parent" technique', *New Scientist*, www.newscientist.com/article/2107219-exclusive-worlds-first-baby-born-with-new-3-parent-technique/ (accessed 31 March 2017).
39 House of Commons, 'Human Fertilisation and Embryology Act', 2008, c. 28.
40 Gibson, *Neuromancer*, p. 87.
41 *Ibid.*, p. 201.
42 *Ibid.*, p. 255.
43 The observation that differences in aging across generations would lead to new possibilities for or risks of incest is not a new one.
44 Gibson, *Neuromancer*, p. 215.
45 Nicola Nixon, 'Cyberpunk: Preparing the ground for the revolution or keeping the boys satisfied?', *Science Fiction studies* 19:2 (1992), www.depauw.edu/sfs/backissues/57/nixon57art.htm (accessed 30 March 2016).
46 *Ibid.*
47 Jean Baudrillard, Sheila Faria Glaser (trans.), *Simulacra and Simulation* (University of Michigan Press, 1994).
48 John von Neumann, *Theory of Self-Reproducing Automata* (University of Illinois Press, 1966).
49 N. Katherine Hayles, *How we Became Posthuman: Virtual Bodies in Cybernetics, Literature and Informatics* (University of Chicago Press, 1999), p. 4.
50 Sherry Turkle, *The Second Self: Computers and the Human Spirit* (Granada, 1984); Sherry Turkle, *Life on the Screen: Identity in the Age of the Internet* (Weidenfeld, 1996).
51 'What is Linden Labs' policy towards incest,' Second Life Forum, https://community.secondlife.com/t5/Abuse-and-Griefing/What-is-Linden-Labs-policy-towards-incest/qaq-p/1309657 (accessed 31 March 2016).
52 UK Government Legislation, Defamation Act 2013, www.legislation.gov.uk/ukpga/2013/26/contents/enacted (accessed 27 June 2017).

Bibliography

Fiction

Gibson, William, *Neuromancer* (Harper-Voyager, 2013)
Heinlein, Robert, *Time for the Stars* (Victor Gollancz, 1963)
Wyndham, John, David Ketterer and Andy Sawyer (eds), *Plan for Chaos* (Penguin, 2012)

Non-fiction

Baudrillard, Jean, Sheila Faria Glaser (trans.) *Simulacra and Simulation*, (University of Michigan Press, 1994)

Clynes, Manfred E. and Nathan S. Kline, 'Cyborgs and space'. *Astronautics* (1960), pp. 26–76

Durham, William H. and Arthur P. Wolf, *Inbreeding, Incest, and the Incest Taboo: The State of Knowledge at the Turn of the Century* (Stanford University Press, 2004)

Dworkin, Andrea, *Pornography: Men Possessing Women* (Women's Press, 1981)

Foucault, Michel, Colin Gordon (ed.), *Power/Knowledge: Selected Interviews and Other Writings, 1972–1977* (Harvester Wheatsheaf, 1980)

Fox, Robin, *The Red Lamp of Incest* (Hutchinson, 1980)

Haraway, Donna, 'A cyborg manifesto: Science, technology, and socialist-feminism in the late twentieth century', in Donna Haraway, *Simians, Cyborgs and Women: The Reinvention of Nature* (Routledge, 1991), pp. 149–81

Hayles, N. Katherine, *How we Became Posthuman: Virtual Bodies in Cybernetics, Literature and Informatics* (University of Chicago Press, 1999)

Herman, Judith Lewis and Lisa Hirschman, *Father-Daughter Incest* (Harvard University Press, 2000)

House of Commons, 'Human Fertilisation and Embryology Act' (2008). c. 28

Irwin, John T., *Doubling and Incest/Repetition and Revenge: A Speculative Reading of Faulkner* (Johns Hopkins University Press, 1975)

Leavitt, G.C., 'Disappearance of the incest taboo: A cross-cultural test of general evolutionary hypotheses', *American Anthropologist* 91:1 (1989), pp. 116–31

Nicolson, Linda, 'The myth of the traditional family', in Hilde Lindemann Nelson (ed.), *Feminism and Families* (Routledge, 1997), pp. 27–42

Nixon, Nicola, 'Cyberpunk: Preparing the ground for the revolution or keeping the boys satisfied?' *Science Fiction Studies* 19:2 (1992), pp. 219–35

O'Connor, Kaitlyn, *Abiogenesis* (CreateSpace Independent Publishing Platform, 2012)

'Offspring, The', *Star Trek: The Next Generation* (Dir. Jonathan Frakes, Paramount, 1990)

Oppenheimer, Martin, *Forbidden Relatives: The American Myth of Cousin Marriage* (University of Illinois Press, 1996)

Paul, A. and J. Kuester, 'The impact of kinship on mating and reproduction', in Bernard Chapais and Carol M. Berman (eds), *Kinship and Behaviour in Primates* (Oxford University Press, 2004), pp. 271–93

Pollak, Ellen, *Incest and the English Novel, 1684–1814* (Johns Hopkins University Press, 2003)

Tomas, David, 'The technophilic body: On technicity in William Gibson's cyborgculture', *New Formations* 8 (1989), pp. 114

Turkle, Sherry, *The Second Self: Computers and the Human Spirit* (Granada, 1984)

——., *Life on the Screen: Identity in the Age of the Internet* (Weidenfeld, 1996)

Twitchell, James B., *Forbidden Partners: The Incest Taboo in Popular Culture* (Columbia University Press, 1986)

von Neumann, John, *Theory of Self-Reproducing Automata* (University of Illinois Press, 1966)

Wyndham, John, David Ketterer and Andy Sawyer (eds), *Plan for Chaos*, (Penguin, 2012)

Websites

'Abiogenesis (Cyberevolution #3)', Goodreads www.goodreads.com/book/show/2052174.Abiogenesis (accessed 30 March 2016)

Bostrom, Nick, 'The transhumanist FAQ: A general introduction', World Transhumanist Association, www.nickbostrom.com/views/transhumanist.pdf (accessed 31 March 2016)

Hamzelou, Jessica, 'Exclusive: World's first baby born with new '3 parent' technique'. *New Scientist*, 27 September 2016. www.newscientist.com/article/2107219-exclusive-worlds-first-baby-born-with-new-3-parent-technique/ (accessed 31 March 2017)

Ketterer, David and Andy Sawyer, 'The corrected and expanded introduction to *Plan for Chaos* by John Wyndham'. HUBbub. http://sfhubbub.blogspot.co.uk/2009/11/revised-and-updated-introduction-to.html (accessed 27 March 2016)

O'Connor, Kaitlyn, 'About Kaitlyn'. http://kaitlynoconnor.com/about_kaitlyn (accessed 29 March 2016)

'What is Linden Labs' policy towards incest', Second Life Forum. https://community.secondlife.com/t5/Abuse-and-Griefing/What-is-Linden-Labs-policy-towards-incest/qaq-p/1309657 (accessed 31 March 2016)

Part IV

The rhetoric of narrating incest

10

'Is't not a kind of incest?'[1] Metaphor and relation in the poetry of Ted Hughes and Sylvia Plath

Charles Mundye

In one of his later and most ambitious of prose works, *Shakespeare and the Goddess of Complete Being* (1992), Ted Hughes attempts nothing less than the construction of an integrated poetics of myth. It is no surprise, perhaps, that the thinking behind this book shapes and is shaped by the preoccupations of his later poetry, but it also informs the relationship of that poetry to the writing of his first wife, Sylvia Plath. This chapter explores aspects of the relationships between texts by Hughes and Plath, and their negotiation of myths and figures of transformation.[2] In doing so it aspires to a liberating close reading of poetic texts, which are too often held captive or overshadowed by the competing and contested agendas surrounding biographical context.

In choosing Hughes's translations of incest narratives from Ovid's *Metamorphoses* as starting points, I trace dialogic exchange across texts by Hughes and Plath, extending the spirit of Eavan Boland's injunction to revel in their mid-century conversation by listening to the voice in Hughes's late works: 'It is a joy to speculate at the end of this century on that mid-century dialogue – how across continents, traditions and sex they spoke as poets and changed each other's poetry.'[3]

Taking a lead from Robert Graves's *The White Goddess* (1948), Hughes's *Shakespeare and the Goddess of Complete Being* attempts to synthesise an understanding of the world through a reintegrating interpretation of poetry, religion and mythology.[4] At its heart is the central and determining importance of the figure of the Great Goddess. Many poems from Hughes's *Tales from Ovid* (1997) and *Birthday Letters* (1998) trace manifestations of this Goddess and other mythic tropes in Plath's texts, and in doing so they further illuminate what Lynda K. Bundtzen has termed 'Plath's overarching themes of death and rebirth, mourning and melancholia.'[5]

Hughes's Goddess is a constant and often seemingly contradictory presence whose essence underlies any number of mythical manifestations:

> The sinister peculiarity of Aphrodite is that, like Inanna before her, she has a 'double' in the Underworld, who shares with her the dying and resurrected god. In effect, the two goddesses are the two poles of the one Great Goddess … In every epiphany of the Goddess the two aspects are present – one latent behind the other. In the foreground they appear to be two, and opposites, but in the background they are one.
>
> These two aspects are the most regular manifestations of the great triple Goddess's three aspects: the Mother, the Sacred Bride, and the Queen of the Underworld.[6]

Hughes identifies a particular manifestation of the Goddess in the character of Isabella from Shakespeare's *Measure for Measure*: 'Isabella is a double deputy for both extremes of the Goddess. She is a high priestess (in effect) of the goddess of fertility and promiscuity … At the same time she is the Diana-like priestess, in all but fact, of a Catholic nunnery.'[7] Isabella's brother Claudio faces the death sentence for sleeping with his fiancée before their proper marriage, a sentence pronounced by the Duke's strict Deputy, Angelo. Won over by her charms in pleading for her brother's life, Angelo offers her an ultimatum: if she sleeps with Angelo her brother's life will be saved. It is whilst arguing with her brother over this particular moral dilemma that Isabella raises the question of incest in kind:

> Wilt thou be made a man out of my vice?
> Is't not a kind of incest to take life
> From thine own sister's shame?[8]

The act, she implies, would be incestuous, in giving metaphorical birth to her sibling's life. Further, if we follow Hughes in the mythic double aspect he ascribes to Isabella, it is possible that a relationship between Isabella and Angelo would be a 'kind of incest'[9] because Angelo's simultaneous capacity for strict chastity and sexual licence, too closely mirrors her own, and they are therefore too alike in kind. Understood in this way, Isabella's question opens up different kinds and metaphorisations of incest, and, further, the problematical nature of its relation to resemblance.

Metaphor is almost always doubly transformative, and in Ovid's tales of metamorphoses this double transformation becomes the subject and process of the poetry itself. Writing about Hughes and Ovid, J.D. McClatchy has observed:

> But more to the point, Ovid goes to the heart of the poetic task. *Change*, things becoming other things, transformations … this is what poems do. Aristotle rightly claimed metaphor as the essence of poetry, and Ovid is the Mother Goose of metaphor, taking the trope and enlarging it into narratives as fantastic as dreams.[10]

Book X of Ovid's *Metamorphoses* opens with an account of Orpheus's descent to the underworld, and his failed attempt to bring his recently-dead wife Eurydice back to the land of the living. The rest of Book X consists of a

'Is't not a kind of incest?'

series of tales sung by Orpheus to the god-inflected natural grove of trees, including the stories of Pygmalion, of Myrrha, and of Venus and Adonis. Hughes translates several of the tales that Ovid sings through Orpheus, although his text disrupts the dynastic sequence followed in the original, and also decontextualises the stories, thereby suppressing the role of the Orpheus narrator and simultaneously inhabiting it with the translation's own narrative voice.[11] 'Myrrha' is one such story, a tale of father–daughter incest, of a girl who lusts after her father, King Cinyras, in place of developing a more natural desire for a husband. Cinyras is son of Paphos, in turn the daughter of Pygmalion and his sculpture-bride:

> And when he asked her just what kind of husband
> She wanted, she whispered: 'One like you.'
> Cinyras understood nothing. He laughed:
> 'My darling, never let anything change your devotion
> To me.' When she heard that word 'devotion'
> Her heart broke up in her body. She stood there
> Like a beast at the altar, head hanging.[12]

Hughes's transformation through translation of this ancient incest narrative is in creative dialogue with Ovid's original text, with Hughes's own poetics of myth, and with the distinct but interrelated personal poetic mythology of Plath herself. Bundtzen has argued that: 'The story of Myrrha's attempted suicide and incestuous affair with her father, Cinyras, is especially pertinent to Hughes's understanding of Plath's suicide and her incestuous love for her father, Otto Plath.'[13] However, as I will further demonstrate, the tale has significance beyond merely biographical cipher as a means through which Hughes explores aspects of the poetic language of myth and metaphor itself.

Hughes's narrator reflects on Myrrha's seemingly paradoxical innocence: lust is something that is visited upon her, delivered by 'One of hell's … sisters' straight 'from the … tarpit', or so the narrator speculates.[14] This explains his figuration of her above as the sacrificial beast, passive in the visitations of destiny. The next narrative simile works proleptically to prepare the way for the inevitable denouement of the tale:

> Like a great tree that sways,
> All but cut through by the axe,
> Uncertain which way to fall,
> Waiting for the axe's deciding blow,
> Myrrha,
> Bewildered by the opposite onslaughts
> Of her lust and her conscience,
> Swayed, and waited to fall.
> Either way, she saw only death.[15]

The tree in the wind figuration once more underlines the ways in which this is an inevitable circumstance visited upon her. She is unable to have agency over her behaviour in just the same way that a tree cannot help being cut down by an axe, but, whether the fall is to the left or to the right, death is the inevitable conclusion for both comparator and compared, Myrrha and tree (who become one and the same in the eventual literalising of this early simile).

Indeed, Myrrha attempts suicide, but her life is saved by her nurse, who then facilitates the consummation of unnatural desires by leading her to Myrrha's father's bed in the pitch dark over a period of nine nights. On the ninth night the King's curiosity gets the better of him, and he introduces a lamp to their lovemaking. Horrified by the realisation of his unwitting crime, he chases after her with a sword, but she escapes. After nine months she prays to the gods to be relieved of her suffering: she does not want to die, as she fears polluting the dead; neither does she want to live. The gods hear her prayer, and she is transformed into a myrrh tree. Of particular interest is the way in which Hughes renders the scene of transformation:

> She swayed,
> Living statuary on a tree's foundations.
> In that moment, her bones became grained wood,
> …
> Her blood sap, her arms boughs, her fingers twigs,
> Her skin rough bark. And already
> The gnarling crust has coffined her swollen womb.
>
> It swarms over her breasts. It warps upwards
> Reaching for her eyes as she bows
> Eagerly into it, hurrying the burial
> Of her face and her hair under thick-webbed bark.[16]

McClatchy identifies a significant departure from Ovidian style in this particular passage, suggesting that Dryden's translation is much closer to the sophisticated detachment of the Latin original: 'But this same passage in Ovid's Latin ("nam crura loquentis / terra supervenit, ruptosque obliqua per ungues") is a mere thirteen lines, and less feverishly adjectival.'[17] This is well observed, but to see this passage as compromised translation is to miss the ways in which Hughes is engaging with his own creative agenda.

Myrrha is pregnant with her father's child, and once the transformation to tree is complete she gives birth to the infant Adonis. Two particular phrases underline the text's connection to a broader poetics of myth. Consider this metaphor: 'She swayed, / Living statuary on a tree's foundations'.[18] The image of the 'living statuary' at this transitional point is all Hughes's own. Ovid's 'longi firmamina trunci' merely turns her into tree trunk.[19] Metaphorising

Myrrha in this way, Hughes's text is making explicit the familial connection between her and her great grandparents, Pygmalion and his statue wife. It further resonates with any number of Plath's texts which incorporate versions of 'living statuary', including 'Morning Song', to which I will return later.[20] The second phrase contains one of the most extraordinarily vivid combination metaphors in this transformational passage: 'The gnarling crust has coffined her swollen womb. / It swarms over her breasts'.[21] Once again, this is not a direct translation of Ovid, but an embellishment that establishes broader networks of significance. Her 'womb' has become encased in wood, hence the future child Adonis is 'coffined', at least until the point at which Lucina, the goddess of childbirth, splits the trunk open to deliver him.[22] In this the text echoes Plath, especially her poem 'The Arrival of the Bee Box', where she describes taking delivery of a hive of bees: 'I would say it was the coffin of a midget / Or a square baby / Were there not such a din in it'.[23] The 'din' results from the innumerable collective of the insects, which she describes in terms of a swarm, introducing as an adjectival qualification the term Hughes so extraordinarily uses to describe the incursion of bark over Myrrha's skin: 'I put my eye to the grid. / It is dark, dark, / With the swarmy feeling of African hands'.[24] Such echoes might seem coincidental, were it not for a further connection, in which Plath's narrating voice imagines a potential result of standing still in metaphor if the bees were released from their imprisoning box: 'I wonder if they would forget me / If I just undid the locks and stood back and turned into a tree'.[25]

Plath here is writing in a long tradition of bee poetry. The bee's representation often encapsulates what Hughes would see as different facets of the Great Goddess: a simultaneous provider of fertility through pollination, sweetness through the transmutation of nectar into honey, and poison through its sting, which leads to death.[26] That the sting is also associated with love through Cupid is no further surprise, and that different kinds of death result from love a related inevitability.[27] Consider the variation on a theme in the text of this early seventeenth-century English madrigal, where the bees are encouraged to feed on the sweet lips of a mistress, but warned of a potential reciprocal stinging:

> Yet sweet take heed, all sweets are hard to get
> Sting not her soft lips, O beware of that,
> For if one flaming dart come from her eye
> Was ever dart so sharp ah then you die.[28]

Hughes's 'The Bee God' complicates the textual conversation with this tradition, and Plath's particular relation to it. Here there is also the danger of death associated with love: 'When you wanted bees I never dreamed / It meant your Daddy had come up out of the well.'[29] Beekeeping was, Hughes's text implies, a way of making the connection back to Plath's textual father, to the point that 'The Bee God' describes an improper and incestuous reunion between 'Daddy' and the poem's second person: 'But when you put on your white regalia, / Your veil, your gloves, I never guessed a wedding.'[30] The ceremony is taking place in poetic text as well as in the bee garden: 'Your page a dark swarm / Clinging under the lit blossom', where the ambivalence holding together wedding 'page' and poem 'page' returns us once again to the collective of the bees ('swarm'), here figuratively equated with the individual letters on the pages of her poems.[31] The bees become the squadrons in the service of 'Daddy', chasing away the interloper husband through an organised attack: 'That outrider tangled, struggled, stung'.[32] As the bee finds a target, so does the poem.

Elsewhere in *Birthday Letters*, as part of a pattern that steadily conflates husband and father, it is 'Daddy' himself who is stung by the words of Plath's poetry:

> Where
> Did you get those words if not
> In the tails of his bees? For others
> The honey. For him, Cupid's bow
> Modified in Peenemünde
> Via Brueghel.[33]

'Cupid's bow' becomes an instrument of Nazi warfare mediated through representations of renaissance suffering, an extraordinary conflation which underlines the close connection of love, death and horror between father and daughter figures.[34] Hughes's subsequent metaphors further transpose 'Daddy' here into a sacrificial figure in the manner of Saint Sebastian: 'Stark naked full of those arrows / In the bronze of immortal poesy'.[35] This might put us in mind of the ways in which fate and the gods determine the direction of travel for the hapless characters in *Tales from Ovid*: Myrrha stung, according to Orpheus, by the venom from a serpent of hell's horrible sister into lusting after her father (but Orpheus knows it is the nature of blind Cupid's arrows to be indiscriminate in their target); Venus herself stung by her son's arrows into love for Adonis, Myrrha's son.

The theme of such stinging sees Hughes inhabit a further aspect of Plath's poetic imagery in his poem 'The Bee God':

> And I was flung like a headshot jackrabbit
> Through sunlit whizzing tracers
>
> As bees planted their volts, their thudding electrodes,
> In on their target.[36]

This poem has husband and father in dramatic conflict, and yet the stinging creates a further point of connection between the two, conversing as it does with the subject of Plath's 'Lament': 'The sting of bees took away my father / who walked in a swarming shroud of wings / and scorned the tick of the falling weather.'[37] However, Hughes's 'The Bee God' is in most explicit conversation with Plath's poem 'Stings', in which poem it is the bees themselves making the ultimate sacrifice:

> The bees found him out,
> Molding onto his lips like lies,
> Complicating his features.
> They thought death was worth it, but I
> Have a self to recover, a queen.[38]

Whilst both Hughes's 'The Bee God' and Plath's 'Stings' figure three characters, the personnel differs. Plath's poem contains the first-person voice, a bee-seller, and one other, 'a great scapegoat', who is the one who gets stung.[39] Hughes's poem replaces the bee-seller with 'Daddy',[40] and the act of recovery is not concerned with the 'self', or the 'queen', as in 'Stings',[41] but rather with the titular 'Bee God' who is a manifestation of the father, recovered from 'the well'.[42] The closing lines of Hughes's poem return to the fatalism which governs the fall-out from this cold resurrection: 'Deaf to your pleas as the fixed stars / At the bottom of the well',[43] which is a repeat with variation on Plath's own fatalistic conclusion to the poem 'Words', which Hughes as editor located as the final poem of *Ariel*: 'While / From the bottom of the pool, fixed stars / Govern a life'.[44]

In further figuring the act of stinging through electrical metaphor ('the thudding electrodes'[45]), Hughes's 'The Bee God' draws power through invoking Plath's poems concerned with the various significances of electricity, and, perhaps, in particular the 'The Hanging Man': 'By the roots of my hair some god got hold of me. / I sizzled in his blue volts like a desert prophet.'[46] Once again this opening outlines a mythical and fatalistic passivity: the gods are to blame, and the first-person subject is their plaything. Whilst it might be reasonable to assume that one of the points of departure of this poem is Plath's experience of ECT treatment,[47] it is more resonant in its mythic echoes of the biblical story of Absalom. Depicted in Samuel 2.18 as caught by his 'head' in a tree before dying as a result of a conflict with his father, David, Absalom is presented in later tradition as hanged from the branches by his hair.[48] Plath's line, 'A vulturous boredom pinned me in this tree' also further invokes the spirit of Shakespeare's character Ariel, 'confine[d]' in the 'cloven pine' for twelve years until her release by Prospero.[49]

Whilst Hughes's 'Myrrha' resonates with Plath's 'The Arrival of the Bee Box', it is likely that the latter is as much inspired by another metamorphosis into tree occasioned by sexual transgression. An important tale in Ovid, but not translated by Hughes in *Tales from Ovid*, the story of Daphne and Apollo describes the transformation of the virginal Daphne into a laurel tree when she is about to be raped by the god Apollo. In Plath's 'The Arrival of the Bee Box', the escape into the metaphorical tree is an imagined potential escape away from fecundity and the attention of the bees, although it seems that the fear of being the likely target of their stings remains:

> They might ignore me immediately
> In my moon suit and funeral veil.
> I am no source of honey
> So why should they turn on me?[50]

The god Apollo is stung by Cupid's arrow into loving Daphne; she is stung into not reciprocating this love with an arrow of lead. Philip Hardie has pointed out the ways in which Daphne's subsequent plea for chastity marks her out as of a kind with the goddess Diana, who is Apollo's twin sister. Ovid emphasises that this is a quasi-incestuous love by portraying the similarities in appearance and character between Daphne and Diana: 'Ovid's Apollo contends with Daphne in a race for sexual possession. Sibling rivalry has turned into something more troubling, a contest to achieve a quasi-incestuous coupling of Apollo with a Diana look-alike.'[51] This is a further example of Isabella's 'a kind of incest', of a resemblance too close to be allowable.[52]

In arguing that the tale of Apollo and Daphne is a narrative in the manner of the more explicitly incestuous Myrrha story, Hardie identifies a structural rhyme between these two tales of tree transformation. Further, they both signify as a self-reflexive figuration of the relationship between author and text:

> This separation between Apollo and that which he has, through his actions, brought into being, may be conceptualised in the light of a reading of the metamorphosis of Daphne as the conversion of a *puella* into the elegiac *tenuis liber* (549, "bark"/ "book"), the sublimation of sexual desire into art. The relationship between Apollo and this girl-text thus figures the narcissistic and incestuous relationship between author and his book.[53]

The literal ambivalence in Latin of *liber*, which means both book and bark, thus leads Hardie to argue convincingly that this is an instance of an Ovidian appropriation of myth to reflect on the processes of poetry as transformative.

A comparable understanding of poetic transformation underlies Plath's more explicit early engagement with the relationship between wood spirit and poetic creativity:

> "My trouble, doctor, is: I see a tree,
> And that damn scrupulous tree won't practice wiles
>   To beguile sight:
>   E.g., by cant of light

> Concoct a Daphne;
> My tree stays tree.
> "However I wrench obstinate bark and trunk
> To my sweet will, no luminous shape
> Steps out radiant in limb, eye, lip,
> To hoodwink the honest earth[54]

In this, Plath explores a kind of selective writer's block, that might, it seems, be subject for a quasi-comedic session of psychoanalysis. Achieving a certain kind of romantic vision is particularly hard, and possibly not even desirable; in this early poem the world is too stubbornly material to be transformed into visionary poetry, and too literal to be the subject of mythic understanding. That she should metaphorise this struggle as the fruitless search to locate the nymph Daphne within the tree demonstrates the alertness of the text to ways in which this tale of transformation is also a reflection on the process of writing creatively.

In a poem written a year later, however, she had found in the same transformation a different warning against the puritan dangers of chastity. In this instance the transformation of Daphne into a tree precludes creative fertility:

> Ever since that first Daphne
> Switched her incomparable back
> For a bay-tree hide, respect's
> Twined to her hard limbs like ivy ...
> Neglect's
> Given her lips that lemon-tasting droop:
> Untongued, all beauty's bright juice sours.
> Tree-twist will ape this gross anatomy
> Till irony's bough break[55]

Her lips are 'untongued', that is, sexually untouched, but also without the voice of poetry.[56]

Daphne chooses perpetual chastity and becomes a tree, whereas Myrrha, lover of her own father, becomes a tree and then gives birth to her incestuous offspring Adonis, who is both her son and half-brother. Philip Hardie traces a kind of genetic crack across the generations, seeing in Adonis's birth the inevitable consequences of Pygmalion's actions in fathering his own lover in an earlier tale in which Ovid's Orpheus narrates the story of a consummate artist transformationally involved in the processes of his own art. The story of Pygmalion is a kind of reverse image of Myrrha:

> The problem is his [Adonis's] inheritance as the great-great grandson of Pygmalion and his statue; is it surprising that a member of this family should be as pretty

as a picture? Adonis is miraculously born of a tree … His mother Myrrha had undergone the opposite transformation to that of her great-grandmother the statue, from soft living flesh to a hard unfeeling object, in fulfilment of her prayer to be excluded from the worlds of both the living and the dead – as the supremely lifelike work of art is suspended uncannily between the animate and the inanimate.[57]

Pygmalion's creation comes alive, in a literalising of artistic metaphorical representation. Hughes's translation of this moment follows Ovid in rendering Orpheus's extended simile that describes the stone coming to fleshy life in terms of the warm yieldingness of wax:

> But his hand sprang off her breast
> As if stung.
> He lowered it again, incredulous
> At the softness, the warmth
> Under his fingers. Warm
> And soft as warm soft wax.[58]

For Hughes, beeswax here has its own private possible symbolism, to which he adds an additional metaphorisation that only exists in his text: 'But his hand sprang off her breast / As if stung.'[59] This particular interpolation reinforces the presiding sting of Cupid, and yet such a striking imagistic innovation at this point in the translated text also reinvigorates the dialogue between this, Myrrha's transformation through the swarming bark, and all of the beekeeping poems by both Plath and Hughes so far outlined.

But is there also a connection between the sting here, and the pressure of a spider bite? To what extent does this particular stinging flag up the shock of the literatilising of artistic representation and the latent danger in the living, female, statue herself? Pygmalion's actions are both narcissistic, in creating his own image, and incestuous, as father-creator of his bride-to-be. In Ovid's text the narcissistic act results from a degree of latent misogyny. The sacrilegious Propoetides become, according to Venus's revenge, hard-faced prostitutes, and it is in response to their vice that Pygmalion falls back on his own skills as an artist in creating a female statue to his own liking and in his own image, for which he develops an unnatural desire. The misogynistic motivation is intensified in Hughes's text with an extraordinary passage not based on Ovid's text and interpolated into the fabric of the translation:

> He adored woman, but he saw
> The wickedness of these particular women
> Transform, as by some occult connection,
> Every woman's uterus to a spider.
> Her face, voice, gestures, hair became its web.

> Her perfume was a floating horror. Her glance
> Left a spider-bite. He couldn't control it.⁶⁰

The uterus is transformed to an arachnid, which devours the male, and a woman's feminine body signifies the 'web' that lures him there.⁶¹

If Hughes's Pygmalion is motivated into narcissistic creation through fear of female sexuality and generative possibility, then Plath explores a version of female narcissism in a poem that registers the failure of such generation, where, in the manner of a spider, the persona, ivory bodied as a statue, spins a mirror that reflects her own image alone:

> This ivory
>
> ...
>
> Spiderlike, I spin mirrors,
> Loyal to my image⁶².

This particular version of Narcissus only hints at the Pygmalion narrative ('This ivory'), but Plath's earlier text on the same theme, 'Barren Woman', is explicit in its Pygmalion parallelism, and also points up the ways in which for Plath the generative possibilities of childbirth and poetry are variously interconnected.⁶³ As such it is part of a central symbolic and metaphorical image system in Plath's poetics. In 'Barren Woman' a childless woman metaphorises herself as an entire gallery. She is an unfulfilled Pygmalion, and a museum not only without statues of her own, but also tellingly without, but desiring of, an appreciative audience: 'I imagine myself with a great public, / Mother of a white Nike and several bald-eyed Apollos'.⁶⁴

Various poems in *Birthday Letters* examine the significance of maternity, and, perhaps most explicitly, the poem 'Isis' makes the connection to the level of all-encompassing myth. A deal is struck with death, who keeps 'Daddy', whilst life is embraced through birth:

> The great goddess in person
> Had put on your body, waxing full,
> Using your strainings
> Like a surgical glove, to create with.⁶⁵

Whilst the temporary assertion of the positive aspect of Hughes's Great Goddess is manifest here in the shape of Isis, the goddess's many facets are simultaneous, and with the benefit of hindsight and remembrance the presence of death contiguous with motherhood is all too easily discernible. Hughes's poem 'Perfect Light' describes a photograph of its addressee sitting among spring daffodils. A further poem by Hughes entitled 'Daffodils' describes a spring 'custom', an unthinking harvest of daffodils cut with 'wedding-present scissors' for the local shop to sell. In retrospect, 'It sounds like sacrilege, but we sold them'.⁶⁶ It is sacrilegious because these emblems of new life emerging from wintry death are being severed from their root before their time.

In Ovid's *Metamorphoses* the story of Narcissus demonstrates the skills of Tiresias as prophet of the future. He predicts Narcissus's fate, but communicates it in such a way that it cannot be understood until it has been lived through, such is the limited application of epic prophecy. Similarly, the protagonists of the poem 'Daffodils' are unable to read the significance of the flower that is the metamorphosis of Narcissus:

> We knew we'd live forever. We had not learned
> What a fleeting glance of the everlasting
> Daffodils are. Never identified
> The nuptial flight of the rarest ephemera –
> Our own days!⁶⁷

The poem recuperates a variation on the Ovidian theme of failed narcissistic love, identifying the symbolism of their future reflected back at them, the flower cut too soon a mirror of her own destiny, a part of the unrecognised image of the sacrilege of their spring ritual. 'Perfect Light' returns to this narrative with the sitter of the photograph captured amongst the daffodils with her two children, in an image that conflates the catholic manifestation of the Great Goddess with another echo of Ovid's Narcissus:

> Mother and infant, as in the Holy portrait.
> And beside you, laughing up at you,
> Your daughter, barely two. Like a daffodil
> You turn your face down to her, saying something.⁶⁸

She resembles 'a daffodil', because her head droops downwards; she is also like Narcissus, because she is looking down into the face of her child that reflects back to her a version of her own image.⁶⁹

A variation of this particular play on the Narcissus theme is also present in Plath's 'Morning Song', where it is allied to further variations on Pygmalion. In counterpoint to Plath's earlier texts of failed generative possibility, 'Morning Song' is an aubade, a poem in which there is traditionally a particular pattern of action. Anglophone poetry usually takes its lead from medieval France in this, and our generic expectations can reasonably predict the dawn breaking and two lovers having to part after their night of love. Consequently there is a characteristic doubleness to the genre: of arrival and departure, of beginnings and endings.⁷⁰

In Plath's text a new dawn is breaking and a newborn life is emerging into the world, and at its centre is the relationship between mother and child. In examining this most potent of metamorphoses the text is equally preoccupied with metaphoric thoughts relating to both Narcissus and Pygmalion.

'Is't not a kind of incest?'

The room into which the child is born is figured in such a way as to emphasise the artistic, in addition to the maternal, preoccupations. The birth of the child is simultaneous with the birth of the work of art into which the child is born; but the artistic parallelism that highlights this simultaneity draws on images of statuary and display precisely to invoke the Ovidian shadow of Pygmalion:

> Our voices echo, magnifying your arrival. New statue.
> In a drafty museum, your nakedness
> Shadows our safety. We stand round blankly as walls.[71]

The mother-poet has given birth to the child-poem in the manner of Pygmalion giving life to the lover-statue in his own image. The following stanza presents a much more complicated image of child-mother contemplation than Hughes's 'Perfect Light':

> I'm no more your mother
> Than the cloud that distils a mirror to reflect its own slow
> Effacement at the wind's hand.[72]

This extraordinarily beautiful and complex figuration is a repeat with significant variation on the narcissistic metaphor from 'Childless Woman' ('Spiderlike, / I spin mirrors, / Loyal to my image'[73]). Here, the mother is the cloud that sees its own reflection in the puddle that it has distilled onto the earth. But what the mother-cloud sees in that reflection is not just self, but effacement of self. The act of giving birth is progressive in the way that Narcissus's mythic paradigm is not, trapped merely looking back at himself and in love with himself only. Here there is necessary separation and difference (distance, effacement) at the same time as absolute identification (the cloud and the puddle, as the mother and child, are essentially made of the same material).

That the progression is towards inevitable death is of course part of the process; nevertheless the product is the stuff of life, and as the poem turns characteristically towards day, away from night, the metaphoric equation of poem and child going out into the world together is made complete:

> The window square
> Whitens and swallows its dull stars. And now you try
> Your handful of notes;
> The clear vowels rise like balloons.[74]

The style of the muted breaking of the dawn ('[w]hitens') will remind the careful reader of a different but related aubade, 'After a Journey', from that other great poet of 'Lyonnesse', Thomas Hardy: 'For the stars close their shutters and the dawn whitens hazily'.[75] Hardy's voice in this poem is performing a version of the Pygmalion myth, recreating his dead wife in his own preferred image. That he can only bring her back in ghostly form in this poem underlines the restrictions of the marvellous self-regard that he nevertheless achieves. Plath's poem goes self-reflexively further than this: what survives beyond the self are the 'handful of notes', metamorphosed into music from the initial 'bald cry', as both child and poem leave their mother-lover-creator and go out into the world with a voice.[76]

A similar but differently figured preoccupation with creativity characterises Plath's 'Ariel', another aubade from which Plath's collection takes its name. In this the progression from dark to light, and from night to morning, is accompanied by a progression from stasis to movement, a movement that metaphorises creation as a harvest emerging from the chaos of ocean: 'And now I / Foam to wheat, a glitter of seas'.[77] This transmutes the imagery of any number of fertility rites, simultaneously representing the double possibilities of maternal and poetic creativity. The closing sacrificial image metaphorises the self as a version of Cupid's arrow fired into the dangerous heart of a new mythical and apocalyptic dawn:

> And I
> Am the arrow,
>
> The dew that flies
> Suicidal, at one with the drive
> Into the red
>
> Eye, the cauldron of morning.[78]

In tracing the movement from stasis to the metaphorical arrow flying towards the sun, the poem also shadows a symbolic path for the spirit of Shakespeare's Ariel in *The Tempest*.

For Hughes, Shakespeare's Ariel, one-time enforced dryad, is properly a flower spirit, released to her natural airy element by Prospero.[79] Hughes's Ariel is androgynous, but referred to throughout *Shakespeare and the Goddess of Complete Being* as female, and indeed at times representative of the Great Goddess, especially in the scene in which she imposes the storm in Act 3 Scene 3:

> Ariel, in the form of a creature from the Underworld, speaks through all the powers of Nature – the 'seas and shores' and 'all the creatures' – with the voice of 'Destiny.' This is not Jupiter, or Apollo, or Diana, but the Great Goddess herself.[80]

Ariel is relatedly associated with bees, through her song from *The Tempest* Act 5, Scene 1:

> Where the bee sucks, there suck I:
> In a cowslip's bell I lie;
> There I couch, when owls do cry.
> On the bat's back I do fly
> After summer merrily.[81]

Hughes's convoluted arguments associate Ariel's cowslip with the wind-flower, the metamorphosed Adonis, beloved of Venus, a flower suffused by the goddess herself. This is a unifying symbol for Hughes, and one which has a key role in determining the significance of the play:

> [T]he Flower and Storm episodes are, in every case, an epiphany of the Goddess. They are episodes in which she breaks up the tragic order that prevails at the beginning of the play, and re-establishes the new, transcendental order, which becomes possible at the end.[82]

That *The Tempest* represents one of the many interwoven literary and mythical structures through which Hughes constructs and understands his textual relationship to Plath is clearly established in poems such as 'Setebos', and 'Night Ride on Ariel'. However, whereas his interpretation of Shakespeare's late play identifies the Goddess as transcending what he terms 'the tragic equation',[83] his poems in *Birthday Letters* that preoccupy themselves with Plath's 'Ariel' and *The Tempest* more generally, establish a very different pattern. 'Setebos' begins with an unproblematic version of the transcendent comedy, until Sycorax takes over the directing:

> I heard
> The bellow in your voice
> That made my nape-hair prickle when you sang
> How you were freed from the Elm. I lay
> In the labyrinth of a cowslip
> Without a clue. I heard the Minotaur
> Coming down its tunnel-groove.[84]

The problem here is the change in 'script', to the point that they lose sight of which play they are in.[85] Ariel is no longer the presiding spirit, and transcendence is replaced instead with confusion. The already-freighted image of the 'cowslip' has become enmeshed in the 'labyrinth', as the Cretan myth overwrites the Shakespearean play.[86] By the end of the poem they inhabit a mythic conflation of ancient sacrificial rites of burning and dismemberment:

> I heard your cries
> Bugling through the hot bronze:
> 'Who has dismembered us?'[87]

In a late essay collected in the significantly titled *Winter Pollen*, Hughes persuasively reads Plath's poem 'Ariel' as a variation on the Phaeton myth, which metamorphoses into the Icarus myth in what he perceives to be a companion poem, 'Sheep in Fog', with its images of sky and water:

> the far
> Fields melt my heart.

> They threaten
> To let me through to a heaven
> Starless and fatherless, a dark water.[88]

In describing the process of this poem's evolution into its final text, Hughes writes:

> Here that word 'melt' has metamorphosed the sun's chariot and horses into the wax wings of Icarus – who also flew (against his father's warning) too near the sun …
> The 'melting' of the 'Phaeton myth' behind Ariel into the 'Icarus myth' behind this … is done with beautiful, extremely powerful effect, yet without overt mention of either. And one can see how any mention of either would have killed the suggestive power of the mythic ideas.[89]

The beauty and significance of the poem is revealed for Hughes in his reading of that one understated metaphorical gesture, and its accumulative associations. As such their poetry does not have the quasi-incestuous resemblance of Daphne and Apollo, for their practice in metaphor and myth are quite different. Hughes in *Birthday Letters* is in search of explicatory and unifying narratives that, once established, are never sufficiently big or unifying to contain his subject. The restlessness of the quest to contain uncontainable experience is part of the distinctive poetic life of the collection, a life contingent upon a kind of kitchen sink approach to myth and metaphor, with the interweaving and cross-identification in the example of 'Setebos' of *The Tempest*, and Venus and Adonis, and Osiris, and Orpheus, and the labyrinth and Minotaur, to name only a few of the more conspicuous texts. In reading Plath's 'Ariel' and 'Sheep in Fog' Hughes acknowledges the much more subtle mythic and metaphorical approach inherent in these poems, and whilst the poems in *Birthday Letters* are illuminating and powerful in their own right, their dialogic nature valuably returns us to Plath's exquisite 'suggestive power'.[90] But it is in his translations and transformations from Ovid that Hughes suggestively explores the interrelation of myth and poetic practice common to both poets. In this respect the dialogic exchange benefits from the presence of Ovid, whose own sophisticated realisation and examination of the relationship between myth, metaphor and poetry enables Hughes's 'suggestive power[s]'[91] to the full.

In Ovid, the point of transformation allows for detailed reflection on the exchange of values in metaphoric thought, which is at the heart of the poetic act of creation. As Hardie has suggested, there is something inherently and necessarily narcissistic and incestuous in this process of exchange, in the bringing together of resemblances in pursuit of poetry. The exploration of incest myth allows Ovid to examine the processes of poetic imagination and technique, specifically in relation to mimesis and metaphor. Incest is revealing as a way of thinking about the proper and improper relations and boundaries between author and text, art and nature, and this is in one sense what makes Ovid's text sophisticated in its reflection of transformation and metamorphosis, not just as a necessary structure of myth, but as central to the process of poetry itself.

This is a shared motivation in the poetry of both Plath and Hughes: his more explicit engagement through translation takes us back to her more intimate evocations of Ovidian preoccupation, both in terms of subject matter and reflection on poetic process. Metaphor is transformational, and poetry that takes transformation as its subject is doubly metamorphic, and concerned here with a poetics of myth around the cycle of death and regeneration so central to the concerns of both Plath and Hughes. In searching after a myth or layering of myth it is those tales which directly consider the relationship between incestuous and quasi-incestuous narrative and the role of the creator that are most telling in terms of understanding a poetic process common to both poets, but so very differently manifested.

Notes

1 William Shakespeare, Stanley Wells (ed.), *Measure for Measure* (Oxford University Press, 2008), p. 156 (3.1.142).
2 Excerpts from twelve poems by Sylvia Plath are taken from *The Collected Poems of Sylvia Plath*, edited by Ted Hughes. Copyright © 1960, 1965, 1971, 1981 by the Estate of Sylvia Plath. Editorial material copyright © 1981 by Ted Hughes. Reprinted by permission of Faber & Faber (world rights excluding US) and HarperCollins (US rights). Excerpts from 'Myrrha', 'Venus and Adonis (and Atalanta)' and 'Pygmalion' from *Birthday Letters* by Ted Hughes. Copyright © 1998 by Ted Hughes. Reprinted by permission of Faber & Faber (world rights excluding US) and Farrar, Straus and Giroux (US rights). Excerpts from *Shakespeare and the Goddess of Complete Being* by Ted Hughes. Copyright © 1992 by Ted Hughes. Reprinted by permission of Faber & Faber (world rights excluding US) and Farrar, Straus and Giroux (US rights). Excerpts from 'Myrrha', 'Venus and Adonis (and Atalanta)' and 'Pygmalion' from *Tales from Ovid* by Ted Hughes. Copyright © 1997 by Ted Hughes. Reprinted by permission of Faber & Faber (world rights excluding US) and Farrar, Straus and Giroux (US rights).
3 Eavan Boland, 'Ted Hughes: A reconciliation', *PN Review* 25:5 (May–June, 1999), p. 6.
4 See Erica Wagner, *Ariel's Gift* (Faber & Faber, 2000) pp. 149–50.
5 Lynda K. Bundtzen, 'Mourning Eurydice: Ted Hughes as Orpheus in *Birthday Letters*', *Journal of Modern Literature*, 23:3/4 (Summer, 2000), pp. 458.
6 Ted Hughes, *Shakespeare and the Goddess of Complete Being* (Faber & Faber, 1992), p. 7.

7 *Ibid.*, pp. 168–9.
8 Shakespeare, *Measure for Measure*, p. 156 (3.1.141–143).
9 *Ibid.*, p. 156 (3.1. 142).
10 J.D. McClatchy, 'Old myths in new versions', *Poetry Chicago*, 172:3 (June, 1998), p. 154.
11 Lynda K. Bundtzen has persuasively argued that the Orpheus myth is a presiding structural presence throughout Hughes's *Birthday Letters*. Bundtzen, 'Mourning Eurydice', p. 467.
12 Ted Hughes, 'Myrrha', *Tales from Ovid* (Faber & Faber, 1997), pp. 117–18.
13 Bundtzen, 'Mourning Eurydice', p. 460.
14 Hughes, 'Myrrha', p. 114.
15 *Ibid.*, p. 118.
16 Hughes, 'Venus and Adonis (and Atalanta)', *Tales from Ovid*, p. 128.
17 J.D. McClatchy, 'Old myths in new versions', p. 158.
18 Hughes, 'Venus and Adonis (and Atalanta)', p. 128.
19 *Ibid.*, p. 128.
  Ovid, Lee Fratantuono (ed.), *Metamorphoses bk X* (Bloomsbury, 2014), p. 34, l. 491.
20 Hughes, 'Venus and Adonis (and Atalanta)', p. 128.
21 *Ibid.*, p. 128.
22 *Ibid.*, p. 128.
23 Sylvia Plath, Ted Hughes (ed. and introd.), 'The Arrival of the Bee Box', *Collected Poems* (Faber & Faber, 1989), p. 212.
24 *Ibid.*, p. 213.
25 *Ibid.*, pp. 213.
26 Hughes, *Shakespeare and the Goddess of Complete Being*, p. 7 *passim*.
27 See Mary Lynn Broe for a comprehensive exploration of Plath's bee motif as political allegory.
28 Anon. (set by John Wilbye), 'Sweet Honey-Sucking Bees', in Philip Ledger (ed.). *The Oxford Book of English Madrigals* (Oxford University Press, 1978), p. 295.
29 Ted Hughes, 'The Bee God', *Birthday Letters* (Faber & Faber, 1998), p. 148.
30 *Ibid.*, p. 148.
31 *Ibid.*, pp. 148, 149.
32 *Ibid.*, pp. 148, 149.
33 Hughes, 'The Cast', *Birthday Letters*, p. 177.
34 *Ibid.*, p. 177.
35 *Ibid.*, p. 177.
36 Hughes, 'The Bee God', *Birthday Letters*, p. 149.
37 Plath, 'Lament', *Collected Poems*, p. 315.
38 Plath, 'Stings', *Collected Poems*, p. 215.
39 *Ibid.*, p. 215.
40 Hughes, 'The Bee God', *Birthday Letters*, p. 148; Plath, 'Stings', *Collected Poems*, p. 215.
41 Plath, 'Stings', *Collected Poems*, p. 215.

42 Hughes, 'The Bee God', *Birthday Letters*, p. 148.
43 *Ibid.*, p. 152.
44 Sylvia Plath, 'Words', *Ariel* (Faber & Faber, 1999), p. 81.
45 Hughes, 'The Bee God', *Birthday Letters*, p. 149.
46 Plath, 'The Hanging Man', *Collected Poems*, p. 141.
47 For an account of Sylvia Plath's experiences with Electroconvulsive Therapy (ECT) see: Andrew Wilson, *Mad Girl's Love Song* (Scribner, 2013), pp. 10, 53, 214–5, 227–8, 230–1, 238.
48 Christian Standard Bible, 'Absalom's Defeat', *Bible Gateway*, Samuel 2.18, www.biblegateway.com/passage/?search=2+Samuel+18&version=CSB (accessed 20 April 2017).
49 Plath, 'The Hanging Man', *Collected Poems*, p. 142.
William Shakespeare, Alden T. Vaughan and Virginia Mason Vaughan (eds), *The Tempest*, Arden Shakespeare (Bloomsbury, 2011), p. 191 (1.2.274; 1.2.277).
50 Plath, 'The Arrival of the Bee Box', *Collected Poems*, p. 213.
51 Philip Hardie, 'Approximative similes in Ovid: Incest and doubling', *Dictynna*, 1 (2004), http://dictynna.revues.org/166 (accessed 23 June 2011).
52 William Shakespeare, Stanley Wells (ed.), *Measure for Measure* (Oxford University Press, 2008), p. 156 (3.1.142).
53 Hardie, 'Approximative similes in Ovid'.
54 Plath, 'On the Difficulty of Conjuring Up a Dryad', *Collected Poems*, p. 66.
55 Plath, 'Virgin in a Tree', *Collected Poems*, pp. 81–2 [ellipsis mine].
56 *Ibid.*, p. 82.
57 Hardie, 'Approximative similes in Ovid'.
58 Hughes, 'Pygmalion', *Tales from Ovid*, p. 149.
59 *Ibid.*, p. 149.
60 *Ibid.*, p. 145.
61 *Ibid.*, p. 145.
62 Plath, 'Childless Woman', *Collected Poems*, p. 259 [ellipses mine].
63 *Ibid.*, p. 259.
64 Plath, 'Barren Woman', *Collected Poems*, p. 157.
65 Hughes, 'Isis', *Birthday Letters*, pp. 109; 110.
66 Hughes, 'Daffodils', *Birthday Letters*, pp. 125–6.
67 *Ibid.*, p. 125.
68 Hughes, 'Perfect Light', *Birthday Letters*, p. 141.
69 *Ibid.*, p. 141.
70 For more on the 'aubade' see: Kit Fryatt, ' "Horny Morning Mood": The aubade and Alba', in Erik Martiny (ed.), *A Companion to Poetic Genre* (Wiley-Blackwell, 2012), pp. 379–89.
71 Plath, 'Morning Song', *Collected Poems*, p. 157.
72 *Ibid.*, p. 157.
73 Plath, 'Childless Woman', *Collected Poems*, p. 259.
74 Plath, 'Morning Song', *Collected Poems*, p. 157.

75 Ibid., p. 157. Thomas Hardy, Michael Irwin (introd. and notes), 'When I Set For Lyonnesse' and 'After a Journey', *Collected Poems* (Wordsworth, 2006), pp. 284, 317.
76 Plath, 'Morning Song', *Collected Poems*, pp. 157, 156.
77 Plath, 'Ariel', *Collected Poems*, p. 239.
78 Ibid., pp. 239–40.
79 Hughes, *Shakespeare and the Goddess of Complete Being*, p. 472.
80 Ibid., p. 439.
81 Shakespeare, *The Tempest*, p. 291 (5.1.88–92).
82 Hughes, *Shakespeare and the Goddess of Complete Being*, pp. 477–8.
83 Ibid., passim.
84 Hughes, 'Setebos', *Birthday Letters*, p. 130.
85 Ibid., p. 130.
86 Ibid., p. 130.
87 Ibid., p. 131.
88 Plath, 'Sheep in Fog', *Collected Poems*, p. 262.
89 Ted Hughes, William Scammel (ed.), 'The evolution of "Sheep in Fog"', *Winter Pollen* (Picador, 1995), p. 206.
90 Ibid., p. 206.
91 Ibid., p. 206.

Bibliography

Fiction, poetry, and dramatic works

Graves, Robert, *The White Goddess: A Historical Grammar of Poetic Myth* (Faber & Faber, 1999)

Hardy, Thomas, Michael Irwin (introd. and notes), 'When I Set Out For Lyonnesse' and 'After a Journey', *Collected Poems* (Wordsworth, 2006)

Hughes, Ted, *Birthday Letters* (Faber & Faber, 1998), digital edition

——., *Shakespeare and the Goddess of Complete Being* (Faber & Faber, 1992)

——., *Tales from Ovid* (Faber & Faber, 1997)

Ovid, Lee Fratantuono (ed.), *Metamorphoses X* (Bloomsbury, 2014)

——., A.D. Melville (trans.), E.J. Kenney (introd. and notes.), *Metamorphoses* (Oxford University Press, 1998)

Plath, Sylvia, *Ariel* (Faber & Faber, 1999)

——., Ted Hughes (ed. and introd.), *Collected Poems* (Faber & Faber, 1989)

Shakespeare, William, Stanley Wells (ed.), *Measure for Measure* (Oxford University Press, 2008)

——., Alden T. Vaughan and Virginia Mason Vaughan (eds), *The Tempest*, Arden Shakespeare (Bloomsbury, 2011)

Swift, Jonathan, Angus Ross and David Woolley (eds, introd. and notes), *A Tale of a Tub and Other Works* (Oxford University Press, 2008)

Wilbye, John, 'Sweet Honey-Sucking Bees', in Philip Ledger (ed.). *The Oxford Book of English Madrigals* (Oxford University Press, 1978)

Non-fiction

Boland, Eavan, 'Ted Hughes: A reconciliation', *PN Review* 25:5 (May–June, 1999)
Broe, Mary Lynn, 'The bee sequence: ' "But I Have a Self to Recover" ', in Harold Bloom (ed.), *Sylvia Plath* (Chelsea House, 1989), pp. 95–108.
Bruyn, Frans De, 'Absalom', in David Lyle Jeffrey (ed.), *A Dictionary of Biblical Tradition in English Literature* (William B. Eerdmans Publishing Company, 1992), pp. 11–14
Bundtzen, Lynda K., 'Mourning Eurydice: Ted Hughes as Orpheus in *Birthday Letters*', *Journal of Modern Literature*, 23:3/4 (Summer, 2000), pp. 455–69
Farmer, David, 'Sebastian', *Dictionary of Saints* (Oxford University Press, 2011)
Fryatt, Kit, ' "Horny Morning Mood": The aubade and Alba', in Erik Martiny (ed.), *A Companion to Poetic Genre* (Wiley-Blackwell, 2012), pp. 379–89
Hardie, Philip, 'Approximative similes in Ovid: Incest and doubling', *Dictynna*, 1 (2004), http://dictynna.revues.org/166 (accessed 23 June 2011)
Hinnant, Charles H., 'The "fable of the spider and the bee" and Swift's Poetics of Inspiration', *Colby Library Quarterly*, 20:3 (September, 1984), pp. 129–36.
McClatchy, J.D., 'Old myths in new versions', *Poetry Chicago*, 172:3 (June, 1998), pp. 154–64
Plato, W.H.D. Rouse (trans.), Eric H. Warmington and Philip G. Rouse (eds), *Great Dialogues of Plato* (New American Library, 1956), 18n.
Wagner Erica, *Ariel's Gift* (Faber & Faber, 2000)
Wilson, Andrew, *Mad Girl's Love Song* (Scribner, 2013)
Wood Middlebrook, Diane *Her Husband: Hughes and Plath – A Marriage* (Viking, 2003)

Websites

Christian Standard Bible, 'Absalom's Defeat', *Bible Gateway*, Samuel 2.18, www.biblegateway.com/passage/?search=2+Samuel+18&version=CSB (accessed 20 April 2017)

11

'[T]he thing that makes us different from other people':[1] Narrating incest through 'différance' in the work of Angela Carter, A.S. Byatt and Doris Lessing

Emma V. Miller and Miles Leeson

Incest between siblings has been depicted in literature throughout history as both a horrific occurrence, and conversely, a Romantic idyll. Even when the siblings appear to be equals and the sex is apparently consensual, the discovery of incest threatens both the immediate family unit and society at large, structured as it is, upon the legitimacy and functionality of the nuclear family. Incestuous relationships with close relatives increase the risk of reproducing children with hereditary health problems,[2] but those concerned also risk being socially ostracised for committing an act not just illegal in many countries, but also morally and ethically censured, both socially and culturally.[3] Yet as Judith Herman argues in *Father-Daughter Incest*, the prohibition in many patriarchal cultures was shaped by concerns over the sexual appropriation of a man's property, not as a result of anxiety for the emotional and physical welfare of the individuals involved. Herman asserts that the only incestuous liaison that is not clearly condemned in ancient cultures is that between father and daughter, precisely *because* the daughter was viewed as the father's property, and in many cultures this is still the case.[4] However, in terms of heterosexual sibling incest, Leonore Davidoff asserts, 'in cultures which emphasize masculine primacy, all brothers, including the younger, start with power and privilege over all sisters, no matter what the age differences.'[5] It is difficult therefore, in any society where men and women have not had the same rights in society, and continue to be treated disparately (even if this treatment does not initially appear to be related to the family unit) to determine whether a heterosexual incestuous relationship can truly be deemed that of equals. Furthermore, ending an incestuous relationship will be inevitably more complex than a relationship with a person not connected to the family.

Narrating incest through 'différance'

Conversely however, in the arts and culture in general, sibling incest has been historically depicted as the highest elevation of Romantic love, indeed William D. Brewer asserts with reference to Shelley's letter to Maria Gisborne, that 'the brother-and-sister incest portrayed in Shelley's *Laon and Cythna* and Byron's *Manfred* is the "excess of love"; the father-daughter incestuous rape which is at the centre of *The Cenci* is the "excess" of hate'.[6] The siblings' similarities and shared experiences appear to many artists to evoke the perfect union of souls, idealised in romantic love from Plato's description in the *Symposium* of early humans as two creatures physically attached to each other (rather like conjoined twins), later separated by the gods and consequently searching desperately for their other half; to the Victorian enthusiasm for Emanuel Swedenborg's theory of 'conjugal love'[7] which described marriage in the following terms: 'For the male and the female of the human species are so created as to be able to become like a single individual, that is, one flesh; and when united, then they are, taken together, the full expression of humanity. If not so joined, they are two, each being as it were a divided person or half a person.'[8] Indeed, Swedenborg even goes so far as to assert that this connection persists after death and that, 'two conjugal partners in heaven are not called two, but one angel', and he goes on to state that '[m]arriage in the heavens is the conjunction of two into one mind'.[9] When we consider that during the Victorian period, women, according to Mary Lyndon Shanley, had few more rights after marriage than 'children', those 'who were incapable of fully rational activity, and criminals'.[10] The real-life implications for the plight of women, resulting from the romanticisation of the joining of not only two bodies in marriage but two minds, where one party was defined legally, scientifically and culturally as superior to the other, becomes worryingly apparent. Yet, Davidoff comments that '[b]rother-sister incest as an explanation of human origins is found in almost every culture, including the Judaic-Christian' and '[b]ecause of their shared parentage, all siblings, whether of the same or different sex, seem to possess a special quality of "unity in difference", a mirroring of the self, two parts of one whole "split along the fault lines of ambivalence"'.[11]

It is this confusion between the discourses of romance and religion, which can be seen to idealise this dichotomy of sameness and difference, posited against the social, legal and scientific discourses of psychological and societal health that creates the problematic tension in the narration of sibling incest. Sibling incest, unlike parent–child incest, has been narrated in terms of abuse *and* also crucially, mainstream romanticism. As much as research has demonstrated 'that sibling incest often involves coerced, severe, repeated abuse',[12] and that 'older brother perpetrators and younger sister targets' suggest a 'double power imbalance (age and gender)',[13] the glamorisation of the sibling incest bond persists into contemporary literature, even in the writing of authors identified with feminism. By interrogating the central problem of sameness and difference in the symbolic structure of Western culture and how it is expressed through language, this chapter seeks to deconstruct the literary depiction of incest as a romantic, or indeed, Romantic, conceit in the literature of three key literary figures of the second wave of feminism: Angela Carter, A.S. Byatt and Doris Lessing.

'[A]long the invisible gangway between her trapezes':[14] Angela Carter's narration of a taboo betwixt definition

Angela Carter's work is characterised by both its author's feminism and its grotesque textual relationship with the style and content of the Gothic. Carter depicts some of the most disturbing aspects of humanity: rape, incest, paedophilia, cannibalism, to name just a few of the topics she presents in her fiction, generally without any clear ethical structure to guide the reader, and often with startling humour. As Aidan Day has commented, 'Carter's fiction is a bit extreme'[15] and this is true of both her narrative style as well as the content of her writing. Yet despite this, her fiction is widely read and respected, even when, as in *The Magic Toyshop* (1967), she appears to condone a societal taboo. However, Carter's writing is as much characterised by what it is, as what it is not, and her work is balanced, somewhat precariously, upon what Derrida in his discussion of the work of Levinas calls, 'the tears' in 'the seam' of '*the* text'.[16]

Derrida describes the text here, as 'that heterogenous tissue that interlaces both texture and atexture, without uniting them' even if, by embracing tears the writer necessarily opens the text up to the 'risk of contamination'.[17]. The metaphor of the seam then, the place where distinct pieces of fabric are threaded together, is a locale of unity in difference, but it is also a fragile place, where the textual unity is under threat from competing meanings and ever-changing contextual frameworks. The sensitive nature of Carter's subject matter is not on the edge of textual meaning, but embedded within it, yet the issues she describes are understood by their broader context outside of the book's covers, as much as that within the story itself. It is the very lack of a dogmatic morality *within* her writing that opens the text to be considered in the framework of, and opposed to, every discourse available to the reader. Her fictions are therefore subject to both amorality and immorality, but also crucially, to a more rigorous, complex and wide-ranging ethical structure than an author could ever enclose between the covers of an individual book.

The Magic Toyshop (1967) tells the story of fifteen-year-old Melanie who is orphaned suddenly when her parents die in a plane crash, and is consequently sent with her younger siblings, Jonathon and Victoria, to live with her Uncle Philip, his mute wife, Margaret, and Margaret's brothers Francie and Finn

Narrating incest through 'différance'

Jowle. Philip is soon revealed to be a tyrannical sociopath, obsessed with the lifelike toys he makes for the toyshop (which the family live above) but uninterested in the welfare of the people he resides with, exhibiting a violent temper and a vindictive interest in humiliating his subordinates. Philip beats Finn, 'likes ... silent women',[18] will throw a woman out of his shop if she is wearing trousers, and forces Melanie to perform in the role of the victim in a dramatisation of the mythological rape of Leda by Zeus to the entire household. Philip even encourages Finn to rehearse with Melanie by taking the part of Zeus disguised as a swan, an occurrence that Finn interprets as a means to manipulate him into attacking her.

> 'Suddenly I saw it all, when we were lying there. He's pulled our strings as if we were puppets, and there I was, all ready to touch you up just as he wanted. He told me to rehearse Leda and the swan with you. Somewhere private. Like in your room, he said. Go up and rehearse a rape with Melanie in your bedroom. Christ. He wanted me to do you and he set the scene. Ah, he's evil!'[19]

Melanie is agonisingly aware that she is still a child and as such is at the mercy of her relatives, yet despite their complaints, the Jowle siblings – all three of whom are adults – remain living together, dependent upon Philip for employment and their home. By way of explanation, Francie comments, "'[w]e're very close the three of us ... It is right for brothers and sisters to be close'".[20] Near the end of the tale, Melanie who has grown closer to the three siblings, celebrates Philip's brief absence from the house with them, and at the conclusion of the evening she witnesses Francie and Margaret in 'a lover's embrace, annihilating the world, as if taking place at midnight on the crest of a hill, with a tearing wind beating the branches above them'.[21] Melanie sees the occurrence as poetic, and even employs an imaginative application of the pathetic fallacy to describe the interaction. In comparison with Philip's marriage to Margaret which is controlling and unhappy, this couple who have shared interests and care not only about each other's immediate welfare but that of Melanie and the other children, must seem much closer to the romantic ideal Melanie understood whilst growing up. Melanie's teenage years prior to her parents' death are described as intensely and privately given to romantic and sexual speculation. She demonstrates a rich imaginative life: 'Melanie remembered reading of the marriage of a pair of Siamese twins. They would have needed a very big bed';[22] an appreciation for her developing body, 'she did not want to think she might not be already perfect'[23], and she dresses in her mother's wedding dress to escape into the garden in the night, overcome with the beauty of her relation to her surroundings just like the Romantics were before her: 'She shook with ecstasy. Why? How? Beyond herself, she did not know or care ... The world, which was only this garden, was as empty as the sky, endless as eternity.'[24] Melanie feels very soon after she has entered the toyshop though, that rather than enjoying her solitude, she is instead, 'entirely alone, brother and sister both lost to her',[25] and as she becomes closer to the Jowles this sense of distance from her own siblings increases. Before she left home, Melanie wondered if her five-year-old sister, Victoria was 'retarded'[26] and Victoria continues to be barely capable of stringing a sentence together. She also expects to be dressed and fed like a much younger child, so that she is no ally for Melanie, and Jonathan is soon enticed by the mechanics of model aeroplanes to abandon his sister for Philip's workshop, an event she marks with the observation that, 'she knew in her heart that, if she ever had Jonathan, she had lost him for good'.[27]

The text therefore, initially appears to condone or excuse the incestuous relationship between Margaret and Francie as preferable *because* it is different. Melanie resents that she is at first not asked to join in the Jowles' music evenings, saying she 'felt that nobody in all the world cared whether she lived or died',[28] and so she is consequently delighted when she is encouraged to join their exclusive group, and in Philip's absence 'they all washed together, giggling and splashing water at one another'.[29] It is later that day when Melanie discovers the truth of Margaret and Francie's relationship and Finn comments: "'You know our heart's core now, the thing that makes us different from other people, Francie and Maggie and I.'"[30] This comment is both a plea for a Romantic understanding of their situation, referring back to the definition of sibling incest lauded by Byron and Shelley, but it is also an attempt at justification through difference. Finn wants them to be given dispensation for being unique, rather than criticised for transgressing. This request does affect Melanie, who, desperate for a sense of belonging, frequently thinks back to the comfort of the physical proximity of her own parents, comparing Finn's request to share her bed with 'when she was Victoria's age and saw ghosts at night she would ... snuggle down in the cosy cleft between her parents and sleep securely, locked in by their flesh which was also her flesh'.[31] Beyond the physical needs of the body for survival, Abraham Maslow, whose hierarchy of human needs (1954) is still referred to by social scientists today, identified that human beings 'need to feel that we belong somewhere, and are accepted members of a family ... Feelings of love affection and closeness are involved, and these contribute to a person's growing sense of identity.'[32] In order to survive and mature 'normally',[33] Melanie is seeking this sense of belonging and the affection of her fellow creatures. Her inexperience and her strong desire to be a part of the exclusive group that the Jowles represent, all make her keen to accept their behaviour. Indeed, the incest could be deemed a result of their own earlier unmet needs, and a sign of their consequent struggle for survival. Rather than breaking apart the family bond through sexual activity, Finn indicates that they are united against the rest of the world because of this difference. Although Melanie is not required to commit incest herself, it is unclear whether she would gain admittance to their group without the possibility of a sexual relationship with Finn. Finn includes himself with Francie and Margaret in the description of their incest above, and because Melanie has seen a naked painting of Margaret by Finn, it is reasonable to assume he may also have committed incest with his sister. Melanie is then creating a bond with the Jowles by accepting their sexual relations and being willing to enter into a similar relationship with one of their number herself. Her description of looking at Finn before she realises the nature of Margaret and Francie's relationship, highlights her desire to become one of their family, and to resemble him, 'She sat in Finn's face; there she was mirrored twice.'[34] She sees herself as the same as him, and so when she discovers, 'the thing that makes' them 'different from other people',[35] she too identifies as part of that group, the same as its members but different from outsiders.

Ferdinand de Saussure suggested that '[i]n language there are only differences ... A linguistic system is a series of differences of sound combined with a series of differences of ideas; but the pairing of a certain number of acoustical signs with as many cuts made from the mass thought engenders a system of values.'[36] In other words meaning is derived from what it is not, a word becomes what it is from its difference to the words that surround it. Derrida's theory of *différance* which incorporates both 'to defer' and 'to differ',[37] elaborates Saussure's consideration of difference by extending the methodology to cover all linguistic and pre-linguistic modes of sense and understanding. He explains:

> *Différance* is the systematic play of differences, of the traces of differences, of the spacing by means of which elements are related to each other. This spacing is the simultaneously active and passive (the *a* of *différance* indicates this indecision as concerns activity and passivity, that which cannot be governed by or distributed between the terms of this opposition) production of the intervals without which the 'full' terms would not signify, would not function.[38]

So to interpret 'incest' through this lens at first suggests that, linguistically at least, there may be some validity to Finn's request for a specific and unique understanding of the incest in *The Magic Toyshop*, dependent upon the context of *their* experience. Yet it simultaneously renders such an approach impossible, as the incest that Margaret and Francie experience is not only understood as a word different to other words, but as a concept which is comprehended through its artistic and cultural context and its lack of other artistic and cultural contexts, through its relationship to the history of incest and everything it might become, even if it is also, on a more localised level, understood in the terms of their particular circumstances: the text that forms their relations, the house they reside in, and its relation to the specific culture of that family and their individual and collective past(s) and future(s). It is therefore, anchored to other depictions of incest even as it is defined by its difference from them. So Finn's desire to be free from the constraints of social prejudices against incest but understood within the context of the toyshop, is therefore not possible, their experience, the lexical item that describes it (although never specifically), and the general concept of incest are dependent upon each other, even as they are divisive.

Derrida famously asserted that 'there is nothing outside the text',[39] a phrase which seems a plea for the uniqueness of the particular text, but this is not the case, rather as Maria Baghramian understands it,

> we are not able to access reality directly without language and the context within which it is embedded ... Language is infinite 'play', and meaning is created afresh in the act of reading a text. The meaning of a text is at least partly fashioned by the reader and is dependent on the context of reading. There is then no room left for the idea of an ultimately correct or legitimate interpretation.[40]

This is not to say though that there is complete freedom to interpret, as context makes its own dictates.

> The phrase, which for some has become a sort of slogan, in general so badly understood, of deconstruction ('there is nothing outside the text'), means nothing else: there is nothing outside context. In this form, which says exactly the same thing, the formula would doubtless have been less shocking. I am not certain that it would have provided more to think about.
>
> ... what I call 'text' implies all; the structures called 'real', 'economic', 'historical', socio-institutional, in short: all possible referents. Another way of recalling once again that 'there is nothing outside the text'. That does not mean that references are suspended, denied, or enclosed in a book, as people have claimed, or have been naïve enough to believe and to have accused me of believing. But it does mean that every referent, all reality has the structure of a defférantial trace, and that one cannot refer to this 'real' except in an interpretative experience.[41]

The text then is bound to its context, even though the boundaries of that context will be different for every reader, dependent upon their own knowledge and experience. As Derrida asserts above, 'there is nothing outside the text', but the text cannot and does not exist without its context, this is an integral part of it, even as its existence depends upon its difference from the world around it, to be *this* text, not another. By drawing attention to this dichotomy of difference and sameness, which underlines all depictions of incest, Carter attempts to situate her narration in the place between the signifier and the signified, the definition of the word, and its context, in particular both extremes of the imagined act, as horror and high Romance. By placing Francie and Margaret in the grotesque setting of the toyshop, and juxtaposing their care for each other with Margaret's loveless marriage, their relationship is rendered *almost* comprehensible, as a desire for everyday affection in an emotionally challenging environment. Their plea for justification through difference though complicates this issue, suggesting that they do not desire an escape to the safety of convention, but instead consider themselves elevated by acting in an even more unusual fashion than the tyrannical Philip. Finn even describes Philip as a 'cuckold', suggesting that he might be a victim, manipulated by Margaret and her brothers, something Melanie does not appreciate. The Jowles are in no way obliged to remain at the toyshop and continue to deceive Philip, they are able to leave at any time, but Finn's words imply that they stay only to maintain a facade of social acceptability. Their connection consequently remains both beyond and between definition, neither ascribing to, nor entirely surmounting, the popular and clinical understanding of the taboo.

Yet according to Saussure 'language (which consists only of differences) is not a function of the speaking subject'.[42] Derrida develops this assertion to include all manifestations of meanings: 'the subject, and first of all the conscious and speaking subject, depends upon the system of differences and the movement of *différance*, that the subject is not present, nor above all present to itself before *différance*, that the subject is constituted only in being divided from itself, in becoming space, intemporizing, indeferral'.[43] This implies that the responsibility for interpretation is not on the subject, so that Finn's explanation of the incest in this text cannot be entirely attributed to him, as it is born out of the discourses that exist within the symbolic structure of the environment of which he is a part. The speaker, and the words he or she utters, can therefore be seen in the same fashion as *the text*, as a part of the context and yet known through its distinction from that same context. Furthermore, the speaker is distinct from that which he or she relays even as he or she has created and chosen the words. The speaker then becomes rather like a parent, who has created an independent being but nevertheless will always be associated with the child in some form. Yet, just as with a parent, this does not make the subject exempt from responsibility, as a knowing awareness of circumstances may impact upon the terminology chosen and the way it is narrated in order to attempt to provoke a certain response. Finn may therefore be coercing the naive Melanie to ascribe to the viewpoint of his family, even if what he says relies upon the process of *différance* to be known in whatever manner.

'Expansive and exclusive':[44] A.S. Byatt's différance *in sameness*

Carter is not the only author though who depicts characters trying to explain or justify incest via the complex interplay of difference, sameness and ultimately, *différance*. A.S. Byatt's *Morpho Eugenia*, also depicts incest between siblings, yet in this text the woman engaged in the act, Eugenia, is married to a man who adores her, William Adamson. When Eugenia's husband discovers the relationship between her and her brother, Edgar, she defends it by saying, 'It was just something – secret – that *was* you know – like other things you must not do, and do. Like touching yourself, in the dark'.[45] By likening sex with her brother to masturbation she thereby situates her defence in sameness, in that it did not seem to her problematic precisely *because* it was with her own flesh and blood. Yet this sameness actually implies difference, or rather, exclusivity, as the Alabasters are described as 'an ancient and noble family, who had always been very pure-blooded'.[46] Edgar reacts to the news of Eugenia's engagement by saying, 'You are underbred, Sir, you are no good match for my sister. There is bad blood in you, vulgar blood … You are a miserable creature without breeding or courage',[47] Edgar is then attempting to use as a defence his aristocratic privilege, albeit indirectly. As Ellen Pollack explains: 'incest had long been held a prerogative of kings determined to preserve their royal lines'.[48] The numerous children Eugenia brings forth whilst married to William all resemble *her* family, the Alabasters, not that of her husband's, suggesting that these are all the children of her relationship with her brother. William considers, 'the child, like all five children, was an Alabaster, a pale, clean-cut, nervous creature'.[49] Unlike Eugenia's sister, Rowena, who is unable to conceive after her marriage to the outsider, Robin, Eugenia reproduces rapidly, even having numerous multiple births, a consideration that occasions William to remark with some distaste: 'Five [children] in three years was, even in those days, a large and rapid family, a mass of tumbling child-flesh, like a litter of puppies'.[50] She even demands that one of her children be named Edgar, saying, 'There was an Edgar in every generation of the Alabasters'.[51] This assertion belies her apparent desire for an unchanging continuity to this family where incest leads to almost excessive fertility, yet intercourse with non-family members (as in the case of Robin) leads to infertility. This attraction of sameness, and the children 'who revert so shockingly to the ancestral type',[52] to such an extreme that they are almost indistinguishable from one another, actually enforces difference, in that they symbolise the rejection by the Alabasters of outsiders. The family wish to remain the same, but they intend their sameness to show they are different and therefore, in their view, superior to others.

As Jane Campbell says in *A.S. Byatt and the Heliotropic Imagination* this text exhibits 'a war of discourses, and this conflict reveals the failure of language ever to reveal the "hard idea of truth" '.[53] 'Classification, and the final impossibility of rigid categorisation are central' to this tale.[54] Byatt situates her depiction of incest in this novella betwixt and between, in a morally ambiguous locale, a 'tear' in the 'seam'.[55] In discussing the work of Lévi-Strauss, Derrida identifies the seam in his work as 'the prohibition of incest', and considers the possibility that '[t]he condition would be a "scandal" … only if one wished to comprehend it *within* the system whose condition it precisely is'.[56] Such is the character of Eugenia Alabaster's defence of incest, refusing to see it within the system of its condition (the social order), as a transgression. The ancestral family home and the privileges of aristocratic difference it affords, offer her a peculiarly individualised environment, where like the rare butterflies her husband nurtures in the artificial safety of the conservatory, she can live according to a set of rules that would not survive easily in the real world. Indeed, every time somebody threatens the exposure of their secret, to judge it and define it by outside factors, she retreats even further into her own world. As William observes after his discovery of Edgar and his wife *in flagrante delicto*, 'her attention [was] already sliding away from him, with a pretty little sigh of relief'.[57] Yet, for Derrida there is no 'frontier' between 'nature and culture', except an illusory one brought about by a refusal to engage in 'real analysis'.[58] It would seem then that, whatever Eugenia's motivation is, her continued desire to appear ignorant is disingenuous; as an adult she can no longer avoid the reality of her situation even as she refuses to acknowledge it.

William, like Philip in *The Magic Toyshop* is a 'cuckold',[59] and much of the narrative is told from his perspective. Consequently Byatt elicits the reader's sympathy for him, yet although William is not a violent man, it is unclear whether he is entirely exempt from blame, and if Eugenia herself deserves censure. Eugenia is depicted as very much a product of her time and more specifically of her social class. Whereas upper-class Victorian boys were expected to be active decision makers, girls were passive, infantile possessions, owned and passed from man to man. As Ginger S. Frost explains:

> Boys went to boarding school and then to university to be fitted out for careers. Some boys might skip university to go into the family business ... Girls stayed at home as 'children' of the house until they married, which could be into their twenties or even longer ... In short, affluent children legally came of age at twenty-one, but they remained dependent on their parents for longer than this.[60]

There was then a marked difference between the experience of growing up as an upper-class boy and an upper-class girl, Eugenia may physically resemble Edgar, but she has had a vastly different upbringing to him. Frost asserts that from her studies of Victorian memoirs, 'boys were clearly superior to girls, and parents did not apologise for their obvious favouritism'.[61] Whereas boys were being prepared for an active life in the world at large, they prepared 'girls to be self-sacrificing and to perpetuate the cycle into the next generation'.[62] As Judith Herman asserts, '[i]t is no accident that incest occurs in the relationship where the female is most powerless',[63] which would have been the case between Eugenia and Edgar.

Eugenia is younger than Edgar but even as a married adult she would have been subject to the desires of the men in her life. Despite her evident sexual experience – during their honeymoon night she is sexually assertive, 'asking for more, and more, and still more' – Eugenia is depicted as strangely inanimate away from the intimacy of the sexual act, an 'immobile ... sleeping beauty'.[64] She is childlike, relying on others to make decisions for her and care for her. Her upbringing has also been forcefully Christian, and the family not only attend church daily but their father is in the midst of writing a theological treatise. This may initially appear to be an unlikely environment in which to commit incest, yet as Jennifer L. Manlowe comments, 'The wording of the biblical law makes it clear that incest violations are not offenses against the women taken for sexual use but against the men in whom the rights of ownership, use and exchange, are vested'.[65] This therefore can be interpreted as supporting the patriarchal regime, where women were governed by their male family members until they were 'given away' in matrimony. However, even ignoring William's claim to Eugenia – and Edgar does just this – her father would still have greater authority over her, than her brother. Yet as Frost states this system actually fostered '[g]enerational conflict (e.g. between fathers and sons)' and this became 'a perennial part of growing up'.[66] Edgar, then, in refusing William consent to marry Eugenia, and appropriating his sister as his property, is exercising his future claim to be head of the household, and the owner of its female inhabitants.

Although, obliquely, William does demonstrate his awareness of his uncertain position as a male dependent, even if he is married to Eugenia: '[i]f he had a place, it was in the spaces between, the cushioned family softnesses and the closed away servile hierarchies in the attics and cellars and backrooms'.[67] William then occupies a space between, he does not fit into a group or class, and he is different, despite his efforts to conform to sexual and social norms. The incest here, despite its socially transgressive nature, is actually a part of the recognised but unacknowledged fabric of the house, and of the preservation of the aristocracy more generally. However, although the incest is part of an understood framework, this alone cannot explain it without further more detailed application of the convoluted context of any and all incest encounters.

Derrida tells us 'there is nothing outside the text' or indeed, 'there is nothing outside context'[68] and although Byatt's text highlights the rationalisations for Eugenia and Edgar's transgression as comprehended by Edgar and William, it cannot be understood as a text without appreciation of the implied but unknown narratives which are connected to this text. Perhaps most noticeably, Eugenia is not given the opportunity to relate her experience fully, rather the men that surround her both possess her body and consume her tale into their own narratives. Her narration of her lived experience of incest, however, is ambivalent, disconnected and does not clearly indicate complicity. In disjointed phrases, expecting to be misunderstood she says, 'you could not possibly understand', and describes it as beginning in childhood, 'as a game'. She then states that although she wanted to stop, she could not stop because Edgar was so 'strong',[69] an assertion that may refer as much to physical force as it could to coercion. Much as Eugenia does not explicitly state that she has been physically forced, recent research on sibling incest questions whether consensual sexual contact can occur between brothers and sisters. Paul B. Naylor et al. write that:

> Canavan, Meyer and Higgs (1992) suggest that incest may occur consensually when partners provide nurture and safety to one another in abusive and painful family conditions. It could, in theory, be argued that such incest may be non-abusive if the partners have equal access to resources of power. Typically, however, incest involves the repeated use of power, threats and force by the more powerful perpetrator as a precursor to, during or after the acts of abuse.[70]

Indeed, William has witnessed Edgar's sexually aggressive behaviour toward the servant, Amy, who is described as 'no more than a child ... who has never had a childhood'. When confronted, Edgar accounts for his actions by saying: 'The servants in this house are no concern of yours, Adamson. You do not pay their wages ... She is a nice little packet of flesh.'[71] Amy however, when asked by Edgar if he was hurting her, replies 'No, Sir. No harm',[72] despite this clearly not being the case. It is likely that Eugenia is or has been in a similar position, aware of the power imbalance and unable to articulate a complaint through confusion over the measure of her own guilt and fear of what might happen next. Indeed, it has been reported that perpetrators of incest whether by force or manipulation, will continue the sexual relationship with the victim regardless of age or circumstances if the opportunity arises. As Richard Johnson, the co-ordinator of Incest Crisis Line has stated, 'incest is something that will continue well into adulthood if the abuser knows that he or she can get away with it and can still control the person that he or she is abusing'.[73] Eugenia, firstly as a dependent in her own home, then married to a dependent, is unable to escape the situation she has grown up conditioned to acquiesce to, but she has also been given an inferior education and she is therefore unable to narrate her experience with the same eloquence that William can employ to condemn it.

The text then cannot be fully known without what Derrida describes as 'all possible referents',[74] which would include the knowledge of Eugenia's experience even if she is unable to fully articulate it or to even acknowledge it, and it would also include contemporary and past scientific and medical theories on sibling incest. This novella's portrayal of incest then requires more than the text encompasses to fully comprehend the taboo it presents, yet these wider issues are suggested in the text, and the responsibility lies with the reader to determine, what Derrida terms the 'real' 'in an interpretative experience'.[75]

Incest and Doris Lessing's 'unattainable beauty'[76]

The Golden Notebook (1962) is perhaps Doris Lessing's best known and most widely critiqued novel. Earlier criticism on this text, by Ellen Brooks, Elaine Antler Rapping and Harold Bloom, amongst others, has focused on the role of women in the novel, much to Lessing's chagrin, who asserted that 'the book was instantly belittled, by friendly reviewers as well as by hostile ones, as being about the sex war, or was claimed by women as a useful weapon in the sex war'.[77] However, although the text's commentary on gendered sexual issues cannot be entirely ignored, and Lessing would not have had it that way, saying that even though the novel 'was not a trumpet for Women's Liberation. It described many female emotions ... It put them into print'.[78] *The Golden Notebook* however, need not be examined *solely* through the lens of second wave feminist issues, indeed this is not the only or the most controversial site of difference in the novel. The incest between the 'unattainable beauty',[79] Maryrose, and her brother, has not received extensive critical attention, yet, although it receives very little narrative space, it is one of the most transgressive acts in the whole novel, enacted by its most conventional depiction of feminine aspiration.

Maryrose, a former model is a cultural ideal of 1950s Western society. Dating manuals of the period encouraged women to '[b]e childlike and feminine at all times', to '[l]ove him, feed him, sympathise with him, soothe him, admire him' and to '[f]an the flames of his ardour gently, but always leave him a little unsatisfied. Thus you will lead him to the altar'.[80] It is easy to see how Maryrose fits this ideal. Described as 'a tiny slender girl', she is 'good-humoured'[81] and marked out by her 'fragility and vulnerability'.[82] Maryrose is desired by all, but like the maidens of chivalric romance she is also sexually unavailable, transforming her admirers into 'swains'.[83] However, this ideal of femininity is juxtaposed by Lessing with what we have already determined earlier in this chapter as the act that is at once the ultimate societal transgression and yet has also been depicted as the highest elevation of literary romance: sibling incest. This is undoubtedly a divisive political move by Lessing, designed to challenge the understanding of what constitutes conformity and non-conformity, and, if these apparent extremes can exist concurrently. Maryrose's story is then essentially an experiment in narrating cultural sexual difference, and exploring through this the expression and comprehension of the concept of cultural truth through *différance*.

Harold Bloom has remarked that '[n]either [Iris] Murdoch nor Lessing is proficient at depicting memorable personages ... Lessing because she cannot be bothered, since she has ceased to believe that we have (or ought to have) individual personalities'.[84] Although this is perhaps provocative for its own sake, there is a degree of truth to the notion that Lessing in this novel adopts

Narrating incest through 'différance'

an insular approach to characterisation where the lives of the characters are often players in Lessing's broader vision, rather than the novel being what Iris Murdoch described as, 'a house fit for free characters to live in'.[85] Yet, this is surely apt and perhaps intentional, as the contentious definition of freedom is one of the central tenets of this novel, in that freedom is a term defined by its context, and understood within society, it is an idea gifted to some individuals, but not to others. The novel develops a complicated network of contrasting concepts of freedoms understood in relation to societal, cultural and geographical locales, which often jar against each other, creating narrative and political tension. However between these understandings of freedom, Lessing posits the possibility of a real freedom that rests on the belief that an individual can experience a truth which is untouched by the ideological demands of social structures. Naturally this is fraught with difficulty, and nowhere more so than in the depiction of the character of Maryrose.

Maryrose with her 'shining hair'[86] and 'her sweet smile', who was 'much in demand because of how she looked',[87] performs the role expected of her as a result of her socially idealised feminine appearance.

> The men patronized her, they thought nothing of her capacity for political thought ... There is a type of mind, like Willi's that can only accept ideas if they are put in the language he would use himself ...
>
> [S]he grew uneasy and appealed: 'I'm not saying right, but you see what I mean...' Because she had appealed, the men were restored, and Willi said benevolently: 'Of course you say it right. Anyone as beautiful as you can't say it wrong.'[88]

Later in the black notebook Anna goes on to say that Maryrose, like '[v]ery many professionally pretty girls' had 'this gift for allowing themselves to be touched, kissed, held as if this is a fee they have to pay to Providence for being born beautiful. There is a tolerant smile which goes with a submission to the hands of men, like a yawn or a patient sigh'.[89] This description of Maryrose is juxtaposed with a discussion on her being sexually unattainable because she is still in love with her dead brother. This small section of text, which includes very little information, is fraught with interpretative difficulty, and although she seems to agree that her 'broken heart' is the reason for her sexual reticence, it is Willi who first suggests it.[90] As the reader already knows that Maryrose will acquiesce with the opinions of men to ease a social situation, it is possible that this is not the primary reason of her reticence.

Similarly convoluted is the description of the incest itself. The depiction of Maryrose's relationship with her brother is only partially narrated and the reader's understanding of what has occurred is fragmentary and disjointed, spaced out between different stories and other narrative perspectives so that the truth is unknowable, and its closest assimilation is constantly shifting and dependent upon interpretation. The novel is, in perhaps the broadest sense, journalistic, being concerned with a specific set of political and gendered questions, of which Maryrose's incestuous relationship with her brother is an essential component in examining and challenging the feminine ideal. However, it is also journalistic in the way the narrative draws together disparate threads into a cohesive whole, from numerous lives, the numerous notebooks and different geographic locations. Anna tells us that the modern novel 'has become an outpost of journalism, in that we read to *find out what is going on*' and it records 'the existence of an area of society, a type of person, not yet admitted to the general literate consciousness' – by which she means the development and description of new or unknown ideological and political ideas.[91] This is not a new phenomenon, but it is the construction of the separate – yet juxtaposed and connected – narratives and how they highlight these various discourses, that is most striking. It is here then that *différance* is most apparent, as the varying ideas, and indeed the characters, slip between and through the cracks and margins of the notebooks, and thus the notebooks are characterised as much by what they do not contain as what they do, so that the omitted, ignored, or misconstrued becomes an integral part of each narrative, and consequently essential to the fabric of the whole. Indeed this reflects upon the narrative understanding of taboos in the real world, known through fragments, not discussed openly or at length, and often dismissed as unpleasant or even unlikely occurrences.

The primary site of the incestuous narrative occurs early on in the novel in Africa where Anna is living in a ramshackle community described in the first extract from the black notebook:

> She said to us – and I remember the sense of shock we felt, as we always did with her, because of her absolute but casual honesty: 'Yes, I know I fell in love with him [a young man] because he looked like my brother, but what's wrong with that?' ...
>
> 'Anyway,' observed Maryrose, 'I don't see the point. I keep thinking about my brother.'
>
> 'I've never known anyone be so completely frank about incest,' said Paul. He meant it as a kind of joke, but Maryrose replied, quite seriously, 'Yes, I know it was incest. But the funny thing is, I never thought of it as incest at the time. You see, my brother and I loved each other.'
>
> We were shocked again. I felt Willi's shoulder stiffen, and I remember thinking that only a few moments before he had been the decadent European; but the idea that Maryrose had slept with her brother plunged him back into his real nature, which was puritanical.[92]

For Maryrose the remembered event is apparently both a fond memory connected with love and also an erotic event that shapes her later sexual development and causes her to look for a return to that lost, forbidden love. For Willi his sexual bravado is immediately eradicated by the impact of the non-normative: through the 'stiffening' of his shoulder (rather than any other part of his anatomy). The dark humour at work here is not just to challenge what may have been seen as Maryrose's supposed chaste status, but to highlight Willi's limited capacity for difference. As in response to this revelation rather than the suitor being given the 'cold shoulder' of bodily disgust: the idealised maiden has become the object to be shunned. Neither of these ways of capturing Maryrose though presents her as she really is, rather her complex and real humanity is lost between known and accepted categories, just as her narrative is misplaced between the fragments of narrative presence.

Willi's displeasure, and his deferral of pleasure is marked in the text with a turn toward another 'Other', the invisible other which watches and judges, the ultimate definition of which Sartre referred to as God.[93] Maryrose's tale then, has been subsumed into Willi's sphere of socially acceptable patriarchy, as Anna has already been, and her narration, by including his shoulder stiffening, gives that social condemnation prominence. Moreover his position as the dominant male within the group is reinforced as directly after this scene he gives George, twelve years his senior, political information regarding the situation in the immediate environment. Willi is considered to be the intellectual superior and, hence, the dominant force; the intensely personal revelation of Maryrose has become subsumed into the power of Willi, by his silent but nevertheless communicated judgement of her situation. It appears however that she is not only open about her sexual history – again a site of *différance* as sexuality becomes liminal and transgressive both linguistically and actually – but that she seeks to view the relationship in ethical terms: 'Yes, I can see why you are shocked. But I think about it often these days. We didn't do any harm, did we? And so I don't see what was wrong with it.'[94] It is this justification and her comment that she thinks about it 'often' which shocks Paul into joking that if she sleeps with him 'she might be cured'.[95] By defending the relationship with her brother Maryrose has challenged the patriarchal social structure and suggested that the categories it has assigned to her, firstly as a social ideal then as a transgressive social outcast, do not necessarily have to apply to her.

By remaining sexually detached from everyone apart from the one man who resembles her dead brother – and this happens outside the narratological framework of the novel – she initially appears to inhabit a radical site of difference outside of the normative patriarchal rhetoric on the novel. Yet, Maryrose's story can also be interpreted as an exaggeration of the patriarchal system of sexual ownership and control of women, whereby Maryrose, without a patriarch to decide upon her sexual future remains in a state of sexual stasis, paralysed by a past she can never revisit and a future she refuses herself permission to explore. As discussed earlier in this chapter, in relation to Byatt's *Morpho Eugenia* the brother would historically in patriarchal culture assume a superior position in the household to his sister, and even if they were treated as equals within the domestic space, during the 1950s women had vastly fewer social rights than men. Her brother therefore, is not exempt from the role of either controller or abuser. Anna tries to explain Maryrose's relationship with her brother by saying they were united against a common enemy: 'they had the tenderest of bonds because of their impossible, bullying, embarrassing mother'.[96] Her mother has, according to Anna, 'sapped all of the vitality out of the girl'.[97] Indeed, Maryrose 'never laugh[s]', although she states that she did when she was with her brother because they were 'happy'.[98] Yet, Maryrose's story is shown to the reader only through the medium of Anna's narration, and therefore we must remain sceptical. We are told that she eventually married a man '[s]he did not love' because '[h]er heart had gone dead when her brother' died.[99] By remaining emotionally tied to her deceased brother, and unable and/or unwilling to develop and explore away from home a loving sexual relationship with another adult, Maryrose demonstrates a desire to retain a link with her childhood and a lack of interest in engaging fully with the adult world as an individual, yet it does not necessarily follow that the relationship was one of equals. Her apparent depression and vulnerability could be just as easily the continued effects of an unhealthy attachment or an abusive relationship as they could that of an unrelenting grief. Anna's presentation of Maryrose's history though is just one 'interpretative experience', and if we accept Derrida's assertion that 'there is nothing outside context', then we must also consider 'all possible referents' in our reading.[100] Lessing asserted that 'the essence of the book, the organisation of it, everything in it, says implicitly and explicitly, that we must not divide things off, we must not compartmentalise' and this extends to Maryrose as a woman as well as the acts she has engaged in. To read this novel critically then, requires in Derridean terms, an awareness of its broader framework – historically, culturally and socially – the scope of which is constantly changing. This adds weight to Lessing's description of 'the inner Golden Notebook' as, 'formlessness with the end of fragmentation',[101] as in Derridean terms the text cannot be anything else.

Although for Derrida all meaning is determined by the interplay of *différance*, this is particularly noticeable when considering the narration of taboo topics. It is a challenge to the writer to convey highly sensitive and controversial material such as incest, especially when, as in the case of Carter, Byatt and Lessing, they were writing in a time period of dramatic social and cultural change not just in relation to the ability to discuss incest at all, but also in renegotiating the parameters of just what incest had been, was understood at the time of writing, or how it might be judged in the future. The sibling incestuous relationship is for writers one of the most problematic to frame ethically, as it is often unclear, in literature and in life, how far the relationship may be abusive and how far, consensual. All three authors considered in this

Narrating incest through 'différance'

chapter situate their artistic representation of the sibling incestuous relationship within numerous disparate discourses, particularly, the literary Romantic history of sibling incest, taboo sexuality, and abuse, demonstrating through the tensions, frictions and the resonances between the particular incestuous liaison and the wider understandings of sex and romance how incest is both amalgamated into our cultural discourses, as well as rejected as a site of social and personal disturbance.

Notes

1. Angela Carter, *The Magic Toyshop* (Virago, 1981), p. 195.
2. A.H. Bittles, 'Inbreeding and fertility', in Michael R. Speicher, Stylianos E. Antonarakis and Arno G. Motulsky (eds), *Vogel and Moulsky's Human Genetics* (Springer, 2010), pp. 516–20.
3. For an overview of the issues see: Anil Aggrawal, 'Incest', in Anil Aggrawal, *Forensic and Medico-legal Aspects of Sexual Crimes and Unusual Sexual Practices* (CLC, 2009), pp. 319–33.
4. Judith Lewis Herman and Lisa Hirschman, *Father-Daughter Incest* (Harvard University Press, 1981), pp. 59–61.
5. Leonore Davidoff, 'The sibling relationship and sibling incest in historical context', in Prophecy Coles (ed.), *Sibling Relationships* (H. Karnac, 2006) pp. 20–1.
6. William D. William, *The Shelley-Byron Conversation* (University Press of Florida, 1994), p. 66.
7. This chapter will consider in detail the relationship in *Morpho Eugenia*, one of two novellas in A.S. Byatt's *Angels and Insects* (1990).
8. Emanuel Swedenborg, John Chadwick (trans.), *The Delights of Wisdom on the Subject of Conjugial Love, followed by The Gross Pleasures of Folly on the Subject of Scortatory Love* (The Swedenborg Society, 1996), p. 40.
9. Emanuel Swedenborg, *Concerning Heaven and its Wonders* (Otis Clapp, 1854; John Allen, 1854), p. 203.
10. Mary Lyndon Shanley, *Feminism, Marriage and the Law in Victorian England* (Princeton University Press, 1993), p. 10.
11. Davidoff, 'The sibling relationship and sibling incest in historical context', p. 19.
12. Paul B. Naylor, Laurie Petch and Jenna V. Williams, 'Sibling abuse and bullying in childhood and adolescence: Knowns and unknowns', in Christine Barter and David Berridge (eds), *Children Behaving Badly* (Wiley, 2011), digital edition, pp. 53.
13. Naylor et al., 'Sibling abuse and bullying in childhood and adolescence', p. 50.
14. Angela Carter, Sarah Waters (introd.), *Nights at the Circus* (Vintage, 2006), p. 15.
15. Aidan Day, *The Rational Glass* (Manchester University Press, 1998), p. 1.
16. Jacques Derrida, 'At this very moment in this work here I am', in Robert Bernasconi and Simon Critchley (eds), *Re-Reading Levinas* (Athlone, 1991), pp. 26–7.

17 Derrida, 'At this very moment in this work here I am', p. 26.
18 Carter, *The Magic Toyshop*, p. 63.
19 *Ibid.*, p. 152.
20 *Ibid.*, p. 40.
21 *Ibid.*, pp. 193–4.
22 *Ibid.*, p. 15.
23 *Ibid.*, p. 9.
24 *Ibid.*, p. 17.
25 *Ibid.*, p. 82.
26 *Ibid.*, p. 7.
27 *Ibid.*, p. 93.
28 *Ibid.*, p. 93.
29 *Ibid.*, p. 185.
30 *Ibid.*, p. 195.
31 *Ibid.*, 170.
32 B. Chatkow-Yanoov, *Social Work Approaches to Conflict Resolution: Making Fighting Obsolete* (Howarth Press, 1997), p. 46.
33 Chatkow-Yanoov asserts that 'If basic human needs are not satisfied, personal pathologies or social problems tend to develop', Chatkow-Yanoov, *Social Work Approaches to Conflict Resolution*, p. 45.
34 Carter, *The Magic Toyshop*, p. 193.
35 *Ibid.*, p. 195.
36 Ferdinand de Saussure, Wade Baskin (trans.), Perry Meisel and Haun Saussy (eds), *Course in General Linguistics* (Columbia University Press; The Philosophical Library, 1959), p. 120.
37 See Jacques Derrida, Stephen David Ross (ed.), David B. Allison (trans.), 'Différance', *Art and Its Significance* (State University of New York Press, 1984), p. 435.
38 Derrida, 'Différance', p. 24.
39 Jacques Derrida, Samuel Weber (trans.), *Limited Inc.* (Northwestern University Press, 1988), p. 136.
40 Maria Baghramian, *Relativism* (Routledge, 2004), p. 83.
41 Derrida, *Limited Inc.*, p. 136–48.
42 Saussure quoted in Derrida, 'Différance', p. 423.
43 Derrida, 'Différance', p. 423.
44 A.S. Byatt, Morpho Eugenia, in A.S. Byatt, *Angels and Insects* (Vintage, 1995), p. 72.
45 *Ibid.*, p. 151.
46 *Ibid.*, p. 22.
47 *Ibid.*, p. 62.
48 Ellen Pollack, *Incest and the English Novel, 1684–1814* (Johns Hopkins University Press, 2003), p. 160.
49 Byatt, *Morpho Eugenia*, p. 72.
50 *Ibid*, p. 72.

51 *Ibid.*, p. 72.
52 *Ibid.*, p. 151.
53 Jane Campbell, *A.S. Byatt and the Heliotropic Imagination* (Wilfred Laurier University Press, 2004), p. 147.
54 *Ibid.*, p. 149.
55 Derrida, 'At this very moment in this work here I am', p. 7.
56 Jacques Derrida, Gayatri Chakravorty Spivak (trans.), Judith Butler (introd.), *Of Grammotology* (Johns Hopkins University Press, 2016), p. 112
57 Byatt, *Morpho Eugenia*, p. 159.
58 Derrida, *Of Grammatology*, pp. 112–3.
59 Carter, *The Magic Toyshop*, p. 195.
60 Ginger S. Frost, *Victorian Childhoods* (Greenwood, 2009), p. 31.
61 *Ibid.*, p. 29.
62 *Ibid.*, p. 29.
63 Herman, *Father-Daughter Incest*, p. 4.
64 Byatt, *Morpho Eugenia*, p. 69.
65 Jennifer L. Manlowe, *Faith Born of Seduction* (New York University Press, 1995), p. 62.
66 Frost, *Victorian Childhoods*, p. 31.
67 Byatt, *Morpho Eugenia*, p. 75.
68 Jacques Derrida, *Limited Inc.* p. 136.
69 Byatt, *Morpho Eugenia*, pp. 150–1.
70 Naylor et al., 'Sibling abuse and bullying in childhood and adolescence', p. 48. M.C. Canavan, W.J. Meyer and D.C. Higgs, 'The female experience of sibling incest', *Journal of Marital and Family Therapy* 18 (1992), pp. 129–42.
71 Byatt, *Morpho Eugenia*, p. 107.
72 *Ibid.*, p. 107.
73 Richard Johnson, Incest Crisis Line Coordinator, quoted in Dick Thompson and Peter Boyes, *Portraits in Courage* (Littlehampton Book Services, 1986), p. 30.
74 Derrida, *Limited Inc.*, p. 148.
75 *Ibid.*, p. 136.
76 Doris Lessing, *The Golden Notebook* (Harper Collins, 2007), p. 92.
77 Lessing, 'Preface', *The Golden Notebook*, p. 8.
78 *Ibid.*, pp. 8–9.
79 Lessing, *The Golden Notebook*, p. 92.
80 Pamphlets such as, *How to Get Your Man*, by Grace Hall, quoted in Virginia Nicolson, *Perfect Wives in Ideal Homes: The Story of Women in the 1950s* (Penguin, 2015), digital edition, Kindle location 1323.
81 Lessing, *The Golden Notebook*, p. 108.
82 *Ibid.*, p. 82.
83 *Ibid.*, p. 127.
84 Harold Bloom, 'Introduction', in Harold Bloom (ed.), *Bloom's Modern Critical Views: Doris Lessing* (Chelsea House, 2003), p. 6.

85 Iris Murdoch references Henry James's discussion of the house of fiction here. Iris Murdoch, Peter J. Conradi (ed.), George Steiner (foreword) 'Against dryness', *Existentialists and Mystics* (Penguin, 1997) p. 156. Henry James, 'Preface', *A Portrait of a Lady* (Oxford University Press, 1998), pp. 3–18.
86 Lessing, *The Golden Notebook*, p. 127.
87 *Ibid.*, p. 110.
88 *Ibid.*, p. 99 [Third ellipsis in the original].
89 *Ibid.*, p. 109.
90 *Ibid.*, p. 109.
91 *Ibid.*, p. 79 [Italics in original].
92 *Ibid.*, pp. 110–11.
93 Jean-Paul Sartre, *Being and Nothingness* (Routledge, 2003), p. 313.
94 Lessing, *The Golden Notebook*, p. 111.
95 *Ibid.*, p. 111.
96 *Ibid.*, p. 109.
97 *Ibid.*, p. 106.
98 *Ibid.*, pp. 379–80.
99 *Ibid.*, p. 110.
100 Derrida, *Limited Inc.*, p. 148.
101 Lessing, 'Preface', *The Golden Notebook*, p. 7.

Bibliography

Fiction

Byatt, A.S., *Possession: A Romance* (1990)
——., *Morpho Eugenia* and *The Conjugial Angel*, in A.S. Byatt, *Angels and Insects* (Vintage, 1995)
Carter, Angela, *The Magic Toyshop* (Virago, 1981)
——., Helen Simpson (introd.), *The Bloody Chamber and Other Stories* (Vintage, 2006)
——., Sarah Waters (introd.), *Nights at the Circus* (Vintage, 2006)
Lessing, Doris, *The Golden Notebook* (Harper Collins, 2013)

Non-fiction

Able, Elizabeth, 'Resisting the exchange: Brother-sister incest in fiction by Doris Lessing', in Carey Kaplan and Ellen Rose (eds), *Doris Lessing: The Alchemy of Survival* (Ohio University Press, 1988)
Aggrawal, Agril, 'Incest', in Agril Aggrawal, *Forensic and Medico-legal Aspects of Sexual Crimes and Unusual Sexual Practices* (CLC, 2009), pp. 319–33
Antler Rapping, Elayne, "'Unfree women": Feminism in Doris Lessing's novels, *Women's Studies* 3:1 (1975), pp. 29–44
Baghramian, Maria, *Relativism* (Routledge, 2004)

Bittles, A.H., 'Inbreeding and fertility'; 'Inbreeding and fetal loss rates'; 'Comparitive fertility in consanguinous and nonconsanguinous couples'; 'Consanguinity and adult mortality and morbidity'; 'Incest'; 'Mortality and morbidity estimates for incestuous matings', in Michael R. Speicher, Stylianos E. Antonarakis and Arno G. Motulsky (eds), *Vogel and Moulsky's Human Genetics: Problems and Approaches*, 4th edn. (Springer, 2010), pp. 516–20

Bloom, Harold, 'Introduction', in Harold Bloom (ed.), *Bloom's Modern Critical Views: Doris Lessing* (Chelsea House, 2003), pp. 1–7

Brewer, William D., *The Shelley-Byron Conversation* (University Press of Florida, 1994)

Brooks, Ellen W., 'The image of women in Doris Lessing's *Golden Notebook*', *Critique: Studies in Modern Fiction* 15:1 (1973), pp. 101–9

Campbell, Jane, *A.S. Byatt and the Heliotropic Imagination* (Wilfred Laurier University Press, 2004)

Canavan, M.C., W.J. Meyer and D.C. Higgs, 'The female experience of sibling incest', *Journal of Marital and Family Therapy* 18 (1992), pp. 129–42

Chatkow-Yanoov, B., *Social Work Approaches to Conflict Resolution: Making Fighting Obsolete* (Howarth Press, 1997)

Christensen, C.W., 'A case of sibling incest: a balancing act', *Journal of Strategic and Systematic Therapies* 9:4 (1990), pp. 1–5

Clark, Robin E., Judith Freeman Clark and Christine Adamec, Richard J. Gelles (introd.), *Encyclopeadia of Child Abuse*, 3rd edn. (Infobase, 2007)

Davidoff, Leonore, 'The sibling relationship and sibling incest in historical context', in Prophecy Coles (ed.), *Sibling Relationships* (H. Karnac, 2006), pp. 17–48

Day, Aidan, *The Rational Glass* (Manchester University Press, 1998)

Derrida, Jacques, Stephen David Ross (ed.), David B. Allison (trans.), 'Différance', *Art and Its Significance* (State University of New York Press, 1984), pp. 410–36

———., Samuel Weber (trans.), *Limited Inc.* (Northwestern University Press, 1988)

———., 'Biodegradeables: Seven diary fragments', *Critical Inquiry* 15:4 (1989), pp. 812–73

———., 'Différance', in Peggy Kapft (ed.), *A Derrida Reader: Between the Blinds* (Harvester Wheatsheaf, 1991)

———., 'At this very moment in this work here I am', in Robert Bernasconi and Simon Critchley (eds), *Re-Reading Levinas* (Athlone, 1991), pp. 11–48

———., Gayatri Chakravorty Spivak (trans.), Judith Butler (introd.), *Of Grammotology* (Johns Hopkins University Press, 2016)

Frost, Ginger S., *Victorian Childhoods* (Greenwood, 1998)

Herman, Judith Lewis and Lisa Hirschman, *Father-Daughter Incest* (Harvard University Press, 1981)

James, Henry, 'Preface', *A Portrait of a Lady* (Oxford University Press, 1998), pp. 3–18

King, Jeannette, *Doris Lessing* (Edward Arnold, 1989)

Lyndon Shanley, Mary, *Feminism, Marriage and the Law in Victorian England* (Princeton University Press, 1993)

Manlowe, Jennifer L., *Faith Born of Seduction: Sexual Trauma, Body Image, and Religion* (New York University Press, 1995)

Murdoch, Iris, Peter J. Conradi (ed.), 'Against dryness', in Iris Murdoch, *Existentialists and Mystics* (Penguin, 1997), pp. 287–95

Naylor, Paul B, Laurie Petch and Jenna V. Williams, 'Sibling abuse and bullying in childhood and adolescence: Knowns and unknowns, in Christine Barter and David Berridge (eds), *Children Behaving Badly* (Wiley, 2011), Digital Edition, pp. 47–57 www.myilibrary.com?ID=337297 (accessed 1 April 2017)

Nicholson, Virginia, *Perfect Wives in Ideal Homes: The Story of Women in the 1950s* (Penguin, 2015)

Plato, Benjamin Jowett (trans.), *Symposium* (IndyPublish, 2005)

Pollack, Ellen, *Incest and the English Novel, 1684–1814* (Johns Hopkins University Press, 2003)

Royle, Nicholas, *Jacques Derrida* (Routledge, 2003)

Sage, Lorna, *Doris Lessing* (Methuen, 1983)

Sartre, Jean-Paul, *Being and Nothingness* (Routledge, 2003)

Saussure, Ferdinand de, Wade Baskin (trans.), Perry Meisel and Haun Saussy (eds), *Course in General Linguistics* (Columbia University Press; The Philosophical Library, 1959)

Swedenborg, Emanuel, *Concerning Heaven and its Wonders, and Concerning Hell* (Otis Clapp, 1854; John Allen, 1854)

——., John Chadwick (trans.), *The Delights of Wisdom on the Subject of Conjugial Love, followed by The Gross Pleasures of Folly on the Subject of Scortatory Love* (The Swedenborg Society, 1996)

Thompson, Dick and Peter Boyes, *Portraits in Courage* (Littlehampton Book Services, 1986)

Whittaker, Ruth, *Doris Lessing* (Macmillan, 1988)

12

Avuncular ambiguity: Ethical virtue in Iris Murdoch's *The Black Prince* (1973) and Simone de Beauvoir's *The Mandarins* (1954)

Miles Leeson

> 'Personal morality just doesn't exist ... You can't lead a life in a society that isn't proper.'[1]

The primary motivation for this chapter is to discuss the nature and extent of the play of ethical relations, within both *The Black Prince* (1973) and *The Mandarins* (1954, trans. 1957). Both novels are concerned with the virtuous, and, in part, the acting out of the 'good life' in a rapidly developing post-industrial society. Indeed, these two novels can be placed within the same writing continuum as it is highly likely that in writing *The Black Prince*, Murdoch was influenced by Beauvoir's earlier novel. In her letters to the author Raymond Queneau (a contemporary of Beauvoir and her long-time partner, Jean Paul Sartre), Murdoch states that she is keen to meet the woman who has written such inspiring works. She goes on to review Beauvoir's novel saying:

> [It is] a remarkable book, a novel on a grand scale, courageous in its exactitude and endearing because of its persistent seriousness ... We are struck by the absence of the novelist's traditional furniture: social institutions, customs, the moral virtues. There is no steady and opaque framework. The characters take nothing for granted, and the encounters take place in a sort of social and intellectual state of nature.[2]

Although it is not within the scope of this essay to draw out and open up all of the aspects of Beauvoir's text to which Murdoch has drawn attention, it will consider Beauvoir's political and personal responses in the novel as a *roman á clef*. The primary considerations will, of course, be ethical and will be developed through the thought of Maurice Blanchot, Emmanuel Levinas and Martha Nussbaum to give a reading which does not seek to entrap characters within certain ethical modes of thinking but opens up spaces for ethical discussion. By this I mean that value judgements tied to actions will be read through an ethical lens but should not constrict the reader's attention to merely the outcomes of actions: instead the promotion of extra-textual discussion, and a return to the novels themselves, will be made paramount. In short, it is the aesthetic reading of ethical virtue that is of most importance to this essay and it is to be hoped that the reader will return to both novels with renewed vigour. We begin by placing both novels in context, and discussing the narrative, and then move on to a consideration of feminist ethics, which is crucial for viewing the development of the female within both novels. By discussing these texts, and applying a selection of both authors' theoretical and philosophical work, this chapter draws out the ethical distinctions in their work and places their discussion of the incestuous within the historical period of creation and publication.

The readings of both novels highlight the tension this creates and this chapter will seek to develop and expand upon the ethical discussions that both Beauvoir and Murdoch address. The relationships involve older men on the outer limits of a family group. It is best to start, therefore, with an introduction of both novels to illuminate the critical discussion to follow. As *The Mandarins* is first chronologically we will begin here.

The first narrator of this multi-perspective novel is Henri Peron, a writer in his mid-thirties whose first book made him famous. He edits a newspaper for the socialist Left, and as the novel opens he has made arrangements to travel to Portugal to meet with political activists who wish to remove the dictatorship of Salazar, and to have a break from life in Paris and his unhappy marriage with his wife Paula; Beauvoir bases him on Albert Camus.[3] He has a mentor in Robert Dubreuilh, a great thinker and writer who is in his mid-sixties. In the first chapter Robert is making plans for his next political move; he wishes to unite the communists with the workers in a nonconformist party, the SRL, which mirrors Sartre's own dream to form a leftist movement in the ill-fated RDR (Rassemblement Démocratique Révolutionnaire);[4] he lobbies Henri to join him in this venture. Robert's wife Anne, widely regarded as being modelled on Beauvoir herself,[5] is a practising psychoanalyst and shares the narration of the novel with Henri. At the opening party it is clear that her primary concern is for her teenage daughter, Nadine, who has recently lost her lover to a concentration camp. As the novel develops it is Anne who provides the reader with an intimate analysis of the relationships in the book. Another central character is Paule (Paula) who has been Henri's lover for ten years; her descent into mental illness, and the reflection upon her dismissal by Henri whilst he becomes entangled with Nadine, acts as a commentary on not only Beauvoir's earlier work in *The Second Sex* (published in France just before she began *The Mandarins* in 1949), but the discussion of personal freedom in her essay 'The ethics of ambiguity' (1945). In a letter to her lover, Nelson Algren, Beauvoir writes 'I put a lot of things in it [*The Mandarins*], travels, drunken evenings, young and mature people, some of Koestler, Camus and Sartre, and myself, indeed.'[6]

It is worth noting that as the story develops we learn that Nadine's lover Diego has been killed in a concentration camp, and her promiscuous behaviour is described as a foil to the despair she feels at his passing and her desire to avoid ever falling in love again. When, as readers, we engage with a novel that has been translated the tone of the piece can often be changed by the translator (unless the author does the translation personally) and this is particularly apparent for *The Mandarins* in Friedman's translation of 1957. Nadine's actions toward her mother Anne, and the dialogue she employs, have been reduced by the translator in intensity: this is discussed later in the chapter. If our ethical reading is to be of value we must keep this in mind, as any interruption or amendments, however slight, whether we are aware of it or not, can divert us from the ethical response to the original. With this in mind it is worth noting the clear links between the works of both authors under discussion as regards their approach to feminist issues.

Tammy Grimshaw in her work *Sexuality, Gender and Power in Iris Murdoch's Fiction* (2005) makes clear connections between Murdoch and Beauvoir:

> Beauvoir maintains that women generally do not engage in this struggle [the struggle for reciprocal recognition] with their male partners as they fail to present men with the hard exigencies of a reciprocal recognition. That is, the male confirms his own selfhood in relation to the woman; she does not raise a demand to have her own selfhood confirmed in return by her male partner.[7]

The Mandarins is explicit with regard to these ideas, as would be expected given Beauvoir's relationship with the feminist movement, but *The Black Prince* is rather more implicit in dealing with a range of female responses to notions of male repression through the narration of incest, the specific language use in the narratology, and the presentation of physical restraint. In Murdoch's novel it is only Christian, Bradley's ex-wife, who gives any meaningful resistance to male hegemony. She is the dangerous and unknown element of the plot, estranged from Bradley and also from European culture for some years, who now returns of her own volition. Although the story will be discussed in some detail for those unfamiliar with it, it is worth noting here that the novel is primarily concerned with the actions of a group of friends and associates living in London, who are all, in some way affected by the process of aging and the impact this has on each individual's ego. Bradley Pearson, Murdoch's central character, engages in a quasi-incestuous[8] relationship with the daughter of his friend and protégé Arnold Baffin, not only in an attempt to obtain a reinvigoration that only youth can bring, but also a means to assert his continued dominance over Arnold, his long-time rival. Bradley Pearson's initials (B.P.) link him closely with Hamlet: the original Black Prince;[9] Shakespeare's play is partially driven with the concern of incest, 'O most wicked speed, to post with such dexterity to incestuous sheets!'[10] It is useful to summarise the action of the novel.

The plot of the novel is as follows. Bradley Pearson is a late middle-aged former writer (although he claims to still be writing, doubt is cast on this) living alone in London near the Post Office Tower and spends a great deal of his time in introspection. His closest friend Arnold Baffin – whom he considers to be his protégé – is a famous writer of popular fiction; a fact that confounds Bradley and distracts him from writing, or at least publishing his own work. His judgmental tone concerning his idea of low art is immediately apparent; 'Arnold Baffin's work was a congeries of amusing anecdotes, loosely garbled into "racy stories" with the help of half-baked unmediated symbolism … Arnold Baffin wrote too much too fast. Arnold Baffin was really just a talented journalist';[11] clearly a degree of unmediated jealousy is at work. As with the majority of Murdoch's novels, unexpected figures return from the past. Bradley's ex-wife (Christian) and ex-brother-in-law (Francis) return to not only haunt him but disrupt his life and unexpected events happen with the unlikeliest of people, for example, Bradley finds himself involved for a brief time with Arnold's wife Rachel. Also typically of Murdoch's oeuvre, difficult relatives return – in this instance his sister Priscilla – and most importantly for this chapter, Bradley claims to fall violently in love with Arnold's teenage daughter Julian. This relationship can be viewed as a semi-incestuous relationship, due to her considering Bradley (a frequent visitor to her house and a constant life presence) as her uncle, or indeed a father figure, although they are not blood relatives. For Murdoch, this is clearly a destructive relationship, and following Bradley and Julian's seemingly idyllic escape to the sea, Arnold intervenes and rescues his daughter from the clutches of Bradley. The main focus of the plot is not the accumulation of lovers by Bradley or the relative merits of 'good' art against 'bad' art but Bradley's desire to escape the confines of age and, ultimately, mortality. By taking Julian as his lover he imagines he is escaping the progress of time and its effects on his body, indeed once she has declared her love for him, his opinion of his body is transformed and rather than turning away from it he views it as beautiful. He comments: 'This was no delirium. Those who have loved so will understand me. There was an overwhelming sense of reality, of being real, and seeing the real. The tables, the chairs, the sherry glasses, the curls in the rug, the dust; real.'[12] Here he puts himself into the same 'false reality' as Henri Perron in *The Mandarins*, although that situation has rather a different outcome to *The Black Prince*. With regards to outcomes, Bradley has rather more in common with Nabokov's Humbert Humbert, being of roughly the same age, both admit to being 'monstrous',[13] and both are convicted of murder – Bradley for the alleged killing of his friend and later rival Arnold, Humbert for the murder of his rival, Quilty;

indeed it could be argued that *The Black Prince* engages with, and ridicules, the late modernist form.[14]

One central area of disagreement between Beauvoir and Murdoch is the impact of life writing. Murdoch's novel, which is concerned with fictional relationships rather than the autobiographical impact that Beauvoir uses, is better placed to discuss the ethical in a fictional space. As Murdoch says toward the end of her most famous essay on the state of the novel, 'Against dryness', 'Literature must always represent a battle between real people and images; and what it requires now is a much stronger and more complex conception of the former'.[15] For Murdoch then it is only in purely fictional writing, rather than autobiographical fiction, that we are able to allow ourselves to be truly transported; this is highlighted by Martha Nussbaum whose work is discussed later. This is essential to the continuing debate as regards the ethical impact of different types of fiction on the individual. When asked in interview with Peter Lennon why she was so keen on bringing the incestuous into the majority of her novels Murdoch insisted that the representation of incest in her fiction needed to be situated within the overall context of her novels, 'It was a theme which has a long tradition in literature. Yes it was used in a symbolic way but you must look at the contents of the book.'[16]

For both of the novels discussed here, incest is not the primary narrative drive – that would be personal and political for Beauvoir as the novel is a *roman a clef*, and intertextual and authentic attention to the other for Murdoch. However, the strongly put suggestion of incest is an essential component and would entirely change the text if it were absent even in an implied capacity: consequently it adds to the complexity and richness of both.

Murdoch was amongst the first to take existentialism seriously in Britain[17] and her first published book was an examination of the work of Sartre, *Sartre: Romantic Rationalist* (1953). Although in some ways similar to Sartre's *Nausea* (1938), *The Mandarins* is nevertheless an independently created work of both political and sexual importance. Beauvoir claimed in an interview of 1982, that '[i]t is the book I wrote with the most passion. It is the book I found the most important among my novels … It is the novel that remains alive [to me]'.[18] In her memoirs and in her letters she also states that she found the act of writing the novel deeply personal and protracted, taking four years to complete.[19] Indeed so personal was it that she was very protective of it, commenting that: 'Contrary to my usual habit, I had so far shown none of it to Sartre; I found it painful to wrench it out of myself, and I could not have endured any other eyes, even his, to see those pages that were still warm'.[20] Beauvoir explains the reasoning for this as: 'I wanted it to contain all of me – myself in relationship to life, to death, to my times, to writing, to love, to friendship, to travel; I also wanted to depict the people.'[21] As much as they usually critiqued each other's work, in this instance Beauvoir was so concerned with the personal nature of her writing, that she felt unable to accept Sartre's comments until the full manuscript was complete. Although Sartre later claimed that it would be her best novel to date it nevertheless, he claimed, was poorly constructed, discouraged the reader, there was a lack of suspense, the characters were unbelievable and there was a general inconsistency in the plotting: no wonder she was more reserved than normal.[22] It is then perhaps unsurprising that she did not show him her work earlier.[23] Certainly the novel has proven problematic to categorise, as Blair asserts: 'It is difficult to say with any exactitude just what *The Mandarins* should be described as: part autobiography, part social and political history, part love story and part literary credo – it eludes both category and definition.'[24] Yet it won the Prix Goncourt in 1954 and Beauvoir thought it her best work.[25] Murdoch's novel too was the recipient of a prestigious literary accolade, this time the James Tait Black Memorial Prize in 1973.

Ethical distinctions

The ethical positioning of this essay is primarily concerned with outcomes; with a type of reading that not only produces effects but also illuminates the disconnects between the reader and the text in fictions concerned with incest. Although this may seem rather Leavisite, which is not my intention, it is better understood through Martha Nussbaum's work on ethics and the novel in *Love's Knowledge* (1990). Her work impacts on this essay and provides a base from which to explore the issue of fictional incest:

> As Aristotle observed [literature] is deep and conducive to our inquiry about how to live because it does not simply (as history does) record this or that event happened; it searches for patterns of possibility – of choice and circumstance, and the interaction between choice and circumstance – that turn up in human lives with such a persistence that they must be regarded as our possibilities.[26]

Literature then speaks about us; our hopes and dreams, fears and nightmares. If we read and transform the words on the page into a real situation then we are transported into a world of difficult choices and moral dilemmas. Both novels discussed here offer us an active heuristic working through of the narration of ethical interests and issues – for our purposes incestuous – in an effort to simulate 'real life' events. The difficulty with this is, if we are to take the work of Emmanuel Levinas into account, that we cannot fully comprehend the 'other', or indeed, in this case narrate him or her, as no matter how hard we try to do so they are always outside of our grasp. Andrew Gibson puts Levinas's thought succinctly as 'the other who I encounter is always radically in excess of what my ego, cognitive powers, consciousness or intuition would make of him or her'.[27] If we try to enclose the 'other' within any

Avuncular ambiguity

framework they always escape identification and we are left without right and proper knowledge; these ideas find an echo within Murdoch's own work on the perception of the individual. She writes in 'Vision and choice in morality 'that '[m]oral insight, as communicable vision or as quality of being, *is* something separable from definitive performance, and we do not always, though doubtless we do usually, require performance to be, the test of the vision of the person who holds it'.[28]

For the central character of Bradley in *The Black Prince* then, as we will see as this discussion progresses, there is a disconnect between his vision of Julian as child and pseudo-relative, and his active choice, which is to seduce her. We need, as attentive readers, to find a way of reading novels and other texts that illuminate the ethical within them, as by doing so we increase our own ethical awareness. The theorist and philosopher Maurice Blanchot in his fragmentary text *The Writing of Disaster* (1980) described three different ways of reading that are applicable to both texts under discussion as both novels deal with the implicitly ethical as well as the explicitly concerned with either politics (for Beauvoir) or egotistic escapism (for Murdoch):

> There is an active, productive way of reading which produces text and reader and thus transports us. There is a passive kind of reading which betrays the text while appearing to submit to it, by giving the illusion that the text exists objectively, fully, sovereignly: as one whole. Finally, there is a reading that is no longer passive but passivity's reading. It is without pleasure, without joy; it escapes both comprehension and desire.[29]

This furnishes us then with three very different ways of comprehending a text, and consequently with three very different groups of potential readers. Blanchot wants us to concentrate on the testimony of the characters within novels as this will enlighten the reader to the ethical course of action. Blanchot has, by suggesting that passivity's reading is necessary, expanded the duty of philosophy to encompass the task of reading. How one reads gives different ethical interpretations, so we must pay 'attention'[30] to the liminality of the text itself on the page. In short, what is 'said' on the page is perhaps not as important as the 'saying', as it is the uncanniness of the saying that does not transport us out of ourselves into the character, as Nussbaum would have it, but disrupts our sense of autonomous selfhood: in so doing, the ethics of literature become clear. As we are concerned with the impact of the incestuous on and in both novels, it is worth developing some thoughts concerning this set of ethical positions.

We are going to need then to set out some distinctions between the two works. *The Mandarins* is primarily concerned with the political, the feminine body politic, and the contradictions of freedom in Paris at the time. Murdoch's ethic however is primarily concerned with Platonism, filtered through a range of later ethical thinkers into neo-Platonism, especially the work of Simone Weil; Murdoch dispenses with an existentialist ethic early in her career. This may have something to do with Murdoch's insistence that she, unlike Beauvoir, was not overly concerned with the gender divide. In an interview with Jack Biles she says:

> I don't really see there is much difference between men and women. I think perhaps I identify with men more than women, because the ordinary human condition still seems to belong to a man than to a woman ... I am not very much interested in the female predicament. I'm passionately in favour of women's lib, in the general, ordinary, proper sense of women having equal rights. And, most of all, equal education.[31]

We may consider from a first reading of this that Murdoch was rather unconcerned with the rise of second-wave feminism in the decade before *The Black Prince* was published; Beauvoir was one of the central driving figures with activists (such as Betty Friedan) recognising *The Second Sex* as a primary text for instigating action.[32] However, let us turn to the three principle issues for feminist ethics, as given by Cole and Coultrap-Quinn, as they bring out issues central to both writers here, especially with regards to the fictional writing of incest:

(1) whether an ethic that stresses the centrality of care can be developed into a coherent, persuasive and politically defensible feminist ethic;
(2) whether justice as defined with classical liberal political frameworks can maintain its hitherto orthodox hegemonic role when one is working within a feminist ethical context; and
(3) whether a relational ethic which attaches such importance to personal intimate bonds between people, can be utilised with larger, more impersonal situations.[33]

These ideas are based on the politicisation of the personal feminist ethic, which seeks to break down the (male-centred) boundaries between public and private morality that reinforce the power of a select group of (generally) males. It is clear that in Beauvoir's theoretical and philosophical work we can see that this is indeed the case. In *The Ethics of Ambiguity* (1948) one of the primary points of discussion is that all adolescents are said to be capable of transcending the innocence of their childhood and competent to challenge the myths that place them in a predetermined world. They are expected to rebel and to insist on their position as meaning-giving subjects to those around them and the world at large and this has clear implications for Beauvoir's fictional work. Beauvoir's biographer Margaret Crossland comments that 'In their teenage daughter, Nadine, she recreated the daughter-figure she had had in Nathalie Sorokine, saying that she wanted to take her revenge for the girl's

Avuncular ambiguity

aggressive behaviour in the past; Nathalie's mythomania, her aggressiveness toward Sartre and her tempestuous jealousy.'[34] This aggressive behaviour is perhaps a result of Beauvoir's transgressing of the line between student and young lover; a case of erotic transference. If one is not born but must become a woman, to paraphrase Beauvoir's premise to her feminist polemic *The Second Sex*, this stage of adolescent 'becoming' must also be a time of ambiguity, of questioning and of challenging perceived norms of not just men but older women who have been transformed into inessential 'others' for men to use and abuse as they see fit.

Murdoch: Replete with the incestuous

Both Beauvoir and Murdoch are back in vogue for critical discussion at present and the amount of secondary criticism produced is on the rise.[35] However, aside from the research of Emma V. Miller, little attention has been paid to the incestuous within their fiction.[36] This may strike the reader as rather odd as for Beauvoir sexuality and sexual relationships were central drivers for both her theoretical and fictional work. As Emma V. Miller has argued, for Murdoch it appears that one could examine almost any of her twenty-six novels and find either direct reference to incest, acts of incest occurring, or assumed or implicit incestuous relations.[37] Beauvoir discusses the incestuous in *The Second Sex* (1949) as part of a hermeneutic of female development and sexual awakening although it is given less space than one might imagine. For Murdoch the incestuous was not only political but deeply personal. In Mary Midgley's autobiography (Midgley was a close friend of Murdoch's at Oxford and also a fellow philosopher) we learn of Murdoch's, perhaps fictitious, yearning for not only a sibling but a lover. Midgley is discussing Murdoch's novel *The Red and the Green* from 1965:

> ... but then it was suddenly cut across by some rather implausible-looking incest. At that point for me the whole thing [Murdoch's novel *The Red and the Green* (1965)] just collapsed and I thought 'not again?' She seemed to me to keep using incest or some other scandal to break up one pattern after another as it was forming. And incest in particular appeared to have a special significance for her that I don't quite understand. I remember that once, when I mentioned my brother, she said. 'Oh I do wish I'd had a brother. I'd have had a tremendous incestuous affair with him.' I wanted to say, 'But that's not how it mostly works ...' But there was a dream there that my comments couldn't reach. Because she didn't have siblings I suppose she felt a kind of need there that could never be remedied.[38]

The relationships between Millie and Andrew in *The Red and The Green* (1965), Ilona and Jesse in *The Good Apprentice* (1985), Carel and Elizabeth in *The Time of the Angels* (1966), Harvey and his mother in *The Green Knight*

(1993), Morgan and Peter, and Tallis and Peter in *A Fairly Honourable Defeat* (1970), Nick and Catherine in *The Bell* (1958), Honour and Palmer in *A Severed Head* (1961), Rozanov and Hattie in *The Philosopher's Pupil* (1983) can all be interpreted as incestuous to some degree, and this is only focusing on the most overt. Indeed, Emma V. Miller states that:

> Iris Murdoch was one of the first authors to depict incest directly as an abusive practise, and such an approach was unusual in the decades after World War II … Iris Murdoch's fiction can be seen to respond to these changes in scientific and cultural attitudes to incest in the post-war era, and her writing reflects and challenges the social perspective contemporaneous with her individual works.[39]

In this chapter a focused discussion on the incestuous and ambiguous nature of Bradley Pearson's relationship with the much younger Julian Baffin will highlight what Murdoch, borrowing from the French philosopher and mystic Simone Weil, terms 'attention to the other'; that is the notion that in order to truly 'see' the other person in my midst I must comprehend (or at least try to) their actions not as how they affect me but how they act in the world.[40] It is unknowable if Murdoch's earlier statement about taking her brother as a lover was meant as a humorous aside as she was known for a wide variety of sexual relationships throughout her life. She certainly enjoyed sexual relationships with men and women during her formative years at Oxford and beyond in much the same way that Beauvoir did in Paris: the liberal attitude of both women towards open relationships is undeniable. Both women also fell under the spell of an 'enchanter' figure (one who holds the other characters within their grasp by fear and sexual intrigue) early on in their careers. This was Sartre for Beauvoir and Elias Canetti for Murdoch and each used these relationships to develop their fiction, using the men in their lives either directly (as Beauvoir does in *The Mandarins* with Sartre becoming Robert Dubreuilh or indirectly: Canetti is the inspiration for many of Murdoch's enchanter figures, most notably Mischa Fox in the 1956 work *The Flight from the Enchanter*).[41] There is clearly some crossover, although there are also major differences between both writers, especially as regards the role of women in both fiction and reality as discussed earlier.

So Murdoch, as we have seen, has claimed to be ambivalent to gender difference in fiction, whilst still keeping in mind that Western civilisation and culture remains dominated by men. Her work can be, and has been criticised by Deborah Johnson in her work *Iris Murdoch* (1987) for not developing these central issues as Beauvoir's work does, in particular her political and theoretical work, even though her background would suggest that she has a duty to import these ideas (much as Doris Lessing does) into her fiction.[42] This is not to say that all critics have dismissed Murdoch as being unconcerned, and hence unethical, for leaving women in a firmly heteronormative state. Gary Goshgarian in his work on Murdoch and feminist values claims that she is, 'directly concerned with the artificial mystiques and myths of womanhood that deny women recognition as free, independent, and contingent human beings. Her novels explore not only the forthright belief in female inferiority but the subtler effects of men building fantasies around women who are turned into objects for men's romantic projections'.[43] Goshgarian goes on to use a classic Lacanian idea to claim that the female role within Murdochian fiction is to function as a mirror for male needs. Julian Baffin becomes for Bradley not only a source of erotic excitement and sexual fulfilment – although the fulfilment is brief and truncated – but a physical reminder of his 'victory' (of sorts) over her father. This concept works well up to a point but does not fully satisfy. If this were to be fully developed it would cause Murdoch's female characters to correspond with certain negative female stereotypes, these being emotional, demure, lacking in intelligence, superficial and so on as they would need to correspond to cultural and conventional images of women. Although these may be apparent (to an extent) in Julian's mother Rachel, and Bradley's sister Priscilla, for the other two main female characters, Julian and Bradley's ex-wife Christian, this is not the case. The notion that Murdoch's male characters can then be seen as rather weak-willed and prone to reliance upon female characters for the development of their ego is therefore a reasonable assumption, especially as regards Bradley Pearson. Much depends of course, as discussed earlier, on the nature of the novel. Unlike Beauvoir's *roman à clef* that transposes certain elements from her life and imports a specific historical situation – making it a realist fiction in the 'journalistic' mode as Murdoch would have it[44] – Murdoch's novel is postmodern in its structure. Dooley claims that Murdoch:

> Appears to take full advantage of her readers' demands for the 'illusion of reality and truth' in the novel, only to unsettle and undermine them, not only in the postscripts at the end, but also in the narrator's address to his 'dear friend' P. Loxias which interrupt the narrative from time to time ... The temporal distance between the narrating voice and the narrated events is important here.[45]

The reader is reminded here of Vladimir Nabokov's *Lolita* (1955), and Matthew Pateman's chapter on this novel in this collection details the effects of judging narrative presentation and interpretation. If what Dooley is suggesting is correct, then the reading of incest in *The Black Prince* must not only be linear but also liminal. Two readings are suggested to us in the main body of the text; that Bradley's recollections are the truth or that he is fabricating his evidence and this has clear implications for the ethical reading that we discussed earlier. The postscripts of the novel complicate matters somewhat.

Like Nabokov, Murdoch similarly scatters clues throughout the novel. Her framing devices (the foreword to the novel by the 'editor', and her postscripts by the other members of the cast), are not the only postmodern devices she employs to compare and combine the characters of Bradley and Arnold. At times the two central characters seem to inhabit the same liminal space in the novel and, perhaps, are for both the fictional editor, and Murdoch herself, a doubling of incestuous action. It is even claimed that Julian is a willing participant in this: 'I love my parents. I suppose. Well, of course I do. Especially my father. Anyway I've never doubted it. But there are some things one can't forgive. It's the end of something. And the beginning of something.' [To which Bradley responds] 'Oh Julian, I've brought irrevocable things to you'.[46] This statement by Julian is, in and of itself, not particularly convincing. That Bradley claims that he has made the situation irrevocable with her father, and by extension her mother as well, is not only to detach her from her family but also the normative ethical environment of her youth: she has been inducted into a shifting world with no firm foundation, no grounding in ethical norms. It seems strange then that Julian would look outside of her immediate family for parental affection, especially if she admires her father as a strong character. If we look at Murdoch's philosophical work in *Metaphysics as a Guide to Morals* (1992) she tells us that:

> Falling in love is for many people their most intense experience (certainly my life is incomprehensible but for this event), bringing with it a quasi-religious certainty, and (it is) most disturbing because it shifts the centre of the world from oneself to another place. A love relationship can occasion extreme selfishness and possessive violence, the attempt to dominate that other place so that it (will) be no longer separate; or it can prompt a process of unselfing wherein the lover learns to see, and cherish and respect, what is not himself.[47]

The relationship between Bradley and Julian can be read as being based on Bradley's selfish wish to escape the onset of old age and Julian's naivety and love for her father.[48] Indeed, it is worth questioning if, even subliminally, whether to some extent she views Arnold and Bradley as one and the same person, or perhaps that they fulfil a similar or dual role in her life. It may well be the case that the developing quasi-incestuous relationship owes more to a conflation of father-figures, due to her desire to be truly 'seen' by her father, than it does to her desire for Bradley as both her boyfriends mentioned in the text – before and after Bradley – are of a similar age to herself. In his postscript to the novel Francis Marloe – another Murdochian joke suggesting perhaps that it is Francis who is the editor and arbiter of the narrative although he comes off as fawning and simplistic[49] – says, 'Further: who in reality is this girl? (Father-fixated of course and taking Bradley as a father-substitute, no mystery there.) The daughter of Bradley's protégé, rival, idol, gadfly, friend, enemy, alter ego,

Arnold Baffin. Science proclaims that this cannot be the work of accident. And science is right.'⁵⁰ Of course we must take this information with a hefty dose of cynicism coming as it does from Francis, a rather seedy, disappointed man who clearly has a sexual attraction toward Bradley and lives out his fantasies through his sister's return and disruption of Bradley's life (even if Bradley's postscript goes some way to confirming his own homosexual tendencies). However I do not think we can dismiss his testimony entirely.

Murdoch's playfulness with Marloe's postscript is clearly intended to provoke in her readers a questioning of not only authorial authority but also the reality of the situation. Marloe claims that Bradley is a masochistic, sadistic, repressed homosexual, a view which may well hold some weight when we see his reaction to Julian (an epicene name of course) dressed in male clothing. We are told that Bradley's sexual excitement is peaked by viewing Julian in her new black boots and wearing an outfit that casts her as both virginal Ophelia and Hamlet, 'I tossed and panted and groaned as if I were wrestling with a palpable demon. The fact that I had actually touched her, kissed her ... I felt like a condemned excluded monster. How could it be that I had actually kissed her cheek without enveloping her, without becoming her?'⁵¹ This is further developed in Julian's postscript – Julian, Rachel, Francis and Christian as well as Bradley are allowed to share their thoughts post Arnold's murder (allegedly by Bradley) with us – when she says: 'If my father was the carpenter, Pearson was certainly the walrus.'⁵² This is a reference to the classic nonsense poem by Lewis Carroll featured in *Alice's Adventures in Wonderland* (1865), and an author whose interest in prepubescent girls has been much discussed.⁵³ Indeed, the poem's reference to 'shucking' may refer not just of the young oysters but of young women. That both the walrus and the carpenter take part in this is worth noting in relation to the doubling of Arnold and Bradley. For her part, Rachel believes that Julian was always a little wary of Bradley: 'My daughter always regarded him as a sort of "funny Uncle".'⁵⁴ In any event, with fragmentation of narrative comes difficulties with deciphering authorial intent, and it is clear that Bradley and Julian's relationship does not exist solely in his mind, as Julian confirms in her postscript that they did indeed have a relationship: 'Centuries separate me from these events. I see them diminished and myself as a child. It is the story of an old man and a child.'⁵⁵ It may be useful to return to Nussbaum at this point:

> The 'vulgar heat' of jealousy and personal interest comes between us and the loving perception of each particular. A novel, just because it is not our life, places us in a moral position that is favourable for perception and it shows us what it would be like to take up that position in life. We find here love without possessiveness, attention without bias, involvement without panic. Our moral abilities must be developed to a certain degree, certainly, before we can approach this novel at all and see anything in it.⁵⁶

The ethical weight for the reader then is placed not in the interpretation of the narrative but the underlying ethical truth. For Murdoch this consists of *right* vision, of 'seeing' the other as they really are, a vision necessary for facing truth and for personal and societal health. For Bradley his implicit consideration that he has a right vision of reality is clearly deluded, as he has not dealt with the underlying issue of aging. By involving himself with a rather epicene and ambiguous teenager, Bradley wants to regress chronologically, sexually and morally and even in his postscript he cannot entirely accept his failings:

> I had not willed Arnold's death but I had envied him and (sometimes at least) detested him. I had failed Rachel and abandoned her. I had neglected Priscilla. Dreadful things had happened for which I was partly responsible ... The court saw me as a callous fantasy-ridden man. In fact I meditated profoundly upon my responsibility. But guilt is a form of energy and because of it my eyes glowed. Much later, my dearest friend, it was you who pointed out to me that, without realizing it, I surrendered myself to the trial as a final exorcism of guilt from my life.[57]

We should not be surprised that there is something of the demonic in his final testament to both the reader and his assumed fictional reader, the 'dearest friend'.[58] He also refers to himself as 'a monster'[59] because of his lack of regard for the central female characters. If we move on to Beauvoir's novel we see a marked change in the incestuous relationship with Nadine as the primary instigator, and with Henri as the rather bored Parisian editor. That both Henri and Bradley are considered as 'uncles', even though not genetically related to their implied 'nieces', is suggestive of a violation of trust by a person in a position of authority and care similar to that of incest.

Incest, translation and Beauvoir

We know of course that every translation does, and indeed must, change a text so that it moves towards the form that the translator, rather than the author, has in mind. This is of central concern for the critical interpretation of *The Mandarins*, as how Beauvoir talks about sex, about incest, and about the situations underlying these two is of course of paramount importance. Every translation must change the text that is being examined and, aside from revisiting the French language edition in its entirety, we rely on the accuracy – or perhaps the inaccuracy of the translator. A serious reading needs to take this into consideration as to read and discuss *The Mandarins* without a clear reference to the original would be to do Beauvoir a disservice; we cannot give a mere passive reading to the text as if it were produced in English. Naturally this point is not new as Barbara Klaw has pointed out that several sections of *The Mandarins* suffer from a weakening of the taboo and the vulgar.[60]

For example Nadine is not only dismissive of her mother on numerous occasions but is also prone to lapse into shocking language to separate herself from her influence; that this is toned down in the English language version may not come as a surprise. Klaw takes her case in point from a central section of the text where Nadine is being both assertive and indifferent to the feelings of her mother. In discussing her relationships with boys of her own ages she says 'Comment veux-tu que j'aie des histoires avec des types si je ne baise pas'[61] the literal translation of this being: 'How do you want me to have stories with guys if I do not fuck?' whereas the English translation of the first edition by Beauvoir's most prolific translator Leonard M. Friedman is: 'How do you expect me to have affairs with guys if I don't go to bed with them?'[62] Luise Von Futlow discusses this section in her work on Beauvoir's translations in regard to sexuality and she believes that 'the toning down elides the effect of Nadine's crude discourse, a crucial aspect of her relationship with her mother and an element that reveals her own cynical and alienated condition'.[63] By toning down the vulgar and intimate language of sex used in the novel it is clear that those sections involved with the incestuous will not carry the impact or the serious ethical weight of the original. Klaw confirms this when she refers to a subsequent conversation Beauvoir recorded with her American publisher. In it he says that he 'was happy with the translation of *Les Mandarins* but apologised for having to cut some lines here and there: 'in our country one can talk about sexuality in a book, he explained to me, not about perversion'.[64]

Incest is one of the few sexual taboos recognised and condemned widely throughout the world,[65] and if such issues are unable to be reasoned with and discussed openly due to editorial interference this naturally reduces the impact of the work of art both aesthetically and ethically. If we move on to a key incestuous scene from the novel with this in mind (considering the narrative structure outlined earlier) it will enhance, or at least make us critically aware, of the 'saying' of the text: 'To have said "I'm going out with Nadine" would have brought on so many questions, so many misinterpretations, that he chose not to say it. But it was really absurd to hide the fact that he was meeting that awkward girl whom he had always looked on a sort of niece.'[66] This reflection from Henri is rather more mature in vision than the passionate but foolhardy Bradley. Yet it is Nadine who initiates the movement between platonic relationship – although Henri is rather lecherous in the jazz club – and one of quasi-incest. It is Henri and not Nadine who is left confused by their interaction, saying: 'What happened? I don't understand ... You spiked my champagne with brandy?' She admits, "'I did. It's a little trick I often play on the Americans when I have to get them drunk. Anyhow" she said, still smiling, "it was the only way to have you."'[67] This is, of course, a reversal of power relations, a concept that is brought to the reader's attention at the very beginning of the second section of *The Ethics of Ambiguity* when Beauvoir discusses the existentialist vision of personal freedom in regard to others in the world. She claims that to transit successfully from child to adult – after having been cast into the world through no fault of one's own – one has to make and remake values that are originally imposed as factual and culturally untransgressable:

> With astonishment, revolt and disrespect the child little by little asks himself; 'Why must I act that way? What good is it? And what will happen if I act in another way?' He discovers his subjectivity; he discovers that of others ... Language, customs, ethics and values have their sources in these uncertain creatures. If the child/ adolescent becomes the locus of their own morality and ethical vision they are not giving any 'attention' to those around them 'the individual must at last assume his subjectivity'.[68]

While Julian and Nadine are not 'little' children, they are nevertheless young and inexperienced. This alleged 'offence' is less of an issue for Murdoch's Julian as her transgression is concerned with the idolising of Bradley as a mentor figure who is concerned with 'high art' rather than her father's perceived writing of populist 'low' fiction. For Nadine her role in her own seduction and quasi-incest can be interpreted as a response to her unresolved grief at the loss of her previous lover as well as her issues with male carers and those who stand as figures of power; she wishes to obtain their level of autonomy that she perceives them as having. However, by crossing the unspoken boundary between herself and Henri she not only fails to gain a fuller sense of individuality but breaks down an ethical code of behaviour that sets boundaries for the rest of the group.

Both novels then can be said to be taking part not only in a discussion of the incestuous but also in ethical modes of representation. As we have seen there are real difficulties when subjecting a novel to an ethical reading in translation as the novel becomes a textual artefact, and not quite the artwork the author intended, yet not a product of the imagination of the translator either. The use of incest is for Murdoch and Beauvoir, one implicit and one explicit, a working out of ethical thinking about bodies in relationship to each other and this, necessarily, spills over into the realm of the political. For Murdoch the teenage body of Julian is a site of transgression, from both societal norms and parental control; for Beauvoir the personal becomes political when her own story is transposed into fiction.

Notes

1 Simone de Beauvoir, Leonard M. Friedman (trans.), *The Mandarins* (Collins, 1957), p. 518.
2 Iris Murdoch, 'At one remove from tragedy: Review of *The Mandarins*', *Nation*, 182 (9 June 1956), pp. 493–4.

Avuncular ambiguity

3 Terry Keefe, *Simone de Beauvoir* (Macmillan), p. 107.
4 Sally Scholz and Shannon Mussett (eds), *The Contradictions of Freedom* (State University of New York Press, 2005), p. 84.
5 Edward Quinn, *History in Literature* (Facts on File, 2004), p. 117.
6 Simone de Beauvoir, Sylvie le Bon (compiled and annotated), *A Transatlantic Love Affair* (New York Press, 1998), p. 472.
7 Tammy Grimshaw, *Sexuality, Gender and Power* (Fairleigh Dickinson University Press, 2005), p. 101.
8 Iris Murdoch, *The Black Prince* (Chatto and Windus, 1973), p. 354.
9 William Shakespeare, Anne Thompson and Neil Taylor (eds), *Hamlet*, Arden Shakespeare (Bloomsbury, 2005), p. 129.
10 Shakespeare, *Hamlet*, pp. 157–8 (1.2.158–9).
11 Murdoch, *The Black Prince*, p. 27.
12 *Ibid.*, p. 170.
13 Vladimir Nabokov, *Lolita* (Penguin, 2000), p. 142.
14 Jillmarie Murphy, *Monstrous Kinships* (University of Delaware Press, 2011), p. 25.
15 Iris Murdoch, *Existentialists and Mystics* (Penguin, 1999), p. 295.
16 Grimshaw, *Sexuality, Gender and Power*, p. 143.
17 Miles Leeson, *Iris Murdoch* (Continuum, 2010), p. 20.
18 Deidre Blair, *Simone de Beauvoir* (Jonathan Cape, 1990), p. 424.
19 *Ibid.*, p. 424.
20 Simone de Beauvoir, Richard howard (trans.), *The Force of Circumstance* (Paragon House, 1992), p. 243.
21 Beauvoir, *The Force of Circumstance*, p. 193.
22 Scholz and Mussett (eds), *The Contradictions of Freedom*, pp. 16–17.
23 *Ibid.*, pp. 16–17.
24 Blair, *Simone de Beauvoir*, p. 424.
25 *Ibid.*, p. 424.
26 Martha Nussbaum, *Love's Knowledge* (Oxford University Press, 1990), p. 164.
27 Andrew Gibson, *Postmodernity, Ethics and the Novel* (Routledge, 1999), p. 25.
28 Murdoch, 'Vision and choice in morality' in Murdoch, *Existentialists and Mystics*, p. 83.
29 Maurice Blanchot, Ann Smock (trans.) *The Writing of Disaster* (University of Nebraska Press, 1986), p. 101.
30 Simone Weil, *Correspondence* (Editions l'Age d'Homme, 1982), p. 18.
31 Gillian Dooley, 'Iris Murdoch's use of first-person narrative in *The Black Prince*', *English Studies* 85:2 (2004), p. 61.
32 Betty Friedan dedicated her major work, *The Feminine Mystique*, to Beauvoir.
33 Eve Cole and Susan Coultrap-Quinn (eds) *Explorations in Feminist Ethics* (Indiana University Press, 1992), pp. 1–2.
34 Margaret Crossland, *Simone de Beauvoir* (Heinemann, 1992), p. 381.
35 For Murdoch see: Nick Turner, *Post-War British Women Novelists and the Canon* (Continuum, 2010). For Beauvoir see: Alison Holland, *Excess and Transgression* (Routledge, 2009).

36. Emma V. Miller, Literary Incest: Intertextuality and Writing the Last Taboo in the Novels of Iris Murdoch (PhD thesis, Durham University, 2011), http://etheses.dur.ac.uk/1400/ (accessed 15 February 2017).
37. Miller, *Literary Incest*, p. 5.
38. Mary Midgley, *The Owl of Minerva* (Routledge, 2005), p. 183.
39. Emma V. Miller '"We must not forget that there was a crime": Incest, domestic violence and textual memory in the novels of Iris Murdoch', *Journal of Literature and Trauma Studies* 1:2 (2013), p. 66.
40. Iris Murdoch, *The Sovereignty of Good* (Routledge & Kegan Paul, 1970), p. 34.
41. Peter Conradi, *Iris Murdoch: A Life* (Harper Collins, 2001), p. 345.
42. Deborah Johnson *Iris Murdoch* (Harvester, 1987), p. 8.
43. Gary Goshgarian, 'Feminist values in the novels of Iris Murdoch', *Revue des Langues Vivantes* 40:5 (1974) pp. 519–27.
44. Murdoch, *Existentialists and Mystics*, p. 291.
45. Dooley, 'Iris Murdoch's use of first-person narrative', p. 135.
46. Murdoch, *The Black Prince*, p. 250.
47. Iris Murdoch, *Metaphysics as a Guide to Morals* (Chatto and Windus, 1992), pp. 16–17.
48. A view supported by Gillian Dooley. See: Dooley, 'Iris Murdoch's use of first-person narrative', pp. 137–8.
49. Christopher Marlow and Francis Bacon have both been suggested as the author of Shakespeare's texts. For more on this see H.N. Gibson, *The Shakespeare Claimants* (Routledge, 1962).
50. Murdoch, *The Black Prince*, p. 346.
51. *Ibid.*, p. 206.
52. *Ibid.*, p. 358.
53. Katie Roiphe, 'Just good friends?', *Guardian* 29 October 2001, www.theguardian.com/world/2001/oct/29/gender.uk (accessed, 13 April 2017).
54. Murdoch, *The Black Prince*, p. 354.
55. *Ibid.*, p. 357.
56. Nussbaum, *Love's Knowledge*, p. 162.
57. Murdoch, *The Black Prince*, p. 335.
58. *Ibid.*, p. 335.
59. *Ibid.*, p. 335.
60. Barbara Klaw, 'Sexuality in Simone de Beauvoir's *Les Mandarins*', in Margaret Simons (ed.), *Feminist Interpretations of Simone de Beauvoir* (Penn State Press, 1995), p. 197.
61. Simone de Beauvoir, *Les Mandarins* (Gallimard, 1954), p. 350.
62. Beauvoir, *The Mandarins*, p. 373.
63. Luise von Futlow, 'Translation effects: How Beauvoir talks sex in English', in Melanie Hawthorne (ed.), *Contingent Loves* (University of Virginia Press, 2000), p. 11.
64. Barbara Klaw, 'Sexuality in Simone de Beauvoir's *Les Mandarins*', p. 197.

65 Anon., 'Inbred obscurity: Improving incest laws in the shadow of the "sexual family"', *Harvard Law Review*, 119:8 (June, 2006), pp. 2464–85.
66 Beauvoir, *The Mandarins*, p. 62.
67 *Ibid.*, p. 66.
68 Simone de Beauvoir, *The Ethics of Ambiguity* (Citadel Press, 1980), p. 36.

Bibliography

Fiction and plays

Beauvoir, Simone de, Leonard M. Friedman (trans.), *The Mandarins* (Collins, 1957)
Murdoch, Iris, *The Black Prince* (Chatto and Windus, 1973)
Nabokov, Vladimir, *Lolita* (Penguin, 2000)
Shakespeare, William, *Hamlet* (The Arden Shakespeare, 2005)

Non-fiction

Anon. 'Inbred obscurity: Improving incest laws in the shadow of the "sexual family"' in *Harvard Law Review* 119:8 (June 2006), pp. 2464–85
Beauvoir, Simone de, Richard Howard (trans.), *The Force of Circumstance: Volume 1, After the War, 1944–1952* (Paragon House, 1992)
——., H.M. Parshley (trans.), *The Second Sex* (Jonathon Cape, 1953)
——., *The Ethics of Ambiguity* (Citadel Press, 1980)
——., Sylvie le Bon (trans.), *A Transatlantic Love Affair* (New York Press, 1998)
Biles, Jack, 'Interview with Iris Murdoch' in Gillian Dooley (ed.), *From a Tiny Corner in the House of Fiction: Conversations with Iris Murdoch* (University of South Carolina Press, 2003), pp. 56–69
Blair, Deirdre, *Simone de Beauvoir* (Jonathan Cape, 1990)
Blanchard, R., A.D. Lykins, D. Wherrett, et al., 'Paedophilia, hebephilia, and the DSM-V', *Archives of Sexual Behaviour* 38:3(2009), pp. 335–50
Blanchot, Maurice, Ann Smock (trans.), *The Writing of Disaster* (University of Nebraska Press, 1986)
Cole, Eve and Susan Coultrap-Quinn (eds), *Explorations in Feminist Ethics: Theory and Practice* (Indiana University Press, 1992)
Conradi, Peter, *Iris Murdoch: A Life* (Harper Collins, 2001)
Crosland, Margaret, *Simone de Beauvoir* (Heinemann, 1992)
Deane, Marion, 'Dangerous Liaisons', *Proceedings of the Harvard Celtic Colloquium* 23 (2003), pp. 52–79
Dooley, Gillian, 'Iris Murdoch's use of first-person narrative in *The Black Prince*', *English Studies* 85:2 (2004), pp. 134–46
Gibson, Andrew, *Postmodernity, Ethics and the Novel: From Leavis to Levinas* (Routledge, 1999)
Gibson, H.N., *The Shakespeare Claimants* (Routledge, 1962)

Goshgarian, Gary, 'Feminist values in the novels of Iris Murdoch', *Revue des Langues Vivantes* 40:5 (1974), pp. 519–27

Grimshaw, Tammy, *Sexuality, Gender and Power in Iris Murdoch's Fiction* (Fairleigh Dickinson University Press, 2005)

Holland, Alison, *Excess and Transgression in Simone de Beauvoir's Fiction: The Discourse of Madness* (Routledge, 2009)

Johnson, Deborah, *Iris Murdoch* (Harvester Press, 1987)

Keefe, Terry, *Simone de Beauvoir* (Macmillan, 1998)

Klaw, Barbara, 'Sexuality in Simone de Beauvoir's *Les Mandarins*' in Margaret Simons (ed.), *Feminist Interpretations of Simone de Beauvoir* (Penn State Press, 1995)

Leeson, Miles, *Iris Murdoch: Philosophical Novelist* (Continuum, 2010)

Midgley, Mary, *The Owl of Minerva: A Memoir* (Routledge, 2005)

Miller, Emma V., ' "We must not forget that there was a crime": Incest, domestic violence and textual memory in the novels of Iris Murdoch', *Journal of Literature and Trauma Studies* 1:2 (2012), pp. 65–94

——., 'The madman in the attic: Playing with gendered literary identity as object and muse in Iris Murdoch's *The Good Apprentice* and *The Message to the Planet*', *Forum: University of Edinburgh Postgraduate Journal of Culture and the Arts* 2 (August 2008), pp. 1–19

——., 'Literary Incest': Intertextuality and Writing the Last Taboo in the Novels of Iris Murdoch.' Doctoral thesis, Durham University, (2011). http://etheses.dur.ac.uk/1400/ (accessed 15 February 2017)

Murdoch, Iris, At one remove from tragedy: Review of *The Mandarins*, *Nation* 182 (9 June 1956), pp. 493–4

——., *Metaphysics as a Guide to Morals* (Chatto and Windus, 1992)

——., *Existentialists and Mystics* (Penguin, 1999)

Murphy, Jillmarie, *Monstrous Kinships: Realism and Attachment Theory in the Nineteenth and Early Twentieth Century Novel* (University of Delaware Press, 2011)

Nussbaum, Martha, *Loves Knowledge: Essays on Philosophy and Literature* (Oxford University Press, 1990)

Quinn, Edward, *History in Literature: A Reader's Guide to 20th-century History and the Literature it Inspired* (Facts on File, 2004)

Roiphe, Katie, 'Just good friends?' *Guardian*, (29 October 2001), www.theguardian.com/world/2001/oct/29/gender.uk (accessed, 13 April 2017)

Scholz, Sally J. and Shannon M. Mussett (eds), *The Contradictions of Freedom: Philosophical Essays on Simone de Beauvoir's The Mandarins* (State University of New York Press, 2005)

Todd, Richard, *Iris Murdoch* (Methuen, 1984)

Turner, Nick, *Post-War British Women Novelists and the Canon* (Continuum, 2010)

Von Futlow, Luise, 'Translation effects: How Beauvoir talks sex in English', in Melanie Hawthorne (ed.), *Contingent Loves: Simone de Beauvoir and Sexuality* (University of Virginia Press, 2000)

White, Duncan, *Nabokov and His Books: Between Late Modernism and the Literary Marketplace* (Oxford University Press, 2017)

Index

abuse (sexual) 2–6, 24, 118–19, 122, 129, 133, 139, 142, 146, 150
   child 3, 5, 10, 22–3, 37–8, 101, 121, 137, 147
Acker, Kathy 47
Algren, Nelson 270
Allen, Sheila 29, 30
Amis, Martin 47
Anderson, Ellen 122
Andrews, Guy 37
Angelou, Maya 5
anti-semitism 189, 209
Appel, Alfred 102
Archibald, Elizabeth 1
Aristotle 146
Armstrong, Elizabeth 2
Aubrey, James 30

Bach, Johann Sebastian 163
Bailey, Beth 2
Banks, Iain 11
   Steep Approach to Garbadale, The 180–94
Banks-Smith, Nancy 26
Barnes, Elizabeth L. 8
Bass, Ellen 70
Baudrillard, Jean 192, 213

Beauvoir, Simone de 134, 141
   Ethics of Ambiguity, The 270, 276, 284
   Mandarins, The 11–12, 269–84
   Second Sex, The 270, 276–7
Becker, Judith V. 3
Behm, Barbara 122
Bell, Eleanor 182–3
Bell, Vikki 5, 70
Benjamin, Walter 163, 176–7
Bennett, Cyril 29
Bergman, Ingmar 23
Berlusconi, Silvio 164
Biles, Jack 276
Blanchot, Maurice 269, 275
Bloom, Harold 258
Boland, Eavan 225
Bowlby, John 4
Bradley, Mike 37
Brink, Andrew 108
Brontë, Emily 1
Brooks, Ellen 258
Broughton, Linda 51, 53
Brown, Laura S. 54
Brown, Margaret Wise 127
Brownmiller, Susan 53–5, 134, 141
   Against Our Will 134, 141
Bulger, Jamie 38
Buntzen, Lynda K. 225

Burney, Fanny 187
Byatt, A.S. 11, 246, 248, 253–7, 261, 262
Byron, George Gordon (Lord) 187, 188, 247

Cairns, Craig 182, 183, 184, 189
Callil, Carmen 58
Campbell, Jane 254
Camus, Albert 270
Canetti, Elias 278
Cantor, Paul A. 1
Carrol, Lewis 281
Carter, Angela 47, 121, 145, 147, 246, 262
  Magic Toyshop, The 6, 11, 248–53, 255
Caruth, Cathy 71–2, 75, 80
Champagne, Rosaria 71
Chapman, Jessica 38
Chateaubriand, François-René de 1
childhood 2–3, 22, 27, 56, 61–2, 67, 71–2, 77, 79, 81, 83, 85, 108, 205, 257, 262, 276
Childs, Peter 56
Churchill-Brown, Leah 83
Cixous, Hélène 51
Clarke, Alan
  Scum 23
Climbié, Victoria 38
coercion (sexual) 23, 126, 257
Coleman, Emily M. 3
consent (sexual) 2–3, 23, 58, 143, 256
Cooke, Lez 23, 31–2
Cormier, Robert 118
Crew, Gary 123
Crossland, Margaret 276
Crutcher, Chris 118
Cullen-DuPont, Kathryn 3

Damasio, Antonio 164
Davidoff, Leonore 246, 247
Davis, Joseph E. 4
Davis, Laura 70

Day, Aidan 248
Defoe, Daniel 187
Deleuze, Giles 172, 174
deMause, Lloyd 2
Dennett, Daniel C. 161–2
Derrida, Jacques 11, 98, 248, 251, 252, 254–7, 262
de Sade, Donatien Alphonse François 109
Doane, Janice 8
Dooley, Gillian 279, 286n.48
Dryden, John 228
Duggan, Robert 11
Dundes, Alan 144

Ellis, Bret Easton 47
Ellis, John 32–3
Eve, Trevor 34

fairy tales 10, 77, 100, 120–6, 136–41, 143–8
False Memory Syndrome (FMS) 7, 8, 10, 70, 71, 73, 82
femininity 52–3, 61, 216, 258
feminism 5, 48, 62, 133–4, 141, 258
Fielding, Henry 187
Fine, Anne 133
Finlay, Frank 21, 29, 33
FMS *see* False Memory Syndrome
Ford, John 188
Foucault, Michel 201
Fox, Robin 199
Freeman, Michael 5
Freidan, Betty 276
Freud, Lucien 32
Freud, Sigmund 2, 4, 6, 22, 23, 25, 37, 38, 70, 71, 127, 130n.24, 134, 148, 162, 165
  Oedipus Complex 24, 47–9, 52, 55–9, 70, 75, 126–7, 161–3, 172–3, 185, 188
Freyd, Peter and Pamela 7
Friedman, Leonard M. 283
Fritzl, Elisabeth 6
Fritzl, Joseph 6, 43n.124

Index

Frost, Ginger S. 255
Fry, Deborah 5
Futlow, Luise von 283

gender anxiety 60, 62
genetic sexual attraction (GSA) 185
Gibson, Andrew 274
Gibson, William
    Neuromancer 11, 198, 201, 212–14
Gieni, Justine 10
Gilman, Sander 189
Goldsworthy, Andy 32
Goshgarian, Gary 279
gothic 1, 49, 52, 55–6, 187, 199, 248
Grant, Deborah 33
Graves, Robert 225
Grimshaw, Tammy 271
Guattari, Feliz 174

Haffenden, John 49, 61
Hamilton, Ian 56
Hamilton, Richard 32
Haraway, Donna 199–200, 203
Hardie, Philip 232–3, 240
Hardman, Charlotte 5
Hardy, Thomas 237
Harrison, Kathryn
    Exposure 10, 69, 72, 76–81, 83, 84
Hartman, Geoffrey 135
Hartnett, Sonya 118
Hayles, N. Katherine 215
Head, Dominic 47
Herman, Judith 22, 24, 33
Hermannsson, Casie 123
Hillis Miller, Joseph 98, 102
Hirschman, Lisa 70
Hitchcock, Alfred
    Psycho 49
Hodges, Devon 8
Holocaust, the 135, 147
Homer, Sean 144
Hughes, Ted 11, 225–41
Hurd, Clement 127
hysteria 2, 4, 22, 24, 71

Irons, Jeremy 111
Irwin, John 205
Iser, Wolfgang 99, 103

Jeram, Anita 128
Johnson, Deborah 278
Johnson, Richard 257

Kacandes, Irene 146–7
Kafka, Franz 165, 168, 172
Katz, Boris 98
Keats, John 165
Kelman, James 193
Kennedy, A.L. 193
Ketterer, David 208
King, Nicola 147
Kinsey, Alfred 3
    Kinsey reports, the 22
Kirson Weinberg, Samuel 4
Klaw Barbara 282–3
Koestler, Arthur 270
Krafft-Ebing, Richard von 4
Kristeva, Julia 51, 127–9, 169–70
Kubrick, Stanley
    Lolita (film) 97, 103–4, 110, 112, 114n.70

Lacan, Jacques 134–6, 139–40, 144, 148–50, 165
Lanagan, Margo 8
    Tender Morsels 10, 118, 133–50
    Touching Earth Lightly 134–5
Law of the Father, the 58, 59
Lawrence, Stephen 38
Lay, Samantha 37–8
Leeson, Miles 11
Lehner, Stefanie 193
Lennon, Peter 273
Lessing, Doris 246, 248, 278
    The Golden Notebook 6, 11, 258–63
Levinas, Emmanuel 248, 269, 274
Levi-Strauss, Claude 169–70, 185–6, 254
Lewis, Matthew "Monk" 1

Lewis, Wyndham 11
Lin, Ying-Chiao 73
Loftus, Elizabeth F. 7
Lowe, Sophie 83
Lukenbill, Bernard 118, 119
Lury, Karen 30, 31, 38
Lynch, Joan 21
Lyne, Adrian
　Lolita (film) 25, 97, 101, 110–12, 114n.70
Lyotard, Jean François 99, 106–8

McBratney, Sam 128
McCabe, Richard 188
McEwan, Ian 8
　Cement Garden, The 6, 10, 47, 49, 55–6, 60, 62, 188
　Homemade 49–55, 56, 59–60, 62
McGraw, Sheila 128
McKinley, Robin 119–20
Mack, Michael 10, 213
McPherson, Joanne 119
Maggi, Armando 164–5, 174
Mallory, Thomas 1
Manlowe, Jennifer L. 256
March, Cristie 181
Marcuse, Herbert 148
masculinity 48, 50, 54–6, 58–60, 62, 71, 148
Maslow, Abraham 250
Masson, Jeffrey 4
'Memory Wars' 69, 71, 76
　see also False Memory Syndrome
Menninghaus, Winfried 170
Merleau-Ponty, Maurice 140
Michaux, Henri 175
Middleton, Thomas 1
Midgley, Mary 277
Miller, Emma V. 10, 11, 199, 277, 278
Mills, Alice 10
Moore, Thomas 208
Moorhouse, Jocelyn 72, 74, 80–3
Moravia, Alberto 164
Morrison, Toni 70, 136

Moussaieff Masson, Jeffrey 4
Mulvey, Laura 81
Mundye, Charles 11
Munsch, Robert 128
Murdoch, Iris 258–9
　Black Prince, The 11–12, 269–84
mythomania 277

Nabokov, Vladmir
　Lolita 6, 8, 10, 25, 97–112, 272, 279–80
Nairn, Thom 182
Naylor, Paul B. 257
Newman, Andrea
　Bouquet of Barbed Wire, A 9–10, 21–38
Nicolson, Linda 201, 210–11
Nixon, Nicola 213
Norris, Hermione 29
Nussbaum, Martha 269, 273, 274, 281

O'Connor, Kaitlyn
　Abiogenisis 11, 198–207, 212, 215, 217
O'Dair, Sharon 80, 82
Oedipus complex see Freud, Sigmund
O'Sullivan, Chris 5
Ovid 11, 143, 225–9
　Metamorphoses 1, 146, 225–8, 230, 231, 233, 234, 236, 237, 240–1

paedophilia 22, 36, 37, 60, 97, 108, 113n.30, 248
Pasolini, Pier Paolo 10–11, 161–77
Pateman, Matthew 10, 25, 279
Pearce, Ashley 22, 30, 33–4, 37
Pearson, Claudia 127
Penhaligon, Susan 21, 35
Petkovic, Nicola 165
Petrie, Duncan 192
Pheasant-Kelly, Frances 9–10
Picknell, J.E. 7
Pilinovsky, Helen 120–1

Index

Plath, Sylvia 11, 225–41
Plato 178n.53, 247, 275–6
Poe, Edgar Allan 49, 105, 108, 114n.65
Pollitt, Katha 71
Pollock, Ellen 254
Poots, Imogen 34
posthuman incest 11, 198–217
post-traumatic stress disorder (PTSD) 146–7, 150
Potter, Dennis
   Brimstone and Treacle 23, 31
PTSD *see* post-traumatic stress disorder
Pullman, Philip 134

Queneau, Raymond 269

Ragland Sullivan, Ellie 148
Raitt, Fiona.E 7, 70
Rank, Otto 185–6
rape 2, 3, 6, 31, 47, 49, 51, 53–7, 62, 74, 101, 102, 104, 109, 110–12, 133–5, 137, 139, 141, 142, 145, 150, 232, 247, 248, 249
   see also sexual violence
Rapping, Elayne Antler 258
Rawls, John 5
Ray, John 101, 103, 105
Recovered Memory 70
   see also False Memory Syndrome
Richardson, Alan 188
Rider Haggard, Henry 52
Riggs, Shannon 122
Rodi-Risberg, Marinella 72, 75–6
Roger, Angela 57
Roiphe, Katie 75, 80
Ronen, Omry 98
Rothberg, Michael 135
Rush, Florence 4
Rutledge, Amelia 120
Ryan, Kiernan 49
Ryan, Ray 192

sadomasochism 28, 55
Salmond, Alex 192

Salter, Michael 7
Sartre, Jean-Paul 269–70, 273–4, 278
Saussure, Ferdinand de 251, 253
Savile, Jimmy 6, 22, 38
Schiff, Stephen 110
Schweighauser, Philipp 104
Second Life (game) 202, 215–17
Sellers, Peter 110
Sendak, Maurice 123
sexual violence 4, 6, 9, 47, 48, 50, 53, 55, 142
   see also rape
Shakespeare, William 1, 11, 72, 226, 238–40, 271
   King Lear 70–5, 144–5
   Romeo and Juliet 127, 129
Shanley, Mary Lyndon 247
Shelley, Mary
   Frankenstein 49, 187
Shelley, Percy 1, 187, 247
Showalter, Elaine 145
Siciliano, Enzo 161, 164
Silverman, Kaja 48
Slay, Jack 47
Smiley, Jane
   Thousand Acres, A 6, 10, 70–85
Smith-D'Arezzo, Wendy 122
Smithson, Robert 32
Sophocles
   Oedipus Rex 75, 88n.94, 162, 165
Spillers, Hortense 75
Stead, William Thomas 2
Stoker, Bram 1, 52
Swain, Dominique 101
Swedenborg, Emanuel 247

Tatar, Maria 143–4
Taylor, Damilola 38
Thomas, Dylan 167–8
Thompson, Susan 122
Thornburg, Newton
   Beautiful Kate 82
Thurschwell, Pamela 24
Toibin, Colm 58

Vickroy, Laurie 147
Viner, Brian 32, 36–7

Waldorf, Heather 118
Walker, Alice 70
Walker, Janet 25, 32
Walpole, Horace 187
Ward, Rachel
  Beautiful Kate 10, 69, 72, 76–80, 81–3, 85
Warhol, Andy 32
Warner, Marina 138
Webster, John 186
Weil, Simone 276, 278
Wells, Holly 38
Westermarck, Edward 185

Wharmby, Tony 29
White, Rebecca 10
Whitehead, Anne 135, 147
Whittier, Nancy 5
Wigmore, John Henry 71
Williams, Raymond 22, 23, 25, 31, 32, 194
Windling, Terry 121
Woolf, Virginia 6
Wyndham, John
  Plan for Chaos 200–1, 207–12, 215

Yolen, Jane 121

Zeedyk, Suzanne 7, 70
Zollars, Jaime 122

EU authorised representative for GPSR:
Easy Access System Europe, Mustamäe tee 50,
10621 Tallinn, Estonia
gpsr.requests@easproject.com

www.ingramcontent.com/pod-product-compliance
Lightning Source LLC
Chambersburg PA
CBHW071403300426
44114CB00016B/2160